CAGLIOSTRO
THE UNKNOWN MASTER

A Critical and Historical Study of High Magic

Dr 'Marc Haven' (Dr Emmanuel Lalande)

TRANSLATED by PAUL FERGUSON

EDITED by PHILIPPA FAULKS

Foreword by JONATHAN BLACK, author of the best-selling
The Secret History of the World

Lewis Masonic

First published by Lewis Masonic 2020

ISBN 978 0 85318 595 6

All rights reserved. No part of this book may be reproduced or transmitted in any form or by any means, electronic or mechanical, including photocopying, recording, scanning or by any information storage and retrieval system, on the internet or elsewhere, without permission from the Publisher in writing.

© Philappa Lee and Paul Ferguson 2020

English Translation copyright 2015 Paul Ferguson

Edited by Philippa Faulks

Cover design: Rowan Lee Foyster
Text design Alan C. Butcher

The moral rights of the authors has been asserted.

Published by Lewis Masonic

an imprint of Ian Allan Publishing Ltd, Shepperton, Middx TW17 8AS.
Printed in England.

Visit the Lewis Masonic website at www.lewismasonic.co.uk

Copyright

Illegal copying and selling of publications deprives authors, publishers and booksellers of income, without which there would be no investment in new publications. Unauthorised versions of publications are also likely to be inferior in quality and contain incorrect information. You can help by reporting copyright infringements and acts of piracy to the Publisher or the UK Copyright Service.

Paul Ferguson, comes from the Channel Islands and has spent most of his working-life as a translator for publication in the Benelux and Switzerland. He feels passionately that the wealth of Continental esoteric writings from the 16th century onwards is an essential part of our culture that needs to be made available to a wide audience in modern English translations. His most recent work include several translations from French, German and Latin for the alchemical scholar Adam McLean, treatises by Gerhard Dorn, and some of the less well-known Rosicrucian manifestos.

Philippa Faulks (also writes as Philippa Lee) is an author, ghost writer, editor, and researcher specialising in non-fiction. Her passions are history/social history, Egyptology, psychology, esoterica and Freemasonry. She has written eight titles including *The Masonic Magician: the Life and Death of Count Cagliostro and his Egyptian Rite* (Watkins 2009).

Philippa is currently the Editor of *The Square* magazine, an online monthly journal for all Freemasons worldwide.

www.philippalee.com

FOREWORD by JONATHAN BLACK

Author of *The Secret History of the World*

In the dark heart of eighteenth century Europe, where high life and low life came together, there lived an adventurer. Magus, fraud, saint, trickster, healer, pimp, alchemist, thief, reformer of Freemasonry and dispenser of the Oil of Wisdom – there are many glittering facets to the life and career of Cagliostro. He was originally Giuseppe Balsamo, a poor boy from Sicily who went on to dazzle royalty and became a popular hero yet find himself embroiled in argument and scandal, until he finally died in prison in Rome, condemned for being a Freemason. He is one of the most mysterious and enigmatic figures in history. It was said of him that in order to understand him, you have to *be* him, and he has always fascinated me. In *The Secret History of the World*, I wrote of an encounter between Cagliostro and another mysterious figure, the Comte de St Germain. Shortly afterwards I was intrigued to inspect Cagliostro's magic ring, on display in the library of Freemasons' Hall in London, in the company of Philippa Faulks, prime mover behind the republication of the present volume.

At the time I had already – in 2003 – published one exceptionally well-reviewed biography of Cagliostro, Ian McCalman's *The Seven Ordeals of Count Cagliostro*. What I admired about that book is that the author remained silkily and suavely agnostic on the question of whether or not Cagliostro had supernatural powers. What I admire about *this* book is the opposite: the author marshals all the evidence and arguments to show that Cagliostro was indeed a miracle-worker.

Some adepts are playful and present themselves to the world in the guise of a trickster or a fool. The Cagliostro of this book was not like that. One of the great occult laws of the universe is that whenever someone tries to act in a way that is purely good, then forces of pure evil rise up to oppose him, and the Cagliostro of this book was destroyed by the malice of enemies who rose up to oppose him at every turn.

The author aims to understand Cagliostro's world-view, the philosophy behind his wonder-working, which he sets squarely in the context of the Western esoteric tradition. Cagliostro believed that in addition to the five senses, we possess others as yet in an embryonic state, but which can be developed to that we can perceive and interact with a whole series of forces.

In his work, Marc Haven shows, crucially, how a plan to speed up the evolution of these spiritual powers lay behind Cagliostro's ambitions for Egyptian Rite Freemasonry.

This book is packed with fascinating esoteric lore, even down to the very copious notes.

EDITOR'S PREFACE

My first encounter with the enigmatic figure of Count Alessandro di Cagliostro was when doing research for my book, *The Masonic Magician: the Life and Death of Count Cagliostro and his Egyptian Rite*.

He immediately came across as something of a mystery, a chimera, one of those flamboyant personalities that compel further investigation. What started as a fascination with this bombastic character soon turned into something of a historical detective story. Once I had established who he was – alchemist, traveler, Freemason and healer – my research then uncovered the makings of a tragic tale. Adored and vilified in equal measure, this was a man who left ripples wherever he went. He careered, from patronage by some of Europe's finest nobles, to persecution by his dissenters. Most dangerously, he attracted the attention of the Roman Catholic Church and its feared Inquisition. Labelled a heretic, Freemason and occultist, Cagliostro had caught their eye and garnered their resentment for many years. His overt spiritual assertions of the immortality of the soul, the path to divinity without a priest and the formation of his *Egyptian Rite of Freemasonry* made him a suitable target. During his later life and ultimately his trial, the Church went to great efforts to denounce him. The chapter headings of this book echo these same calumnies – 'the Imposter', the Quack', 'the Charlatan', 'the False Prophet' – all these 'titles' were judgments passed by those who did not understand a man well ahead of his time.

A question I am frequently asked with regard to Cagliostro is, 'was his true identity Guiseppe Balsamo, the common thief and forger from Palermo, Italy?' My response is ever the same – I really don't know! There are certainly documents provided by the Inquisition (several of which are reproduced in the pages that follow) that may persuade us that this man of apparent integrity and ideals could indeed have been born into a simple family, took a turn for the worse and fled Sicily when his 'scams' went wrong.
Towards the end of his book, Marc Haven writes:

At the beginning of this chapter we said that the question of the unknown life of Cagliostro was of no importance, and we say it again now at the end, hoping to have proved it. Even if we join his enemies in accepting, without proof, that Balsamo really was Cagliostro, we do not find in this hypothesis anything, which in any way sullies the beauty and nobility of his remarkable life.

A book, *La Vie de Joseph Balsamo*, was published by the Inquisition and described by Haven, 'as an *apologia* for its actions, [and] is a masterpiece of hatred and hypocrisy'. Steeped in contempt and filled with ludicrous assertions, it was the metaphorical nail in Cagliostro's coffin. The era was already one of suspicion and fear, with the French Revolution just months away at the time of Cagliostro's arrest. His supposed involvement in events such as the 'Affair of the Diamond Necklace', the formation of the Bavarian Illuminati, through to his alleged support of the revolutionary overthrow of the monarchy, meant that his confused and torture-induced confession literally 'damned him if he did and damned him if he didn't.' Originally condemned and sentenced to death by the Inquisition, this was later commuted to life imprisonment in the Fortress at San Leo in Tuscany. On 26 August 1795, four years after his incarceration, he died aged 56, a broken and unrepentant man. The Holy Fathers who oversaw his burial penned this bitter epitaph:

On the 28th August in the year of grace 1795,

Joseph Balsamo, known as the Conte di Cagliostro, born in Palermo, baptised a Christian but a notorious non-believer and heretic, after having propagated all over Europe the impious dogmas of the Egyptian sect, and having acquired, through his fame and eloquence, an almost innumerable crowd of followers; having undergone various mishaps from which he emerged safe and sound thanks to his magical arts; having been finally condemned by sentence of the Holy Inquisition to perpetual imprisonment in a fortress of this city in the doubtful hope that he would eventually repent; and having with the same obstinacy borne the sufferings of prison for a period of 4 years, 4 months and 5 days, but being finally struck down by a violent attack of apoplexy, which is not unexpected in a man with such stubbornness of heart and unrepentance of soul, died without having given any sign of repentance and without showing any regrets, outside the Communion of our Holy Mother Church, at the age of 52 years, 2 months and 28 days. He was born in misery, lived in greater misery, and died in the greatest misery on 26th August of the aforesaid year at 3 o'clock in the morning. This day, a public supplication was ordered to petition God to, if it were possible, show mercy upon this piece of clay kneaded by His hands.

As a heretic, excommunicated and unrepentant, burial in consecrated ground was denied to him: instead he was buried at the very top of the hill on the side where it inclines towards the west, more or less equidistant from the two structures which were built for the sentinels and which are known as Il Palazzetto and Il Casino, on the soil of the Roman Apostolic Curia, on the 28th day of this month at 11 o'clock in the evening.

Even after years of research, Cagliostro remains an enigma to me, a character almost frozen in time. This is the reason why the legend of Count Cagliostro still tantalises us and continues to evoke such strong opinions amongst both his champions and detractors. Researchers love a mystery, always hoping there will be untold hidden depths to their subjects – I was lucky enough to find those depths in the long forgotten manuscript of Cagliostro's *Egyptian Rite of Freemasonry*, which I then had translated. Along with my co-author Robert L.D. Cooper, we brought his dimly wavering flame back to life.

In this seminal work, *Cagliostro, The Unknown Master*, Dr. Haven is likewise intrigued and yet still often surprised by the Count's adventures and achievements. Haven obviously identified with Cagliostro. He was also a man of healing, with a utopian view of life, who later in his life, tried to establish a community with similar aims to the Count's proscribed 'way to enlightenment' – through meditation, prayer, occult learning and Freemasonry. At medical school Haven had become a friend of Dr. Gérard Encausse (known as 'Papus') who at a relatively young age was already well established in esoteric circles for his treatises on Kabbalah, Tarot and occult subjects. In 1894, Papus introduced Haven to the famous healer Nizier Anthelme Philippe ('Maître Philippe de Lyon'). Maître Philippe's life appears to have closely mirrored Cagliostro's; he was a healer, occultist, was deeply spiritual and seemingly unswayed by public opinion. Maybe this is why Haven felt compelled to help rehabilitate the Count's reputation with the publication of his book. Throughout the pages Cagliostro appears all at once as both Master of magic and the archetypal rogue – he plays with our sensibilities yet enriches our opinion of him, even where it seems incredulous. He was an unquenchable flame of a man, existing ahead of his time, worshipped and condemned in equal measure. His detractors poured venom on his reputation whilst his supporters fanned the flames of his successes. And succeed he did, for after nearly 220 years, his memory and Masonic ritual lives on. Whether it is ridiculed or revered, that he left his mark on history is without doubt.

Perhaps you are already well versed in the life of Cagliostro, or merely a lover of eighteenth-century historical figures. Maybe you are drawn like a moth to the bright flame of the Enlightenment era; or possibly have an interest in the occult, Rosicrucianism or Freemasonry. It is fair to say that, wherever your interest lies, Marc Haven's book gives a fascinating and unique view of each aspect of this remarkable man.

For the past 8 years I have wanted to shed more light on the life of Cagliostro and it is thanks to the sensitive translation skills of Paul Ferguson, that we can offer the English version of this important book. This text will peel back another layer of the magic and mystery that surrounds Count Alessandro di Cagliostro, while simultaneously deepening the enigma and legacy of this great man. Replete with copies of letters from dignitaries praising Haven's subject and including tales from the mouths of his contemporaries, *Cagliostro, the Unknown Master*, is a testimony to be reckoned with.

Read on and decide for yourself – Master of magic or seller of snake oil?

Philippa Faulks, 2014

CAGLIOSTRO

—

THE UNKNOWN MASTER

A Critical and Historical Study of High Magic
by
'Dr. Marc Haven' (Dr. Emmanuel Lalande)
translated from French by Paul Ferguson

But ye denied the Holy One and the Just, and desired a murderer to be granted unto you; And killed the Prince of life, whom God hath raised from the dead; whereof we are witnesses.

Acts of the Apostles, III.14-15

Cagliostro. Portrait engraved by Leclère
(*Galerie Historique,* Museum of Versailles).

TABLE OF CONTENTS

A CHRONOLOGY OF THE AUTHOR'S LIFE 15
AUTHOR'S INTRODUCTION 19
Cagliostro and High Magic

AUTHOR'S FOREWORD 23
CHAPTER I – THE ADVENTURER 29
Cagliostro's early travels

CHAPTER II – THE IMPOSTOR 33
A portrait of Cagliostro

CHAPTER III – THE SWINDLER 45
Cagliostro in London – first visit

CHAPTER IV – THE WIZARD 59
Cagliostro in Russia

CHAPTER V – THE QUACK 93
Cagliostro in Strasbourg

CHAPTER VI – THE CHARLATAN 119
Cagliostro in Lyons

CHAPTER VII – THE FALSE PROPHET 145
Cagliostro in Paris

CHAPTER VIII – THE EXPLOITER OF PUBLIC GULLIBILITY 177
Cagliostro in London – second visit

CHAPTER IX – THE PROFANER OF THE ONE TRUE CHURCH 193
Cagliostro in Switzerland and Rome

CHAPTER X – SOME OBSERVATIONS UPON THE LIFE AND DEATH OF
CAGLIOSTRO 221
The spirit of the shadows

CHAPTER XI – WAS CAGLIOSTRO REALLY JOSEPH BALSAMO? 223

AFTERWORD – THE UNKNOWN MASTER 231

APPENDIX I 136
Specific documents on the origins and person of Cagliostro

APPENDIX II 243
General documents – letters and reference material

BIBLIOGRAPHY 248

LIST OF ILLUSTRATIONS

PORTRAIT OF CAGLIOSTRO BY LECLÈRE
THE AUTHOR WITH COLLEAGUES
BUST OF CAGLIOSTRO BY HOUDON, IN PROFILE
CAGLIOSTRO'S HOUSE IN STRASBOURG
PAVILION BUILT BY CAGLIOSTRO AT RIEHEN
SEAL OF THE LA SAGESSE LODGE OF LYONS
PORTRAIT OF CAGLIOSTRO BY CHAPUY
PORTRAIT OF CAGLIOSTRO BY BOLLINGER
BUST OF CAGLIOSTRO BY HOUDON, FRONT VIEW
LETTRE DE CACHET FOR THE ARREST OF CAGLIOSTRO
PORTRAIT OF CAGLIOSTRO BY BARTOLOZZI
CAGLIOSTRO'S COUNTRY-HOUSE IN BIENNE
CAGLIOSTRO'S SEAL
A, B, C: CAGLIOSTRO'S SIGNATURES
CAGLIOSTRO'S CERTIFICATE OF BAPTISM
CAGLIOSTRO'S CERTIFICATE OF MARRIAGE
CAGLIOSTRO'S COATS OF ARMS
FAMILY-TREE OF JOSEPH BALSAMO
MAP OF CAGLIOSTRO'S TRAVELS

AN IMPORTANT WORD ABOUT THE FOOTNOTES

Dr. Marc Haven's book contains almost as many footnotes as text. In the original these are placed at the foot of each page. In this translation they are placed for convenience at the end of each chapter. Although some are simply references, others are much more substantial and repay careful study. We would therefore suggest that the reader read the book at least twice: the first time simply ignoring the footnotes and then a second time browsing through them to find material of particular interest.

Of course, Marc refers to the (almost exclusively French-language) texts and editions that were most readily available to him. We have retained these references and the relevant page-numbering. Many of the texts to which he refers will readily be found on the Internet. Some of these texts will also be found there in English translation, e.g *La Vie de Joseph Balsamo*, from which Marc quotes extensively, will be found as a free Google Book (www.books.google.com) under the title *The Life of Joseph Balsamo, Commonly Called Count Cagliostro*; his memoir to the French Parlement will also be found at Google Books as *Memorial, Or Brief, for the Comte de Cagliostro, Defendant: Against the King's Attorney-General, Plaintiff: in the Cause of the Cardinal de Rohan, Comtesse de la Motte, and Others*; while Funck-Brentano's *L'Affaire du Collier* is available at the Archive website https://archive.org/details/diamondnecklace00funcrich under the title *The Diamond Necklace*. Information about Cagliostro's involvement with the English aristocrat George Gordon will also be found at Google Books in *A Complete Collection of State Trials and Proceedings for High Treason and Other Crimes and Misdemeanors from the Earliest Period to the Year 1783: With Notes and Other Illustrations, Volume 22* (search term: Cagliostro). The English-language versions of the scurrilous *Courrier de l'Europe* will also be found at Google Books (volumes 19 and 20 are the most relevant).

Where it was possible to suppress one of the original footnotes by including the content of the note within the text then we have done so. Occasionally, where certain things in the text would not make as much sense to a modern reader as they would have done to one of Marc's contemporaries (e.g. references to contemporary French scholars or occultists), we have added footnotes of our own. These are indicated by a capital T (for Translation) after the number, e.g. Note 114T at the end of Chapter IV. Our own additions to Marc's existing footnotes appear in square brackets.

Standing, from left to right: Jean Chapas, Dr. Gérard Encausse ('Papus'), Dr. Emmanuel Lalande (pen-name: 'Dr. Marc Haven'). Seated: Nizier Anthelme Philippe ('Maître Philippe de Lyons').

Dr. Marc Haven

—

A chronology of the author's life

based largely upon the reminiscences of his brother, the distinguished philosopher André Lalande (see André Lalande, *Marc Haven*, Pythagore, 1934)

1868
'Marc Haven' is born as Emmanuel Marc Henry Lalande in Nancy (Lorraine) on 24th December to Charles Marc Lalande, Director of Studies at the Lycée de Nancy, and Marie Julie Amanda Labastie, whose own mother – Julie Mallein – was a first cousin of Henriette Gagnon, the mother of the novelist Stendhal. He was given the relatively unusual first-name of Emmanuel in homage to the renowned local architect Emmanuel Héré.

1869
The family move to Rouen, where Charles Lalande takes up a similar post. He enjoys an interesting and stimulating childhood moving around different parts of France as his father develops his career.

1874-5
Moves with his family to the Yonne where he acquires a love of the mountains that he will never lose (see Author's Introduction).

1876
As a pupil at the Petit Lycée in Montpellier he shows precocious literary talent by writing a schoolboy-novel in diary form.

1880
Marc falls in love with the Russian Nihilist movement as a result of reading too much pulp fiction.

1883-1884
First becomes acquainted with the works of the esoteric novelist Joséphin Péladan, whose books his father had bought on a whim.

1887
After completing his secondary education at the Lycée de Sens and having become, amongst other things, an accomplished Latinist, Marc moves to Paris to study medicine rather than the engineering course recommended by his family. Initially lodges in Rue des Fossés-Saint-Bernard in the Latin Quarter.

1888
Moves to Rue Le Goff, where he lodges with his elder brother Julien, a recent product of the École Normale Supérieure. He frequents the most popular Latin Quarter cafés, especially the 'Vachette' on the corner of Rue des Écoles et Boulevard Saint-Michel, the café where the 'Roi de la Bohème' – the 'King of the Bohemians' – is elected and a popular haunt of writers such as Verlaine, Mendès, Huysmans, Mallarmé, Barrès and Maupassant.
In the Latin Quarter cafés Marc is also able to indulge his passion for gambling, especially poker. While playing late one night he experiences a strange combination of déjà vu and apparent precognition:

One of my partners suddenly said, 'OK, I'll raise you five'. Of course I'd heard this phrase so many times before that it had become quite commonplace, but somehow I felt that I'd heard exactly *the same 'call' before in* exactly *the same place and with* exactly *the same feelings being aroused in me. Then a second player said, 'OK, I'll raise you five.' This simply intensified my original feelings, and it was with a sense of mounting anxiety that I found myself thinking, 'Now the third player's going to say, 'Ah! He must have an Aces Full then!" And you know, that's exactly what he* did *say, and with precisely the same timbre, intonation and facial expression that I'd just imagined. It was all over as quick as a flash and I must say that it wasn't a pleasant sensation at all, although the effects disappeared almost immediately.* (1T)

1890
Marc spends the summer at Saint-Briac-sur-Mer with the painter Paul Signac aboard the latter's yacht *Le Mage*. Signac shares Marc's interests in synaesthesia and the psychological effects of colour, as well as in numerology and other esoteric subjects.

1891
A childhood friend of Marc's, a Monsieur Lefort, introduces him to the occultist circle associated with a bookshop at 29 Rue de Trévise, the *Librairie du Merveilleux*, founded by Lucien Chamuel. Through Chamuel he meets Dr. Gérard Encausse ('Papus'), also a medical student. Although still in his mid-twenties, Encausse has already published books on the Sepher Yetzirah and the Tarot as well as an elementary introduction to occultism and several articles in the two journals he has helped to found, *Initiation* and *Le Voile d'Isis*.

1892
Chamuel publishes a collection of Marc's poems, *Turris Eburnea*. The titles of some of the poems, e.g. *The Sphinx*, *The Seven Degrees*, are redolent of the direction in which his thought was moving at this time.

Formally adopts the pen-name 'Marc Haven'. 'Haven' is the Spirit of Dignity in the First Hour of the *Nuctemeron* of Apollonius of Tyana, just as 'Papus' is the Spirit of Medicine in the same hour of that system.

1893
Moves out of his brother's apartment to live with a group of friends who share his esoteric interests in a house in Rue Durand-Claye. Influenced by Papus, he becomes increasingly interested in homeopathy and alternative medicine. One of his fellow-lodgers is the alchemist, homeopath and pharmacy student Abel Thomas.

Papus introduces him to the poet and occultist Stanislas de Guaïta (1861-1897), co-founder with Joséphin Péladan of the *Ordre kabbalistique de la Rose-Croix*. Marc is elected a member of the Order's Supreme Council and is initiated as a Master Cabalist by Papus and de Guaïta.

Subsequently, as *Supérieur Inconnu* of the Martinist Order, he replaces Maurice Barrès (1862-1923) as one of the symbolic 12 members of its Supreme Council.

1894
Papus introduces him to the famous healer Nizier Anthelme Philippe ('Maître Philippe de Lyon').

1896
Qualifies as a medical doctor and becomes an extern, but his independence of mind, distaste for some of the favouritism that he has witnessed in the recruitment process for the Paris hospitals, and a passion for research cause him to abandon his plans for an internship. However, his doctoral dissertation, on the mediaeval doctor and alchemist Arnold de

Villanova, is most impressive: at 192 pages it far exceeds the usual five-page efforts and wins a silver medal as one of the best medical dissertations of the year. It is subsequently published by Chamuel as *La vie et les oeuvres de maître Arnaud de Villeneuve* (a modern edition was published by Slatkine in 1972).

Marc does not start practising medicine immediately, but instead tries to establish a Utopian community where part of the day is devoted to manual work and the rest to meditation, art, and research into the occult sciences. Unfortunately circumstances conspire against the idea and eventually he moves to Lyons, where Papus is seeking a medically-qualified associate for the famous healer Maître Philippe. Marc is entranced by Maître Philippe's powerful personality and tremendous gifts. Maître Philippe, born in modest circumstances in Savoy, has married a wealthy widow and heiress in her own right, a Madame Landar. This leaves him free to work as a healer without payment. Unfortunately it doesn't prevent him having a number of brushes with the law due to his lack of formal medical qualifications. As a qualified doctor Marc is able to help by signing off Philippe's prescriptions and sheltering him from criticism by the authorities. Although Marc has his own practice and is also appointed to the local hospital, the Hôpital St-Luc, Maître Philippe's house is very much the focal point of his activities.

Marc falls in love with the charming and uncomplicated Victoire, the daughter of Maître Philippe and Madame Landar.

Marc felt that, in some respects, Maître Philippe's life closely mirrored that of Cagliostro, another much misunderstood and reviled healer, and the two books on Cagliostro that he subsequently published were intended as a tribute to his memory.

1897
2 September: Marc marries Victoire.

1900
Édition l'Initiation of Paris publishes Marc's edition of 13 letters from Albert Poisson under the title *L'Initiation alchimique*.

1903
Bibliothèque Chacornac of Paris publishes an expanded edition of *La Cabbale* by Papus with contributions by Marc.

1904
Marc experiences tragedy with the early death of his wife Victoire.

1905
Marc suffers another blow with the death of Maître Philippe. He withdraws increasingly from public life to concentrate on writing. Marries for a second time, this time to the Moscow-born Olga Chestakoff, who would later write her own short tribute to Maître Philippe entitled *Lumière Blanche, Évocation d'un passé* under the pen-name Marie-Emmanuel Lalande.

1906
Bibliothèque Chacornac of Paris publishes *Interprétation de l'Arbre de la Cabale*, co-authored by Marc.

1909
P. Dujols & A. Thomas of Paris publishes Marc's facing-page translation from Latin of the *Archidoxis Magica* by Paracelsus.

1910
Librairie Hermétique publishes his *L'Évangile de Cagliostro*.
H. Durville *fils* of Paris publishes his translation of Agrippa's *Arbatel*.

1912
Dorbon-aîné of Paris publishes the first edition of his *Cagliostro: Le Maître Inconnu*, of which this present book is a translation.
Bibliothèque universelle Beaudelot of Paris publishes *Profonds mystères de la Cabale divine* co-authored by Marc.
1926
Marc dies at his home in the suburbs of Paris.

NOTES
(1T) Cf. Élisabeth Czoniczer, *Quelques antécédents de 'A la recherche du temps perdu': tendances qui peuvent avoir contribué à la cristallisation du roman proustien*, Librairie E. Droz, Geneva, 1957, p. 150.

AUTHOR'S INTRODUCTION

CAGLIOSTRO AND HIGH MAGIC

Cagliostro! Is there any name that piques more interest or arouses more curiosity? If any name is better known then I'd very much like to know what it is. Talk to people in the street, even those without any literary pretensions, or talk to great scholars and people in powerful positions, talk to them about Simon Magus, Cornelius Agrippa, Paracelsus even, and just a few perhaps may have heard something about them but to the majority they'll be completely unknown or evoke only vague recollections. But then try talking to those same people about Cagliostro and just see the difference! Absolutely *everyone* will have heard of him, to a greater or lesser extent, for better or for worse. Whether they're learned scholars or complete ignoramuses they'll all know something about him. For some he'll be the man who predicted winning lottery-numbers, for others a magician who summoned up the spirits of the dead, or a healer who cured the incurable, or an *éminence grise* who changed the destinies of princes and, perhaps, of entire nations. For others he'll be an alchemist, a hypnotist, or the Unknown Grandmaster of Freemasonry. But whatever the specific title or identity, to all of them Cagliostro is a familiar personality.

Personally I think that the famous populariser of science Louis Figuier put his finger on it: every Hermeticist and every thaumaturge has their speciality, their particular field of study, but Cagliostro had the extraordinary talents and abilities of all of them put together – there wasn't a single one of the various branches of occult science that was foreign to him. In every field he achieved wonders, and consequently all esoteric groups claim him for their own. What's more, although some would deny that he ever exercised any meaningful political influence he certainly played an important part in the major intrigues of the age.

Also, unlike Apollonius of Tyana, Albertus Magnus or Nostradamus, who are already lost in the mists of time, Cagliostro is our near-contemporary. The Diamond Necklace Affair and the French Revolution happened only yesterday. At the time of writing (1912) Freemasonry and the study of hypnotism have been in existence for just two hundred years, and the rapid changes they have undergone are the work of scarcely two or three generations. Our grandfathers were Cagliostro's contemporaries – they can talk to us about him, they knew his disciples, and they retain oral traditions of them that have all the freshness and charm of personal recollections.

And yet in spite of all this Cagliostro, the man everyone feels qualified to talk about, remains an enigma. Having had, in his day, as many enemies as he had admirers, he has suffered from the clash of contradictory opinions. His life is still the subject of bitter discussion, which is just another way of saying that his memory is thoughtlessly attacked, for critics always prefer to destroy their old icons rather than create new ones.
Historians in particular have dealt harshly with him: to them he's just an intriguer, an impostor, or a skilful and deceiving conjurer, just another flamboyant adventurer stranded in the wastelands of the 18th century.

Even occultists, who are always so keen to learn more about their illustrious forebears and who often don't have very much brilliance of their own to display, and who should really be his staunchest defenders, speak of him with reserve for fear of compromising themselves or committing some indiscretion. Depending on their affiliation they'll see him as a Hermeticist, as a secret envoy of the Templars or, more simply, as a medium with a talent for healing. This difference of opinion amongst the self-styled 'adepts', amongst the varied devotees of exactly the same doctrines, will occasion no surprise.

Occultism, indeed, is neither a precise doctrine nor a homogeneous sect. It is in fact just a fictitious grouping, bringing together people of all intellectual stamps, from the most uncompromising Positivist to the subtlest mystic. Many of them are complete ignoramuses, puffing themselves up on the basis of a few poorly-understood books that they claim to have read. Others are more ambitious, a small cluster of scientists engaged in a ceaseless quest for unity, the true Wandering Jews of the learned world. Rarer still are those of good will, the best of the bunch, who seek in occultism exactly what they would seek anywhere else: an opportunity to do useful work on behalf of God or man. All these different groups sit side by side, engaging in brotherly love with all due ceremony, splitting from one another violently, and passing from intense mutual admiration to equally intense mutual hatred, their blessings being as sudden and unexpected as their excommunications – and just as noisy. The occult is a market-place rather then a temple: so how could all these people possibly have a common opinion about anything, let alone about Cagliostro? Some may think me too harsh, but in the twenty-five years that I've lived amongst occultists, of all sects and classes, I've learned that there's really only one thing that brings them together, only one thing that they have in common: all of them, whatever their outward appearance or statements of principle, seek the phenomenal, i.e. they all want to acquire exceptional power over matter and life or, at least, they want to persuade others that they have acquired it. It was this selfish curiosity, this desire for domination over others which, in days gone by, caused a crowd of disciples to gather around the powerful Cagliostro. It is these same feelings which, in our own times, cause so many people of different kinds, under the vague title of occultists, to gather around some rather less qualified Masters.

To study Cagliostro effectively therefore requires an understanding of the psychology of occultists, especially since his followers came from such a wide range of countries and cultures. We need to undertake this study astutely, trying to avoid conflict or the awakening of hostility in those who, if we carried out these investigations amongst contemporary occultists, might feel that they were being targeted for their beliefs or that their interests were being compromised. We shall also need to examine the innermost nature of magic in all its forms, for nobody (as even Cagliostro's enemies acknowledged) has fulfilled the vocation of Magus to a greater extent than he did, and no one before or since has ever performed thaumaturgy so consistently or so publicly. But if we tried to study magic before we had marshalled all the evidence then we would rapidly be lost in a purely speculative field of enquiry that is insusceptible to criticism and, frankly, largely devoid of interest. Examining the archives, analysing an actual life and the known facts are therefore the only ways of achieving genuine illumination and getting at the truth. By taking Cagliostro, his life, his teachings and his actions as our subject of study we shall therefore get as close as possible to a truly scientific examination of the miraculous and the mysterious.

But – a good three-quarters of humanity will exclaim in chorus – miracles are just a joke and mysteries don't happen anymore! This is a very immature protest, just a form of the simple bravado beneath which humanity often hides its fear of the unknown. The miraculous and the mysterious are all around you, watching over you. Can't you feel it, you poor people, in the evening when you fall asleep, in the morning when you wake up, every time your heart beats or your mind is agitated, in every one of your hidden emotions if you're an artist, in every unforeseen event of your life if you're a man of the world, in every one of your deals if you're a businessman, in every one of your experiments if you're a scientist?

The real joke is the way that people rely upon scientific or religious dogma to explain extraordinary events and so obtain some mild reassurance. This is simply insane. By all means deny the mysterious, deny the unknown world of the spirit, deny the miraculous for as long as you want, but eventually there will come an hour of crisis, that worrisome evening when you suddenly find yourself thinking, as it were, in another language, when you finally have to acknowledge your doubts and you search around desperately for something that provides some measure of stability. If, in that situation, you want to challenge mysterious reality with frank denials and whimsical 'systems' then go ahead: you won't interfere with the course of nature in doing so, but nor will you do anything to reduce the profound disquiet at the bottom of your heart.

It was thoughts such as these that prompted me to publish this study of Cagliostro. I reflected upon the fact that remarkable occurrences are often seriously misunderstood and attempts made to explain them often self-deceiving. I was motivated especially by that irresistible attraction that the miraculous and the marvellous have for every human soul, by the anguished questions we find ourselves asking when, suddenly and without apparent reason, a corner of the veil is lifted. Then something happens that compels your attention – everything suddenly changes, the world seems fresh and new, and all your former beliefs, all your accepted systems of ideas, just collapse. A giddiness overwhelms you. You feel ready to submit to anything. Now vulnerable to any infatuation you seek out the craftsman of this miracle, whether he is a genie to be drawn to you by simple sacrifices or a devil to be entreated by violent exorcism.

Sometimes travellers in the mountains have experiences just like this. When, towards evening, and with an ascent ahead of you the following day, you finally reach one of those little chalets lost in the snows to await the dawn then you may often, through the excess of excitement generated by your climb, be unable to sleep or may awaken well before the time you were due to set off, and may rise from your bed and sit in darkness in front of the chalet-door. The absolute silence and stillness of a moonless night enfold you in their impenetrable veils. Only with difficulty can you hear from afar an occasional stone rolling down the mountainside dislodged by the foot of the chamois or drops of water falling from the rock into the stream below. Everything is utterly dark, formless, lifeless. There may be some creatures surrounding you, mute observers lurking in the shadows. But if you try to pierce the darkness, if you try to make sense of the shapes and the fleeting shadows, if you try to make out the outlines of the dark masses that surround you then it's only through the closest and most persistent attention that you'll see anything at all, and in any case what you think you can see is often only the work of your feverish imagination.

Time passes – you may even have fallen asleep for a time – and then, suddenly, the sky is bright. From the background, where previously there was only a stagnant darkness, there emerge peaks, valleys and forests. The mountain-tops stand out against the sky, the ice is iridescent. Where previously the shadows congealed into an impenetrable mass, now a thousand forms take shape and are thrown into relief. It's a world that's emerged from nothing, a re-creation. Your senses are confused, dazzled, you're ready to fall to your knees to seek out, in the brightening sky, the Craftsman who created all this magic, be it an angel or a sun, so as to adore him and to come closer to him.

And yet, what has actually happened? Not much to be honest: a ray of sunlight has simply pierced the night and changed everything. Heaven has sent to Earth, towards us poor blind creatures, a little of the force that we call light in the firmament or, in the world of morals, Truth, and this trifling thing has brought about the most marvellous blossoming of a new day in the heart of man and upon the Earth.

I well remember having a magical experience of this kind one morning in the Alps. What, in comparison with this magical evocation of a world emerging from darkness, is a table moved by spirits, a piece of lead changing into gold, an unexpected cure, or the actions of a hypnotised subject? This daily miracle, if we would but reflect upon it, has so much to tell us about all kinds of other phenomena that we think of as strange only because they occur less frequently. In fact, I believe that this miracle carries within it the secret of all the great manifestations that have caused such deep disturbances at sundry times in history and which have brought upset to so many. By meditating upon it I have found that many of my thoughts about the spirit world, about high magic, about miracle-workers, and about their words and deeds have become so much clearer to me. And very often, while writing this book, I have found myself constantly reminded of those precious secrets that the dawn revealed to me that morning on the mountain-side.

Dr. Marc Haven.

CAGLIOSTRO – THE UNKNOWN MASTER

FOREWORD

by DR. MARC HAVEN

I shall never forget a newspaper article from the early years of the twentieth century which contained a biography of one of my contemporaries and which also included a photograph of him. His biographer, a hundred years hence perhaps, will certainly consider this article to be one of his most important sources of information. Yet the photograph was actually of some unknown individual, or certainly someone unknown to me, and the biography claimed that the hero of the article had been born in a harem in Constantinople, whereas he'd actually first seen the light of day, as the son of small farmers, in a village in France. Mercifully I've forgotten the other details.

This memory has constantly haunted me during my researches into the life of Cagliostro. If errors of that kind can be printed in our own time and can receive such widespread exposure, and if we're living in the midst of events whose character we cannot fully appreciate or which we often do not even get to hear about, then what fog of illusion and world of fantasy must we inevitably encounter when we have to deal with the events and personalities of the past?

When we're dealing with a personality who's played a relatively minor role in history we often find ourselves confronted with special difficulties caused by the sheer remoteness of the events, by prejudice, and by accepted opinion. The partiality of the personality's contemporaries assumes all the more significance as time passes, and makes it harder and harder to check the accuracy of their statements. A 'general opinion' – often that of the most attractively-written or best-selling book on the subject – will take root, and later authors will feel obliged to adhere to it just because the idleness or credulity of the masses has failed to seriously challenge it.

This is exactly what has happened with Cagliostro, and with him more than anyone else. From his own times onwards those who saw him at work, who observed him and questioned him, were forced to acknowledge, if they were level-headed people of a philosophical turn, that it was impossible to give an opinion on him [1]: some revered him like a god, others detested him as the greatest enemy of mankind [2]. No one has ever inspired greater devotion or greater fury, and no one has ever remained more enigmatic, even to his close friends, and even to the magistrates to whom fell the weighty task of judging him.

Consequently, around him more than any other person calumnies have accumulated and legends have grown. Even when he was alive they began to spread, and after his death religious hatreds – which are always the most persistent and which survive even the grave – made sure that they endured. Historians have been struck by his sudden appearance on the eve of the French Revolution but, unable to find any obvious and immediate connection with his actions, and nothing that explained his role, they've neglected to make any effort to understand him, and have therefore relegated him to the ranks of incidental historical figures of no importance.

Then the creative writers got hold of him, and finally a view of him took shape that we can still find today, and which has become the traditional view of him simply through repetition. Extracted from history and turned into a legendary figure, half-wizard, half-conjurer, both cunning swindler and ridiculous buffoon, Count Cagliostro has become an exhibit in the Museum of Puppetry [3] to be found somewhere between Robert Macaire [4T] and Pulcinella.

Many people are content to leave it at that: it's enough for them to get to know the charming Cagliostro of Gérard de Nerval or the impressive magician depicted by Alexandre Dumas, but those who have sometimes felt, if only briefly, that there is more to life, who feel that there's a world of mystery around them, cannot be satisfied with such a superficial view – they will want something more. But what exactly can we do to find out the truth about Cagliostro and to acquire a deeper understanding of his mind and spirit?

The first step in this process is obviously to track down the best sources of information. But what sources do we have on the life of Cagliostro? First, and very numerous of course, are the satires and lampoons from the pens either of his adversaries in the various lawsuits that he had to undergo (and, in particular, the Diamond Necklace Affair), the personal enemies that he made by his great frankness of speech or the unusual character of his actions, or the Inquisition which, at the time of his capture, knew that they had in their hands one of the heads of Freemasonry (either a secret chief or an openly-acknowledged one) and would therefore be able to kill two birds with one stone. On the one hand they'd be able to sully forever the memory of this representative of the liberal ideas that at that time were simmering in the minds of so many and on the other discredit the entire Order of Egyptian Freemasonry by bringing down its Grandmaster.

The book known in French as *La Vie de Joseph Balsamo* [5T], published by the Inquisition as an *apologia* for its actions, is a masterpiece of hatred and hypocrisy. The lampoons of Sachi, Morande and Madame de la Motte pale into insignificance beside it [6], and yet these three characters also did not spare him. The task of demolishing Cagliostro's reputation, however, assumed new proportions in the perfectionist hands of the Inquisition: all the most defamatory material that they could get their hands on from the three writers we have just mentioned was added to whatever compromising details they could extract from Cagliostro and his wife either by false promises or by torture [7]. If we add to this everything that, in 1791, the fevered imagination of Italian priests, scared stiff by the French Revolution, could invent against Freemasonry in general and the founder of a Mystical Rite in particular, then we'll get some idea of just how violent an attack on Cagliostro the *Vie de Joseph Balsamo* really is. The skill with which the author, by simply playing with words, deliberately confuses religion and Catholicism, atheism and heterodoxy, liberalism and scepticism, means that if readers are not fully alert to his trickery then they will unconsciously fall into line with his argument and accept his conclusions. Not only is the book a hate-filled summary of the case against Cagliostro, not only is it riddled with errors where the statements are verifiable [8] and with obvious inventions where they are not, but in developing his argument the author falls into such blatant contradictions that they positively leap off the page. In fact, the French translator of the work, however hostile to Cagliostro he might have been, and even though Cagliostro inspired in him nothing but scorn and sarcasm, cannot prevent himself in certain places from drawing attention to certain contradictions that outrage justice and even common sense [9].

There is therefore virtually no material that we can use from the *Vie de J. Balsamo*, any more than from the earlier lampoons, and if we do have to quote them here then it will only be with many caveats. We can say the same of many of the other biographies, either stand-alone or interpolated into more general works [10], all of which rely heavily for their documentation on that little book, that tissue of lies and stupidities, that the Apostolic Chamber ordered to be printed in Rome.

The publication of the Fontaine documents by the French scholar Campardon [11] has encouraged a number of writers to investigate Cagliostro more closely. Funck-Brentano was the first, and he wrote with impartiality. A more recent author [12] has turned to the subject, but his book, unlike Funck-Brentano's, and like the old lampoons, is suffused with exactly the same spirit of hatred that inspired the Jesuit Marcello to write the *Life of J. Balsamo*.

To arrive at a true picture of Cagliostro we also have to eliminate all the frippery with which certain novelists have chosen to weigh him down: Alexandre Dumas, Gérard de Nerval and Jules de Saint-Félix [13] have all added, to a character who was certainly in no need of embellishment, and to all the established traditions about him, certain features drawn from other characters in history or legend. Already in the time of Cagliostro chroniclers were happily piling the utterly incredible on top of the simply miraculous – in several lampoons of the time, for example, we find the following story:

With a cry of surprise Cagliostro suddenly halted in front of a carved wooden crucifix. He couldn't understand how the artist, who must certainly have never seen Christ, had been able to achieve such a perfect resemblance.

'So you knew Christ then Cagliostro?'

'Yes indeed, we were very close. Oh, how many times we walked together on the wet sand on the shores of Lake Tiberias! His voice was of an infinite gentleness... But he simply wouldn't listen to what I had to say: he ran along the sea-shore, got together a group of beggars, fishermen, paupers and people in rags, and preached to them – and, of course, came to a sticky end in the process!'

Then, turning to his servant, he said, 'Do you remember that evening in Jerusalem when they crucified Jesus'?

But the servant simply said, with the most profound reverence: 'No Sir, I'm afraid I don't. A clever man like you must know that I haven't been in your service for the last 1500 years!' [14]

All these stories, including that of the rejuvenation of a maidservant whom he allegedly turned back into a little girl, and that of the Banquet of the Ghosts [15], circulated in his time. Baron de Gleichen, who was an honest man, explains them as caricatures invented by jokers [16], some of whom tried very deliberately to use ridicule to neutralise the prestige that surrounded a man of exceptional abilities, while others genuinely confused the stories in good faith. From the moment that Cagliostro first revealed his abilities as an alchemist or healer this was considered ample justification to attribute to him the transmutations of a Joseph-François Borri, the occult activities of a Federico Gualdi, or the terrible mysteries of the spirit Gablidone [17T] [18].

Finally, some of Cagliostro's own followers and admirers, whose judgement was corrupted by credulity, enthusiastically swallowed all the latest stories and hawked them around, distorting them still further in the process [19].

From all these legends, exaggerations and distortions the mythical character of Cagliostro the magician was gradually constructed, and we have to accept that the literary men, who took over the image of him in what was already a very distorted state, distorted it even further. Of course, I'm not saying that I expected to find documentary evidence about Cagliostro in what the novelists have had to say about him: I am simply mentioning them here because it's important not to approach our subject with the preconceived image of the 'literary Cagliostro' before our eyes, and because we shouldn't forget that this distortion of the truth began with Cagliostro's contemporaries.

Above we have discussed all those sources – sullied as they are with errors, calumnies and legends – which we ourselves must simply ignore but which, unfortunately, have been the sole inspiration for the majority of writers on the subject. So what remains to us?

1. Genuine information and assessments provided by competent witnesses, either people who knew him well or those who only knew him in passing but who noted shortly afterwards their impressions of their visit to Cagliostro [20].

2. Documents drawn up during official investigations: these in particular will be able to provide us with invaluable dates and texts [21].

3. Personal correspondence, open-letters, requests and memoranda written either by Cagliostro himself or at his direct request [22] and which have been systematically neglected. In particular, the response to the Public Prosecutor which he wrote at the time of the Diamond Necklace Affair was ridiculed and misunderstood, as the more literate section of the general public mistook it for a boastful work of fiction and therefore laughed it to scorn. And yet if these critics, given better advice, had made the effort to fathom the sense of these writings and to separate facts from symbols then they would have seen Cagliostro appear to them as clearly as he ever did through his actions, for its pages, held in such disregard, shed a singular light on some of the more obscure aspects of his personality.

Official texts, assessments by impartial contemporaries, and letters and requests written by Cagliostro himself are therefore the only sources – not very abundant maybe, but clear and sane – on which scrupulous critics can draw if they are eager to restore to its true form and show in its true light the fascinating figure of a man who foretold the French Revolution, healed the allegedly incurable, and was sufficiently versatile to be a friend of Lavater and the spiritual counsellor of the Cardinal de Rohan.

Unfortunately, this is not the line of enquiry that the professional historians have followed. Instead they've focused on the satires and lampoons, so very numerous, so rich in scandal and so amusing to quote. That was enough for them; they didn't look any further, and even if some have occasionally questioned Cagliostro's attempts to defend himself, or the recollections of contemporary observers, then it has always been in a weak and prejudiced manner [23].

As a result neither the biographies, all replete with exactly the same errors and calumnies, nor the superficial comments interpolated here and there in more general texts, nor even the pages that more enlightened minds have devoted to Cagliostro provide us with even an approximate idea of what he was really like: the odious swindler, the naive madman, the subtle manipulator of souls, the coarse oaf – we're introduced to hundreds of different characters, none of them having very much connection with reality, and none of them intellectually satisfying. What's more, the same author often presents us with completely contradictory facts or assessments just a few lines apart! Such nonsense is simply an insult to our common sense.

We therefore have every reason to begin our study of the man with a blank sheet of paper. A new biography of Cagliostro, conceived along different lines to the existing ones, is therefore an historical necessity. It was while I was trying to study this fascinating character with a view to reaching some definite conclusions about him that I saw the need for new research. I must confess that, as I took a closer look at the character and achievements of the man he grew enormously in stature and also became easier to understand. My reason for writing this book is therefore something rather more than mere curiosity: I feel, quite simply, that I have a duty to fulfil.

NOTES
(1) '*Vere aenigma est iste, de quo non licet judicare*', i.e. 'That man was a true puzzle, about whom one simply cannot draw conclusions', cf. Anon., *Liber memorialis de Caleostro* [sic], Venice. p. 36 (translated into French by Dr. Marc Haven as *L'Évangile de Cagliostro*, Paris, 1910, p. 86). Cf. also the letter by Blessig in Weisstein, *Cagliostro à Strasbourg*.
(2) De Breteuil and Meiners both thought of him as 'a man...about whom I would like to warn the entire world', cf. Meiners, *Briefe über die Schweiz*, part II, in Mirabeau, *Lettre sur MM. de Cagliostro…*, Berlin, 1786, p. 14.
(3) This is almost the exact expression used by that English answer to Joseph Prud'homme whom we know as Thomas Carlyle. Cf. Fraser's Magazine, July 1833, pp. 19-28, and ibid. August 1833, pp. 132-155. [Joseph Prud'homme was a character invented by the actor and humorist Henry-Bonaventure Monnier to satirise the smug Parisian middle class, cf. Verlaine's poem of that name in his *Poèmes saturniens*.]
(4T) A fictional character renowned in French culture as the archetypal villain, created by Benjamin Antier in his play *L'Auberge des Adrets*, which was performed for the first time in 1823 and much imitated. The French government became so concerned by the character's popularity that they eventually banned him from the stage.
(5T) Readily available on the Internet in the 1791 English translation entitled *The Life of Joseph Balsamo, Commonly Called Count Cagliostro*.
(6) Sachi and his various disagreements with Cagliostro are discussed in Chapter V, *Cagliostro in Strasbourg*; Morande in Chapter VIII, *Cagliostro in London*; and Madame de la Motte in our account of the Diamond Necklace Affair in Chapter VII, although history has sufficiently unmasked and condemned these last two characters that we have had no need to refute their self-interested assertions.
(7) Cf. the section on Rome in Chapter IX of this book.
(8) If we look solely at questions of fact in that part of Cagliostro's life for which official documents do exist – a period of approximately ten years – then we can identify more than thirty definite errors of dates, names or events. We can thus see what degree of confidence can be placed in accounts of Cagliostro's youth in which the author gave even freer rein to his imagination, as any corrections for this obscure period are obviously an impossibility.
(9) In his preliminary note, pp. iv and v, the translator felt he had to excuse himself for translating the death sentence pronounced on Cagliostro, whatever he might have been and whatever he might have done. He admits that his logical sense rebels against the arguments of the Holy Office and the clamouring of the Inquisitors who were still, in 1791, demanding blood to protect the Holy Roman Church, see op. cit., notes to pp. 96, 86, and 82.
(10) Christian, *Histoire de la magie*, Paris, Furne, pp. 170 et seq. Figuier, *Histoire du merveilleux*, Paris, 1861, vol. IV, pp. 1 et seq.
(11) Campardon, *Marie-Antoinette et le procès du collier*, Paris, Plon, 1863, pp. 410 et seq.
(12) D'Alméras, *Cagliostro*, Paris, 1904.
(13) J. de Saint-Félix, *Aventures de Cagliostro*, Paris, Hachette, 1855.
(14) Funck-Brentano, *L'affaire du collier*, Paris, Hachette, 1902, p. 89.
(15) *Mémoires authentiques*, Paris., 1786, pp. 18 et seq. *Gazette d'Utrecht* of 2nd August 1787.
(16) De Gleichen, *Souvenirs*, Paris, 1868, pp. 125-126. Lord Gower, who is identified as the author of the caricature we have just mentioned, may not have invented it specifically for Cagliostro: in the *Chronique de l'Oeil de Boeuf* by Georges Touchard-Lafosse, which deals with the court of Louis XIV

and Louis XV, we find, in Chapter XXII, exactly the same story attributed to the Comte de Saint-Germain. The story of the extreme rejuvenation is also associated with Saint-Germain, while that of the crucifix will be found in *Magie de Cagliostro*, 1789, p. 18.

(17T) Cf. *Protokoll über den spiritus familiaris Gablidone* by Lavater, Frankfurt/Leipzig 1787.

(18) Cf. *Gazette de Leyde*, no. 72 of 9th September 1785. *Ma correspondance*, no. 73, 2nd September 1785 and *Essai sur la secte des Illuminés*, 1789, pp. 129-134. 'It was said that at the end of each month he would shut himself up for 48 hours. When he finally emerged he would send a gold ingot to the goldsmith's to be sold. The gold of these ingots was always finer than that of French gold coinage', *Souvenirs du duc de Lévis*, quoted in Chaix d'Est-Ange, p. 6.

(19) His friends and defenders caused him as much grief as his enemies: thanks to their stupidity, foolish gossips made Cagliostro the target of fresh ridicule.

(20) Even so we must still make allowance, when examining these texts, for the inevitable prejudice that arose in the minds of officialdom and indeed all seriously-inclined individuals against a person with such incredible charisma, whose words were so thought-provoking, and whose strange behaviour often jarred against the high tone of 18th century French society. Many people saw Cagliostro simply as a fool – and that is not unreasonable, as long as you mean the sort of Fool you find in the Tarot, i.e. someone to amuse the children but also someone whose symbolic gestures remind the truly wise of certain eternal verities.

(21) We're referring here to the following official documents: *Interrogatoire à la Bastille, Lettres ministérielles* of 1783, *Débats du procès du Collier*, and the *Verdict* of 31st May 1786. These were to be found at the time of writing (1912) in the *Archives Nationales* and at the *Bibliothèque de l'Arsenal*. See the Bibliography at the end of this book for details.

(22) Several documents by Cagliostro's lawyer Maître Thilorier were inspired and, some say, even partly written (in Italian) by Cagliostro, cf. *Gazette de Leyde*, no. 18 of 3rd March 1786. Borowski, *Cagliostro, einer der merkwürdigsten Abentheurer*, Königsberg, 1790, p. 5.

(23) An excellent writer, Funck-Brentano, in his book on the Diamond Necklace Affair, was obviously obliged to mention Cagliostro, but he speaks about him only in passing, dealing with just a few months of his life and with an event in which Cagliostro was only very slightly involved. On the other hand this author has unfortunately followed common opinion in seeing Cagliostro as the entertaining originator of the whole affair and hasn't shrunk from accentuating these negative character traits by readily assigning to him some pretty dubious anecdotes. In a word, he has not really penetrated any further into the heart of Cagliostro's personality. He wasn't under any obligation to do this of course and so he hasn't felt the need to shed light on certain questionable aspects or dispel certain calumnies if they are directly concerned with the subject of his book. Apart from these reservations his book is certainly the best and most balanced account of Cagliostro that has appeared to date (1912).

CHAPTER I

—

'THE ADVENTURER'

CAGLIOSTRO'S EARLY TRAVELS

I think it's fair to say that no one has ever taken literally Cagliostro's obviously allegorical account of his childhood travels. Almost everyone has seen it as nothing more than a particularly pretentious attempt to impress. His enemies, in an attempt to catch him in the act of lying about himself and to neutralise the positive effects of his philanthropy and amazing achievements, immediately set about finding a more likely origin for him and digging up a more mundane account of his youth.

Sachi was the first to undertake this task, announcing that Cagliostro's real name was actually Thiscio, that he'd been born in Naples the son of a coachman, that he'd been a wigmaker, and that he'd also exercised, here and there, some rather less honourable professions. Other writers said he was a Portuguese Jew. Madame de la Motte adopted these accounts and republished them. Later, Morande and Police Commissary Chesnon identified him as Joseph Balsamo, and published an account of his youthful adventures that was enough to discredit him forever. Although superficially this may appear to be a quite different story, it exhibits all the same hallmarks and the same richness of detail as the previous one, and used source-documents of the same integrity. This second version achieved even greater notoriety than the first, and was quickly and widely disseminated thanks to the so-called newspaper known as the *Courrier de l'Europe*. We find it in the works of almost all the biographers and historians.

The goal of all these accounts, however heavily fictionalised, was the same: to pierce Cagliostro's veil of anonymity and, in particular, to cast so much doubt and opprobrium on the unknown portion of his life that his current reputation would be harmed. As a result the established version of his life, even when it showed him in the most virtuous possible light, became a matter for grave suspicion.

Nothing can resist a destructive process of this kind: calumny, even the most whimsical, gives birth to doubt, and doubt is a universal solvent even more powerful than that of the alchemists. Defamatory facts can be completely self-contradictory, assumptions can rest on nothing, imagination can be given free rein, but the reader, either out of curiosity or indifference, does not stop with the obvious dishonesties, but instead laps up whatever is offered to him. The mischief is then complete, and mistrust has made itself at home. The hero falls, and nothing and nobody can get him back on his feet again either in his own time or, indeed, for centuries thereafter.

That is what happened to Cagliostro: his youth, which no one knew anything about, was blackened with calumnies, and the first years of his life, which he wanted to leave enshrouded in mystery, were studded with scandalous stories and criminal intrigues without limit, without evidence, and without scruple. It is with this kind of introductory chapter that all Cagliostro's biographers begin.

We shall not of course follow them down that road. We shall study the various assumptions about his mysterious birth and the unknown part of his life, but we shall do that in the place that is appropriate to our study, i.e. after we've carefully followed his life, step by step, from the hour when his life becomes known to history [1] until his dying-day. This will give us, in contrast to the image that emerges from the works of self-interested lampoonists or unreflective critics, a flesh-and-blood figure to stand comparison with the purely imaginative creations fed to the general public to fill the vacuum of this unknown period of his life. This is far preferable to basing our account, as they have done, on suppositions and poorly-evidenced facts so as to create a novelistic figure which would simply cast a shadow of unjustified mistrust across the living, breathing figure that we shall present. We feel that passing from the known to the unknown in this way is an altogether more scientific and equitable approach. It will also enable us to avoid excessive length and repetition, because in order to judge the value of the various assumptions about him we need to find out who was responsible for formulating them: if we are to follow Cagliostro in his work and struggles in Strasbourg, Paris and London we will need to discuss those writers who were the first to try to raise the veil of mystery in which he was enshrouded.

Without therefore wasting time trying to find out whether Cagliostro ever visited Egypt, passed through Rhodes on his way to Malta, was born in Messina or somewhere else, or whether he lived for a time in Naples – all quite secondary matters since Cagliostro never really appeared in any of these places and since, in addition, we consider most of his statements on these topics to be purely symbolic in character [2] – we shall begin our study with the first appearance of Cagliostro in London in 1777. It is only from that date onwards that we have any documentary evidence that originates either with him or with his adversaries and which is sufficiently precise and open to discussion.

Before his first stay in London there were certainly some events in his life that were already a part of history and which seem well established: his stay in Malta [3] and his work with the Grandmaster Pinto, who was an amateur of hermetic science; his marriage in Rome; his friendship with Chevalier d'Aquino [4]; and a visit he made to Spain [5] are all facts that he himself acknowledged and which his enemies accepted even if the latter did distort the details. We must therefore ourselves accept and re-state them.

Cagliostro certainly spent an active youth: he began travelling in Western Europe at an early age but no real evidence remains of his work as no one who knew him at that time refers to him in their writings. Since he certainly did not achieve in any of these places anything remotely comparable to the extraordinary accomplishments that were to make him famous later on we can only mention certain statements that are rightly accepted by other authors, unless we wish to fall into the same trap that we have criticised other writers for falling into. We shall not however dwell on these events for too long. These travels, which lasted several years, brought him eventually to London in 1777, and that was the true beginning of his career.

NOTES
(1) In England in 1777, when he was approximately 33 years of age.
(2) We say 'most of his statements' because not all of them are purely symbolic, as we explain later.
(3) 'The information we have from Malta confirms the arrival in that island around 1766 of a Sicilian priest accompanying a youngster aged about ten to twelve whose description corresponds to that of Cagliostro, and who then travelled further with Chevalier d'Aquino', *Ma correspondance*, no. 59, 22nd July 1786. Cf. also Borowski, *Cagliostro... etc.*, p. 31. The priest, who was wearing the insignia of the Sovereign Order of Malta, had travelled extensively in the Middle East and was called Puzzo, while the child's name was Michael.
(4) *Mémoires pour le comte de Cagliostro*, Paris, 1786, pp. 18 & 19. In 1783 Cagliostro travelled to

Chapter I

Naples to be with Chevalier d'Aquino, who was dying.

(5) *Mémoires pour le comte de Cagliostro*, p. 22. Don Luis de Lima Vasconcellos, Grand Prior of Majorca, brother of Don Jaime de Majonès de Lima de Sotomajor, the Spanish Ambassador to France 1747-1764, was a disciple of Cagliostro, cf. *Souvenirs de la marquis de Créquy*, Paris, 1834, 3 vols., vol. III, pp. 223 et seq.

CHAPTER II

—

'THE IMPOSTOR'

A PORTRAIT OF CAGLIOSTRO

During his time in Europe (i.e. 1777 to 1787) Cagliostro was known as a man of slightly below-average height [1], square-shouldered, with a broad and convex chest, exuding an overall impression of good health and strength. His impressive head was covered with wavy, slightly-dishevelled black hair, which he wore brushed back [2]. He stood ramrod-straight, often even pulling his shoulders back exaggeratedly, a stance that displayed a neck that was round and muscular and yet also remarkably gracious [3]. In contrast with his broad chest his hands and feet were small, and his wrists and ankles slender [4]. An incipient plumpness, which became accentuated only in the final years of his life, in no way compromised a natural vivacity. His gait was lively and nimble [5], full of *joie de vivre* and a muscular energy that always seemed to be seeking an outlet. His face was full, his complexion fresh, his forehead broad and lofty. His physiognomy, very broad at the level of the cheekbones, narrowed towards the base, with the lower maxilla less developed. His features were quite symmetrical and integrated: his nose was well-rounded, his ears delicate and refined [6], his upper lip protruded over his lower lip, and his mouth, often half-open, revealed a set of strong and dazzling teeth. Beneath a median dimple his chin swelled proudly.

Cagliostro's eyes were very dark, expressive, and sparkled with life [7]. If he fixed them on you to examine you closely then you were forced to look away, so piercing was his gaze. When he spoke passionately about something, his pupils would dilate and his eyelids rise beneath the high arch of his brows as his voice grew louder. His gestures were accentuated: when he walked, he shook his hair like a mane, and when he stood still his whole body seemed to vibrate in sympathy with his thoughts. Vermilion blood circulated beneath his skin, giving his face a radiant luminosity [8]. Sometimes he would drop this leonine 'prophet's head', as he momentarily laid aside his terrible majesty to become softer and display some merciful or tender feeling. When that happened you would be left wondering whether, with his gentle voice and tender expression so full of benevolence, he was indeed the same man as the one who just moments before had been thrilling minds and galvanising bodies with the resonance of his voice, the flash of his eyes and the grandeur of his words.

His facial expressions changed constantly, but his face always remained lively and attractive. That was something his contemporaries are unanimous about [9]. Even before he had spoken, his expression made it clear that this was an intelligent, energetic and sympathetic man. When he eventually began to speak the timbre of his voice, his gestures, his cadences all served to confirm your initial judgement. You also got an impression of authority and power to which the majority were happy to yield without thinking, in a rush of spontaneous sympathy, though there were some who struggled against it.

On the eve of his death, when old age, his many struggles, the privations he endured in the Bastille and the tortures that he underwent in Rome had taken their toll, causing his features to deteriorate and his formerly robust body to become decrepit, Cagliostro undoubtedly lost much of the heroic allure that he had enjoyed as a young man. We can see a change in him already in the London portrait [10].

In recent times the medium Helene Smith [11T], well known for her work with Professor Flournoy and for the religious paintings she has produced under the stimulus of specific visions, suddenly found herself painting a portrait of Cagliostro in his last days (perhaps even his last hours), which doesn't resemble in the slightest the portraits of him with which we are familiar, except for the bony structures of the face and the expression [12]. What people seem to find especially striking about the Smith portrait is the expression of suffering that's etched upon his emaciated face, and which contrasts so strikingly with the intelligent gleam of his large wide-open eyes and his general impression of energy. Although this painting has no documentary value for those of a critical turn of mind, we ourselves find it very interesting and instructive. The evocation by spiritual means of an image from the past is no longer considered an inadmissible phenomenon and an insult to logic. Indeed, perhaps in the years to come it will find acceptance as an everyday accepted mode of historical enquiry [13]. We are very sorry that Helene Smith has refused to communicate with us or allow us to reproduce this distressing image which, if more widely disseminated, would perhaps have inspired some worthwhile reflections in the more observant, and would in any case have aroused in many people some justified feelings of compassion for the Martyr of San Leo.

Cagliostro, no matter what the legends say, dressed simply [14]. This statement will no doubt surprise many readers. We are so used to unthinkingly following the novelists in depicting him as covered in braid and studded with diamonds, plumed like a general, turning the heads of astonished passers-by with his opulent clothing [15]. Indeed, some writers have loaded him down with all the jewels that the policeman Chesnon found lying in his writing-desk and with all the fine costumes of Saint-Germain, plus a few missing details to make him look like some ridiculous travelling-acrobat, and this is how he has been presented it to the public. Here again, as elsewhere, when we start examining the received opinions on Cagliostro we find that the truth is more likely to be found in their precise opposite. If we can we should make a clean slate or, if we cannot manage that, then at least try to provide a less whimsical interpretation of the facts. For is anything more firmly established in the public mind than the ridiculous ostentation and bad taste of Count Cagliostro? But what exactly were the origins of this legend?

First it was a product of his intense generosity and lack of selfishness. People saw him showering money on the unfortunate and asking nothing in return and that alone was enough to inspire criticism. He also talked a lot about alchemy, and knew the Hermetic secrets of gold and diamonds. The envious couldn't help speculating about the 'occult treasure' that must lie hidden in his coffers or how much even the smallest stones in his bracelets must be worth. When Cagliostro became associated in the public mind, quite unjustly, with the Diamond Necklace Affair, in which of course millions of pounds were involved, Madame de la Motte rushed to exploit the situation. It was she who first wrote [16] about Cagliostro's costumes, the scandalous luxury of his wife's lifestyle, his diamonds, and his generally poor taste. These allegations were repeated without scrutiny, were accepted and amplified, and as a result in modern writers we find nothing except long-winded descriptions of 'the charlatan's sumptuous costumes'.

The truth, however, is very different and the historians, if they had not been so insincere, could easily have found out what it was. In Russia Count Moszyński, who certainly never lost an opportunity to attack his *bête noire*, tells us that Cagliostro affected an 'extraordinary' simplicity of dress [17]. In Strasbourg, a very observant and not especially sympathetic Swiss notes that his manner of dress was very simple and natural [18]. This same gentleman had reproached Cagliostro for, amongst other things, spending too much time with VIPs instead of dedicating himself exclusively to the common people, and especially to the citizen of an independent Switzerland who had paid him the compliment of travelling all that way to see him – that was the burden of his complaint! In the *Évangile de Cagliostro* [19] we find the same opinion. These are varied testimonies, supplied over a period of several years in different places by people with no very great love of Cagliostro. However, no one has wanted to take any notice of them, and of course we can say the same for all the other aspects of Cagliostro's life! Not only did he dress simply he even affected, as one of his enemies tells us, 'a negligence in dress that often bordered on cynicism' [20]. Our so-called historians, confronted with this statement, should feel very ashamed. For us, on the contrary, it simply provides confirmation of our thesis: Fashionable conventions were beneath him.

Indeed, he thought about absolutely everything except his appearance, and if you followed him into his laboratory, as our quoted author did, or surprised him in his room after a night of hard work, or came to him unexpectedly to ask him to help with a patient in danger, then he might appear in his working-clothes, without powder or ribbons, his collar half-open [21], his sleeves rolled up and his hair dishevelled, even if it meant shocking some petty marquis or pastor in a white cravat who had come to visit him. His clothes were of little interest to him: they seem to have been generally clean [22], but whether he was smartly dressed or not, whether the weather was good or bad, whether it was his conscience or his sense of duty that was summoning him outside, he would simply get up and go. One day De Gleichen saw him 'running along the road in the middle of a downpour, wearing a very beautiful outfit, to help a dying man and without even taking the time to grab an umbrella' [23].

Yes, here is the real Cagliostro, Cagliostro as he was meant to be, as he was. This contempt for worldly things was not an affectation: it had its origin in events, in the fact that he had more important things to think about than what time it was or what the weather was like. It was not a studied attitude or a deliberately provocative one. When he went out into the world he wore the costume that was appropriate to his rank and historical period, the sort of clothes that he could wear anywhere without embarrassment and which did not make him stand out from the crowd. It was these clothes, simple and appropriate, and suitable for wearing around town, that the authors we have mentioned have described him as wearing. His Versailles portrait [24] shows him thus attired, whereas the engravings of Basset show him in indoor or working-clothes [25].

CAGLIOSTRO. Bust by Houdon.
Museum of Aix-en-Provence

Those who got to know him well – which was by no means an easy task as he adopted a generally brusque and abrupt attitude towards the idly curious, the big-headed and the pretentious – were immediately struck by his pride. He never deliberately abased himself to make 'the slightest effort to obtain the favour of important people' [26]. He would even reject their advances if he suspected an ulterior motive, or if he discerned, in their approaches, the slightest trace of impertinence [27], especially towards his wife the Countess. Even his enemies remarked upon it, and his independence of manner towards everyone, great and small, male and female, often led to breakdowns in relationships. 'He is hostile to schemers', acknowledges one of his more violent detractors with some amazement, 'and seems almost happy to alienate those people who might be most useful to him' [28].

Ladies in high society, diplomats, worldly abbés and people of refinement at the Court of Louis XVI were often startled by his brusqueness, and initially thought they would be glad to get away from him, but Cagliostro's gaze was so majestic and his words so captivating that very soon all they wanted to do was remain in his presence, 'such was the impact that the man made' [29]. He was naturally imposing, radiating a mysterious grandeur and power, and all those who met him left his presence 'deliriously proclaiming all his wonderful qualities' [30]. 'Even those who did not join his inner circle and saw him only in passing could not deny this extraordinary air of authority' [31]. Sometimes even the most malicious sceptics found themselves drawn to him despite themselves. 'Those who paid him a visit merely to catch him out left full of wonder at his wisdom' [32]. As for his patients, those poor wretches who came to pour out their hearts to him and assail him with unceasing requests for assistance, they found in him a patience that would withstand any test and an ability to help that was simply miraculous. Whatever their station in life they were unanimous in their praise for his extraordinary powers and, above all, for his kindness [33].

But Cagliostro's kindness was not the philanthropic pity of the doctor or the philosopher for the travails of mankind: it was something greater than that. He did not love only those in his own intimate circle – his darling wife [34], his disciples and his friends [35] – and nor was his charity confined to his patients, the poor or to prisoners [36]: he even extended it to two most hateful creatures, two miserable wretches who never stopped making his life as unhappy as possible and who indeed were the architects of all his misfortunes: Sachi and Madame de la Motte. Blessed with as much love as wisdom he raised his voice in both their favours when human justice was poised to strike them down. He intervened to save Sachi from imprisonment and he tried to get Madame de la Motte's punishment reduced, not wishing to add anything to their misfortunes and forgiving them entirely and publicly for their crimes and misdeeds [37].

'He was not known to have any kinds of financial resources or letters of credit and yet he lived in great comfort [38]'. His house was swarming with people seeking help from morning to night. Countess Cagliostro, gentle, pleasant, diffident, as plain-living as her husband, a true home-body [39], welcomed at her table all those that her husband brought to her, whether friends, the merely inquisitive, scroungers, the poor seeking help, even high aristocrats too sometimes. The Cagliostro's always kept a good table, with a certain abundance indeed [40], always ready to welcome the anticipated flow of guests. Cagliostro liked to entertain people at table and would let his guard down more readily in the cordial atmosphere of these informal meals than elsewhere: he spoke more than he ate, always arrived at the last moment, often late, having rushed about all morning, on foot or in a carriage, and always seemed to be ready to set out again. He ate only macaroni and drank only water, and indeed the first course had hardly been served when his own meal was over.

While the courses followed one after the other with the guests tucking in eagerly Cagliostro would chat and answer people's questions pleasantly and even cheerfully until it was time for the coffee that he loved so much and which he would always make a point of taking with his guests [41].

His energy was extraordinary. He was always on the go and never seemed tired. The whole Cagliostro household was a hive of activity, and he never stood still: he would go out in the morning to visit patients, return to see others, receive visitors, and then chat with his closest friends. At nine in the evening he would tell people that he was withdrawing to his room or laboratory to rest, but in fact would continue working hard far into the night [42]. He often never went to bed, instead slumbering for just a few hours in an armchair [43], then reappearing the following morning refreshed and ready for a new day. But he always kept these night-time hours strictly to himself for solitary meditation, and it was only exceptionally that he would stay up late chatting and working with a few disciples [44].

His philanthropy was well known: not only did he give his advice, his time, his help and his abilities to those who needed them, but also, as we know, he would prepare or buy remedies for them and give money to the poor, often paying the rent and others debts of those crushed by misery [45]. From the rich he refused to accept anything, and those who wanted to give him some token of their esteem, however small, whether directly or via the Countess, would have a struggle to do so and would often have to resort to subterfuge [46]. If they did succeed, then those who had given Cagliostro what they thought was a gift of considerable value would find him, just a few days later, giving *them* a gift worth many times the value of their own, which, of course, they would not dare to refuse. This fact is well established [47]. And if he did sometimes accept gifts from especially obstinate donors then what was that besides the wealth that he distributed every day to the poor and needy?

Surrounded, lionised and adored by women, he nonetheless passed amongst them imperceptibly, attracting them no doubt, but never being subject to their influence. He was surrounded by a swarm of women of all kinds – rich, beautiful, intelligent, powerful [48] – but none ever distracted him. From St. Petersburg to Rome, during those ten years when his private life was under hourly scrutiny, when even the smallest details of his life were being uncovered, no one ever found the slightest evidence of a love affair. 'Nobody has purer morals', Labarthe wrote to Séguier [49], and nobody, one might add, understood better the hearts of men, the souls of women and their respective dangers.

He was amiable and often made jokes. He sometimes displayed a refined tenderness when dealing with the emotions of the social elite [50], bestowing on them, in just a few minutes of spiritual release, more real love than he himself would enjoy in a whole lifetime of human affection, but he also knew how to guard himself against dangerous personalities: in those situations the severe and impenetrable *persona* of the Master would immediately reappear [51]. Neither schemers like the petty Madame de la Motte nor beautiful socialites like the Marquise de Branconi [52], who long held a grudge against him, could add him to their conquests. His ambitions were too vast and his mind too lucid to feel comfortable wasting time on life's journey dreaming instead of acting.

Cagliostro spoke fluent French. Foreigners who spoke to him in Italian testified that he spoke that language extremely well and that it was certainly his native tongue [53] but Bode, who used to speak to him in Portuguese, states that it was that language he spoke best [54]. In any case, it was French that was most generally useful to him and the language with which he was most at ease: his depositions in Paris during the Diamond Necklace Affair and his letters are proof of that, as is the general testimony of all those who frequented him. The

French in France, like the Italians in Italy, noticed only that, in their respective languages, he had a foreign accent which they couldn't quite place. Sometimes he spoke a dialect that no one could identify but which, according to a contemporary [55], seemed to be half-way between French and Italian [56]. He knew Latin, as his interrogations in Rome prove [57], and according to Laborde he sometimes quoted Arabic [58].

In whatever language he was expressing himself he always spoke in a lively fashion: the images flowed, and he would speak volubly about all manner of things, covering a thousand different topics, religion, the sciences, ethics, without any apparent link between them, but always with originality, offering keen and intelligent insights, never being content to remain within the humdrum framework of small talk or lapsing into the dreariness of private sermons. He broke down the barriers of scientific dogma, the closed doors of theologies and the façades of fashionable morals, causing the walls of all the prisons of truth to tremble. What he said was lively, with a personal slant: if he sometimes seemed to be adhering to some system or other he would suddenly set himself free from it by following another route. From the subject of Heaven and its many mansions he would pass to chemistry, from gangrene to the importance of loving one's neighbour, from the nature of the Sun to the intrigues of his enemies. Those who heard him for the first time, whether on leave from their regiments, easing off their boots after a hunt, or coming back from the theatre, left him with their head in a whirl, returning home to tell their friends that there was no twaddle that had ever been spoken that equalled that of Cagliostro [59]. Twaddle?! A superficial and lazy judgement to be sure, for quite serious men have called any form of metaphysics complete twaddle. To a Brittany peasant the higher mathematics is a tedious piece of twaddle, and according to the judgment without appeal of Tribulat Bonhomet [60T] the verse of Mallarmé and the pages of Jakob Böhme are pure twaddle as well.

All the historians speak mockingly about Cagliostro's inflated, pretentious and vacuous literary style, but if we examine the direct quotations from him which his contemporaries have left us and if we read his memoirs then we certainly find some very beautiful and sometimes impressive passages. In his legal petitions and letters, we find taut argumentation, tending even to a certain dryness here and there. Finally, if there are certain passages with an exaggeratedly cadenced tone where rhetorical artifice is apparent we must remember that they date from a time when writing assumed a garb that is now largely obsolete, and that Cagliostro simply gave his lawyer Maître Thilorier a general outline of his defence [61] for him to re-cast in its final form. The lawyer of the 18th century, however meritorious he might be, was prone to minor defects of literary style. Compare his submission in the Diamond Necklace Affair with the others: if there are any differences then they are all in Cagliostro's favour [62].

Cagliostro's prose contains individual words, turns of phrase and even occasional sacred transports that will simply exasperate the level-headed and the serious. Not everyone, however, can or should be as cold and clinical in their manner of expression as a notary determining the fate of someone's life-savings. When an envoy of God is talking about his fatherland, his life, his passions, then linguistically 'the wind bloweth where it listeth', his sentiments will no longer be time-bound, and his voice, an echo of the Eternal Word, will sometimes vibrate with strange sonorities. Cagliostro spoke and acted with a lofty detachment, in the name of the power that had been given to him by God as he himself said [63], and in such a way that everyone could grasp something of his teachings – some more, some less. Cagliostro did not speak to the imagination but to the spirit. He didn't repudiate rationality [64] but he had no time for haughty and ignorant quibblers whose minds are systematically closed to anything with which they are not already familiar. They alone were to accuse him of unintelligibility. Those whose minds were more open, more impartial, even if they were outside his circle of disciples, appreciated his knowledge and found nothing but charm in his conversation [65].

Those who were fortunate enough to hear him speak often and who then reflected upon his words would begin to understand him better and better: apparent contradictions would be eliminated and the links between the different subjects with which he dealt, which seemed to be missing at the outset, would become apparent as they reflected upon them. His life was seen to be in harmony with his words, his doctrine explained his powers, and his actions demonstrated the truth of his theories. Whether he was in his laboratory, was busy with a patient, or was out in the world, Cagliostro became increasingly comprehensible, greater in stature, and more charismatic and attractive. He always encouraged his listeners in their efforts to understand him, appearing to these people of good will in a light of which others would not have suspected him capable. In the depths of his lectures, in the middle of his digressions and in his actions such people managed to tease out certain unchanging principles and discern certain moral laws to direct their conduct. They caught a glimpse of the initiatory road about which Cagliostro often spoke, the road that leads to immortality and total power. To keep digging, to keep sowing – and allow others to reap the harvest – to try always to go one step further, to accept all the tasks that others reject [66], sure in the knowledge that Nature will not conceal anything and that Heaven will impart all its strength to anyone who shows himself incapable of using it for selfish purposes, to become master of one's soul through patience – that was the doctrine that Cagliostro taught.

But was it, we might ask, a doctrine in the strict sense of the term? The word is surely inappropriately dry and scholastic: it was a school of energy, of abnegation, of firm confidence in the future. Cagliostro's pupils felt stronger both physically and morally when they were around him. They left him full of ardour, but after trying to live out his example for just a short while they would return, rapidly exhausted, to drink once more, this time even more eagerly, from the fountain of life. Every struggle made them eager to receive more, every new shaft of illumination made their souls stronger. They would experience something, verify it for themselves, and see their faith grow as their suppositions were confirmed.

In the presence of a Master whose acts were no less marvellous than his doctrines, a man towards whom everyone felt a debt of gratitude that they would never be able to repay, it was impossible for a certain spirit of competition not to arise. Within the tiny coteries of Cagliostro's disciples it was all a question of who would be the first to bring to the world some new *dictum* or, even better, some previously unheard-of action, as further proof of Cagliostro's miraculous abilities. Gradually, as people's imaginations went to work and vanity came into play, the legends and exaggerations made their way into the minds of enthusiasts. From there, thanks to the need to spread the word but a lack of skill in doing so, these legends made their way into the outside world. There they expanded and became so badly distorted in the process that, far away from the circles of disciples in which they had originated, a vast tornado of rumour and supposition arose. People who had never even met Cagliostro or had had only the briefest of encounters with him but who were full of second-hand information that they believed to be true would exchange the most conflicting and self-contradictory statements and the most unlikely assertions, and all with an air of total assurance, about this man about whom everyone was talking, about his religion, his occult mysteries, his personal appearance, his mannerisms. For some he was just a braggart, for others the Devil incarnate. He was an Italian Rosicrucian, a Sufi mystic, a Portuguese Jew. Everyone had total confidence in his own opinion, however unrealistic, and often claimed to have proof. Some had no doubt that he was the famous Cosmopolite or Peregrini risen from the grave and arrived straight from Austria, while for others Cagliostro and the Comte de Saint-Germain were one and the same – after all, they'd heard it from Cagliostro himself! But the most serious question that people wanted an answer to was whether he really had attended the wedding in Cana of Galilee as some had said, or if he really was Simon Magus or one of the Apostles [67].

Inevitably, all these ridiculous stories found their way back to Cagliostro's disciples. For some of them the question of whether Cagliostro really had lived before, if he really was the reincarnation of some historical figure, coincided with their own thoughts, unsettled them, led them into serious discussion and in some cases motivated them – as audacious a step as it was – to actually put the question to Cagliostro himself. The answer to that question would vary, depending on how the question was put and who was asking it. If he was asked, 'Master, is it true that five (or perhaps twenty-five) centuries ago you were already on the Earth and were called such-and-such' he would answer evasively and sometimes recount some unknown fact from the period in question [68] which, without being particularly specific, would simply confirm the questioner's suppositions. He would never say categorically that such was the case, but nor would he ever go to much trouble to dissuade the questioner from whatever it was that they genuinely seemed to believe.

In doing so, wasn't he simply acting as any self-respecting Sage would? Only a person who understands the mysteries of the spirit can speak authoritatively about the evolution of souls: it is for that person alone that phrases like 'I was or was not this person or that' have any real meaning. But those who asked Cagliostro such questions had no knowledge or understanding of the spirit world and could not therefore receive from him any other answer other than one that, without actually doing violence to the truth, would encourage them to seek further. If on the other hand Cagliostro was asked, 'Master, who exactly are you?', he would simply reply, 'I am who I am' [69]. Nor did he ever conceal from anyone the fact that the name Cagliostro, which he had personally chosen, or his title of Count, or the rank of colonel that he allowed some to assign to him in various places [70] were mere fictions, just token attributions that he changed several times, and that the only dignities of which he was genuinely proud and which he claimed for himself was to be the friend of God, someone who had God's ear, and who was his faithful soldier. Then, shaking his head in a gesture that was simultaneously sympathetic and valedictory, he would cut the conversation short and leave his disciple deep in thought as he watched this mysterious, all-powerful man with the unfathomable gaze and the power to perform miracles walk nobly but nimbly away from him and disappear into the crowd. What sort of being had he just been talking to, and what was this strange light in which his soul was suddenly bathed that made him feel so weak and yet so joyful and so profoundly secure in the presence of Count Cagliostro?

NOTES
(1) Five feet one (!) says police-officer Bernard in the *Courrier de l'Europe*, no. 29, 1787. Cf. also *L'Évangile de Cagliostro*, Paris, 1910, p. 85. Also *Ein paar Tröpflein aus dem Brünnen...*, 1781, p. 2. De Gleichen, *Souvenirs*, p. 135.
(2) Cf. Langmesser. *Jacob Sarrasin*, Zurich, 1899, p. 54, remark by Schmidt.
(3) We can see these features in the portrait by Chapuis and the bust by Houdon, both of which are reproduced in this book.

(4) Cf. Gedike and Biester, *Berliner Monatsschrift*, vol. IV, July-December 1784, *Le pseudo comte Cagliostro*. Also *Cagliostro démasqué à Varsovie*, 1786, p. 32.
(5) In Roveredo, in 1787, this vitality had struck the author of the *Liber memorialis* just as it had already astonished the people of Northern Europe in 1778. Cf. *L'Évangile de Cagliostro*, p. 85 and Langmesser, loc. cit., p. 55.
(6) *Berliner Monatsschrift*, 1784, December issue, *Observations d'un voyageur*.
(7) Letter from Bürkli in Funk, *Cagliostro à Strasbourg*, p. 14. 'He had the piercing eye of a falcon'. Langmesser, loc. cit., p. 54: 'His gaze was *verschlingend*', i.e. 'devouring'.
(8) 'When he spoke, in his mellifluous voice, with his highly expressive gestures and his eyes rolling heavenwards, he reminded you of the God-intoxicated mystics of the Middle Ages', *L'Évangile de Cagliostro*, p. 86. Cf. *Lettres sur la Suisse*, De Laborde, Langmesser, *Jacob Sarrasin*, Zurich, 1899, p. 54., *Ibid*. Testimony of Schmidt, p. 55, and *Notice* of 1788, p. 3.
(9) 'He had a very fine head – indeed it could have used as a model to represent the profile of an inspired poet', De Gleichen, *Souvenirs*, p. 136. 'The boldness of his countenance made it very prepossessing', Casanova, *Mémoires*. 'Cagliostro had a very pleasing countenance', *L'Évangile de Cagliostro*, p. 85.
(10) Painting by Bartolozzi in 1787, engraved by Macquart, and reproduced in this book.
(11T) Her real name was Catherine Elise Muller. 'In the late 1890s, Smith was studied by a number of leading investigators, most notably Theodore Flournoy, a Swiss professor of psychology. Flournoy, using psychoanalytic techniques, spent five years sitting in on séances, researching Smith's personal history, and corroborating historical information she provided at her séances. Flournoy described the takeover of Cagliostro as a gradual process. First, Smith felt as though an invisible force seized her arms and she could not move them. Then, pain arose in her neck at the base of her skull. Her eyelids drooped, and her chin dropped and formed what appeared to be a double chin, giving her a resemblance to portraits of Cagliostro. She took on a pompous bearing, made Masonic signs with her hands, and spoke in a slow, deep, masculine bass voice with an Italian accent. Cagliostro addressed everyone as 'thou' and acted as though he was 'the grand master of secret societies', according to Flournoy' (From: *The Encyclopedia of Demons and Demonology* by Rosemary Ellen Guiley, Checkmark Books, 2009, article on 'Helene Smith'). For Flournoy, see R. E. Goldsmith, *The Life and Work of Theodore Flournoy*, Ph.D. thesis, Michigan State University 1979.
(12) Portrait painted in thirteen weeks from 23rd November to 13th April 1908. Cf. *Initiation*, 1908, p. 208.
(13) Psychometry is a very fascinating applied science which is providing us with a lot of new information. Many striking examples of divination can be explained by this incidental perception of traces of the past. The scholar Campardon told me a most charming story one day. Apparently one of the most erudite and hard-headedly rationalistic of modern historical researchers, tired of his ceaseless and fruitless searching for an essential document on the life of the French Revolutionary figure Jean-Paul Marat, was persuaded by some unfathomable impulse to go and see a trance-medium to find out where this obscure document might be found. The medium described a provincial town, a square, a fountain, a house opposite the town hall, an attic… 'That's Amiens!' shouted the historian. He immediately rushed off there, made a forcible entry into an old attic and found the famous document! Similar facts are not rare: every family has some personal experience of such matters via telepathy or psychometry. It would be premature to try to explain this phenomenon, but to blame it on pure coincidence is absurd.
(14) *L'Évangile de Cagliostro*, p. 86.
(15) Lenotre portrays him thus.
(16) *Réponse pour la comtesse de Valois Lamotte*, Paris, Cellot, 1786, pp. 26 & 37. Cagliostro's 'secret treasure' was announced, to general public mistrust, in his first memoir, Cf. *Mémoire pour Cagliostro*, 1786, p. 61.
(17) *Ein paar Tröpflein*, p. 3.
(18) Letter from Bürkli in Funk, *Cagliostro à Strasbourg*, p. 19.

(19) *L'Évangile de Cagliostro*, p. 86.
(20) *Ein paar Tröpflein*, p. 2, 'He's actually rather negligent in the way he wears his hair and clothes, but without in any way being indecorous', says Borowski in contrast in his *Cagliostro*, p. 137.
(21) See his portrait later in this book and the *Letter from Bürkli* in Funk, *Cagliostro à Strasbourg*, p. 19.
(22) Testimony of an observer in Roveredo, *L'Évangile de Cagliostro*, p. 86. No doubt this was because his wife made sure that they were.
(23) De Gleichen, *Souvenirs*, pp. 135-136.
(24) The portrait is reproduced as the frontispiece to this book.
(25) Lenotre, without providing any references, says that in Paris he wore, until long after the warmer weather arrived, a fur-lined dress-coat, which he had brought back no doubt – if the story is to be believed – from his stay in Russia, cf. Lenotre, *Vieilles maisons*, p. 163. Lenotre has taken this detail from the memoirs of the Marquise de Créquy which, as we know, are apocryphal and are actually the work of the Comte de Courchamps.
(26) Georgel, *Mémoires*, p. 52 and elsewhere: 'He did not pay court to anyone'.
(27) When the Cardinal, before he had even been introduced to Cagliostro, summoned him to Saverne out of sheer curiosity Cagliostro replied: 'If His Eminence is sick then let him come here and I will cure him. If he's feeling alright then he doesn't need me, nor I him'. In Paris he refused invitations from the Duc de Chartres and the Comte d'Artois, both of whom wanted to attend their *salons*, cf. Georgel, *Mémoires*, p. 46.
(28) *Cagliostro démasqué*, pp. 50-51. In another lampoon we read: 'What strikes us most about his behaviour is a pride without equal and an absolute lack of anything in the way of everyday good manners or education', *Ein Tröpflein*, p. 2.
(29) Georgel, *Mémoires*, p. 52.
(30) Georgel. *Mémoires*, p. 48, and *L'Évangile de Cagliostro*, p.7. Baroness d'Oberkirch, initially offended by his off-handedness, was subsequently completely won over: 'I found it difficult to free myself from a fascination which, even now, I have difficulty understanding, but which I cannot deny', *Mémoires*, vol. I, p. 135. The Cardinal, from his very first meeting with Cagliostro, was – as he himself admits – filled with a religious awe.
(31) Gedike and Biester, *Berliner Monatsschrift*, vol. IV, July 1784. De Gleichen and the envoys of the *Philalèthes* felt this masterful influence and, on their return to the lodge, testified to the other brethren about the great impression that Cagliostro had made upon them, cf. *Acta Latomorum*, 1815, vol. II, p. 114.
(32) *L'Évangile de Cagliostro*, p. 5. See below for the story of the students who came to trick him but left him convinced of his clairvoyant abilities. A police-agent sent from Paris to Strasbourg to cross-examine him fell to his knees in awe during one of his meetings with him.
(33) 'It's the good Lord who is leaving us', the people cried when he left Strasbourg.
(34) Cf. *Mémoire contre Chesnon*, Paris, 1786, p. 16, *L'Évangile de Cagliostro*, p. 81, Sophie Laroche, *Tagebuch einer Reise*, p. 297.
(35) Letter from Bürkli in Funk, *Cagliostro à Strasbourg*, p. 1. 'He has shown himself to be full of kindness towards us'.
(36) His philanthropy in Strasbourg, Paris and London is the only thing about Cagliostro which no one has ever disputed.
(37) Cf. *Requête à joindre au mémoire*, Lottin, 1786, p. 6. For Madame de la Motte, see *Mémoire contre le procureur général*, 1786, p. 73.
(38) Georgel, *Mémoires*, p. 46.
(39) 'She never went out, never went to the theatre. She was always seen wearing the same dress', Letter from Bürkli in Funk, *Cagliostro à Strasbourg*, p. 14. These sources flatly contradict the lies spread by Madame de la Motte, and rebut accepted opinion.
(40) Sophie Laroche, *Tagebuch einer Reise*, 1788, p. 315. In Paris the Cardinal often turned up without warning. If he brought lots of people with him then sometimes he'd send round some platefuls

of food from his house.
(41) Sophie Laroche, *Tagebuch einer Reise*, 1788, p. 314. 'After dessert he always has a *caffè mocha*', Letter from Séguier in Funck-Brentano, *L'Affaire du Collier*, p. 90. Cf. also *Ma correspondance*, no. 73, of 5th September 1785.
(42) *Cagliostro démasqué*, p 11.
(43) Letter from Bürkli in Funk, *Cagliostro à Strasbourg*, p. 24.
(44) In Strasbourg he stayed up late with Sarrasin preparing medicines, in Paris he was often up late with Cardinal de Rohan, and in Roveredo with his hosts. Cf. *L'Évangile de Cagliostro*, p. 26.
(45) See letter from Görge in *Oberrheinische Mannigfaltigkeiten*, 1st Quarter of 1781, p. 113 et seq. and *Lettre au peuple anglais*, pp. 5-9.
(46) Isaac Iselin, *Ephemeriden*, November 1781, Langmesser, *J. Sarrasin*, p. 38, *Lettre de Langlois*, Archives Sarrasin, vol. XXXIII, shelf-mark 13, folio VI, and Chapter III of this book, *Cagliostro in London, First Visit*.
(47) Cf. Chapter III of this book, *Cagliostro in London, First Visit*. The Duc de Choiseul wanted Cagliostro to accept a diamond-encrusted snuffbox, but was only able to persuade him to accept it by receiving a more valuable snuffbox in return, cf. Spach, *Cagliostro à Strasbourg*, Works, vol. V, p. 75.
(48) Cf. Chapter VII of this book, *Cagliostro in Paris*, the section on women's Freemasonry, p. 172 et seq.
(49) Letter dated 1787. Cf. Funck-Brentano, *L'Affaire du Collier*, p. 99.
(50) *Liber memorialis de Caleostro* [sic], French translation by Dr. Marc Haven, Paris, 1910, p. 53, and von der Recke, *Nachricht von des berüchtigten...* 1787, p. 80.
(51) In Italy a lady in high society once tried to seduce Cagliostro with a two-pronged attack: her beauty and a huge personal fortune. The upshot was that she never saw him again. 'Doesn't she know me!', he screamed. 'She doesn't know or understand either me or what I have to say! She will never see me again until the blindfold that covers her eyes has fallen!', *Liber memorialis*, p. 45 of the French translation.
(52) Cf. Chapter IX of this book, *Cagliostro in Switzerland*.
(53) Letter from Blessig in Weisstein, *Cagliostro à Strasbourg*; *Elsaß-Lothringische Zeitung*, 1882, no. 37; and Heyking, *Cagliostro parmi les Russes*, in *Initiation*, August 1898, p. 129. Countess von der Recke published a letter in Italian from Cagliostro addressed to her in 1779. This is reproduced in the Appendix to this book.
(54) *Ein paar Tröpflein*, p. 2. The author sees this as proof that he was Portuguese.
(55) *Liber memorialis*, French translation, p. 7.
(56) Was this the *lingua franca* that Cagliostro said was essential for anyone visiting the Maghreb, or a Provençal dialect? Unfortunately we don't have a specimen of it to enable us to judge.
(57) *Vie de Joseph Balsamo*, p. 190.
(58) He had some Arab manuscripts amongst his papers, but Bode, who reports the fact (*Ein paar Tröpflein*, p. 3) says there was no doubt that he couldn't read even the first line of them. Bode's opinion is curious to say the least. The fact that Cagliostro didn't want to answer Norbert (Letter from Blessig, p. 23) when he spoke to him in Arabic proves only that he was annoyed about being probed as a suspicious character under the guise of courtesy. The impartial witness in Roveredo tells us, on the other hand, that he often withdrew to his room to write in Arabic, cf. *Liber memorialis*, French translation, p. 16.
(59) 'If pure twaddle can be sublime then nobody is more sublime than Cagliostro', *Vie de Joseph Balsamo*, p. 171, footnote. Beugnot admits that the first time he met him he was left dumbfounded, cf. *Mémoires de Beugnot*, p. 46, 1889.
(60T) A philistine and excessively rationalistic doctor who is the eponymous anti-hero of a series of stories by Auguste de Villiers de L'Isle-Adam (1838-1889).
(61) 'It is claimed that Count Cagliostro composed this memoir himself in Italian and that all Maître Thilorier did was translate it. That is very likely. Count Cagliostro has sufficient intelligence and, his friends claim, sufficient candour as well to write his life-story with plenty of freshness and interest

without needing the help of a lawyer', *Ma correspondance*, 24th February 1786, no. 18.

(62) Let us judge from this sample taken from *La dernière pièce du fameux collier*, p. 1: 'And so the great Cagliostro left, and in his flight disgorged after him the Elixir of Empiricism distilled in the Furnace of Calumny'. The author of this masterpiece was ill advised to treat as mere gossip the *Mémoire de Cagliostro*, where we can read things like this: 'I have written what suffices for the law and for any sentiment other than idle curiosity. Is that not enough? Will you insist on me being more specific, and on knowing the name, motives and financial resources of this unknown person? What does all that matter to you my dear Frenchmen? My fatherland is, for you, the most important place in your great empire, the place where I submitted respectfully to your laws; my name is the name I have made honourable amongst you; my motive is *God*; and my financial resources are my Great Secret. When, in order to comfort the infirm or feed the poor, I come to seek admission to your professional medical bodies or your official charities then – and only then – may you question me, but to perform in the name of God all the good that I can do is a right that requires neither name, nor fatherland, nor evidence, nor financial security', *Mémoire pour le comte de Cagliostro accusé*, 1786, p. 74. Twaddle? I really don't think so!

(63) *Interrogatoire de Rome. Vie de Joseph Balsamo*, pp. 117 & 127.

(64) His detractors wrongly accused him of irrationality: 'His technique is not to say anything that appeals directly to the reason – the imagination of his audience is left to form the interpretation', *Vie de Balsamo*, p. 39, note.

(65) 'His general conversation is pleasant and instructive', De Gleichen, *Souvenirs*, Paris, 1868, p. 135. Cf. Letter from Bürkli in Funk, *Cagliostro à Strasbourg*, 1905, p. 15; judgements by Pfeffel, Schlosser, Iselin and Lavater in Langmesser, *Jacob Sarrasin*, pp. 1, 38, 51, 68; Letter from Bürkli in Spach, Works, vol. V, p. 76.

(66) This was the aphorism of the Hermetic Masters: 'Seek the primary matter amongst things most vile, amongst the refuse which men tread underfoot each day'.

(67) Cf. *Liber memorialis*, French translation, p. 25; *Gazette de Leyde*, no. 72 of 9th September 1785; cf. also *Tableau mouvant*, vol. II, p. 307: 'He's a beneficent sylph, he's a 1,400-year-old man, he's the Wandering Jew, he's the Anti-Christ'; *Mémoire pour Cagliostro*, p. 55.

(68) Letter from Bürkli, in Funk, *Cagliostro à Strasbourg*, p. 5.

(69) *Rituel de la Maçonnerie Égyptienne*, Mss. Papus, p. 75.

(70) *Mémoire pour le comte de Cagliostro*, 1786, p. 23; Von der Recke, *Nachricht von des berüchtigten…*, p. 112; *Lettre au peuple anglais*, pp. 56-57; Letter of Blessig to Countess von der Recke: 'He clearly explained that his title of 'Count' does not refer to his lineage but to his occult knowledge'. Cf. also Weisstein, *Cagliostro à Strasbourg*, p. 7.

CHAPTER III

—

'THE SWINDLER'

CAGLIOSTRO IN LONDON – FIRST VISIT

According to the journalist Morande, 'Cagliostro survived in London by exploiting the credulity of gamblers whom he had tricked into believing that he knew how to predict winning lottery-numbers, and even how to make gold. In this way he managed to extort considerable sums from them. However, when none of them saw that their ambitions were being fulfilled they realised that this was nothing more than an imposture, denounced him as a swindler, and had him thrown into jail on more than one occasion. Balsamo decided to swear a false oath to extricate himself from the matter: he swore (and persuaded his wife to do the same) that he had never received any money from these people, and so escaped the hands of justice'.

This is the same view that we find in the *Vie de Joseph Balsamo* and other lampoons, as well as in many literary treatments of Cagliostro's life [1]. Are we therefore to assume that his first visit to London was nothing more than a catalogue of swindles, of mugs being exploited, people being financially ruined, and rascals bribing judges to persuade them to jail the innocent? Alas, it is indeed! We are fully in agreement with the opinion of Morande and his imitators as expressed above, but with one slight nuance: in our view it was *Cagliostro* who was the exploited innocent party, and the only swindlers were his so-called victims. And if our dear readers will have the courage to follow us into this world of crooks, burglars and bailiff's men, from judges' chambers to solicitors' offices, from courts to prisons, then they'll see that the person who was accused of being a swindler actually distributed money with largesse to enrich other people while keeping nothing for himself; that nowhere did he display greater ingenuity, trustfulness and patience than during his time in England; and that in no other country would he have been persecuted by those whom, after all, he had actually enriched. Cagliostro came to England rich and left it poor, leaving his fortune in the hands of English rascals and judges who were obviously determined to have a share of it right from the outset.

Below we shall recount the facts as they occurred, almost on a day-to-day basis. The details may seem long-winded, but that is the only way we can remove the opprobrium that has been heaped on Cagliostro, for all his enemies exploited his various entanglements with the law to impart to him a reputation for dishonour that subsequently opened the door for all the later malevolence that he had to endure.

Cagliostro, honoured in Courland, Russia and Strasbourg, a triumph in Lyons, celebrated and officially acquitted in Paris was, in all these phases of his life, invulnerable to his enemies. The only Achilles' heel he ever offered his enemies was that he had legal judgments made against him in London in 1777, and yet that was enough to compromise him as a swindler and instantly tarnish all his merits and accomplishments. Morande understood that all too well, and exploited it for all it was worth. Everyone came to believe the utterly fallacious version of Cagliostro's life in London in 1777 as reported at the start of this chapter. Despite Cagliostro's protests, no one ever thought of challenging it. But, let us tell our readers what *really* happened, so that they can judge for themselves.

Cagliostro arrived in London in July 1776 [2] without letters of introduction, bringing with him more than £3000 in cash and jewellery. He rented an apartment with his wife at 4 Whitcomb Street, the home of a Mrs. Juliet. Spotting the couple as rich and probably generous as well, she soon recommended some companions to them in the form of a destitute and sickly Portuguese lady called De Blévary, [3] who lived in the same building, and an Italian called Vitellini, a former schoolmaster and amateur chemist, who had been reduced to poverty by gambling. Cagliostro and his wife took them under their wing, lodging them, clothing them and feeding them [4]. Cagliostro also took on Vitellini as his secretary, while the Countess hired De Blévary as her companion. Although Cagliostro went out little, preferring to work for his own pleasure on chemical experiments at his lodgings [5], the indiscreet nattering of Vitellini, who enjoyed hanging around in cafés [6], and the equally injudicious gossip of De Blévary ensured that everyone in the area rapidly learned that a remarkable man, a true adept, immensely rich, and willing to share both his secrets and his wealth with anyone who needed it was living locally.

It didn't take very long for the inevitable results of such indiscretions to manifest. People in need of various kinds of help flocked to his door. Some were kindly received, but they only returned in greater numbers and with even more pressing demands. Cagliostro tightened his purse-strings and tried to slam the door on them, but as soon as he stopped being generous with them (or not generous enough, depending on their whim) the beggars turned into bitter enemies [7].

Cagliostro, partly in an attempt to come to help some of these wretches [8] and partly to try out a new system of calculation that interested him [9], had on several occasions predicted the winning-numbers in the English lottery [10]. This acted as the trigger for the beggars and spongers to try – through supplications, gifts, entreaties, anything – to pester him for even more help. Cagliostro later recalled the problems that he had with two of his most persistent and troublesome importuners:

Scott and his girlfriend, a Miss Fry who liked to style herself 'Lady Scott', initially pursued me in vain, but then Scott changed tactics and tried to win me over with gifts. He gave my wife a short fur cape worth four or five guineas. Obviously I didn't want to embarrass the man by refusing it, but that same day I reciprocated by giving him a gold box worth about twenty-five guineas. To avoid further annoyance I banned both of them from my premises, but a few days later the bogus Lady Scott managed to get hold of my wife. In a flood of tears she told her that she'd been ruined yet again, that her husband was a crook, that she'd taken up with him simply out of weakness of character, that he'd stolen their joint lottery winnings, and that he'd abandoned her along with the three children she had had by him. Countess Cagliostro, who was not so much angered by the fraud that had been perpetrated on Lady Scott as touched by the sad fate of this poor creature, was kind enough to speak to me on her behalf. I sent Lady Scott a guinea and told her to put it on number 8 for the lottery on 7th December. Lady Scott scraped together all the money she could and put it all on number 8 as I'd instructed. And as I predicted, number 8 was the winning number.

It's at this point that the details in Vitellini's diary become interesting. Vitellini was at the house of Miss Fry when she returned there with her lottery winnings. He himself counted some 421 guineas along with £460 in notes. Miss Fry gave Vitellini 20 guineas and then

Chapter III

came to see me in the first flush of excitement to offer me her entire fortune. The answer I gave her will be found in Vitellini's diary, but here it is verbatim: 'I don't want anything. Take it all. My advice, my good woman, is to go and live in the country with your children. Take it all I say. The only favour I ask of you is that you never darken my door again'. Vitellini makes it clear that Mr. Scott won 700 guineas on the same number I had given Miss Fry, which shows that their alleged disagreement was fabricated or, at least, had not been of long duration. What is certain is that, from this time onwards, they always acted in concert.

Since Miss Fry's greed had not yet been satisfied, she looked for ways of obtaining new numbers. No doubt thinking that the best way would be to persuade my wife to accept a gift from her, she offered her a small ivory toothpick-box stuffed with banknotes. After my wife made it clear to her with some formality that she wouldn't accept any gifts, Miss Fry acted in concert with Vitellini to find a way of making her a gift she couldn't refuse. They both went to a Mr. P., a jeweller in Princes Street, where Miss Fry bought a necklace of brilliants costing £94 and a double-lidded gold snuffbox for £20. She put the necklace in one half of the box and filled the other with a herbal powder resembling snuff which was supposed to be good for the so-called 'fluxions' (an inflammation of the lungs) from which my wife was then suffering. Miss Fry, seizing a moment when my wife was alone, went to see her on the pretext of thanking her. During the conversation she took out the box without affectation and offered her some snuff. My wife was unfamiliar with snuff of this kind, but she said that she did like the scent of it. Miss Fry then offered her the box containing it. Vitellini was also present. My wife refused it several times. Miss Fry, seeing that her insistence was fruitless, threw herself at my wife's feet in a flood of tears. My wife, not wishing to offend her, finally agreed to accept the snuff-box. It was only on the day after this scene that she realised that the snuff-box was actually double-lidded, and that one half contained a necklace of brilliants. She then explained to me what had happened on the previous day. I made no secret of my displeasure and would gladly have immediately returned both the box and the necklace to Miss Fry if I'd not wanted to avoid upsetting and humiliating her with this late restitution [11].

At the beginning of January 1777 I changed lodgings [12], renting the first floor of a house in Suffolk Street. Vitellini had tipped off Miss Fry about this, and so she rushed to rent the second floor, which meant that – no matter how much annoyance it might have caused me – I was unable to avoid bumping into her. She claimed to have invested her money unwisely and was once again financially embarrassed. She mentioned a trip to the countryside which she was anxious to take, for which she needed 100 guineas. She asked me to give her some numbers for the French lottery. I replied that her request was sheer madness. However, to get rid of her I arranged for my wife to give her the equivalent of 50 pounds 8 shillings in Portuguese money and begged the landlord not to put any obstacles in the way of her departure, adding that, immediately she had left, he should bring me an account for everything that she might owe.

On the following day, 6th February, I sent her a message asking whether she'd finally decided to leave. She replied that the sum that I'd given her was insufficient and that she would be going into town to see whether she could recover a debt of £400 which she said she was owed. In the evening she came round, found my wife alone, burst into tears and told her she had no money. She once again asked her to persuade me to give her the winning lottery-numbers. When this final attempt failed she resolved to carry out, starting the following day, a scheme that she'd been planning for quite some time.

You need to know that Miss Fry had another apartment in the city which she shared with

Scott. Vitellini often saw them both, but in the greatest secrecy. He had been indiscreet enough to tell them about some chemical experiments that I'd told him about and, as he was presumptuous by nature, he'd assured them that if he could get his hands on a certain powder that I used in my experiments [13] then he could, in a very short time, make his fortune and theirs as well. As for the lottery-numbers, he also claimed that if he could get hold of the relevant secret manuscript then he could predict them just as accurately as I myself could [14]. Scott and Miss Fry had enough influence over Vitellini to persuade him to tell them where the cupboard was located in which I'd concealed the gold box which contained the powder along with the manuscript to which I have just alluded and my other precious papers, and also which drawer of the cupboard contained them.

At this point Scott and Miss Fry conceived a plan to steal everything from me and to force me, essentially through torture, to share with them the secret knowledge that Scott supposed I had. For this purpose they joined forces with a lawyer, a disgrace to his profession by the way, who has since undergone the shameful punishment of the pillory for swindling and perjury. Mr. Reynolds (for that was the lawyer's name) appointed himself head of this little enterprise. All that was missing was a witness who was willing to affirm anything that they might want him to affirm. For this task a Mr. Broad was chosen: he lived with Miss Fry and passed himself off as her servant. There was also a need for some sort of back-up. Reynolds designated another lawyer of a similar calibre to himself, someone who, for money, was willing to swear to just about anything as many times as one might wish. This was a man called Aylett, who has also recently undergone the same humiliating punishment as his colleague, also for the crime of perjury.

Now that everything had been planned it was agreed that Miss Fry would take out a writ [15] against me, and that Scott, Reynolds and Broad would enter my premises furtively along with the bailiffs and take advantage of the ensuing tumult to launch the attack they'd been planning.

I was at home with my wife and Vitellini when, on 7th February at ten o'clock in the evening, I saw a bailiff enter accompanied by five or six bailiff's men who told me that I was under arrest for a debt of £190 sterling upon the petition of Miss Fry. Even though I already had a very poor opinion of this girl I certainly didn't expect such impudence and perfidy. Having recovered from the initial shock I was getting ready to follow the bailiff when I heard a noise in the next room [16]. It was Reynolds and Scott breaking into my cupboard. Reynolds tried to impress me by telling me that he was the Sheriff of London [17] and that he had every right to do what he was doing. The bailiffs, who were obviously in on the plot, allowed Scott to snaffle the manuscript, the gold box to which I have alluded above, and several papers, including the promissory-note for £200 sterling signed by Scott and Miss Fry.

I followed the bailiff to his house where I spent the night. Not having any sureties to offer I deposited with Saunders – for that was the bailiff's name – some jewellery and some Portuguese currency amounting to some £1000 sterling. Amongst the jewellery was a walking-cane, in the head of which was a repeater-watch surrounded by brilliants, as well as the box and necklace that Miss Fry had presented to my wife.

I left Saunders' house during the evening of 8th February. The following day, at midnight, a constable called at my house with his escort and told my wife and myself that we'd been arrested under the terms of a warrant [18] issued against us at the request of Miss Fry. I asked what crimes I was accused of. The constable told me that I myself was being arrested as a conjurer and my wife as a witch. We were then taken to a guard-house while they waited for the Justice of the Peace who had issued the warrant to get out of bed. It was a cold night

Chapter III

and I succeeded, with the help of some guineas that I had on me, in persuading the constable that he wouldn't be failing in his duty if he allowed us to return home until the Justice of the Peace had got up. This he agreed to.

The next morning, being alone in my apartment, I saw Reynolds arriving. He paid me the greatest compliments on my alleged secret knowledge and asked me, in the gentlest manner possible, to teach him and Scott exactly how to use the manuscript and the powder. To help persuade me he told me that he was in complete control of the situation and would help me to get my property back. Scott, who was hiding behind the door eavesdropping on the conversation and could see that the honeyed words of Mr. Reynolds were having no effect on me whatsoever, then rushed in, drew a pistol from his pocket, pressed it against my chest and told me that he would kill me if I didn't show him how to use the objects he had stolen from me. I did not reply.

Reynolds then disarmed him, and the two of them began entreating me once more. I told them that what they were asking me was impossible, that the objects they had stolen would always be useless to them, and that I was the only person who could use them effectively [19]*. 'Return them to me', I said to them, 'and I will let you keep not just the £200 promissory-note that you took from me but all the effects deposited in the hands of Saunders'* [20]*.*

Scott and Reynolds agreed to this, and left to find Saunders. No doubt they subsequently regretted having accepted my offer, as they failed to bring anything back and I heard no more of them. As for my good self, after appearing before the Justice of the Peace I successfully appealed against the warrant in the Court of King's Bench and, with the help of two sureties that I was able to lodge, no longer had to fear a visit from the constables [21]*.*

Cagliostro hoped that he was going to enjoy some peace at last, but unfortunately this was only the start of his problems. From that day onwards – 10th February 1777 – there began a struggle, unceasingly renewed, in which Cagliostro was assailed every day with threats, arrests and new seizures of assets, sometimes on this pretext, sometimes on that, with on each occasion new sureties having to be lodged and fresh expenditure having to be made [22].

Fed up with being constantly arrested and followed around he acted decisively – actually on the advice of Saunders – and went to live permanently at the bailiff's house. Now that he was the bailiff's permanent and voluntary prisoner he and his wife were able to prevent the continual invasion of their privacy by police-officers and bailiff's men [23]. While he was there, in June and July 1777, he got to know a lawyer called Priddle, a friend of Saunders, who said that he wanted to take on his defence and help Cagliostro sue his accusers for the return of his possessions. The case was to be heard on 27th June before Lord Mansfield, Chief Justice of the King's Bench, but then the lawyers agreed amongst themselves to appoint an arbitrator in the form of a Mr. Howarth, and he it was who heard the case on 4th July.

And now we have yet another betrayal. The lawyer who took his case on disappeared and Cagliostro, not knowing a word of English, was obliged, at no notice at all, to plead his own case – with Vitellini acting as interpreter – against Miss Fry, represented by the weaselly Reynolds. As a result Cagliostro's case, which was cast-iron enough to have been a foregone conclusion if he'd had a competent barrister to represent him, became so muddled through the subtleties of Reynolds' advocacy that the arbitrator handed down a sentence that was both inadequate and unclear – even absurd. The arbitrator made no judgment on the writ of 7th February (arrest for a so-called debt of £190), nor on the warrant of 9th February (arrest for the crimes of magic and sorcery), nor on the writ of 24th May (arrest for theft of £200 in gold coins), even though all these charges had been submitted to him for arbitration, had been discussed in front of him, and had been shown to be meaningless. Without actually discharging Cagliostro he pronounced only that he *had to return* to Miss Fry a gold box and a necklace of brilliants which he had in his possession, and to pay her costs, without even noticing that Cagliostro had already offered to pay these before the lawsuit began, and also overlooking the fact that, during the course of the hearing, Cagliostro had stated 'that he knew perfectly well that he was entitled to keep the box and the necklace, either because they'd been given to Countess Cagliostro, or because Miss Fry owed him, in respect of a loan, double and triple the value of these two objects, but that he did not want to exercise his right to retain them, and that he agreed to return them to her, just as he had always offered to do'.

Has there ever been a legal judgment more iniquitous in content and more vicious in form? What's more, the judgment was not confirmed and became final only a few months later, in November [24]. Until then Cagliostro had to live as a permanent defendant, remaining constantly on his guard, and having to maintain his guarantors who were becoming nervous as a result of the constant delays.

One of the men who'd agreed to stand surety for him, a certain Badioli, regretted having done so, and secretly wanted to be released from his obligations. On 9th August he arrived at Cagliostro's lodgings in a carriage and suggested that he might like to go for a drive with him. Cagliostro was not suspicious and agreed to do so. The carriage stopped in front of a building that Cagliostro did not recognise. Badioli got out and Cagliostro followed him. The door opened, Badioli asked Cagliostro to go ahead of him, the door closed again, and then someone told Cagliostro that he was now in the prison of the King's Bench and that his sureties were formally discharged [25]. Cagliostro remained there for one month, during which time he was assailed by a new shower of writs. A young barrister called Sheridan, brought along by Cagliostro's friend O'Reilly, came to his aid, found him new guarantors, lodged a deposit as surety with the warden of the prison, and finally won him his freedom, but at a steep price: 3,500 guineas.

Finally, in November 1777, the Howarth judgment was published. This final injustice, coming on top of the continual persecutions that he'd undergone in anticipation of a remedial judgement, sickened him to the point where he refused to continue with any lawsuits, paid off everything and everybody, formally cursed England [26], and decided to leave the country. His only other act was to assign power of attorney to his friend O'Reilly so that, with the assistance of the barrister Sheridan, they might try either by judicial decision or by negotiation to recover the stolen powder-box and manuscript. Having nothing left out of his personal fortune other than 50 guineas [27] and some jewellery, he left for Brussels where, as he says, Providence enabled him to improve his financial situation [28].

The lawsuit against Scott that O'Reilly launched after Cagliostro's departure ended while he was on his travels. He was in Strasbourg (1780) when he learned that Scott was in prison, having been found guilty of burglary and facing hanging if the judgment followed its course. Cagliostro intervened 'as he did not want to be responsible for the death of a man' and withdrew his complaint against him [29]. Scott paid the costs of the action and then disappeared without ever returning the manuscript or the box, even though Cagliostro had offered him a further 500 guineas for them. As for those who had persecuted him during his year in England the ends that they came to are rather interesting. Here is what, less than ten years later, Cagliostro wrote for the edification of Monsieur Morande [30]:

Chapter III

In my life I've found that God's justice always manifests sooner or later, and that the wicked always come to a sticky end. If Monsieur Morande should for just one minute doubt the truth of this assertion – so terrible for them, but so comforting for those of good intent – then let him reflect upon the fates of those whose cause he has defended and whose horrors he has himself exceeded.

Madame de Blévary, as a reward for my kindness towards her, delivered me into the hands of two rascals. She is <u>dead</u>.

Miss Fry, my relentless enemy, did not get to enjoy the fortune that she owed to my advices. After using it up suborning witnesses and corrupting law-officers she fell into the most abject misery. She is <u>dead</u>.

Mr. Broad acted as friend, spy and witness for Miss Fry: he is <u>dead</u>.

Lady Gaudicheau, the sister of Miss Fry, was her accomplice and that of Scott also: she is <u>dead</u>.

Mr. Dunning, the barrister acting for Miss Fry, was chosen to ensure that a patently unjust cause triumphed: he is <u>dead</u>.

Mr. Wallace, my own lawyer, instead of defending me, had me delivered up to the mercy of the arbitrator that Miss Fry had chosen: he is <u>dead</u>.

Mr. Howarth handed down an unworthy judgement, which condemned the innocent while letting perjury go unpunished. He is <u>dead</u> (drowned while crossing the Thames).

The Justice of the Peace of Hammersmith had my wife and I arrested for an imaginary crime. He was expelled ignominiously from his profession and is now <u>dead</u>.

Mr. Crisp, Marshal of the Prison of the King's Bench, along with Aylett, swindled me out of 50 guineas in silver. He lost his job, was reduced to beggary and ended up in an almshouse: he is <u>dead</u>.

Finally, Vitellini betrayed my trust. His culpable indiscretion made him an accessory to a theft of which he thought he would one day reap the benefit. He was confined to a prison for vagabonds, where he <u>died</u>.

All the ten people I have just named, with the exception of Madame de Blévary, were in the first flush of youth. Four years after my departure only one remained alive.

Of all my persecutors from those days there remain alive today only four individuals, whose existence is such that death would actually be a blessing to them.

Reynolds, lawyer for Miss Fry and the accomplice in Scott's robbery from me, suffered the infamous torment of the pillory for perjury.

The lawyer Aylett, who extorted from me 80 guineas on the pretext of me actually being Balzamo [sic] of London, has just undergone the same punishment for a similar crime.

Saunders the bailiff was mixed up in the plot against me. His fortune was dissipated in just a short time. He has been in prison for several years now for corruption.

As for Scott, if I have not been misinformed, he is currently living all alone, without family, without friends, in the depths of Scotland, where, haunted by remorse and experiencing simultaneously the worries of great wealth and the anguish of great poverty, he will torment himself with his attempts to use an asset whose benefits constantly elude him, until eventually he will die of inanition in the presence of the object of his greed, which has become the instrument of his persecution.

Such has been the fate of the fourteen individuals who joined forces against me and who violated in my person the sacred vows of hospitality. Some of my readers will see in this series of events only coincidence, but I myself recognise there the Divine Providence that has sometimes made me a target for the arrows of the maliciously inclined but which, ultimately, has always destroyed the weapons that it had used to test me [31].

One must wonder how, from such simple truths, Morande could have produced the repellent story with which we began this chapter. It was easy for him to do so of course: by simply recounting the lawsuits in which Cagliostro was unable to obtain justice for himself it was an easy task to portray the muddled debates in an unfavourable light, and even in the more difficult cases certain lying witnesses, well paid for their services [32], enabled charges to stick.

Of course, an imbroglio of this kind, with its books of Cabalistic [33] calculations and mysterious red powders, was tailor-made for a satirical journalist like Morande. And who was in charge of these wonders? A self-styled healer, some crazy wretch who has come from goodness knows where, who gets himself out of jail and then immediately goes back there. What an easy task it must have been for a man like Morande, with a pen dipped in acid, to transform this brilliant savant into a vulgar charlatan, to turn a man of good will into a criminal. And Morande made an excellent job of it: the leaders of the campaign paid well, the general public had some fun and the *Courrier de l'Europe* increased its circulation.

We shall not comment on how he went about these things. We leave it to our readers, now better informed, to decide for themselves where the truth lies and what we should think about those people who perverted the truth by such means. There is however one point on which we need to insist. Many will smile at Morande's jests or shrug their shoulders when they read that Cagliostro predicted the correct lottery-numbers the day before they were drawn [34]. 'An absurd claim!' some will cry. But the facts are there, plain for all to see. 'Pure coincidence!' the sceptics will reply. But quite apart from the bad impression that the whole idea of gambling leaves on the serious-minded – just a 'tax on stupidity' as some will claim – Cagliostro's predictions might also cause some of our readers to question his good faith, and we most certainly want to avoid that, as such categorical judgements should never be made lightly. To the scoffers I will simply present the bare facts of the matter [35] with a challenge to explain them. To the more reflective amongst my readers I would like to submit the following observations.

Everyday language makes a distinction between the words 'forecast' and 'prediction' which is not very much in conformity with their etymology. 'Forecast' suggests to us the idea of a logical deduction from cause to effect, whereas 'prediction' suggests a mysterious coincidence between an unreasoned assertion and a fact whose cause we cannot explain. But are these associations of ideas legitimate? Is there really any contradiction between the two terms? We do not think so. When Christopher Columbus, about to be killed by the Indians, won their respect by telling them an eclipse would occur, he had predicted the future to those who were threatening him. When a chemist predicts that mixing two colourless liquids will cause a red solid to precipitate at the bottom of a test-tube is this not, to an ignoramus, a genuine prophecy of a miraculous event?

Let's take a more complex example: when a doctor examines a patient's throat and tells him he has scarlet fever, and that on the third day the eruption will cover his entire body, is he not making a genuine prediction? But because the chemist or the doctor will be able to explain to the initiated, in accordance with the theories of the day and using the appropriate terms of art, exactly why they think the ensuing phenomenon will occur, we would never refer to something of this kind as a prediction or prophecy but as a 'forecast'. Immediately we are intellectually satisfied and we do not see what has happened as anything other than a very natural occurrence. If however the doctor – and this is often the case – had not been able to base his diagnosis on characteristic, clear-cut symptoms provided by his examination of the patient's throat or by taking the patient's temperature but, even so and thanks to one of those special flashes of intuition that illuminate the mind, he had made the same forecast, then he could not have given his colleagues any plausible reason for his prediction, however accurate. In that case, would the word 'forecast' still be applicable, or would we have to admit that we had departed from the scientific domain and entered the nebulous world of prophecy?

In the example we have given, a 'certain feeling' steered the doctor in a particular direction, and then a conviction, impossible to justify, formed within him. But what is this 'certain feeling'? And whence is this conviction born? Isn't this just a confused perception of certain vague feelings derived from the world of forces that surrounds us, the greatest part of which evades our meagre awareness? Without a criterion to classify them, without a language into which to translate them, the doctor nonetheless experienced an impression of them that was sufficient for him to formulate a certain conviction within him.

Isn't the intuition of the so-called 'clairvoyants' [36] of the same order? They too cannot explain or justify their convictions, but they certainly experience them with exceptional profundity They affirm them and often, as we know, their predictions prove to be correct. Let us therefore exclude from our imaginations this illusion that there is some sort of antithesis between 'predictions' and 'forecasts': both these words, essentially synonymous, signify the application of knowledge, whatever form that knowledge might take, to the task of determining the outcome of a sequence of facts.

For a forecast to be possible we need constant relationships linking a state A of a system of forces to another (later) state B, C, or D in the same system, and it is sufficient for us to know accurately 1. the state A; 2. the law that links state A to state B, C, or D. In simple cases, such as the calculus of functions in mathematics, or experiments in physics [37], the forecast is easy: it is what we call 'scientific determination'. If the facts become more complicated then resolving the equation becomes more difficult, but it always remains possible if we have sufficiently precise and numerous data to be able to transform the additional unknowns into knowns, and so progressively reduce the problem to a simpler type [38]. In biology [39] the degree of complexity is so great that problems are generally regarded as insoluble: the relationships between the very numerous data, more or less clearly perceived, more or less expressible, elude us and we can no longer draw conclusions. Even so, we can see that the problem is merely very complex and does not involve logical insolubility. If our forecasting ability is faulty in this case it is not because of an apparent spontaneity that contradicts the law of general causality or because the solution depends upon an unfathomable continuity between the facts, but simply because of the poverty and inadequacy of our initial knowledge of the facts of the problem. The laws that connect the facts in a continuous series from cause to effect, and the constant relationships between things, are everywhere manifest if we make the effort to identify them.

The universe is a whole. The narrow solidarity of beings, their participation in one and the same universal life in which every individuality, the synthetic principle of a group of inferior unities, is a constitutive element of the superior unity, creates such a bond between them that no action is isolated and nothing ever happens by chance [40]. A being, however negligible, cannot undergo any modification without the whole world feeling the effects of that modification, in the same way that every general action has its repercussions upon the smallest parts of the universe. Man does not choose his place in the universe, any more than a rock does: his life is linked to that of his environment. A man calls forth certain events around him just as a social crisis calls forth the man necessary for its solution and just as a landscape determines its flora and fauna, for does the environment not modify the creatures that inhabit it up to the point of actually determining their shapes and colours [41]?

Familiarity (what the French call *connaissance*) with these relationships, which run from mineral to man, from matter to thought, constitutes knowledge (what the French call *savoir*). The sciences, in the form in which we currently possess them, are only partial classifications, empirical collections of facts. The forecasts that knowledge enables us to make surpasses scientific forecasts just as much as knowledge itself surpasses a specific science, e.g. botany or linguistics. Knowledge, the emergence of a hero, the extinction of a sun, the storm that devastates a region or the discovery of a new physical force, are not peculiar accidents but the consequence of other facts, to all appearances very remote from one another. Their realisation is, necessarily, characteristic for such-and-such an epoch and such-and-such an environment. It is not an isolated fact without any linkage with those that preceded or any relationship to the unity, for no word ever emerges from a person's mouth and no stone ever rolls into a torrent without underlying causes determining those events, and anyone who can perceive these causes can also predict the event.

Is it however given to man to attain this entire knowledge of life and to become aware of all these relationships? Yes, replied Cagliostro, and he was echoing the Sages of all times and places when he said so. The potential for the development of man's faculties is unlimited, and man the microcosm can find within him all the heavens and their inhabitants, and the Earth and its forces. His aim must be to know everything and to forecast everything.

But Cagliostro was not content simply to enunciate this truth: he gave evidence of it as well. This knowledge was something he actually possessed. If he sensed that a person was suffering from the most recondite diseases or the most deeply-concealed moral anguish, if he announced events happening hundreds of miles away at the moment they were taking place, if he could forecast, years in advance, the career of a man or the destiny of a society, it was because, for him, these facts were not isolated and because their realisation occurred as the necessary consequence of present states, the multiple interrelationships of which his mind readily comprehended.

If therefore he decided, during his time in London, to choose as his particular subject of study the determination of the numerical series in lottery-draws this was simply to give an example of what is possible for the human mind [42], namely the resolution of one of those complex and ungraspable problems that the intelligence rebels against analysing, and which man, purely out of a sense of powerlessness, relegates to the vague realm of chance, to the 'junk room' of our sciences and the 'unclassified' shelf in the encyclopedic repertory of our knowledge.

By achieving precision in this realm of facts Cagliostro also showed how nonsensical it is to ascribe the word 'chance' to the logical and perfect sequence of phenomena which only appear to be undetermined and introduced us to the possibility of a form of knowledge of which our technical understanding and scientific methods are only very rough sketches. When he wrestles with these transcendent problems and follows life and its development as far as spheres in which we ourselves can only see cold abstractions and can only churn up lifeless formulae, he appears to us to be as great as when he is mastering a disease, transmuting matter or teaching humanity – perhaps even greater – and the sarcastic remarks of certain petty minds fall pitifully before this triumphant wisdom the way that the

Chapter III

blasphemies of naughty children fall lifeless at the foot of a God whose love gave them life and who, despite their blasphemies, will never fail to call them to His arms.

NOTES

(1) *Courrier de l'Europe*, April 1787 and subsequent issues. Cf. also *Vie de Joseph Balsamo*, p. 35, D'Alméras, *Cagliostro*, p. 65, et seq.

(2) 'For the first time in my life', says Cagliostro. All these passages are taken from the *Journal* of Vitellini, who played one of the most important roles in the Cagliostro story and who, in a fit or remorse on his death-bed, bequeathed these documents to an Irish gentleman, a Mr. O' Reilly, who sent them to Cagliostro. The *Journal* was used in the drafting of the anonymous *Lettre au peuple anglais*, 78 pp. (Paris, Lottin, 1787) which is the final and peremptory answer that Cagliostro gave to Morande's calumnies. It is to this work and edition that all the references in this chapter will be made unless otherwise indicated. The anonymous English work *Life of the Count Cagliostro*, London, 1787, provides information about the events of 1776-1777 that agrees very closely with that contained in Vitellini's *Journal*.

(3) *Lettre au peuple anglais*, 1787, p. 5.

(4) Cagliostro generously accommodated those who came to see him, cf. *Lettre au peuple anglais*, pp. 7 & 8.

(5) *Lettre au peuple anglais*, p. 8.

(6) *Lettre au peuple anglais*, p. 6 & p. 13.

(7) A certain Pergolezzi, more daring than the others, was the first to try blackmailing him. He published an account of Cagliostro which was pure fabrication and which the attorney Aylett and then, after him, Morande made use of, the former to swindle 80 guineas from Cagliostro and the latter to defame him, *Lettre au peuple anglais*, p. 6.

(8) It is at this point that two crooks enter the scene who extorted more than £200 from Cagliostro by recounting their misfortunes: one was called Scott, who styled himself 'Lord Scott', and the other a Miss Mary Fry, who called herself 'Lady Scott'. These two rascals had been introduced to Cagliostro by Madame de Blévary, cf. *Lettre au peuple anglais*, pp. 8, 9 &10.

(9) 'Through detailed examination, study and sheer hard work I had succeeded in achieving 100% accuracy in some astrological procedures for predicting lottery-draws', said Cagliostro in the preamble to the demand for restitution which he made against Fry and Scott. He had written his calculations down in a notebook which he kept in his bedroom in conditions of the utmost secrecy. This manuscript, which was obviously much coveted, was written either in a secret code or with deliberate interpolations which made it impossible for anyone other than Cagliostro to use it, cf. *Lettre au peuple anglais*, p. 9.

(10) 'The draw for the English lottery began on the 14th. Jestingly I told people what the first number would be. No one in my social circle wanted to take the plunge, but as luck would have it the number I predicted was the one that came up. For the draw on the 16th I gave the number 20. Scott wagered a small amount and won. For the 17th I gave the number 25: number 25 it was, which won Scott £100. For the 18th I gave the numbers 55 and 57, both of which were correct. The winnings for the 18th were shared between Scott, Vitellini, and the self-styled Lady Scott'. Cagliostro, having thus verified that his calculations were correct then decided, *out of discretion*, never to use this procedure again, cf. *Lettre au peuple anglais*, p. 9.

(11) This would have created a very awkward situation for the Countess.

(12) To get away from the assorted rascals and the traps that they were setting for him.

(13) This was probably the pink powder, known as the 'consolidating powder', which Cagliostro also used in the composition of certain medicines, cf. Chapter V of this book, *Cagliostro in Strasbourg*.

(14) It is this claim and the rumours surrounding the manuscript that gave rise to books containing all sorts of far-fetched procedures for choosing winning lottery-numbers that appeared from 1790 onwards, e.g. *Le Gros Cagliostro, Le Vrai Cagliostro, La Cabale de Cagliostro*, etc.,

(15) Permission to have someone imprisoned which in England could be granted to any creditor,

whether real or alleged, on simple oath, whether true or false.
(16) Which had a separate entrance, cf. *Lettre au peuple anglais*, p. 15.
(17) The Sheriff of London did indeed have a delegate with the same surname as attorney Reynolds.
(18) In French this would be known as a *prise de corps*.
(19) See note 9 above.
(20) It should be noted that these objects were worth £1,000 and that they contained the box and the necklace that he was accused of having swindled and even sold!
(21) *Lettre au peuple anglais*, p. 17.
(22) *Lettre au peuple anglais*, p. 18.
(23) 'Thanks to this expedient my person became sacrosanct and I was sure of being able to sleep in my own bed. I occupied the most beautiful apartment in his house, kept open table there, and paid the bills of some of the other prisoners. I even paid off the debts of some of them so they could be released from prison. My ordinary expenditure was 7 to 8 guineas per day, and regularly – every evening in fact – I settled up with my host', *Lettre au peuple anglais*, p. 20. We understand that Saunders was sorry to see him go and tried to return to Cagliostro's house and arrest him again as soon as he could.
(24) *Lettre au peuple anglais,* p. 26: the courts were in summer recess.
(25) Such was the law of England.
(26) 'I resolved to flee forever a country where the basic rules of justice, gratitude and hospitality are thus ignored', *Lettre au peuple anglais*, p. 28.
(27) *Lettre au peuple anglais*, p. 29.
(28) In December 1777. According to the memoirs of Countess von der Recke, Cagliostro repaired the damage done to his personal fortune by the law-courts and thieves of London by purifying or augmenting diamonds in Brussels, cf. Von der Recke, *Nachricht von des berüchtigten Cagliostro*, 1787, p. 11.
(29) *Lettre au peuple anglais*, p. 29. We can see how much Cagliostro's conduct must have disconcerted his friends and alienated good will towards him. Here was a man who had fought for his best interests for three years, finally obtained victory, and who then, at the last minute, by withdrawing his complaint simply cancelled out all the results he had so painfully achieved. Mr. O'Reilly, who seems to have had some involvement in the drafting of *The Life of the Count Cagliostro*, cannot help but let drop, here and there, a number of complaints about Cagliostro's incomprehensible behaviour.
(30) We in our turn offer it to his latter-day successors as a subject for reflection.
(31) *Lettre au peuple anglais*, p. 74, et seq.
(32) Morande received money from France for this purpose. He was seen, along with Monsieur Dubourg, the *notaire* at the French Embassy, hanging round various ale-houses and dives looking for stooges of this kind. Dubourg was paid fifty guineas for this noble enterprise. Priddle and Saunders were also involved (*Lettre au peuple anglais*, p. 19). Morande offered 100 guineas to O'Reilly, the owner of the Freemasons' hotel, *to merely state* that Cagliostro had left his premises without paying (*Lettre au peuple anglais*, p. 47). O'Reilly refused and later recounted the fact.
(33) This is the usual term, although it has nothing to do with the Cabala.
(34) The lotteries at this time were similar to the Government-run weekly draws that are still (1912) held in Italy: five numbers were drawn from the first ninety numbers and, depending on their sequence or connection, the ticket-holders who had chosen them could win ten, a hundred or a thousand times their stake.
(35) *Lettre au peuple anglais*, pp. 9, 10 & 11.
(36) We are using this word (French, *voyants*), however vague it might be, in preference to that of 'mystics' (*mystiques*) or visionaries (*illuminés*) which are vaguer still and which, according to certain writers, denote very different spiritual states.
(37) Experimentally one maximises the simplicity of the secondary state by eliminating the additional variables (pressure, temperature, etc., which are assumed to be constant) which could make the problem more complex.

Chapter III

(38) Equations with several unknowns, problems of dynamics in mathematics, analysis of organic compounds and mixtures in chemistry.

(39) Both the biology of individuals and that of groups.

(40) For us a fortuitous event is a coincidence of two facts where the causes of those facts are both unknown to us. As soon as the relationship is known then the element of chance disappears. The superstitious relationship which is a subject of ridicule then becomes a forecast which is a subject of respect.

(41) Adaptation and mimicry are everyday observations in biology.

(42) Cagliostro wanted only to demonstrate truths positively and indisputably on the basis of facts: he never exploited the truth for his own benefit and never allowed his knowledge to be abused in favour of others. He could have spent the rest of his life drawing from the lottery revenues (i.e. from the pockets of the losers) the money that he needed for his philanthropy, but did not do so. 'Whatever the cause of these bizarre prognostications', he says ironically, when discussing the relentless accuracy of his lottery forecasts, 'I believed out of scruple that it was my duty to abstain from giving out any numbers in the future', *Lettre au peuple anglais*, p. 9.

CHAPTER IV

—

'THE WIZARD'

CAGLIOSTRO IN RUSSIA

Cagliostro in Mittau

We shall not be following Cagliostro's various wanderings throughout Europe too closely. His journey from lodge to lodge – a journey on which he was welcomed, listened to and honoured by Freemasons of all Rites; where he met both sincere seekers after truth and many others of dishonest intent; and where his influence helped to revolutionise Masonic ideas – was characterised primarily by his influence on those around him, and we shall be examining this in detail in Chapter VI, which is devoted to Egyptian Freemasonry [1]. Suffice it to say that this stage of his European travels ended in Mittau (the present-day Jelgava in Latvia) in what was then Duchy of Courland [2]. He arrived there at the end of February 1779 [3] on his way from Königsberg [4] and remained there for several months. When we last saw him he was in England, isolated and virtually unknown, fighting petty personal battles within a restrictive environment that offered him little scope. Now we find him in the middle of the expansive world of Courland, and with a new identity too – that of a miracle-worker. It was in Mittau that Cagliostro first emerged as a man of remarkable ability and a master of unknown and unseen forces, and where he had the good fortune to be surrounded by educated and cultivated disciples whom he dominated with his mysterious fund of knowledge and enchanted with his immense personal charm. In Mittau too he adopted a new mode of action, so why should we be in any way surprised if he also appeared under a new name [5]?

Finding out exactly how Cagliostro spent his time in Courland is a rather more difficult task than is the case later on in his life: documents, especially detailed and reliable ones, are lacking, and all we really have to go on are the notorious satirical accounts. These of course are distorted by ignorance and malice and in some cases are complete forgeries published a long time afterwards during the Diamond Necklace Affair [6]. An honourable exception however is the book by Countess von der Recke, *Nachricht von des berüchtigten Cagliostro* (1787). Although its date of publication and its basic intentions place it firmly in the category to which we have just referred, i.e. of fundamentally hostile books published long after the events, it has one saving grace: it includes an earlier memoir dating from 1779 in which the authoress, writing under the immediate influence of the events she describes, does her best to record, on a virtually day-to-day basis, those actions and words of Cagliostro that especially caught her attention. Unfortunately she later added to it a commentary more voluminous than the memoir itself in which she sought to undermine the significance of Cagliostro's miracle-working and explain it away by finding a rational explanation for it in terms of conjuring and trickery. According to her novel opinion, Cagliostro was nothing more than a skilful tool of the Jesuits [7], a man whose pernicious doctrines, feigned virtues and power to deceive had taken advantage of that Order's trustfulness.

As we shall see, even if she must be criticised for her subsequent change of heart, which occurred under pressure from external influences and was used as ammunition by Cagliostro's enemies and caused many readers of their books to lose faith in him, her earlier memoir of 1779 remains, in its entirety, a document of great interest for anyone seeking an impartial account of Cagliostro. We shall therefore be quoting from it frequently.

We can even find some grains of truth in the reluctant admissions and unintentional self-contradictions of the lampoonists and pamphleteers. Since Cagliostro did not confine his miracle-working to his time in Russia we can also find important testimonies dating from his visits to Strasbourg, Lyons and Paris which we can use to acquire a better understanding of his life and work in Courland.

At that time in those parts of the world the more open-minded section of the population ran great intellectual risks: Illuminism, a vague mystical trend composed of equal portions of idleness, egoism and credulity, was very much in vogue, and all people seemed to be able to talk about were celestial visions, communications with angels, revelations, conjurations and evocations. While one's mind could easily be led astray into the realms of illusion by Swedenborg, one's will could just as readily be perverted into superstition by Scieffort and Weishaupt and their respective secret sects [8]. Germany in particular was riddled with secret societies. Even in little Mittau one Dr. Stark, a professor of philosophy and the head of a very exclusive sect of Illuminati, taught his followers a form of ceremonial magic about which people spoke only with trepidation [9]. Countess von der Recke [10], who will play a very important part in our story, was also completely immersed in these mysterious studies. Her principal motivation seems to have been a desire to communicate with the soul of her late brother [11]. She'd used the ideas of Swedenborg and Lavater to construct a confused mystical system of her own to which she was very much attached and of which she was extremely proud. Within her own social circle she was recognised as an authority on esoteric subjects [12].

Meanwhile, the Masonic lodges had also developed a passion for investigations of this kind and were permeated by esoteric influences: as a result they had largely abandoned their social purpose and split into warring sects of absolutely no use to humanity and positively dangerous to those who were sucked into their sphere of influence. One danger was that the more superficial and overbearing type of personality, if he managed to acquire a leadership role, would tend to over-react to such follies by going to the opposite extreme, destroying amongst these dreamers any form of belief in a spiritual life and thus reducing them to the narrowest and most debased type of sensuality [13].

Cagliostro would have none of this: he knew exactly how to nourish a person's inner life by providing them with a healthy spiritual diet that was appropriate to their ability to assimilate it, and to steer their curiosity in a direction that would lead them to a true and accurate understanding of the laws of nature. He knew that he had to teach and demonstrate to many of the seekers tottering blindly along the path of truth that our knowledge of the world is relative and very erroneous; that our senses furnish us only with quite conventional subjective ideas about natural phenomena; and that such concepts are inevitably incomplete because our perceptions are limited to what is revealed to us by touch, hearing, sight and smell. It is our other senses – which are as yet embryonic – which, developed under special conditions, can enable us to contact a whole series of unknown forces, open up to us a world of phenomena unperceived by the majority of human beings, and so push back the frontiers of the knowable. That, of course, was what, more than anything, remained to be proven: the reality and value of such phenomena had to be made perceptible to observers.

This is what Cagliostro sought to do by surrounding himself with all the extra conditions that his disciples, most of whom were followers of specific esoteric systems, might consider indispensable. He was dealing with two kinds of occultists: some were alchemical enthusiasts

Chapter IV

[14] who thought only of transmutation, the Elixir and the Powder of Projection, and who awaited the single word of power that would give them the key to the Hermetic enigmas and the mastery of which they dreamed, while others, without specifically rejecting alchemy, saw that only as one branch of magic, and initially were only interested in rites and rituals that might enable them to command the Spirits [15].

This was the raw material with which Cagliostro had to work if he wanted to speak to his audience persuasively. Each one of his disciples had a practical and very personal goal. All kept strictly to the letter of it and, despite their declarations of disinterest, their ambition refused to allow them to shake off the chains of selfishness and materialism [16]. Cagliostro's starting-point with these men and women therefore had to be the point that each of them had already reached by their own efforts [17]. He had to speak to them in language they could understand and to begin by holding before them the possibility of realising their own narrow spiritual ambitions, before gradually leading them to an appreciation of much wider horizons. During this preliminary stage of their spiritual education – at the same as trying to get them interested in searching for the magical treasure of Wilzen [18], the propagation of gold, the Elixir of immortality or the privileges of the Third Circle of Initiates – Cagliostro knew he had to address them in a symbolic language so pure that his very words were enough to reveal profound truths to everyone who had ears to hear.

But let's get back to more mundane matters. Cagliostro had been told to present himself on his arrival to the Marshal of the Nobility -, a Herr von Medem. In his turn Von Medem introduced him to his brother, Count von Medem, and to the *Oberburggraf* (the supreme burgrave), Chamberlain von Howen. All three men were Freemasons [20].

Cagliostro first gave them proof of his various Masonic degrees and then told them of his ambition to found a mixed lodge in which he would reveal to them many of the secrets that they were seeking. His hosts were certainly interested but also somewhat wary. To set their minds at rest Cagliostro then performed, in their presence, an alchemical operation that filled with them enthusiasm. Cagliostro followed this up with a magical demonstration which they found even more impressive [21]. As a result they were very eager to follow Cagliostro's instructions. A mixed lodge was duly formed [22].

The usual working of this lodge was as follows. In a chamber decorated with symbols the Members of the Lodge, all initiated Egyptian Freemasons, would meet at an agreed place and time, all of them duly prepared according to the instructions of the Grandmaster, and without swords or any other metallic objects upon their persons. The chamber communicated by a door with another, smaller room, a sort of tabernacle, containing a table covered with a white cloth, a chair and – on the table – several lights arranged in a triangle surrounding a carafe of white glass filled with water. In front of the carafe was a piece of paper covered in strange symbols [23].

Grandmaster Cagliostro, in Masonic regalia and with sword in hand, would then lead a young child [24] into the larger chamber and, after consecrating them before the whole assembly by the laying-on of hands, anointing them with something he called the Oil of Wisdom [25], and uttering a verbal formula describing the goal that he wished to achieve, would ask the child to enter the smaller chamber and sit in front of the carafe. He would then leave the smaller chamber, closing the door behind him, and stand in front of the door of the larger chamber. The 'dove', for that is what the child was called, would therefore be alone in the tabernacle. The Grandmaster and those present would then recite one of the Psalms and spend some time collecting their thoughts in silent prayer [26]. Cagliostro would then ask the child if he or she could see anything in the carafe. The child would often reply with something like, 'Yes, I can see an angel… several angels…' [27]. Cagliostro would then thank his spiritual visitors and announce that those assembled were free to ask whatever questions they wished. Cagliostro would pass these questions on to the angels who would answer either with signs or words that only the child could perceive or with moving pictures that the child would then describe [28].

Many of these answers have come down to us in the memoirs of the time, many of which were written by the questioners themselves. In Russia, in Strasbourg and in Lyons the same sort of events seems to have occurred, and all of Cagliostro's biographers have described at least some of them. Here are some examples taken more or less at random from contemporary authors.

One lady asked what her mother, who was then in Paris, was doing. The answer was that she was at the theatre seated between two elderly men. Another questioner tried to trap Cagliostro: she wanted to know how old her husband was. No answer was forthcoming, which produced great cries of enthusiasm from those assembled, because the lady in question was unmarried! After the failure of this attempt to trick Cagliostro no further efforts of a similar kind were ever made [29]. Sometimes questions would be put secretly. On one occasion the dove – a boy this time – was handed a folded slip of paper. He didn't open it, but immediately read in the water of the carafe the words 'No, you will *not* obtain it'. The slip of paper was then unfolded. The question on it was whether the lady would be successful in obtaining a commission for her son in a particular regiment. The accuracy of this answer also impressed those present [30]. Sometimes answers could relate to future events. The famous prophecy of the French Revolution and the death of Louis XVI were made in this way via a young dove [31].

The angels sometimes made their presence felt to the doves in more tangible ways. So great was the angels' materiality that the doves could actually touch them [32], clasp hands with them and exchange material objects with them. One of the most impressive magical sessions of which we still have a record was held in Warsaw. Cagliostro had asked those present to sign a piece of paper. He then burnt it. Shortly afterwards the dove – a young girl – saw an envelope sealed with wax fall at her feet. She gave it to Cagliostro, and when it was opened each person recognised their signature on the document that it contained [33].

Once Cagliostro's disciples had come to understand, through repeated experiments, the significance of these phenomena both for the general well-being of humanity and for the expansion of their spiritual knowledge they still needed to be persuaded that, however much astonishment and religious awe these strange events might inspire, they were not unnatural or even supernatural in character but involved the use of faculties that anyone who wished to acquire them could master.

Cagliostro achieved this enlightenment by slightly modifying his experiments here and there by changing the concomitant conditions or the character of his demonstrations so as to firmly establish in his disciples' minds that their perception of spiritual phenomena and the direct action of the human will upon them were the natural prerogative of the regenerated man. He therefore gradually reduced and then eventually eliminated the ceremonial, the drapes and curtains, the lodge-decorations and the mysterious formulae [34]. The magic circle, which those attending lodge meetings had previously not been allowed to step outside of, was sometimes walked across or even omitted altogether. Countess von der Recke, who was extremely observant by nature, quotes Cagliostro as saying to her: 'Do not judge me. If you had the power to command the Spirits then you would understand the purpose of the magic circle. I have the right to change the rules that I give you, to modify my conduct, to act differently depending upon the people involved. But I shall of course be held responsible for any abuse of those powers' [35]. Despite the clarity of this response, which is so much in conformity with the plan that Cagliostro always followed in his demonstrations, Countess von der Recke saw it only as an incomprehensible meddling with the ritual. Later she would rely on this alleged contradiction in Cagliostro's behaviour to prove that all these activities were the merest charlatanism.

One of the changes that Cagliostro made was to decide that the lights were no longer necessary: Cagliostro simply sat the child down in front of the carafe. On other occasions 'he performed the experiments without the carafe, simply placing the dove behind a folding-screen which represented a sort of small temple' [36].

Here is another example of these simplifications. It concerns an experiment in which the dove had just seen, in the carafe, the questioner's town-house: 'Even though the carafe had been removed the dove said that he could still see the town-house, and even a person who was then in one of the rooms. No sooner had the owner of the house heard him say this than he rushed round to his house and found that everything the dove had said was perfectly true' [37].

As we have said, in the early days the dove was always a child with all the innocence of the first flush of youth. He or she would be formally prepared for the ceremony at least one day in advance. However, Cagliostro gradually decreased the number of requirements, using as doves whomever was presented to him, immediately and without preparation [38]. 'Someone who suspected that there was some sort of clandestine communication going on between Cagliostro and his doves told him that he wanted to bring a young girl for him to work with, someone who was wholly unknown to him. Cagliostro readily agreed to the arrangement, adding that everything that occurred in the demonstrations was due entirely to the action of divine grace. The new dove was brought to him and the subsequent demonstration was very successful' [39].

The fact that Cagliostro could accept whatever doves were brought to him, without having seen them before, and could immediately transform them into clairvoyants, with the resulting demonstrations being every bit as successful as they had been with the others completely removes any suspicion of complicity and destroys the childish hypothesis that Cagliostro and the doves were simply acting out a script, which is the basic assumption underlying Countess von der Recke's systematic slander. Her sad apostasy does not, therefore, even have the excuse of a plausible reason for her doubts.

In Paris, Cagliostro often used teenagers as doves [40]. He even offered to use fifty young girls simultaneously to prove that his power over those he used as doves did not depend solely on the fact that the dove was in some way special or abnormal [41]. The inevitable conclusion was that the qualities required for an effective dove – and especially the requisite lucidity of mind – were present in everyone, and not just in exceptional individuals. Convincing evidence of this was the fact that those attending the demonstrations as members of the audience rather than as doves might also suddenly find that they were witnesses to the manifestations [42] or sometimes even witnessed them when no dove (or 'medium' as we would say in modern parlance) was present. In those situations, it would seem, it was solely the will of Grandmaster Cagliostro that was the determining factor.

At Versailles, before leading members of the aristocracy, Cagliostro summoned up not just the images of people who were absent or dead whose names had been given to him and who were visible only to the dove but also enabled these people to be seen in the form of animated and apparently living phantoms by all those present [43].

In Strasbourg, Cardinal de Rohan witnessed a similar demonstration arranged especially for him in which the image of a woman who was dear to him was manifested [44]. And 'in Lyons Cagliostro once held a whole roomful of Freemasons spellbound by showing them the ghost of their late Brother, Worshipful Master Prost de Royer, an eminent magistrate, who had just died' [45].

As case after case is cited, these phenomena become more and more credible. We're no longer concerned with isolated and minor cases of hydromancy (divination by water) or crystallomancy unconsciously occurring in abnormal subjects, but with the blossoming and practical implementation of a new faculty revealed to humanity solely by the power possessed by Cagliostro: the Master simply gives a command and the spiritual eye of the disciple, or even of a disinterested individual, slowly opens, just as his hand would move if the Master ordered it. A truly terrifying power that caused many to fall to their knees in awe!

Cagliostro did not however want the excessive admiration of his disciples to be transformed into some sort of fetishistic devotion either towards him or towards the powers that they witnessed. His aim was to develop their hearts and to encourage them to reflect. He explained to his disciples that this power that they regarded with such terror was not strictly limited to him and that he could transfer it under certain circumstances to particular people provided that they were pure in heart and well-intentioned, and as long as God agreed to grant this grace to them. Was this not, after all, the goal of Egyptian Freemasonry?

Once, in the early days, he had asked a third party to consecrate and question the dove [46]: the selected experimenter and those assembled were thus able to note that Cagliostro's powers had been successfully transmitted to his representative and that the requisite phenomena had still been accomplished perfectly. And Cagliostro did more than that: after choosing some disciples who had been carefully-instructed, who were reliable, and who devoted all their efforts towards the pursuit of the good and the true he transferred his powers to them not just temporarily for use in his presence but permanently, even for use in his absence [47].

Cagliostro's wife, when fiercely cross-examined by the Inquisition in Rome, testified that her husband had, on several occasions, transferred all or part of his powers to his disciples and that she herself had been granted the right to use such abilities 'by the power that she had received from the Grand Copht' – but in respect of certain human subjects only [48]. What is more, this power that some were able to acquire from him was so thoroughly and completely their own spiritual property that they could themselves delegate the use of it and assign it to substitutes or successors in accordance with the orders and precepts of the Master [49].

Finally, Cagliostro delivered teachings on the actual form of the revelations and demonstrations and the nature of the knowledge thus obtained. This undoubtedly went over the heads of many of his disciples. His many critics were of course no more responsive, the vast majority of people being more strongly drawn to the bizarre and the outlandish. Cagliostro undoubtedly acted wisely in making these teachings too subtle for consumption by the vulgar, but we feel obliged to briefly outline them here.

Knowledge, Cagliostro taught, is not the same as erudition. True knowledge is entirely personal in nature and does not require the intervention of another human being, elementary spirit or angel [50]. Even less does it demand some unspecified deployment of procedures and rituals. Cagliostro found this direct knowledge within himself, marshalled it through his keen clairvoyance, and manifested it through his prophecies. Few people understood it; perhaps even he himself did not. Always with Cagliostro one finds oneself searching for the

Chapter IV

presence in the background of some mysterious formula, sylph, devil or angel that would explain the man. It is certainly hard to conceive of him without the presence of a familiar spirit. Yet the evidence that he possessed the power of *direct* clairvoyance is huge: his contemporaries have told us about several instances, and Countess von der Recke mentions some of them [51]. His announcement in Strasbourg of the Empress Maria Theresa's death in Budapest at the precise moment it occurred is well-known [52], and Monsieur de Laborde, a *fermier-général* [53T] tells us, in his *Lettres sur la Suisse*, an even more striking story about the revelations and predictions that Cagliostro made in Warsaw concerning a young lady of the Court [54].

Such are the facts, and we cannot ignore them. Any disciple who had followed Cagliostro progressively in his series of demonstrations would be forced to conclude that these phenomena, however remarkable, were real, and that it was possible for knowledge to exist that was beyond the bounds of generally accepted science. Further than that, such disciples would draw the logical conclusion that external forms were of no use and that everything depended solely on the spiritual presence and will of Cagliostro, in whom an unlimited knowledge and power were to be found. Even so, the Master himself declared: 'Any human being who is willing to follow the same road with energy and patience will acquire the same powers, for God has given everything to man' [55]. There was therefore no need for human beings to seek out any other path to enlightenment.

What could be said against all this? Admittedly, even in Cagliostro's time, there was no shortage of sceptics: straightforward deceit, conjuring tricks, optical illusions and coincidence were all put forward as likely explanations [56]. Close observation and mature reflection will however show that these explanations are not even worthy of discussion. The sheer number of separate events, their apparent authenticity, the special circumstances under which they occurred and, in particular, the fact that his often prophetic revelations came to pass, suggest that any form of illusion must be discounted. Conjuring tricks can simulate any natural event – they can move a table or light up a room, but they can never illuminate a mind. Have not all the latest scientific discoveries initially been greeted with accusations of trickery? When the gramophone was first presented to the *Académie des Sciences*, didn't one of the most eminent scientists of the age accuse the demonstrator of being a ventriloquist? No, a chance event that continually occurs or an apparent illusion that always turns out to be reality can no longer be termed a chance event or an illusion. Cagliostro's clairvoyance and his ability to transfer at least some of his powers to his disciples are indisputable facts.

Some of his critics alleged (and some still do) that the phenomena could be explained by animal magnetism, but this was not one of Cagliostro's interests [57]. One of Cagliostro's disciples who was still living in 1850 wrote a quite interesting but very little known letter on this subject which we feel obliged to reproduce here, as it confirms the validity of our thesis. Louis Cahagnet [58T], having mentioned in his magazine *Le magnétiseur spiritualiste* [59] that a friend of his, Comte Brice de Beauregard, liked using magic-mirrors consisting of a globe of clarified water which he would then influence and subsequently cause to be influenced by spirits which would write the answers to questions in such a way that they could be read by clairvoyants, and having likened him to other animal magnetisers such as André Saturnin Morin and the crystal-gazers of ancient times, accepted the following rather indignant response for publication [60]:

> Sir,
> I read with interest in your excellent magazine an article on magic-mirrors, in which my name was linked to that of Monsieur Morin.
> An attentive reading of your article would suggest, if I'm not mistaken, that following the successes in crystal-gazing achieved by Cagliostro, Comte de Laborde and Baron Dupotet I myself then set to work along very different lines. That is far from being the case.
> In September 1827 I was initiated into Cagliostro's mysteries by one of his disciples who had known him and had actually been initiated by the Grandmaster himself. From that time onward I have followed, and continue to follow, the same procedures as Cagliostro.
> I believe that I am the only person in Europe to know the secrets of this subject, because all Cagliostro's disciples have since died and have taken those secrets to the grave with them. Since 1827 I have only met one man who knew them. I have met literally hundreds of people who have allowed their imaginations to run riot, coming up with all sorts of new theories, but I have not met a single expert of the 'old school'.
> Monsieur Dupotet should not try telling us that he discovered magic; in 1827, a long time before he arrived on the scene, I knew something about this science and I produced certain facts that he was unaware of and will perhaps always be unaware of.
> You say, 'Monsieur Morin greatly simplified this experiment'. I contest that. Monsieur Morin, whom I have the honour to know neither personally nor by name, could not simplify something that he doesn't know anything about, or which he knows only imperfectly simply on the say-so of intriguers who spoke to him about me by boasting that they were familiar with my secret when they weren't.
> Sir, let us not confuse things: clairvoyance is not trance-mediumship, and a theurgist is not a hypnotist. Monsieur Morin performs animal magnetism. He is therefore a hypnotist pure and simple. You yourself stated this and acknowledge it in good faith. I, on the other hand, perform a kind of hypnotism which I term 'angelic', which is something quite different. I therefore refuse to be bracketed with Monsieur Morin and declare formally that we have nothing in common. We do not practice the same skill nor do we believe in the same doctrines.
> You can take my word for all this. It is now some thirty years since I was admitted to the Société de magnétisme de Paris founded by the Marquis de Puységur, and it is now some thirty years that I have been performing hypnotism for the benefit of humanity..., so I think I am allowed to have an opinion on this subject and to say what hypnotism is and what it isn't.
> But let us return to Monsieur Morin. All he practises is vulgar hypnotism. What Cagliostro did was clairvoyance, or what you would call, in default of not knowing the correct term, 'spiritual hypnotism'. I look forward to sharing the Beatific Vision [61] with Monsieur Morin , but I don't hold out much hope,
> I remain Sir, etc.
> Comte Brice de Beauregard,
> Secretary-general, Société de magnétisme de Paris, Belleville, 25th June 1850.

Figuier put it very well when he said that Cagliostro combined in one person the prodigious gifts of many kinds of exceptional people – miracle-workers, healers, alchemists – without belonging exclusively to any of those categories. Cagliostro didn't try to explain his achievements in terms of mysterious fluids, he never boasted about his work, nor did he seek to conceal it beneath elaborate showmanship. He was happy to produce results which were all the more impressive because their cause and origin were unknown [62].

I am quite happy for people to give whatever name they wish to this incredible power and unblemished knowledge which commanded the spirits, ordered matter to come to life and then forced it to obey his laws, as long as the name they give them is a new one. But please don't assign to them some poorly-defined label taken from a purely artificial classification of the human sciences. We often mislead ourselves by using empty words. Back in 1830 people thought they were speaking meaningfully when they referred to 'somnambulistic lucidity' or 'animal magnetism'. Today our critical scientists will explain Cagliostro in terms of hypnosis, suggestion and the externalisation of motricity, and will declare themselves satisfied. Oh what a vain and empty tangle of words! All we've done is change the terminology: the secret of the spirit remains hidden from us. We are no closer these days to explaining Cagliostro's most trivial prophecy or most unchallenging cure – even using Monsieur Grasset's polygon [63] – than we were back in the days of Cagliostro's fame, when it was all explained away by the Mesmeric fluid or, fifty years later, by spirit mediumship.

Let's be quite sure about this: in Cagliostro's work we find neither superstition nor narrow practices that might be associated with hypnotism, nor a foreshadowing of Spiritualism nor an error-strewn form of ceremonial magic that is ultimately degrading for the human spirit. There is nothing in his work that is not certain, comprehensive and infinitely extensible. Basing himself on contemporary ideas, using contemporary language, and respecting the milieux in which he found himself, Cagliostro sought to gradually lead his disciples to concentrate exclusively on the regeneration of humanity and to focus their efforts solely on increasing the power and dignity of their souls by teaching them that, however great the marvels they might perceive, if they found the angels themselves standing before them – yes, even the Seven Great Angels that stand before the face of God – then 'one should not worship them but rather tell them to worship God, along with the Brothers' [64].

He taught them also that you should never try to pierce the veil that separates us from the world of spirit unless you can speak like a Master, and that you should never supplicate or abase yourself when doing so, 'because man was made in the image and likeness of God. Man is the most perfect of His works, and God gave him the right to command and dominate those creatures that come immediately after him' [65]. Finally, he taught that ultimately there is no need for lights and candles, hieroglyphs or magic formulae, but only for a 'pure heart and a doughty soul, and a desire to love, to do good and to be patient' [66].

These were the beautiful and noble lessons that Cagliostro taught while he was in Courland, and we can easily imagine the enthusiasm that they aroused. So great was the esteem in which he was held that if he had wanted to conquer a whole kingdom with his ideas then Courland would have let him. Indeed, the author of the *Vie de Joseph Balsamo* claims that the throne of Courland was secretly offered to him, and that if he turned it down it was only out of fear of the consequences [67]. That last phrase, which was obviously written for the benefit of crowned heads and was intended to justify in their eyes the persecution of someone who must have struck them as a terrifying adventurer, was not something that Cagliostro ever himself uttered: he *did* say that if he had wanted to become king then that was entirely up to him, but he also added that he had rejected the idea because such an ambition was not part of his plan, and because he felt it was essential always to respect the established order and sovereign of each country [68]. Once again we can see that the author of the *Vie de Joseph Balsamo* completely distorted Cagliostro's words and actions. Indeed, so hostile was the French translator of this book that he was unable to prevent himself from protesting against this insinuation.

What certainly is true is that Cagliostro had won the veneration of many in Courland, and that the entire local nobility had come over to his side [69]. The Lodge, however, was composed exactly as it had been at the outset. Founded by Countess von der Recke, her aunt Frau von Kayserling and her cousin Frau von Grotthaus, it also included Herr von Medem and his brother the Marshal, who was Worshipful Master; Herr von Medem von Tittelmunde (i.e. Tetelminde), the Marshal's son; the Aulic Councillor Schwander; Dr. Lieb; Hinz the notary; Herr von Howen; Major Von Korff; and later, Frau von der Recke's mother-in-law [70]. Cagliostro's other disciples were able to visit him and listen to his lectures, but they did not attend Lodge-workings, which remained secret. During the last few weeks of his stay in Courland Cagliostro actually lived at Von Medem's house [71], devoting all its time to the instruction of his disciples rather than practising medicine [72].

Lodge meetings were held every evening, with Cagliostro performing various demonstrations and giving lectures. In her book, Countess von der Recke published a few pages of rather confused notes made during these lectures which unfortunately often display a misunderstanding of the material, but which it is interesting to compare with the Ritual of Egyptian Freemasonry and other material by Cagliostro. In his farewell speech he urged his disciples to think often of him, to remain loyal, to work hard, and to keep silent. This last recommendation was aimed especially at Countess von der Recke and he repeated it to her in private [73]. We shall see below how much attention she paid to it.

When Cagliostro left Russia, Countess von der Recke wrote him a letter 'that he still has, in which she assures him not only of her affection but also her respect, but whose contents he will only reveal with her permission' [74]. Such feelings, which were shared by all his disciples in Courland, survived his departure: they wrote several letters to him which he answered [75]. More than a year afterwards they were still defending Cagliostro against the scandalmongers [76]. Everyone, especially Countess von der Recke, expected him to return from St. Petersburg [77] and hoped that he would settle permanently in Mittau where he had won such a sympathetic following. Not long afterwards, however, the Countess changed her mind about him, and then everyone followed suit. These are the circumstances in which this sudden and total reversal occurred. In 1782 the Countess, already disappointed in her hopes that Cagliostro would make a dazzling debut in St. Petersburg [78] and hurt that he had preferred to go to Warsaw rather than return to Courland, had a meeting in St. Petersburg with Prince Poni☐ski [79T]. The Prince had just had Cagliostro staying with him as a lodger for one month and, by now very hostile towards his former guest, gave the Countess the worst possible account of her 'Miracle Man'. For Poni☐ski, Cagliostro's transmutations were mere trickery, his evocations pure comedies, and his prophecies merely secret but naturally-acquired knowledge of people and things. Although Poni☐ski had a bad reputation [80], his comments disturbed the Countess. On her return to Mittau she began to review her memories of Cagliostro in an effort to find a rational 'scientific' explanation for everything that had happened [81].

Little by little her former convictions began to disintegrate. The professional sceptics she was surrounded by – people like Hinz and Schwander – played an active role in this process. They argued that the children who had acted as 'doves', who had been unaware of their *état second* (to use Hippolyte Bernheim's terminology) [82] and who were readily suggestive under the influence of their surroundings through fear or self-interest, had simply given answers that confirmed the doubts that the questioners had expressed.

Chapter IV

Eventually Poni☐ski's opinion came to be widely shared – people had simply been misled! Their scepticism was further increased by their reading of the satirical *Cagliostro démasqué à Varsovie*, a copy of which the author had sent Countess von der Recke in 1786 [83], as well as other similar lampoons [84]. The Countess then wrote to Strasbourg, where Cagliostro was then living, asking him what he was doing and what people thought of him there. The man who acted as intermediary to feed all this information back to her, the theologian Laurent Blessig, told her all the current rumours, especially the negative ones, and unfortunately it was those that she preferred to listen to. However she still hesitated: she had seen too many things to be totally sceptical and she did not find either within herself or her entourage sufficient reason for rejecting everything nor, admittedly, any way of explaining everything either [85].

It was the influence of the German man of letters Friedrich Nicolai, whom she got to know during her later travels through Germany [86], that finally overcame her remaining scruples. He was able to transform her regrets into resentment, and her estrangement into hatred. Seven years after the events of 1776, Nicolai and his friends persuaded the Countess to publish first a comment hostile to the Grandmaster of Egyptian Freemasonry in the *Berliner Monatsschrift* for May 1786 and then a book in which she defamed him by accusing him of trickery and ignorance, denouncing him to everyone who would listen as a dangerous tool of the Jesuits.

As we can see, it was not her personal impressions or the results of direct observation that she was publishing – these, all of them singing Cagliostro's praises, had formed the basic text of her journal published in 1779 – but a violent declamation crammed with malevolent suppositions and unfavourable interpretations, bringing together in one volume the snide remarks of a Polish nobleman who spent most of his time ridiculing people (Poni☐ski), the opinion of a dull Strasbourg theologian (Blessig), and the acerbic criticisms of German penny-a-liners who disliked anything that smacked of mysticism (e.g. Nicolai and his circle).

Such was the origin of this little book in which Countess von der Recke disavows her former Master and friend. Although, when Cagliostro was in Mittau, he could not have had any inkling that the Countess would be assailed by such doubts, he does seem to have had some vague premonitions that she might succumb to them. On the first such occasion he wrote to her: 'When I'm no longer there, do not be too anxious always to investigate what I call the 'Why of the Why'... Idle curiosity, vanity and a desire for power can have, as their sequel, misfortune that extends until the thousandth generation... If you are not motivated to study mysticism solely by a desire to do good then please do not study it at all' [87]. On the second occasion, writing on the eve of his departure from Alt-Auz, he once again – this time with magisterial insight – foresaw what was likely to happen. During the last ritual that he performed he suddenly asked the Countess to rise to her feet. He then led her inside the Magic Circle where he was standing, looked at her gravely, and asked the dove what he could see within the tabernacle:

'I'm kneeling in front of Count Cagliostro. He's got a watch in his hand' (this is quite correct). 'There's a spirit here in a long white robe, with a golden crown on his head and a red cross on his breast'.

'Ask the spirit his name', said Cagliostro.

The child complied, but the spirit remained silent.

'Well my child, did the spirit tell you his name?'

'No Sir'.

'Why not?'

'Because he has forgotten it Sir' [88].

Cagliostro looked upset. He wrung his hands, collected himself, pronounced some words which the Countess did not understand, and the meeting continued. When it was finished Cagliostro addressed his disciples:

One of you will be a Judas to me, and will betray me, and seek to harm me. I learned about this sad event just now when the spirit kept silent and refused to reveal his name. I shall not tell you how much my heart is wounded by this discovery. I tremble not for myself but for the unhappy person who will betray me... I shall be greatly saddened by their fall, but I shall not be able to intervene on their behalf. But all of you, pray with me, pray for the traitor, and pray for me as well... [89]

Unfortunately these warnings – although so clear and so precise – proved as incomprehensible to the Countess as Cagliostro's teachings had done.

Cagliostro in St. Petersburg

Cagliostro left Mittau at the peak of his success. At the Lodge everything was going according to plan and all the best people were aspiring to the honour of becoming his disciples, but the enthusiasm of the Courlandais, far from encouraging Cagliostro to prolong his stay in Mittau, actually proved an incidental cause of him leaving it [90].

The brilliant court of Catherine II and the emerging power of the Russian Empire were attracting the nobility of both Poland and Courland. There was nothing wrong with Mittau, but it was not St. Petersburg: there only, in the Russian capital, could ambitions truly blossom. And what greater success than to bring before the Empress a powerful being, an adviser without equal, someone who could protect her in both the visible and invisible realms? Would not such a master-stroke simultaneously ensure the recognition of both the great Empress and the equally great Cagliostro? Surely whoever achieved such a coup would enjoy both earthly good fortune and celestial grace?

Empress Catherine was certainly interested in Freemasonry. 'Whatever one might think of Catherine II from the standpoints of morality and the finer feelings', wrote the Masonic historian Friedrichs [91], 'and however severely one might judge her on these two points, it cannot be denied that she had both the discernment of a great statesman and a colossal intellect. French culture, as personified by men such as Montesquieu, Voltaire, Rousseau, Diderot, d'Alembert and Grimm, enjoyed a monopoly in her country. Is it any wonder then that Catherine studied their works with such enthusiasm? But her natural percipience immediately recognised the impossibility, from the point of view of the everyday life of her people, of implementing the ideas that their works suggested: the materialism, atheism and subversive democratic tendencies that were manifested in their philosophy might well prove perilous for a people as politically unsophisticated as the Russians. Just as she was looking around her for people to provide the firm support she needed for the effective education of her people she thought she had found them in the Freemasons, who had only just been established in Russia and who, in their lodges, waged an uncompromising war against atheism and the immorality preached by the French philosophers, seeking to replace it with a pure faith in the Divinity, and what is more a faith that was not made narrow by dogma. They also required their members to swear allegiance to the higher authorities of the State. Cultivation of the arts, encouragement of the sciences, improvements in public education,

Chapter IV

raising the standard of public health – was this not Catherine's own programme, and was it not the ideal of Freemasonry as well? Were they not natural bedfellows? And so it was that Catherine granted the Freemasons the protection they had asked for' [92].

No one could help more with the expansion of Russian Freemasonry than the Grand Copht. There was no doubt that he would be of invaluable assistance to the Empress and that she in her turn would appreciate what he had to offer. Cagliostro felt motivated to leave Mittau. This was not a difficult decision. He had made Mittau his first stop in his wanderings through Europe and had taken up temporary residence there in such a way as to show himself in the best possible light, but there was no longer anything to keep him there. In Mittau Count Cagliostro had finally stepped out into the footlights: here was a man who could pierce the veil that separated mankind from the world of spirits, who could command those spirits, and even be paid homage by them. As the Grandmaster of true Freemasonry he helped all the unfortunates of the world: the unquiet souls, the grieving hearts, the sick, the halt and the lame. That was the reputation that Cagliostro took with him to St. Petersburg.

Cagliostro had been told to introduce himself, on his arrival in St. Petersburg, to Baron von Heyking [93], but despite the letter of very warm recommendation that he brought with him from Herr von Howen, the Baron received him with the disdain that a man in high society feels for a 'commonplace fellow without a trace of literary culture' [94]. Von Heyking was certainly prejudiced against him. German by both race and temperament, he represented the autocratic wing of the *Große Landesloge* of Berlin [95], which was already in competition with the English lodges and those of the Swedish system which had also been developing in Russia. Not only did he not like Cagliostro as a man, he also feared him as a dangerous political adversary. Cagliostro greeted him fraternally enough and, initially at least, did not take offence at von Heyking's mistrust and hostility.

'I can forgive you your incredulity and your ignorance', he told Von Heyking, 'because after all you're just a little child in the Order despite all your Masonic titles. If I wanted, I could make you tremble.'

'Yes, perhaps I'd tremble if you gave me the 'flu', retorted Heyking ironically.

'Ha! What would a dose of 'flu be for Count Cagliostro, who knows how to command the denizens of the spirit world!' [96]

The conversation continued, Heyking always sardonic, Cagliostro always patient. Like all the would-be intellectuals of this great city, which liked to copy Paris in so many ways, the Baron prided himself on his 'healthy' knowledge of science [97] and his elegant scepticism, two characteristics that would obviously make any contact with Cagliostro somewhat problematical.

From Freemasonry the conversation moved on to chemistry. Von Heyking made a fine show of his knowledge of the subject, once again seeking to impress and subdue his interlocutor. Here, according to Von Heyking's memoirs, is how the conversation unfolded:

'For anyone who possesses the secrets of alchemy', said Cagliostro, 'chemistry is really pretty much nonsense [98] *and alchemy is a thing of naught for anyone who can command the spirits. As for me, I have plenty of gold'* (he said this while jingling the ducats he had in his pocket) *'and I also have diamonds aplenty'* (showing me a ring with badly-set carbonadi) [99] *'but personally I place no trust at all in things like that, but instead stake my happiness on the power that I can exert over the beings that form the class immediately above we mere humans'.*

I couldn't help smiling.

'Your incredulity doesn't annoy me in the slightest', said Cagliostro. 'You're not the first

know-all that I've subdued and reduced to dust [100]. Tell me, which of your late relatives would you most like to see again?'

'My uncle', I replied, 'but on one condition'.

'And that is?'

'I'd like to fire a pistol at him. As he's only a spirit it won't do him any harm'[101]).

'No!' cried Cagliostro. 'You, Sir, are a monster! I refuse to show you anything. You are simply unworthy of it!'

Cagliostro jumped up from the table and left the room abruptly, as if offended. Countess Cagliostro was also present, and she began trembling, knowing Cagliostro's formidable powers. She was certainly weighing up the Baron's rashness, but as Cagliostro's wife she knew that, in her husband's case, wrath was not something that followed the usual train of events or that overwhelmed his soul and became an obsession: he only allowed himself to be carried away when it suited him, and he was not vengeful by nature.

And, indeed, Cagliostro returned just a few minutes later, all smiles as if nothing had happened.

'I see you have guts, Baron von Heyking', he said simply. 'That's a fine thing, a very fine thing indeed. But in time you will come to know Count Cagliostro and the mighty power that he wields'.

And from that moment on he never discussed esoteric or spiritual matters with the Baron, whom in any case he saw on very few further occasions [102].

Cagliostro received a rather warmer welcome from certain other local personalities. There was Chevalier de Corbéron, France's *chargé d'affaires* in Russia [103], who sensed when he first met Cagliostro that he was indeed a Master and was utterly won over by him, and who presented him at Court. Lieutenant-General Melissino, a Hermeticist and proponent of the Masonic rite that bears his name, General Golitsyn and Prince Potemkin [104] also became his followers and remained loyal to him.

Some, like Melissino, were keen to pick his brains about Freemasonry. Cagliostro's teachings enabled them to acquire some understanding of its true foundations and aims. They no longer saw the work of the lodge as a round of trivial ceremonies and mundane celebrations but as an exercise in theurgy: nothing less than the regeneration of man was the goal, and the wonderful means to attain that goal was the assistance of the spirit world.

Others, of a more philosophical and Hermeticist turn, found in Cagliostro the adept they had so long awaited, the only person who could help them to find their way through the mass of contradictions in the authors they had read and so resolve their doubts. Cagliostro did not waste their time repeating the lessons of the old alchemists such as Bernard Trevisan or Geber but instead looked directly into Nature's laboratory, saying: 'This is how you must find what you are seeking, this is what is missing in your work' [105].

When Cagliostro did not want to answer questions in person he would use a child as an intermediary, just as he had done in Courland. Whether the questions concerned hieroglyphics, Hermeticism, research into the past, forecasts of the future or advice on the present, the spiritual beings would appear to the dove and provide answers.

But, even more than spiritual anguish or unfulfilled intellectual curiosity it is disease and physical suffering that make people unhappy and cause them to avidly seek help and healing. Even if Cagliostro had never thought of practising medicine he would certainly have been prevailed upon to do so. Was he not a man of immense erudition and power? Everyday experience proved it: after all, Cagliostro had more servants in the spirit world [106] than the

Chapter IV

Empress had in the whole of Russia. What doctor could be expected to achieve as much as Cagliostro?

Patients hastened to him, and he consoled and cured both rich and poor with the same disinterest. 'It was in St. Petersburg that Cagliostro began healing the poor and giving them money. Amongst this class of unfortunate just to give them some food is enough to heal them, as hunger is what their diseases start with. A man of particular integrity decided to give the 'new doctor' a try: his life was saved and he wanted to pay him, but Cagliostro simply gave him his money back' [107].

Cagliostro's medical services were increasingly in demand, and for the first time he practised medicine consistently. It was still, however, a secondary occupation for him. Laboratory work, carried out in his inimitable way, was what chiefly occupied him at his time.

His medical cures brought him all the more fame because they were often achieved in the face of desperate illness and without recourse to standard medical processes. Cagliostro cured a court official called Ivan Isleniev of an ulcerated cancer of the cervix which had been written off as incurable. This cure is well attested [108]. Also, 'in St. Petersburg Cagliostro cured Baron Stroganov, who suffered from bouts of insanity with a neurological basis, as well as Gelagin, Madame Bouturlin and others' [109].

Rarely, if ever, did he use drugs to treat disease. He was content to ask Heaven for a cure or to question the doves about the cases with which he was dealing. Sometimes he simply ordered the disease to leave the patient – and it did so. 'Ah! Auto-suggestion' the superficial-minded will exclaim at this point, but I can only think of one case in Cagliostro's entire medical career where he used the power of suggestion and that was, appropriately enough, in St. Petersburg. This is what happened, told in Cagliostro's own words:

In the city named after Peter the Great one of the Ministers of the Empress had a brother who'd lost his reason. He actually believed that he was greater than God. No one could restrain his violent outbursts in which he would shout and scream, blaspheming and threatening to destroy the whole world. He was kept a virtual prisoner. The Minister begged me to cure him [110].

When I entered his room he immediately fell into a fury, scowling at me ferociously. Even though he was chained up he managed to twist his arms as if he wanted to hurl himself onto me. Then he screamed, 'May he who dares to appear before Almighty God, the God who dominates all the other gods and who drives them far from His face, be hurled into the deepest abyss!' But I, repressing any emotion, simply went up to him in all confidence and said, 'Will you not be quiet, you lying spirit? Do you really not know who I am, the God who is above all other gods and whose name is Mars? Do you not see this arm which contains all the strength required to act from the very summit of the heavens to the very deepest abyss of the earth? I came to you to take pity on you and to make you well again, and this is how you welcome me! Obviously you do not know that, although I have the power to heal you, I also have the power to destroy you – utterly'. And I immediately gave him such a thump that he fell backwards onto the ground. After the guards had picked him up and he had calmed down a bit I ordered a meal and began eating, forbidding him to eat with me. When I saw that he was suitably humbled I said to him: 'Your salvation lies in humility, and in being deprived of all power before me. Come here, and eat'.

After he had eaten something we boarded a carriage and drove out of the city, along the banks of the River Neva. The guards had got a boat ready on my orders and were sitting on the embankment. We embarked, the crew started rowing, and off the boat flew. Then, with the aim of throwing him in the river to effect a cure by means of shock – I had taken the precaution of posting people in appropriate places to come to his aid if necessary – I grabbed him, but since he in his turn suddenly encircled me in his arms we both fell into the water, where he tried to drag me down to the depths while I, who was above him, sought to control him with my bulk. After a struggle which lasted longer than I would have liked I finally managed to extricate myself and swim for safety while he was rescued by the guards and placed in a sedan-chair.

When we'd returned from our little adventure and had changed into dry clothes he said to me, 'Truly, I now recognise that you are indeed the god Mars and that there is no power equal to your own. I shall be subject to you in all things'. 'My friend', I answered, 'you are not a rival to Almighty God and neither am I the god Mars, but just a man like you. You have the demon of pride within you and he has driven you mad. I have come to snatch you from the clutches of this evil spirit. If you really want to be subject to me in all things then just do what any ordinary mortal would do'.

And from that day onwards he allowed himself to be cared for and so eventually returned to the state he was in before his reason degenerated into delirium [111].

Now we are willing to admit that in this particular case Cagliostro *did* use the power of suggestion. But when we find Cagliostro curing cancer patients who had been given up for dead like Isleniev, or when Cagliostro, sitting in an armchair at Prince Potemkin's house, says – referring to a patient in full fever who is delirious in a hospital-bed, 'At this very moment we hereby order the fever to dissipate', something they were able to verify for themselves as having occurred when they went to visit the patient one hour later, then I would argue that to use the word 'suggestion' in such cases is to take liberties with language and to seek dishonestly to explain away a deeply thought-provoking occurrence by means of a superficial explanation.

That Cagliostro enjoyed great success in St. Petersburg [112] is beyond dispute. Even his detractors, who find a thousand nasty things to say about his time in Mittau and Warsaw, cannot find anything to criticise about his time in Russia. Proof of his fame can be found in the jealousy that was shown towards him by members of the local medical profession, and more particularly in the anger shown towards Cagliostro by the chief medical adviser to the Empress, a Scot called Dr. John Rogerson [113T]. The following anecdote is telling in this regard:

One day Rogerson visited Cagliostro in a state of absolute fury and began insulting and taunting him. 'I said to him', as Cagliostro later amusingly recalled [114], 'that if he was visiting me in my own person as Cagliostro then I would call my servants and have him thrown out of the window, but if he was taunting me in my capacity as a fellow medical-man then it was as a medical-man that I would give him satisfaction. 'I'm taunting you as a medical-man', said Rogerson, clearly frightened – and, indeed, I had a large posse of servants at my disposal at that time. Then I said to him, 'In that case let's not fight with swords but with something from the medical armamentarium. You will swallow two arsenic tablets that I shall give you while I shall swallow whatever poison you choose to give me. Whichever of us dies shall be regarded in perpetuity as a pig'. 'Pig' was Cagliostro's favourite epithet for people he didn't like.

Rogerson declined Cagliostro's offer. The Empress managed to calm Cagliostro down and was subsequently able to keep Rogerson at a safe distance. The 'duel with poisons' never took place [115].

As long as the Empress looked favourably upon Cagliostro and extended her protection towards him in her desire to expand Freemasonry in Russia no one would make a move against him, but his enemies were keeping a watchful eye on him. They found a propitious moment to close in on him when the astute Empress, uncharacteristically, had a sudden change of heart and lost interest in the Masonic Lodges [116]. At that time Cagliostro had just accomplished another amazing cure: a two-year-old girl was not only saved from death but was so transformed within just a few days that her mother scarcely recognised her – and that of course provided Cagliostro's enemies with an opportunity to allege that another child had been substituted in her place [117].

The Russians, a fickle people, easily enthused and just as easily demotivated, lost all interest in Cagliostro the miracle-worker. Dark rumours began circling around him: it was said that he was receiving money secretly and that his wife was involved in all sorts of sordid intrigues [118]. There were mutterings too about a political conspiracy, and in Tsarist Russia the word 'conspiracy' had an almost magical power. Cagliostro's friends, sensing probable persecution, summoned him to Warsaw [119] – and he went.

Much later, in 1786, all these rumours and mutterings were gathered together and embellished with the most malicious and risqué imaginings to produce the story that Cagliostro had actually been thrown out of St. Petersburg on the orders of the Empress and at the request of Monsieur de Normandez, the King of Spain's *chargé d'affaires* [120]. This legend, like so many others, has persisted. It is important to destroy it. Baron von Heyking, who as we know did not exactly see Cagliostro surrounded by an aura of sanctity, nonetheless reports the Monsieur de Normandez affair with greater impartiality and reduces it to its just proportions. We should remember that the events in question occurred right at the outset of Cagliostro's visit to St. Petersburg, in fact the day after his arrival [121]. Apparently the Spanish *chargé d'affaires* wanted to see him to check on his various titles and qualifications and, it would seem, to make sure that he would not claim to be a colonel in the military service of Spain [122]. After this interview Cagliostro remained in St. Petersburg for several months enjoying the protection of the Empress, the support of the nobility and the respect of the general population [123]. The intervention by Monsieur de Normandez would not, therefore, seem to have had much impact. In fact, Cagliostro's titles and qualifications mattered little: his actions and personal magnetism were enough to enable him to achieve recognition and approval. As for his departure from the city, far from being thrown out he received tokens of the most exceptional and genuine gratitude [124]. Warm letters of introduction for use in Warsaw and a passport in due order were granted to him at his simple request. Cagliostro was willing to show the passport to anyone who wanted to see it as late as 1787 [125].

He retained a number of good friends in St. Petersburg. During the Diamond Necklace Affair he was able to call upon the testimony of Baron de Corbéron, at that time Minister Plenipotentiary to the Duc de Deux-Ponts, regarding his life in St. Petersburg, what memories people had of him there, and the honourable circumstances under which he had left that city.

Cagliostro in Warsaw
In April 1780, at the insistence of Prince Poni☐ski [126], Cagliostro moved to Warsaw. Prince Adam Poni☐ski, founder of the Warsaw Templar Lodge known as *Charles of the Three Helmets* [127], was a keen alchemist. He had come to know Cagliostro through mutual friends in St. Petersburg and was very keen for him to join his circle and to have him direct their work. Poni☐ski was surrounded by alchemists of all kinds. Hermeticism was very much in vogue in Poland [128] and, of course, no group of esotericists is more diverse than alchemists.

At the bottom of the alchemical scale you have the humble *souffleur*, as the French call them, the simple bellows-operator, often quite ignorant, sometimes superstitious, always very materialistic, with a natural interest in chemistry, enjoying working with furnaces and suchlike for its own sake, astonished at every turn by events that are all too familiar to others but which are completely unfamiliar to him, burning his charcoal and wasting his life quite at random, and always expecting the unexpected. Such people have been numerous in the history of alchemy, but if they were responsible for any major discoveries at all then these have been very few in number.

The *mystical* alchemist is a very different creature: his home is not cluttered with chemical equipment as his sole concerns are symbols and the world of dreams. The fire that burns in his laboratory is the fire of a gentle and constant flame. The mystic seeks the Philosopher's Stone within himself, and his athanor is the human being. We can also include in this class what one might call the *socially aware* alchemist, the reformer, who conceals his bold ambitions beneath a veil of chemical symbolism. This is the type of alchemist who was most dreaded by the clergy and the ruling class in the Middle Ages, but out of fear of allowing any of these different types of alchemist to escape the Inquisition targeted all of them in their relentless pursuit.

Occupying the highest level of alchemical culture is the Hermetic philosopher, who observes nature, seeks to fathom her laws and mysteries, and always works in collaboration with her. This is the true scientist who, on the basis of observations, rises to the challenge of formulating a general hypothesis before verifying it in a series of experiments and enshrining it in law. It is to these Hermetic philosophers that we owe most of the chemical discoveries that make up our present scientific culture.

Researchers in all these categories, along with the simply inquisitive, were to be found in Poni☐ski's entourage, conversing and experimenting with him, and all of them looking forward keenly to the arrival of Cagliostro, a man who intrigued them and who was supposed to be a great Adept. Although Cagliostro never described himself as a 'Son of Hermes' [129], people were already talking excitedly about his Elixir [130], his Luminous Stone [131], his secret processes for enlarging diamonds [132], softening marble and amber, working them and then restoring their hardness, or for giving cotton and hemp the sheen and smoothness of silk [133], as well as the evidence that he had given of his power over matter. Much was expected of him: it was known that in the spirit world he had access to a most excellent source of all the information that was useful for the Hermetic art, and *souffleurs*, mystics and scientists were all counting on him to help them achieve their differing goals. Poni☐ski in particular was drawn to Cagliostro. Poni☐ski did not do things by halves, and ardently desired occult powers [134]. In return, Cagliostro was interested in the Prince: he knew that, beneath a stormy exterior, he had a heart of gold and that, even if he was sometimes prone to violence, he also had finer feelings.

And so it was that Cagliostro came to Warsaw and lodged with the Prince. Poni☐ski arranged for his country-house at Vola to be converted into a laboratory. No expense was spared and Cagliostro 'who refused to accept any money, gave Poni☐ski in return all the information that he needed to furnish the laboratory to the highest standards' [135].

While Vola was being transformed into a chemical laboratory Cagliostro was astonishing his hosts with his conversation and miracle-working. The difference in surroundings meant that he came across as even more impressive than he had done in Mittau and St. Petersburg: the truths that he embodied and taught may have been the same, and of course the laws of matter, nature and the spirit had not changed, but now he was surrounded by people for

Chapter IV

whom the search for the Philosopher's Stone was the only miracle that really mattered. It seems that in this less spiritual and more materialistic milieu, less tinged with philosophical speculation than that of Russia, Cagliostro worked especially hard to plant the seeds of spiritual development. Before the very eyes of the *bon viveurs* and the sardonic grins of the sceptics he conjured up phenomena that were specially chosen to challenge their assumptions. To the *souffleurs* he spoke of a Hermetic philosophy which was not to be found in books; to everyone he presented something new, something surprising; he did not flatter anyone, was no respecter of persons, and spoke, as he acted, with complete independence, unconcerned about alienating anyone he encountered [136]. He enjoyed great social success, his wife's birthday being elaborately fêted [137]. He was also received by the King [138]. As a contemporary wrote: 'Count Cagliostro was in Warsaw for some time and had the honour of audiences with the King on several occasions. The King held him in high esteem and paid homage to his intelligence, talents and knowledge. However, a sceptical young lady of the Court who one day heard the King expressing these positive views burst out laughing, said that Cagliostro must be a charlatan, and set him the challenge of telling her certain things that had happened to her. The following day the King told Cagliostro about the challenge. Cagliostro answered coldly that if the young lady would like to make an appointment to see him in His Majesty's presence then he would give her the greatest surprise of her life. The invitation was accepted and, at the agreed time, Cagliostro told the young lady everything that she had thought it impossible for him to be able to tell her. This surprised her so much that she immediately became such a keen admirer of him that she entreated him to tell her what would happen to her in the future. Initially Cagliostro refused but, won over by the young lady's entreaties and perhaps persuaded also by the King's curiosity, he made the following prediction:

Soon you will leave on a great journey. Your carriage will break down at some of the staging-inns in Warsaw, and while it is being repaired your manner of dress and hairstyle will cause such hilarity amongst those around you that they will pelt you with apples. You will go from there to a famous spa where you will meet a man of high rank whom you will like so much that you will marry him a short time afterwards. Despite the efforts that will be made to get you to see reason you will be tempted to hand over to him all your fortune. You will marry him in a city where I myself shall be, and despite the efforts that you make to get to see me you will not succeed. You are threatened with grave misfortunes, but here is a talisman for you: as long as you have it on your person no harm will befall you, but if it proves impossible to prevent you from handing over your fortune through a contract of marriage then you will immediately lose the talisman, and as soon as you lose it then it will be in my pocket wherever I might happen to be.

'I do not how much credence the King and the young lady attached to these predictions, nor what went through their minds as the events unfolded, but I do know that everything happened exactly as Cagliostro said it would. Cagliostro actually showed me the talisman, which he had found in his pocket on the very day the young lady signed the marriage contract by which she handed over her entire personal fortune to her new husband' [139]. The famous magical session at which the burning parchment was rematerialised and restored to those attending [140] also took place in Warsaw around this time.

Cagliostro often held meetings of the Egyptian Lodge with those who wished to become his disciples: he gave a course of lectures which were initially concerned with chemical operations but which later included Hermetic medicine [141], thus preparing his disciples for the practical work which was to follow. As soon as the laboratory was ready, the real work began. The first task was the transmutation of a pound of mercury into sterling silver. This was done at a public meeting in front of spectators [142]. On this occasion Cagliostro promised that he would later give his disciples the formula for the red powder that he had used in the transmutation. In return he insisted that his disciples show enthusiasm, respect and a degree of spiritual elevation. He also put the scoffers and hard-headed sceptics firmly in their place [143].

Unfortunately we have very little information about the sequel to these interesting experiments and about Cagliostro's alchemical work in Warsaw in general. Even so, what information that has come down to us has been maliciously distorted. In 1786, at the time of the press campaign against Cagliostro, a lampoon appeared without the name of the author or publisher entitled *Cagliostro démasqué à Varsovie* ('Cagliostro unmasked in Warsaw') [144]. We now know that the author was August Count Moszyński [145], who had been delegated to assist Cagliostro in his work at Vola. His pamphlet repeats lots of stories which were intended, the author says, 'to unmask an impostor who has already abused public credulity for far too long' [146], in other words to corroborate the attacks made by Cagliostro's enemies and to try to make him look a preposterous and shameless charlatan. Although the pamphlet is riddled with trivia and stupidities it is actually a more interesting document than others of its kind, as it gives us a glimpse of Cagliostro at work in his laboratory.

Count Moszyński tells that he was an eye-witness to a transmutation. He accepts that such an event occurred, but claims that his eyes must have deceived him and that Cagliostro must have used subterfuge. Cagliostro asked for some mercury to be poured into a crucible, added to it a pinch of red powder, and then asked for the crucible to be luted and placed it in the furnace. When it was removed from the furnace a few minutes later it was found to be cracked and to contain a silver ingot and a small amount of gold.

This is something that Moszyński actually saw, which was performed in front of a large gathering, and where most of the operations were performed by a third party acting in Cagliostro's presence. Moszyński saw all this but refused to accept it and tried to explain it by using his imagination, claiming that Cagliostro must have added gold to his mercury and have swapped the crucibles, replacing the initial one by another in which the silver ingot had been placed in advance, with Countess Cagliostro being assigned the task of getting rid of the old one. Finally the red powder – which would have served no purpose if we accept Moszyński's version of the facts – was probably just carmine.

Such are the entirely gratuitous assumptions of Count Moszyński, made in the face of facts which were obtained under sound experimental conditions. We could examine them one by one to show just how inane his comments are, but that would take far too long. Let us merely note as a blanket statement that what he has to say consists solely of simple-minded and malevolent assumptions – none of which is proven or even well-founded, and some of which are flatly contradicted [147] – formulated in a desperate attempt to explain away incontestable and, for him, deeply embarrassing facts as a simple act of deceit.

So here we have on the one hand a personal enemy of Cagliostro who hides behind a cloak of anonymity, who witnesses a transmutation and yet alleges, without any evidence, that the whole thing was a fraud, and on the other Cardinal de Rohan, who himself witnessed several similar experiments and who says that they were genuine [148]. Why should we accept the doubtful assumptions of the former, thus rejecting the clear and multiple testimonies of the latter? Should we not, on the contrary, regard as deeply suspect the statements of a man who, at the same time as he was pretending to be helping Cagliostro in his work, was doing his best to ensure that it failed [149]? He had also made up his mind that Cagliostro was going to lose the good will of his protector Prince Poniński and had a vested interest in ensuring that this occurred, and deployed all the means at his disposal to achieve that.

In his criticisms Moszyński shows an equal amount of bad faith: if an alchemical operation is instantaneous then, according to him, it must be false; if Cagliostro takes weeks for a *passage* [150] then that is simply a pretext for wasting time and stringing out an experiment which was not going to succeed anyway [151]. In another part of his pamphlet he tells us that Cagliostro's powder of projection 'which he no doubt got from some alchemist or other' [152] had been stolen from him by 'one of his girlfriends' in London, whereupon he performed a transmutation in front of her. We went into some detail elsewhere in this book about the Scott and Fry affair [153] and we can see from that just how much confidence we can place in a writer who distorts the truth in this way.

We can fully understand the subsequent events. When Moszyński's animosity became even more intense, when he starting laying traps for Cagliostro and even started defaming Countess Cagliostro and trying to turn the Prince against his Master, Cagliostro decided to finish once and for all with this traitor who was quite happy to hypocritically act respectfully towards him in front of others. There was a violent row [154]. Cagliostro saw that Moszyński's calumny had been successful and that his disciples' confidence in him had been shaken. Accordingly he decided to abandon the Prince, the Polish aristocracy and his new laboratory [155]. Bigheads like Moszyński and his partisans obviously had no need for him, and so he departed, leaving them to their sarcasm and the facile satisfaction of an apparent victory.

From June to September 1780 we find Cagliostro in Strasbourg, saddened no doubt and eager to forget the recent past. He spent this time in seclusion with one of his disciples, Countess de H., whose personal doctor he was and whose spiritual counsellor he was to remain [156].

We might well ask why Cagliostro didn't make more effort to convince people of the legitimacy of his alchemical work. While his acts of clairvoyance, of prediction of the future, of stimulated visions and of many incontestable and remarkable cures have been credited to him just about everywhere, we find only rare accounts of his alchemical achievements. Were his abilities in this direction limited or were his Hermetic doctrines on life and matter incorrect?

No, Cagliostro's power and freedom were limitless, and the ability of the mind to act upon matter is a truth as undeniable as the power of a hypnotist's will to act on the brain of his subject even though, like hypnosis, it has not yet become part of 'official' scientific doctrine. But whereas, in his psychic experiments, Cagliostro initiated humanity into the use of faculties whose evolution entailed at that time a perfectly natural and general development, in his laboratory researches into the life of matter and its transformations he was far ahead of his time, penetrating more deeply into the sanctuary of nature and unleashing forces that neither the people of his time nor those of many generations hence would understand and use. All he could do was outline the general principles and offer his disciples a glimpse of the road that he had opened up to them.

But who were his disciples? What exactly did they want from him? Like all searchers for the Philosopher's Stone they wanted to see a base metal transmuted into the purest gold in just a few hours or days and to learn the formula for the operation, so as to then to be able, thanks to this secret, to fulfil their ambitions of becoming rich and having everyone admire them for their exceptional knowledge. Their eyes were focused on this one aim alone – nothing else mattered to them. But was this the goal that Cagliostro himself sought? Could such a frame of mind as his alchemical students obviously had really allow him to achieve for them the rapid miracles they sought? Whereas in the experiments with the dove or the theurgic meetings in Courland those attending were disinterested and respectful, listened devotedly, and accepted without ulterior motive what was revealed to them, in the laboratory work at Vola the experimenters wanted just one thing: gold. That was all they really wanted, and they took umbrage at Cagliostro's insistence that they should closely observe phenomena that they considered as devoid of interest, and that they follow long and involved methods to attain their goal. Yet it was only in these intermediate and unstable states of matter that Cagliostro could have offered them instruction. He would have achieved this by making them closely observe certain new phenomena. A knowledge of these phenomena should have been revelatory for them, and realisation of them would certainly have been possible in the light of the state of science at that time [157].

Let me explain. Between the human body, the most advanced on our Earth, and the more primitive mineral body we have the bodies of the animal and vegetable kingdoms. Of course, no one ever bothered to ask Cagliostro to try to influence the behaviour of an animal or to help it evolve, or to modify a plant [158], although I am sure that Cagliostro would have been quite happy to have undertaken work of this kind, which is obviously purely scientific and disinterested, and very satisfying for the intellectually curious observer. If a start can be made on developing man's spiritual powers – and Cagliostro's revelations as well as recent experiments prove that it can – then the sphere of action of these powers will begin to expand beyond the human kingdom, initially into the animal kingdom and then into the vegetable kingdom, and will only reach the mineral kingdom at its most extreme boundary, if indeed it needs to extend that far. The order of nature requires that this be so, and evolution demands it if its laws are to be fulfilled – it is the safeguard of progress.

If we can conceive, by means of a logical development of this idea, of the possibility of the mind acting on that form of matter that we term 'inorganic', then we should regard it only as a limit that is, as yet, indeterminable for us, even though we are today witnessing the blossoming of this power within the human kingdom. We should also remember that this 'limit' was even more distant for Cagliostro's contemporaries. Even, therefore, if Cagliostro's disciples had not had within their hearts certain obstacles to the satisfaction of their desires, no higher reason could have urged him to perform before their very eyes a wide range of extraordinary alchemical transmutations even though he undoubtedly had the ability to do so.

NOTES

(1) Cf. Chapter VI of this book, *Cagliostro in Lyons*.

(2) At this time an Independent state under Prussian protection.

(3) Countess von der Recke, *Nachricht von des berüchtigten Cagliostro Aufenthalte in Mitau*. Berlin, 1787, p. 6.

(4) Cagliostro made a short stop in Königsberg. Arriving on the 25th February 1779 he checked in at the Schencken inn in Kehrwiedergasse. He was received, though not without some suspicion, in some of the better households, but Chancellor von Korff, who detested the Jesuits, thought Cagliostro might be one of their spies and warned everyone about him. Cagliostro, for his part, made no effort to counteract such accusations or to get the city on his side. He left soon afterwards, feeling that he would never be able to do any worthwhile work because of the ill-will of the locals. Cf. Borowski, *Cagliostro, einer der merkwürdigsten Abentheurer...* 1790, pp. 52-53. Von Korff later revised his opinion of Cagliostro and showed much kindness towards him in Mittau, cf. Von der Recke, op. cit., p. 6.

(5) He had travelled under the names of Count Fénix (or Phoenix) and Count Harat but introduced himself there as *Cagliostro*. 'It is the right of any traveller', he used to say, 'to remain anonymous'. Cf. *Mémoire pour le comte de Cagliostro contre le Procureur général*, p. 23, and Anon., *Lettre au peuple anglais*, p. 57.

(6) Cf. *Cagliostro démasqué à Varsovie*, 1786; *Ein paar Tröpflein aus dem Brunnen der Wahrheit,* Im Vorgebirge, 1781 (actually 1786); and *Le charlatan démasqué*, Paris, 1786. These lampoons were collected and reproduced, with additions, by the author of the *Vie de Joseph Balsamo*, Paris, 1791.

(7) Von der Recke, op. cit., pp. 26, 107 et seq. &148.

(8) Von der Recke. op. cit., pp. 155-156. Also De Luchet, *Essai sur la secte des Illuminés*, pp. 90, 102, 117.

(9) Von der Recke. op. cit., p. 50. Countess von der Recke quotes the *Anti-Saint-Nicaise* who expresses the same views on Stark.

(10) Anne-Charlotte von Medem, born 3rd February 1761 in Mesothen (present-day Mežotne), Courland, died 20th August 1821 in Loebrehan. She was the daughter of Count von Medem and Elise von der Recke, herself a talented poetess and an ascetic writer, who was his third wife. She married Pierre de Biren in 1779. She was extremely beautiful, had a keen intelligence, and was involved in several political intrigues, some of them after the death of her husband.

(11) Her older brother, Count von Medem, who shared the same mystical ideas as his sister, had died in Strasbourg in 1778. Countess von der Recke, persuaded that her brother's spirit would appear to her, spent night after night in cemeteries invoking it, cf. Von der Recke. op. cit., p. 5 and p. 167. 'You do not like Magic for itself', said Cagliostro to her one day when he was reading what was in her heart, 'you do not seek magical powers in order to develop and to acquire the ability to help millions of people without distinction, but simply because death has robbed you of someone to whom your heart was bound and whom you would like to recapture', cf. ibid., p. 52. And, elsewhere: 'If you're not willing to detach yourself from everything, if you remain exclusively and narrowly attached to a living being or even to a branch of knowledge then you will never be able to achieve complete development and freedom. In such a case you might reach the very highest level of any art or science, and I will help you to achieve that, but you must give up magic. I leave the choice to you', ibid, p. 103.

(12) When she first encountered Cagliostro she treated him as her equal, advising him, sometimes even reproving him, convinced that she could conceal some of her thoughts from him (op. cit., pp. 62-63). A person of integrity, but at odds with some features of Cagliostro's system, and shaken in some of her beliefs by some of the things that he said to her, her opinion of the miracle-worker was in constant evolution: one day she was convinced by him and very much his champion, while the next she would refuse even to listen to him (op. cit., pp. 135, 167). As she was effectively in control of his entourage the majority of the incidents in Cagliostro's stay in Courland were built around these hesitations and volte-face.

(13) This would be all the easier for him as a rationalist reaction against these excesses was already taking shape; even in the milieu of the Von Medem family such a reformer would find willing allies, such as the Aulic Councillor Schwander, who was Countess von der Recke's intellectual director, and the notary Hinz, a regular visitor to the household. Cf. op. cit., pp. 8, 9, 26, 28, 77.

(14) The Countesses von Medem and Von Howen had collaborated with the Hermeticists Muller of Mittau, Schmidt of Jena, and Freund of Strasbourg, op. cit., p. 3.

(15) 'We were more eager to communicate with spirits than to witness transmutations', cf. Von der Recke, op. cit., p. 10.

(16) This was as true of Countess von der Recke as of any of the others. Although she professed the strongest detachment from material things (op. cit., p. 11) she applied pressure on Cagliostro for several days to obtain for her, by Hermetic means, a certain amount of money without the knowledge of her family which she needed not for some charitable enterprise but to spend on herself. Cagliostro refused, initially pleading material difficulties, but finally saying to her: 'To be able to develop yourself so that Heaven entrusts to you even greater treasures – those that you desire so much – you must first learn how to resist the temptations offered by the riches of this world, just as Christ did', op. cit.

pp. 12-13. Cf. also p. 52. Even so, Countess von der Recke persisted, apparently not being aware of the self-contradiction.

(17) Schlosser understood this and, in his article on Cagliostro, supports our thesis that Cagliostro, wanting to free his disciples from the illusions in which he found them immersed, needed in the early stages to speak to them in a language they could understand, to go through certain magical questions with them, to descend to Hell with them in order, subsequently, to accompany them back to the surface once more. Cf. Borowski, op. cit., p. 149., Von der Recke, op. cit., p. 112.

(18) Von der Recke, op. cit. pp. 32 et seq.

(19T) The Marshal of the Nobility was the elected head of the aristocracy in administrative regions of the Russian Empire. The position was created by Catherine the Great in 1785.

(20) Initiated in Halle in 1741, op. cit., pp. 3 and 7.

(21) The magical experiment proceeded as follows: Cagliostro, after consecrating by means of some rituals the six-year-old son of Von Howen, told him to look at Cagliostro's hand. 'Without the child's knowledge Cagliostro asked my uncle what apparition he wished to see. My uncle said that, in order that his son might not be frightened, he wanted to be able to see the child's mother and sister who were then at home. Ten minutes later the child said that he could see his mother and sister. Cagliostro asked him: 'What is your sister doing?' and the child answered, 'She has her hand on her heart as if she's in pain'. Then the child said: 'Now she's kissing my brother who's just come home'. When these gentlemen had left their homes to attend the meeting my brother's cousin was not in town, and we were certainly not expecting him to arrive that day given that we believed him to be more than seven miles away. But at the moment the child had this vision he did in fact return home suddenly, quite unexpectedly and, what is more, my cousin had just previously had heart palpitations so severe that she had felt quite ill', Countess von der Recke, op. cit., pp. 28, 30-31.

(22) 29th March 1779. Cf. Von der Recke, op. cit., p. 33 and Borowski, op. cit., p. 57.

(23) Op. cit., pp. 63-65, and *Rituel de la Maçonnerie ∴ Égyptienne*, Mss. Papus, p. 58. We cannot help but quote here a passage about these experiments from Éliphas Lévi which shows that he didn't understand a thing about them: 'Cagliostro practised hydromancy, as he knew that water is simultaneously both an excellent conductor, a powerful reflector, and a very refractive medium for the astral light, as the mirages of the sea and mountains prove', Histoire de la Magie, 1892, p. 217. Such pompous phrases, devoid of all sense, are unfortunately quite common in the works of occultists in general, and those of Éliphas Lévi in particular.

(24) These subjects, who could be either boys or girls and who were called 'doves' or 'pupils', had to be very young and of the most perfect innocence. Cagliostro maintained that their ignorance of life and their naivety were necessary preconditions for the manifestation of a pure spirit. They wore a white robe to represent purity to those witnessing the manifestations, cf. *Rituel de la Maçonnerie ∴ Égyptienne*, Mss. Papus p. 31. The first 'dove' was the nephew of Count von Medem, a little boy of six, but without any education: he didn't even know the alphabet, cf. Von der Recke, op. cit., pp. 40, 66.

(25) Op. cit., p. 30.

(26) *Vie de Joseph Balsamo*, pp. 100, 122, 177. Cf. also *Ein paar Tröpflein*, p. 7, Von der Recke, op. cit., pp. 66, 70, 72. Cagliostro recommended the deepest meditation, complete immobility and the suppression of any distracting thoughts or stimuli. Sometimes incense was burned in the outer chamber, cf. *Rituel de la Maçonnerie ∴ Égyptienne*, opening of the workings for the degree of Master, Mss. Papus, p. 64.

(27) Op. cit., pp. 69-70. Cf. also *Vie de Joseph Balsamo*, pp. 122-179 and *Cagliostro démasqué à Varsovie*, 1786, p. 3.

(28) 'Cagliostro explained to us that the child did not always speak on his or her own behalf: a magical spirit (an 'inspiration', a 'mantic force' or a 'control' as we might say in more modern parlance) dictated the answers to the child, who would then often pass them on unconsciously, without actually seeing anything. The doves were sometimes completely unaware of what they had just said', cf. Von der Recke, op. cit., p. 67. This was why Cagliostro formally forbade people to question the doves after the experiments. Countess von der Recke, who did not really believe in psychic phenomena, saw in this

defence a skilful precaution on Cagliostro's part to ensure that his deception was not discovered. Now that we're better informed about such matters we find in Cagliostro's severe admonition only confirmation that he knew what he was talking about, as questioning the dove outside the framework of the séances would involve opening the door to error: one would be coaching the dove to become a cheat. This is something that has been known for a long time. 'But when the soul has been previously disturbed, or is moved in the interim, or the body intervenes, and confounds the divine harmony, then divinations become turbulent and false, and the enthusiasm is no longer true nor genuine' (Iamblichus, *On the Mysteries* III.vii, Thomas Taylor's translation). Nowadays we find the sort of explanation of these events such as was provided by Countess von der Recke, i.e. in terms of conjuring tricks, to be absurd on all points where we have personal experience of the facts, and yet we tend to accept this same form of interpretation in respect of all those phenomena which science has not yet investigated. Is this not absurd? Would not reason, in noting the errors of Countess von der Recke, require us to suspend judgement and at least admit the probability of interpretations of these surprising and as yet unexplained events that do not involve trickery?

(29) This occurred in Strasbourg and was reported by a contemporary. Cf. Figuier, *Histoire du merveilleux*, Paris, Hachette, 1861, vol. II, p. 16.
(30) Figuier, ibid, p. 16.
(31) Cf. Chapter IX of this book, '*Cagliostro in Rome*'.
(32) *Vie de Joseph Balsamo*, p. 136.
(33) *Cagliostro démasqué à Varsovie*, 1786, p. 4, where, needless to say, the author sees it as a simple conjuring trick.
(34) *Ein paar Tröpflein*, p. 6.
(35) Von der Recke. op. cit., p. 79, p. 33. Notice V, and p. 98.
(36) Von der Recke. op. cit., p. 88 and *Vie de Joseph Balsamo*, p. 134. During the experiment performed with the dove 'Henry' in the presence of Prince Joseph and the Prince de Lamballe on behalf of the Duc d'Orléans (see Chapter IV of this book) the vision occurred in a mirror that was 'approximately a foot square' and not in a carafe. It is was in a mirror also that Cagliostro showed the Duc de Richelieu, who had come to see him in disguise, who he was and what he would become.
(37) *Vie de Joseph Balsamo*, p. 148. No doubt hydromancy will be proposed as a so-called physical explanation of this, just as Éliphas Lévi would (cf. Note 23 above)!
(38) *Vie de Joseph Balsamo*, pp. 147-148.
(39) *Vie de Joseph Balsamo*, pp. 134-135.
(40) In Warsaw one of his doves was a 16-year-old girl, cf. *Cagliostro démasqué à Varsovie*, 1786, p. 6. One of his doves in Paris, who was ten years old when the Duc d'Orléans brought him to see Cagliostro, was still living in 1843. He was a public health inspector called Monsieur Henry (see Note 36 above) and lived at 24 Marché des Innocents. Cf. *Initiation*, March 1906, *Travaux de Cagliostro*, p. 257.
(41) *Vie de Joseph Balsamo*, p. 138. Iamblichus says *(On the Mysteries,* III.xii & xxiv) 'that the prophetic power of the Gods...is wholly everywhere present with the natures which are capable of receiving it...It likewise externally illuminates and fills all things, pervades through all the elements, comprehends earth and air, fire and water, and leaves nothing destitute of itself, neither animals nor any of the productions of nature, but imparts from itself a certain portion of foreknowledge, to some things in a greater, and to others in a less, degree...those that are more simple and young are more adapted to divination'.
(42) A sceptical magistrate secretly sent his son to his house to find out what his wife was doing at that moment. When the boy had left, the father addressed this question to the Grand Copht. The carafe did not provide any information but a voice *that everyone heard* announced that the lady was playing cards with two lady neighbours. This mysterious voice, produced by no visible body, inspired terror in a part of the assembly, and when the magistrate's son arrived to confirm the complete accuracy of the oracle several ladies in the assembly felt obliged to withdraw. Countess von der Recke testifies that, in Courland, the audience could often hear the kisses that the angels exchanged with the doves as a

sign of peace and union with them at the beginning and end of meetings. These were as clearly audible as those given by the dove, op. cit. pp. 85 & 108.

(43) Figuier, *Histoire du merveilleux*, Paris 1861, vol. IV, p. 28. Jean-Pierre-Louis de Luchet, the author of the *Mémoires authentiques*, used these anecdotes and similar ones, as well as certain indiscretions that leaked out about these theurgic evocations, to fabricate the humorous tale of the *Dîner des Treize*. It is sad that the unavoidably satirical character of literary fantasies of this kind meant that the memory of these marvellous events was distorted and held up to ridicule, but this in no way detracts from the validity of the documents themselves.

(44) *Mémoires de Robertson*.

(45) Péricaud, *Cagliostro à Lyons*, p. 2.

(46) *Vie de Joseph Balsamo*, pp. 147, 148, 153. Countess von der Recke, op. cit., p. 89.

(47) *Vie de Joseph Balsamo*, pp. 138, 151, 179.

(48) *Vie de Joseph Balsamo*, p. 178.

(49) Saint Martin confirmed this effective transmission of powers in the Egyptian Lodge of Lyons. *Correspondence de Saint Martin et Kirchberger*, 73rd letter, p. 205. The letter from Count Brice de Beauregard which we quote later on is further proof. *Vie de Joseph Balsamo*, pp. 134, 198 et seq. cites authentic evidence of this.

(50) In response to a question from the Freemason Salzmann, Cagliostro replied that 'in Egypt there are lodges where they work with spirits, and others where only human beings are present'. Letter from Salzmann to Willermoz of 31st December 1780, *Collection of Bréghot du Lut*.

(51) One day Cagliostro described with perfect accuracy the symptoms from which the (then absent) Countess von der Recke was suffering, the work she was doing, and even the location where one would find her on entering her room (op. cit., p. 71). On another occasion he revealed to her the thoughts that were actually in her mind while she was speaking to him about a completely unrelated matter (ibid. p. 78). One evening he announced that a certain gentleman would fall sick the following night, that he would suffer from certain illnesses and that he would send for a certain doctor, all of which proved absolutely correct (ibid, p. 87). In the presence of Count von Medem he sketched out the plan of a forest at Wilzen where he had never been, but which the Count himself knew well, indicating to him paths and even the shapes of certain trees (ibid. p. 58.)

(52) D'Oberkirch, *Mémoires*, vol. I, chapter VII.

(53T) A major tax collector in the tax-farming hierarchy of the Ancien Régime.

(54) An account of this will be found below.

(55) Von der Recke, op. cit., pp. 117, 120, 131.

(56) In her commentary Countess von der Recke is guilty of all sorts of misinterpretations: the assumption that the child was simply acting out a part will simply not do, as we have shown. Cagliostro was happy to use as a dove anyone that was presented to him without further preparations. Elsewhere, the Countess claims that Cagliostro wrote on the talismanic parchment the answers that the dove was to give, forgetting that she herself acknowledged (op. cit. p. 80) that the child could not read and that the questions were submitted by those present after the dove had been locked in the tabernacle. In any case, this form of clairvoyance, the development of a 'magic eye', as Gichtel terms it (*Theosophia practica*, IV, 10, 18, 28) which has been known from time immemorial (*Acts of the Apostles*, XXI, 9; XVI, 16; St. Matthew, VI) has hardly ever been denied except in the early hours of the Positivist crisis which prevailed until the mid-19th century. In our times, when science is less presumptuous due to being rather better informed, cases of telepathy, psychometry and clairvoyance are everyday facts of which no one would any longer dispute the existence. Trying to explain the unknown in terms of trickery strikes us as immature, and Countess von der Recke's book, which is composed entirely of such nonsense, would have been as unimportant as the lampoons of Count Moszyński or Monsieur Motus if, by great good fortune, it had not also included the original text of her journal.

(57) Cagliostro was in Bordeaux in 1783 when Père Hervier was propagating by both word and deed the science of hypnotism, and was even preaching the new doctrines in a cathedral packed with

worshippers. Hervier, by then a hypnotist of repute, decided to engage in a power-struggle with Cagliostro in an attempt to show that the miracle-worker's actions were based solely on hypnotism and could be explained entirely in terms of the science that he himself practised. On this occasion however he was publicly humiliated and was justly censured for his impertinence by all his colleagues. Cf. Figuier, *Histoire du merveilleux*, vol. IV, p. 26.

(58T) Louis-Alphonse Cahagnet (1805-1885) was a journeyman-cabinetmaker who published a remarkable three-volume work on spiritualism. The first volume was *Magnétisme: Arcanes de la vie future dévoilé* (translated into English as *The Celestial Telegraph* and published in 1848). The first volume summarised his experiments with eight trance-mediums as well as spirit communications from 36 entities who claimed to have died over a period dating back some two hundred years. In his book 'Modern Spiritualism' (1902) the spiritualist historian Frank Podmore observes: 'In the whole literature of Spiritualism I know of no records of the kind which reach a higher evidential standard, nor any in which the writer's good faith and intelligence are alike so conspicuous'.

(59) 2nd Year, 1850, No. 8, p. 204.

(60) To be found in the same journal, same year, p. 342.

(61) This was the actual term (*vision béatifique*) that Cagliostro himself commonly used, and which he repeated before his judges in Rome. See *Vie de Joseph Balsamo*, pp. 190-191.

(62) Figuier. *Histoire du Merveilleux*, Paris, 1861, vol. IV, p. 119.

(63T) The neurologist Dr. Joseph Grasset proposed in his *Demi-fous et Demi-responsables* (English translation *The Semi-Insane and the Semi-Responsible*, 1907, freely available on the Internet) a polygonal neurological model, the apex of which represented the seat of mentality. If the neurones were diseased at that location, he argued, then insanity and irresponsibility would ensue.

(64) *Rituel de la Maçonnerie ∴ Égyptienne*, Mss. Papus, p. 41. Cf. also *Vie de Joseph Balsamo*, p. 186. This a phrase that Gichtel would certainly have understood, but Lavater was scandalised by it: 'Pay close attention, my dear friend, regarding the Seven Spirits of God. If the very least of the very least of the servants of the very least of the angels had spoken to me, then what a man I would be! The pretentiousness expressed here is like someone wanting to carry the Sun around in his pocket like a watch', Letter to Sarrasin. Langmesser, *J. Sarrasin*, Zurich, 1899, p. 41.

(65) *Rituel de la Maçonnerie ∴ Égyptienne*, Degree of Master. Mss. Papus, p. 48.

(66) *Rituel de la Maçonnerie ∴ Égyptienne*, Mss. Papus, p. 75. Countess von der Recke once said, 'When Cagliostro was with us he linked religion to magic and Freemasonry in a very clear-cut manner', op. cit., p. 14. Cf. and ibid., pp. 31, 35, 119.

(67) *Vie de Joseph Balsamo*, p. 46, 'He himself acknowledged it', says the author.

(68) This is what he always stated and taught: cf. *Mémoire pour le comte de Cagliostro contre le Procureur général*, 1786, p. 6; *Rituel de la Maçonnerie ∴ Égyptienne*, Catechism of the degree of Master. Mss. Papus, p. 84.; *Mémoire contre Chesnon*, 1786, p. 37.

(69) 'He had turned all the heads in Courland', Von Heyking, *Le comte Cagliostro parmi les Russes*, in *Initiation*, August 1898, p. 129.

(70) Von der Recke. op. cit., pp. 7-8, 25, 105 and Note V, p. 35.

(71) Von der Recke. op. cit., p. 92.

(72) Von der Recke. op. cit., p. 105. On 10th April 1779 the lodge received from Cagliostro the last initiatory degree that he was to give them, ibid., p. 33. Note V.

(73) Von der Recke. op. cit., pp. 105-112.

(74) *Lettre au peuple anglais*, p. 65. This was written in 1787 in response to the fuss that Morande was making about an article hostile to Cagliostro which Countess von der Recke had published in the *Berliner Monatsschrift* (May 1786, pp. 395, et seq.). But Cagliostro appealed to her loyalty in vain: she had already gone back on all her old promises.

(75) Von der Recke, op. cit., p. 146.

(76) Von der Recke, op. cit., pp. 177, 180. They had held them up to ridicule even in Mittau and they had to endure some personal attacks even within their own circles, op. cit., p. 33, Note IV.

(77) Something he had himself raised hopes of, cf. Von der Recke. op. cit., p. 142.

(78) Von der Recke. op. cit., p. 10.
(79T) Adam Poniński (1732 or 1733-1798) was a Polish nobleman, one of the leaders of the Radom Confederation (1767), Grand Treasurer of the Crown (from 1775) and a member of the Permanent Council. Widely regarded as a traitor serving Russian interests, he was stripped of all titles and exiled in 1790 but rehabilitated soon afterwards.
(80) Letter from Salzmann to Willermoz of 22nd November 1780. *Collection Bréghot du Lut.*
(81) 'To seek the Why of the Why' in the terminology of Cagliostro, who wanted to save her from the danger of following this false road, cf. Von der Recke, op. cit., p. 45.
(82) But Cagliostro had forewarned them, see above. Cf. Von der Recke. op. cit., p. 102.
(83) Von der Recke. op. cit., p. 10.
(84) The *Mémoires authentiques*, amongst others. Countess von der Recke recognised errors in these documents relating to subjects with which she was familiar, but was willing to accept calumnies on topics she knew nothing about, cf. Von der Recke, op. cit., p. 20.
(85) 'He has never made any promises to us that, at least to outward appearances, he has not kept', Von der Recke, op. cit., p. 10.
(86) Von der Recke. op. cit., pp. 9, 156. At that time Countess von der Recke was surrounded by German rationalists and French *Philosophes* infused with the new spirit who were sworn enemies of any form of religion, and even of any form of metaphysics. Her book was published by Nicolai who also wrote the Preface.
(87) Von der Recke. op. cit., pp. 46, 47, 48.
(88) Von der Recke. op. cit. p. 106.
(89) Von der Recke. op. cit., p. 111.
(90) Cagliostro left for St. Petersburg at the end of May 1779. On 13th May he was still in Mittau. Von der Recke, op. cit., p. 146. Cf. ibid, p. 25.
(91) Dr. Friedrichs, a professor with the Cadet Corps, in his very interesting book, *La Franc-Maçonnerie en Russie et en Pologne*, Paris, Dorbon-aîné, 1908, p. 32. [The Cadet Corps was a military academy with admission by examination, rather like Sandhurst or West Point, which prepared boys for careers as commissioned officers. It was founded in 1731 by Empress Anna. The course lasted seven years. All instructors had a military rank, and taught a full programme of military preparation. In 1766 Catherine the Great's educational reforms broadened the curriculum to include the sciences, philosophy, ethics, history, and international law.]
(92) In 1763, Catherine declared herself 'Protectress' of the Order.
(93) Henri-Charles, Baron von Heyking, born in Courland in 1751, died in 1809, studied in Germany and entered the service of Prussia. Returned to Russia and in 1779 was a Major of Cuirassiers in the Imperial Guard. Later, under Alexander I, he was disgraced and had to retire to Mittau.
(94) Von Heyking, *Mémoires*, fragment quoted in *Initiation*, August 1898, p. 129.
(95) Cf: *Les enseignements secrets de Martinès de Pasqually*, Paris, 1900, preface, pp. CXX et seq.
(96) Von Heyking, loc. cit., p. 131.
(97) Von Heyking, loc. cit., p. 131. The 'healthy' chemical notions of the time!
(98) What he actually said was that it was 'child's play', but we should remember that the conversation would have been in Italian and that it was translated and reported by someone from Courland, cf. Von Heyking, loc. cit., pp. 13l, 132.
(99) This is scarcely credible given everything that we know about Cagliostro's dazzling jewellery.
(100) What he actually said was 'Che ho soggiocato e sminuzzato'. Von Heyking is known to have written this conversation down immediately after returning from Cagliostro's house, loc. cit., p. 132.
(101) Through his stupidity Von Heyking was simply seeking to justify Cagliostro's judgement that he was just an ignorant child.
(102) This was the same Baron von Heyking who deliberately stoked up animosity against Cagliostro at Court. One person he got his poison into was Count von Görtz, envoy of the King of Prussia. Von Görtz was said to be 'so haughty that he refused to speak to anybody'. *Mémoires de la margrave d'Anspach*, Paris, Bertrand, 1826, Volume I, p. 232.

Chapter IV

(103) Marc-Daniel Bourrée, created Chevalier de Corbéron in 1775 and Baron in 1781, born in Paris on 15th July 1748, played a major role in the difficult dispute with Turkey in 1779 regarding tensions in the Crimea. Highly regarded as a diplomat he was also feared for his caustic wit and intractable character. He first became a Freemason in Paris, and was a 7th (i.e. Final) degree initiate of the Rite of Melissino. He had a sharp mind, keen curiosity and was loyal and sensitive, but he was also a victim of all the worldly passions. He was fond of Cagliostro and openly protected him in Russia, remaining very close to him thereafter. Thanks to his beliefs and loyalty to Cagliostro the Empress always referred to him as a 'dedicated visionary'. Cagliostro's influence changed him utterly by turning his thoughts towards higher things. His biographer, L. H. Labande, noted this transformation without understanding its cause. He quotes a letter from de Corbéron on this subject in which the effects of this initiatory transformation are revealed: 'Baron de Corbéron accepted his disgrace (in 1784) with a philosophical attitude that he would certainly not have displayed in his ebullient youth. 'During my time of feeble service', he wrote, 'if I brought zeal, honesty and disinterest to my work then a love of glory disguised within me a feeling of pride that I mistook for nobility of soul. Far from fulfilling the duties I had been given with the sole aim of doing good I must reproach myself for having had my reputation as my sole concern, and to have become even more vain as a result of my successes while neglecting to abase myself before the Lord, Who is the sole source of our qualities and virtues. This terrifying but always fair-minded judge, this severe but so very good father – and, indeed, a thousand times more than merely good – punished me, but very gently. He punished me in my pride, in my love of myself... O my Father, bless Him for me and with me', *Journal de Corbéron*, preface, p. lxiii. In 1781 Baron de Corbéron got married in Strasbourg. Arrested in Brumaire of Year III, he was very lucky to escape the guillotine and died in Paris on 31st December 1810. Cf: L.H. Labande, *De Corbéron*, Plon, 1901.

(104) Letter from Salzmann of 22nd November 1780, *Collection of Bréghot du Lut*. Alexander Potemkin, born in Smolensk in 1736, General-in-Chief, Prime Minister and official favourite of the Empress since 1774 conquered the Crimea and founded Sevastopol. He died in 1791.

(105) Bode, in his anonymous lampoon, assures us that in St. Petersburg Cagliostro was primarily concerned with alchemy, collaborating especially with 'General G.' (i.e. Golitsyn) who worked with *aqua regia* and with the Water of the Philosophers, and with Prince Potemkin. De Corbéron told Bode in 1781 that he was convinced of Cagliostro's powers and was quite happy to say so (which is tantamount to saying that he had firm evidence of it) but this did not prevent him from making fun of it, without further discussion, in his lampoon, cf. *Ein paar Tröpflein*, p. 10.

(106) Cf. *Liber memorialis*, French translation, p. 78.

(107) *Mémoires authentiques*, new edition, Paris, 1786, p. 12. 'There's no shortage of charlatans prepared to work for nothing!', says the anonymous author of the lampoon *Ein paar Tröpflein*, p. 8. At least this piece of mischief acknowledges that even Cagliostro's bitterest enemies accepted that he always acted in an entirely disinterested manner. Meiners said the same thing about his healing activities: 'Healing people doesn't prove anything. All charlatans heal their patients', *Briefe über Schweiz*, III, p. 424.

(108) *Ein paar Tröpflein*, p. 12.

(109) *Journal de Corbéron* for 2nd July 1781, Volume II, p. 396. 'He doesn't cure everyone', De Corbéron says elsewhere, 'but he does cure most'. MS 3059, Avignon Library, p. 146.

(110) It was Cagliostro himself who told us the story. The reader would be well advised to ignore the pastiche of Gospel diction in which the author of the *Liber memorialis* makes Cagliostro speak and to concentrate exclusively on the medical details.

(111) *Liber memorialis*, French translation, under the title *L'Évangile de Cagliostro*, by Dr. Marc Haven, Paris, 1910, pp. 67 et seq.

(112) Monsieur d'Alméras, who claims the opposite was the case but does not offer any evidence, is content to reproduce the sarcastic remarks of a few lampoonists while entirely ignoring the positive and credible accounts which we have reported above, cf. D'Alméras, *Cagliostro*, p. 163.

(113T) Sometimes spelt Roggerson [which is Marc Haven's preferred spelling], but certainly not

Rugenson 'as certain badly informed authors have called him' (*Vie de Joseph Balsamo*, p. 48), cf. *Journal de Corbéron*, II, p. 372.

(114) Cagliostro himself told this story to some friends and included it in the *Liber memorialis*, French translation, p. 77. The *Gazette de Santé* published the same story in summary form in 1786, cf. Figuier. *Histoire du merveilleux*, 1861, vol. IV, p. 10.

(115) Cagliostro's behaviour has been criticised as unchivalrous and uncalled-for. On the contrary I find a certain nobility in it. The 'medical duel' is the only one that would make sense in the circumstances. Dr. Jacquet, a writer of talent as well as a genuine scholar, in his inconclusive discussions with Professor Hallopeau about the transmissibility of alopecia, recently offered him (*Quinzaine thérapeutique*, 1909, p. 152) a choice between: 1. a contrasting experiment in which he would treat the disease in his own way and Professor Hallopeau in his; and 2. a personal experiment in which he offered to be inoculated with the so-called contagious disease by his opponent, predicting that he would not contract it. All this was done with an irony that might well have been less dramatic than that displayed by Cagliostro but which seems to reflect the same spirit of scientific sincerity that inspired Cagliostro to provoke Rogerson. There are similar examples in medical history and these have not been found to be in any way ridiculous.

(116) Russian Freemasonry collapsed into confusion and enmity as the number of Rites increased: 'Why should the strong-willed Empress Catherine care any longer for something that had become a society divided against itself, drifting from one system to another, composed of worthless people, a 'social club for coachmen and servants' to use the rather blunt expression of Bergmann, the Attorney-General of Riga and commentator on Masonic affairs? Catherine turned her back on them and even started ridiculing her former allies, writing three anti-Masonic comedies, *L'Enchanteur sibérien, Le Trompeur* and *L'Aveugle*, with Cagliostro as the anti-hero', Friedrichs, *La Franc-Maçonnerie en Russie*, Bern, 1908, p. 42. Nicolai published German translations of these plays in Berlin in 1788 under the title *Lustspiele wider Schwärmerey... von J. K. m. d. K. v. R.*

(117) *Cagliostro démasqué à Varsovie* repeated this story much later on, but repeats the allegation only in the form of a hypothesis (p. 62). Madame de la Motte and Morande also repeated it and the calumny took shape. We find it here and there presented as definite fact.

(118) Theodore Mundt wrote a novel based on these allegations called *Cagliostro à Saint-Pétersbourg*, Leipzig, 1858. As a work of pure imagination it is technically beyond reproach but, like all such novels, it has helped to give many people the wrong idea about Cagliostro.

(119) It was Rogerson who orchestrated these intrigues. 'The jealousy of the Court doctor obliged him to leave Russia', cf. *Ein paar Tröpflein*, p. 12 (note 3, following page) and *Ephemeriden der Freymaurerey in Deutschland*, Anno 5785, p. 112.

(120) Mirabeau, *Lettres sur MM. Cagliostro et Lavater*, Berlin, 1786, p. 9. 'This is an old calumny taken from the memoirs of Madame de la Motte which has already been rebutted by Monsieur de Corbéron' wrote Cagliostro in his *Lettre au peuple anglais*, 1787, p. 64.

(121) Heyking, *loc. cit.*, p. 131.

(122) De Normandez would have had a notice inserted in the *Gazette de Saint-Pétersbourg* stating that there was no Spanish colonel called Cagliostro. We should note that De Görtz, the representative of the King of Prussia; Harris, the English Ambassador Plenipotentiary; and de Normandez were all political adversaries of De Corbéron, who was Cagliostro's friend and protector. See the *Journal de Corbéron, passim*.

(123) The King of Sweden, Gustav III, sent Colonel Toll to Cagliostro to question him and invite him to visit the King. The historian Geffroy describes the exquisitely polite but also moving character of Cagliostro's meeting with the King of Sweden's emissary, *Gustave III et la Cour de France*, Paris, 1887, Volume II, p. 258. See also the *Journal de Corbéron*, volume II, p. 396: The Prince of Prussia saw Cagliostro in St. Petersburg. He paid homage to his great learning'. The author of the pamphlet entitled *Ein paar Tröpflein...* which reports at great length on Cagliostro's time in St. Petersburg doesn't tell us why Cagliostro had to leave, and even says that it was *of his own free will* 'that he had decided that it would be a good idea to take his torch of enlightenment elsewhere', p. 12. Needless to

say, if there had been the least breath of scandal then the author would have wasted no time in telling us about it.

(124) The Empress, on his departure, gave him a significant sum of money as a present, cf. *Le Charlatan démasqué*, Frankfurt, 1780, p. 62.

(125) *Lettre au peuple anglais*, 1787, p. 64.

(126) Salzmann, Letter to Willermoz of 22nd November 1780, Archives of Monsieur Bréghot du Lut. Cf. also *Ein paar Tröpflein*, p. 12.

(127) Established in 1745. Poniński was also one of the founders of the Grand Orient Lodge of Warsaw in 1780.

(128) Poland, a country where Cabalist Rabbis were still numerous as late as the second half of the 19th century, was a major centre of occult sciences in the 18th century. Jean de Thoux de Salverte, founder around 1750 of the Warsaw lodge *Au bon pasteur* ('The Good Shepherd') spent five years studying the Cabala and alchemy for the benefit of his lodge, cf. Friedrichs, *La Maçonnerie en Russie*, Bern, p. 55, and *L'occultisme en Pologne*, in: *Initiation*, 1904, an article by Monsieur Erny.

(129) 'For anyone who possesses the secrets of alchemy', Cagliostro once said to Von Heyking, 'chemistry is really pretty much nonsense and alchemy is a thing of naught for anyone who can command the spirits'. Cagliostro was a Master of Fire because he understood the creatures of fire, just as he was a Master of disease because of his knowledge of human beings. He didn't have to touch the patient or even examine them – all he had to do was to issue a command.

(130) If the memoirs of the Marquise de Créquy are to be trusted this was based on potable gold, vol. III, p. 272. Cagliostro's universal medicine came in various forms: as yellow drops, as the 'Wine of Egypt', as 'Jupiter's Beard', as 'Egyptian balm' or 'Egyptian pills', but they all included the revitalising principle which was their active ingredient, cf. Von der Recke, *Nachricht von des berüchtigten…*, p. 56; *Gazette d'Utrecht*, 2nd August 1787; Borowski, *Cagliostro, einer der merkwürdigsten Abentheurer…*, Königsberg, 1790, p. 138; and *Ma correspondance*, no. 73, 1785, 5th September.

(131) 'He spoke to me about a type of stone… which took only five days to make and which, if you buffed it in the darkness with a little saliva would have such a glow that you could actually light a candle with it, and then subsequently extinguish it by wiping it with a handkerchief', Letter from Salzmann to Willermoz of 13th December 1780. *Collection of Bréghot du Lut*.

(132) Madam d'Oberkirch tells an interesting story on this subject. One day Cardinal de Rohan showed her a large solitaire which he wore on his little finger. On it were engraved the coat of arms of the House of Rohan. He asked her what she thought of it. 'Well it's certainly a beautiful stone, Monseigneur. In fact I've admired it for some time.' 'Well *he* made it, do you understand?' replied the Cardinal. 'He created it out of absolutely nothing. I saw it. I was there, with my eyes fixed on the crucible, and I witnessed the whole operation. Is this really what science can do? What do you think, Madame? Don't tell me that he tricked me or took advantage of me, because the jeweller and the engraver have estimated the value of this brilliant at 25,000 *livres*. You'll have to agree with me that it's a pretty strange swindler who makes gifts like that to people.' Madame d'Oberkirch was forced to admit that she was amazed by the whole business. 'And that's not all', continued the Cardinal. 'He makes gold as well. He created some in front of me, about five or six thousand *livres* of it, up there, in the palace-loft' (quoted in D'Oberkirch, *Mémoires*, vol. I, chapter VII. Cf. also Von der Recke, *Nachricht von des berüchtigten*, p. 11). The adamantine work was attempted using both hot and cold procedures and also by the wet way. Before Moissan's work on the electric furnace Albert Poisson and one of his friends spent much time researching this. Papus (Dr. Gérard Encausse) describes a method whereby charcoal is dissolved in wood vinegar (pyroligneous acid) at a high temperature under pressure. It is in the carbon solution thus obtained that diamonds can be augmented. Was this the method Cagliostro used? Personally we don't think so. The Cardinal also saw him making a diamond in the crucible, but this was a special case. Cagliostro did provide a clue to the process he used: he put the diamonds that were entrusted to him for augmentation *into some earth* (*Vie de Joseph Balsamo*, p. 36). That is more in line with his usual technique.

(133) Von der Recke, *Nachricht*, pp. 10, 96; *Ma correspondance…*, 1786, p. 3, 22, 84.

(134) And, it has to be said, for very selfish and not very honourable reasons. Figuier tells us that initially he asked Cagliostro to provide him with a familiar spirit to serve him, and was profoundly irritated when Cagliostro was unable to oblige. Poniński then asked him for help in seducing a woman who was very much on his mind at that time, the beautiful Képinska. Once again, Cagliostro was content to show Poniński her image in a mirror, but this was not enough for the Prince. Figuier, *Histoire du merveilleux*, vol. IV, p. 108.

(135) *Ein paar Tröpflein*, p. 12. The Prince delegated the amateur chemist Count Moszyński to help him in his work. We shall have more to say about him in due course.

(136) The hate-filled author of *Cagliostro démasqué à Varsovie* is forced to acknowledge this sincerity of manner and independence of character, which tally so badly with the picture that he tries to present of a master of cunning intrigue. He is unable to explain the contradiction: 'The majority of impostors', he says, 'are flexible in their manner and seek to attract friends, but Cagliostro seemed to assume a studied arrogance and went around making an enemy of everyone he met. Other charlatans go to great lengths to maintain the connections they've established with the people they take advantage of to carry out their trickeries, but Cagliostro fell out with them over matters of absolutely no importance', *Cagliostro démasqué à Varsovie*, pp. 50, 51.

(137) *Cagliostro démasqué à Varsovie*, p. 50.

(138) Stanislaw August Poniatowski, the last King of Poland, a member of the Masonic lodge known as *Charles of the Three Helmets*, was a fated individual: on the day of his birth a mysterious astrologer predicted his rise to power and also his misfortunes (cf. *Initiation*, 1904, article by Monsieur Erny, *L'occultisme en Pologne*). Cagliostro knew him before his various misfortunes.

(139) *Lettres sur la Suisse adressées à Madame M*** par un voyageur français* (De Laborde). Geneva, 1783, volume I, p. 13. A letter from 1781.

(140) See the description of this event earlier in this chapter.

(141) 'He dictated to us a whole load of 'secrets' which were either completely false or already known to chemistry', *Cagliostro démasqué à Varsovie*, p. 7. What he means is that Cagliostro either taught truths that Moszyński already knew and he scorned them or that he taught him things that were unknown to him and he rejected them. The author criticises, in the same admirable manner, Cagliostro's teachings on medicine.

(142) *Cagliostro démasqué à Varsovie*, pp. 8 et seq. Cf. also *Ein paar Tröpflein*, p. 13: 'Just conjuring tricks', says the author.

(143) *Ein paar Tröpflein*, p. 13.

(144) A publication to which Morande was undoubtedly no stranger: indeed the editor mentions the *Lettre de Mirabeau* and the *Réponse de Madame de la Motte* and also alludes to the allegations that Morande made against Joseph Balsamo in the *Courrier de l'Europe*.

(145) Countess von der Recke identified this anonymous writer, and Borowski confirmed it. Cf. *Cagliostro, einer der merkwürdigsten Abentheurer…*, 1790, p. 142, and Düntzer, *Neue Goethestudien*, Nuremberg, 1851, p. 138.

(146) Cf. the Preface to this book.

(147) Examples: 1. the gold added to mercury, 2. the swapping of crucibles.

(148) Cf. Note 133 above.

(149) He skirts round all these subjects. See *Cagliostro démasqué à Varsovie*, p. 6. The lamp entrusted to his care was found extinguished on 24th June, ibid. p. 36. A myrtle-leaf was found swimming in the contents of the Hermetic Egg which had been entrusted to the Count that same day and had been removed by a third party, ibid. p. 38. A most peculiarly managed operation! Moszyński also swapped a flask, an action that led to a scene between him and Cagliostro, ibid., p. 36, and so on. Moszyński's attitude – sometimes obsequious, sometimes hostile – was always insincere. He ridiculed the reverence that Cagliostro demanded of his assistants, 'who find these childish antics simply unbearable', ibid. pp. 24, 29, 31.

(150) *Passages* is the term used by the French Hermeticists to describe the various transformations of colour and state which matter undergoes while in evolution within the Alchemical Egg.

(151) Moszyński, despite his scientific pretensions, had obviously not read the old Hermetic writers nor the *Journal de Philalèthe* where the Great Work is described as taking at least a year.

(152) *Cagliostro démasqué à Varsovie*, p. 20. So are to assume that it was no longer carmine?

(153) Cf. Chapter III of this book devoted to Cagliostro's first visit to London.

(154) 'Cagliostro had coarse manners', *Ein paar Tröpflein*, p. 6. Cf. also *Cagliostro démasqué à Varsovie*, p. 49.

(155) 27th June 1780. *Cagliostro démasqué à Varsovie*, p. 16. One day Cagliostro confided to Countess von der Recke that he sometimes deliberately sowed seeds of doubt about his work in the minds of spiritually blind individuals who could only be harmed by being brought into the light, and who would inevitably only plunge deeper into error. 'In Warsaw he did not *want* to go ahead with brilliant transmutations, and in fact he deliberately arranged things so that appearances were against him, because he felt that the unworthy disciples of his did not deserve anything more in the way of a reward and because he didn't *want* them to discern anything of his true grandeur', cf. Von der Recke, *Nachricht*, p. 128. He who brought us the light could cope with contradiction and with open struggle as long as it was conducted in a spirit of loyalty, but he could not bear to be surrounded by falseness and betrayal. He was happy to perform his acts of theurgy before ignoramuses, the downhearted, even the rebellious, provided that they were sincere, but he would not profane the blessings of heaven by wasting them on people who mocked the word of God, lived in ivory towers of superiority, and questioned the envoy of God only in an attempt to set traps for him.

(156) This fact alone would be sufficient to neutralise all the silly stories that were made up, a long time afterwards, on his alleged disgrace. If he had been 'uncovered', 'seen through', 'thrown out in shame' by the people of Warsaw as some members of the Fourth Estate have been happy to proclaim, then why was he treated so well by one of the noblest ladies from this same milieu? As soon as we dispassionately and thoroughly examine any of the allegations made against Cagliostro we see that they have no substance whatsoever: we feel sorry for him, and we respect him even more – that is the sole impression that remains.

(157) The Luminous Stone and the augmentation of gemstones fell into this category. Late 19th and very early 20th century experiments revealed these intermediate states of matter, these transitional forms where the processes of material evolution become apprehensible and which make it possible to understand some of their characteristics (e.g. the meta-elements of William Crookes, the transformation of helium and radioactivity.)

(158) A contemporary biography of Cagliostro contains the following sentence, which seems to indicate that Cagliostro did indeed perform demonstrations of this kind: 'I have heard people of good faith maintain, and this long before the famous passage during the Diamond Necklace affair when the Queen appeared to Madame de la Motte (actually, to Mademoiselle de la Tour), that Cagliostro had demonstrated palingenesis to them…' Unfortunately we have not been able to find any further details of this anonymous document, which consists of two pages in quarto, published around 1800.

CHAPTER V

—

'THE QUACK'

CAGLIOSTRO IN STRASBOURG

No sooner had Cagliostro arrived in Strasbourg [1] than he began to devote himself almost exclusively to medicine, attending to all those who came to see him irrespective of social class or financial status. It's been alleged that initially he concerned himself solely with the common people, using their cures as a means of winning the confidence of the wealthy and the aristocratic and so building up his practice amongst them. Certainly his early patients were from the poorer classes, but isn't that perfectly natural? Don't those to whom Fate has dealt a weak hand tend to suffer more, aren't they less embarrassed about seeking help than the fortunate of this world, and aren't they both more worthy of our attention and also more eager to grasp the hand [2] that reaches out to them? Those who found themselves in Cagliostro's presence and could see that he was anxious to help them consulted him in person, but those who were confined to their beds by illness were equally happy to welcome him into their homes. De Gleichen has testified to his dedication in caring for them [3] and the Swiss Bürkli tells us that he often went without leisure – never going to the theatre for example – for fear that some unfortunate person might try to visit him in his absence and have to go away disappointed [4]. The hopeless and the poor found in him a source of material help and, what is even more important, that form of sympathy that is so invaluable to those who are in despair [5]. He went everywhere that suffering demanded it. He did not care whether the illness was minor or severe, or whether the patient was rich or poor, nor did he ever change his appearance or manner to suit the patient [6].

We have little documentary evidence about this first period of his medical career and the cures that he effected. De Gleichen does however report a case in which Cagliostro was summoned to attend to a woman in labour: the obstetricians had given up all hopes of saving her and could not even promise to be able to save the child. Cagliostro announced that he would ensure that she gave birth without any problems, and he was as good as his word [7]. In another case, Spach had questioned an old man from Strasbourg who claimed to have been cured of a serious chest complaint that had afflicted him at twenty years of age, and which would probably have killed him without the intervention of Cagliostro [8].

He must have handled thousands of cases, but we know little about them. His carriage would take him to town and out into the suburbs from early morning – 6 o'clock in winter, 5 o'clock in summer – to 9 or 10 o'clock at night [9]. 'He was surrounded by people with all sorts of disabilities, poor devils of every kind, the gouty, the deaf... and he cured them all. He always received them kindly and then gave them essential oils, elixirs, and sometimes money too. He cured all of them… His staircase and hallway were simply crammed with patients' [10]. But all these patients, being ordinary people of no great fame, have left no records of their cures. Not only did the poor die forgotten, they were also cured without anyone knowing about it. Their diagnoses and the type and number of the cures that Cagliostro achieved will therefore remain forever unknown to us. His reputation, which was starting to grow day by day, is the only evidence that we have that such cures were both numerous and exceptional.

Little by little however, the upper and middle classes also began to consult him. As a result, the successes he enjoyed achieved wider fame and have been recorded in more detail. One of his early cures was that of an officer of dragoons, declared incurable, the victim of a serious illness [11] which had reduced him to the state of a 'ghastly cadaver'. 'This officer', says Baron de Gleichen, was introduced to me by his captain. In the interim he'd put on plenty of weight and was really quite plump. Cagliostro had restored him to perfect health' [12]. In another case, one of the secretaries of the regional *Commandant* [13] had fallen sick. His doctor declared him a lost cause, saying he would be dead in only twenty-four hours. On the orders of the *Commandant*, Cagliostro took him under his wing and restored him to, it would seem, perfect health, to everyone's astonishment [14]. 'I verified this miracle cure for myself', says another contemporary. 'The secretary was dying of gangrene of the leg. All the doctors had written him off as a hopeless case' [15].

Thanks to this undeniable success Cagliostro's fame reached its apogee. Another remarkable cure was that of Madame Sarrasin, the wife of a banker from Basel, who had been growing progressively weaker during eight months of intermittent fever accompanied by chronic icterus. Sleep had become impossible for her. Lying immobile in bed, shivering under fur blankets, her condition was deteriorating from day to day. The finest medical minds of Europe were consulted but all declared her beyond cure. Not only did Cagliostro cure her but, but despite her age, she became pregnant a short time afterwards and gave birth to a

The house, known as the Maison de la Vierge, where Cagliostro lived during his time in Strasbourg. Later 1 Kalbsgasse.

son on 4th April 1782. She and her husband called him Alexandre in honour of her saviour. Madame Sarrasin later recalled with emotion how Cagliostro 'had snatched her from the claws of death' [16]. Monsieur Sarrasin, in his *Journal* [17], also tells us about how one of his sons, Félix, was healed. He had been suffering from a 'gouty disease of the nerves' which no doctor had been able to relieve but which disappeared completely after just one visit to Cagliostro. Bürkli, who'd mocked Cagliostro's healing of an elderly spinster who had been deaf since the age of seven [18], acknowledged that his wife, who'd been in poor health when she arrived in St. Petersburg, received from Cagliostro a degree of care that considerably improved her general health and cured a stomach disease [19]. It was around this time also that Labarthe wrote to Séguier: 'Madame Augeard, a young and very pretty woman from Paris, who is well known to me, and who is very rich thanks to her husband's employment as a tax-farmer, was struck down with a terminal illness and sought out Cagliostro, who gave her as a present an elixir which cured her completely. Her brother tells me that she now enjoys the most wonderful health' [20]. Chevalier Langlois, a captain of dragoons in the regiment of Montmorency, who was dying, was also saved by Cagliostro, and retained a profound gratitude which he expressed in a touching letter in which he describes the benefits that he received from his saviour:

Sir,

I owe everything to Count Cagliostro. The enclosed letter, which I wrote years ago to the staff of the newspaper in Paris and which they kindly printed [21] *will explain to you how he became my saviour. My life had been under threat for some eight years without me experiencing the slightest relief from the various remedies prescribed to me by the most highly-qualified doctors. Given the state I was in an imminent death was actually the least alarming prospect for me and my family, as I was facing the total degradation of my intellectual faculties. Count Cagliostro restored to me my life, my health, my reason and my happiness. I have not had the slightest re-occurrence of the dreadful sufferings and violent fits with which I was formerly tormented. To conclude, my cure was total and radical, as were many others that Count Cagliostro performed before my very eyes which I could tell you about as en eye-witness if you felt it appropriate… etc.* [22].

Wieland [23] also tells us, in open letter, about the miraculous cure of his 29-year-old daughter, who had been reduced to a desperate consumptive condition by chronic ulcerative gastritis. She could no longer eat solid food: a few spoonfuls of milk kept her alive, and that had been her regime for some ten years. She was slowly dying and in continuous pain. 'Until the beginning of 1782 things were going from bad to worse', writes Wieland, 'despite the attentions of the most experienced doctors in our city. It was around this time that Count Cagliostro made a short visit to Basel and, through the mediation of a friend, this kind and splendid man came to see her. Initially he prescribed some remedies which he sent to her from Strasbourg. Her condition immediately improved and, in August, she was well enough to go to Strasbourg to see her benefactor. While there she was completely cured in just a few weeks. You can well imagine our gratitude towards this remarkable man, who was always eager to extend a helping hand to anyone afflicted by diseases which had been written off as incurable but which finally yielded to his sublime art, and whose wonderful soul requires no other reward than that which all truly wonderful souls enjoy: the inexpressible pleasure that comes from having made people truly happy' [24]. It would be tedious to continue: the cures of Baroness von Dietrich [25], Chevalier Montbruel [26] and the Prince de Soubise are reported everywhere.

The last of these cures, however, was so rapid and permanent that it deserves special mention. The Prince de Soubise had a violent scarlet fever and the doctors despaired of his life. Cardinal de Rohan, who was then in Saverne, spoke to Cagliostro about the Prince, who was his cousin. Cagliostro agreed to take the case and immediately rushed off to Paris with the Cardinal. When they arrived, the Cardinal went in on his own to see the Prince and reported back to Cagliostro that he was better, that the doctors' prognosis had improved slightly, and that they were reasonably optimistic. Cagliostro asked to be allowed to return to Saverne, as he was not interested in patients who had been cured. The Cardinal however was extremely concerned and was reluctant to leave. The following day the situation had changed again: the Prince's condition had deteriorated, and this time the doctors and the Prince's entourage had no doubts on the matter – he was dying [27]. This time Cagliostro was in a position to act. Cagliostro got into the Cardinal's coach and returned with him to the Prince's palace. The Cardinal announced that a doctor had come, but did not name him. The Prince's family allowed them free rein. In the Prince's apartment there were just a few servants and no one else. Cagliostro insisted on remaining alone in the dying man's room and his request was granted.

One hour later Cagliostro summoned the Cardinal and said to him, pointing to the patient: 'In two days, if my advice is followed, the Prince will be able to get up and walk around the room. In eight days he will be able to go out in his carriage. In three weeks he'll be paying court in Versailles'. The Cardinal did not know what to say to this. He simply followed Cagliostro out and, later that same day, returned with him to see the Prince. This time Cagliostro brought a small flask from which he administered ten drops to the patient. 'Tomorrow', he said to the Cardinal, 'we'll give the Prince five drops fewer. The day after tomorrow he'll take just two drops of this elixir, and he'll be able to get up that same evening.

And things turned out just as he had said they would. Just two days after this first visit the Prince de Soubise was well enough to receive all his friends. In the evening he asked to be allowed to get up, and was seen, without any fever, walking around his room, chatting quite cheerfully, sitting down again in an armchair, and asking for a chicken-wing, which however he was refused as the doctor brought along by the Cardinal had prescribed a strict diet. The third day went wonderfully well. By the fourth day the Prince was convalescing. And on the evening of the fifth day the Prince de Soubise was able to tuck into his chicken-wing [28]! The Cardinal and Cagliostro then set out for Saverne once more, their stay in Paris having lasted just thirteen days [29].

This cure enjoyed great and wide renown, and from Paris a flood of people in high society – 'some ladies of quality as well as two actresses' says Madame d'Oberkirch, who seems to have been extremely shocked by this strange social mélange [30] – followed Cagliostro to Strasbourg so that their treatments were not interrupted. The undeniability of these marvellous cures [31], the high social standing of those who had benefited from them and the obvious unselfishness of Cagliostro were altogether too novel and too attractive for there not be a huge rush from both North and South of scientists, theologians and the merely inquisitive towards this demigod, both to seek cures and to ask for some crumbs of this wonderful knowledge and some fragments of this power that he dispensed so liberally. And came they did: Strasbourg was thronged with visitors who came to the city just to see him.

After reaching his town-house [32], if you will imagine it, you crossed a passage and a small interior courtyard, went up a few stairs, and then entered a large room which was a cross between a drawing-room and a hallway [33]. There you would find, leaning against the fireplace, a man of average height, with a lively expression, his black hair brushed back, who greeted you with neither excessive aloofness nor timidity, and who maintained with everyone he met the same easygoing charm and frankness of speech. His piercing glance, full of vitality, impressed all his visitors. 'He's a very intelligent and pleasant man, cheerful, unassuming, lively, but aware that he really is somebody, asserting himself well, and therefore able to chat with even the highest ranks of society as someone who can do a lot for them without expecting anything in return' [34].

In Strasbourg he would receive visitors from 5 p.m. to 7 p.m. The men would remain with him: besides his close friends such as Sarrasin, Straub the director of the local munitions factory, and Barbier de Tinan the Muster-Master, you might also find the leading men of the city, such as the Royal Praetor De Gérard; Cardinal de Rohan; Maréchal de Contades, the Governor of Alsace; Monsieur de l'Ort [35], the King's Lieutenant; Baroness von Reich; Monsieur de la Galaizière [36]; scholars such as Professor Ehrmann and Mathieu Béguin, counsellor to the King; members of the nobility such as the Comte de Lutzelbourg, Baron de Dampierre and Baron de Zuckmantel; priests, especially the curé of Saint-Pierre-le-Vieux; and sometimes foreign visitors such as the poet, theologian and physiognomist Lavater, the philologist Breitinger, the pastor Touchon, Jean-Daniel Ullmann, and Salzmann, or VIPs from Paris or Russia [37].

Meanwhile, in a small room at the rear of the house, the ladies would gather around Countess Cagliostro who would enjoy a place of honour beside the fire. Close to her would be her great friend Madame Sarrasin, who was older and more worldly than the Countess [38] and was very much the leading-light of this little coterie. Countess Cagliostro, forced to act as hostess every day because of the huge numbers of people visiting the house [39] and also to keep open table for the passing guests that her husband brought to her, did not feel very much at home even when these visitors had left. The favourites remained: the Sarrasins actually lived with the Cagliostros on terms of the closest intimacy, 'dining with them every day, living with them like the early Christians' [40]. The house, always full, was more like a hotel than a home. When Countess Cagliostro was received by Cardinal de Rohan she had been showered with praise, which sat rather uneasily with her innate simplicity and timidity. Some of the regular male visitors to the Cagliostro household, aware that showing the slightest signs of being attracted to the Countess would cause problems with her husband [41], would sometimes stay in the small drawing-room and join in the conversation with the ladies, but the newcomers, all of them wholly devoted to Cagliostro, remained with him as soon as they had been presented in the large drawing-room. There they questioned, listened to and observed the mysterious miracle-worker. According to some they received rather varied receptions: 'Kind and affectionate towards some, extremely brusque towards others, he manifested from the very first minute of his conversations and consultations either a marked sympathy or an equally marked antipathy' [42]. These caprices were however only superficial: like Wagner's hero Siegfried, inspired by the dragon's blood, he could hear people's souls speaking to him irrespective of what their lips might be saying. He looked into their hearts, indifferent to the expressions and gestures of the body [43], and responded according to these inner thoughts with a tender and suffusing kindness towards some, but with a disconcerting abruptness towards others.

His way of speaking to patients was also extremely varied. Most often he would offer, in a very reserved and simple manner, to join his prayers to those of the patient, urging them not to lose hope. "Some find Cagliostro extremely modest: once he said quite frankly to a lady who had consulted him, 'Madam, the Count knows absolutely nothing about your problems [44], but there is a God in heaven Who, from an insignificant blade of grass, can extract a sap that will restore health to you, and Count Cagliostro will prostrate himself before Him to request some of it" [45]. On other occasions, and not without good reason, he spoke with a self-assurance and an authority that would repel most doctors and philosophers. 'To a patient who threw his arms around his neck he said quite simply, "Sir, you are as unwell as it's possible to be, but have no fears, Count Cagliostro will heal you" [46]. If the circumstances warranted it – if, for example, he had to explain why a friend who his who was present was so lost in thought – Cagliostro might add with a smile, 'Well perhaps I'm being a little bit optimistic in promising a cure. Many cures do not succeed, especially with the deaf and the blind, but no doubt Heaven will do something for us' [47]. In general Cagliostro came across as proud, as if he was always really saying to people, whatever their social status, 'Yes I can be of use to you, but I don't expect anything in return from you' [48].

His conversation turned to various subjects, but generally medical ones. One person would come to see him to ask for a cure for his own condition, while another would have come on behalf of a friend. Cagliostro, always benevolent, did not reject any request out of hand: he would always listen and observe, his face would assume an expression of contemplation, and his eyes would often take on a strange appearance [49] as if his interior life was temporarily absorbing their customary sparkle. Then he would respond, gravely promising to help in whatever way he could. His face would then re-assume its customary good humour and he would address himself to one of the VIPs present, who never thought it beneath them to act as his secretaries – for Cagliostro never wrote a single prescription himself – clap him on the shoulder and say, 'My dear Von Flachsland, or my dear De La Salle, or my dear De Rohan or whatever, please write down what I'm going to say to you'. They would do so and Cagliostro would countersign what they had written [50], sometimes adding explanations.

On those occasions when inquisitive spirits like Cardinal de Rohan, Salzmann or Ramond de Carbonnières were able to steer the conversation away from purely medical subjects they would try to cross-examine Cagliostro about his mysterious powers and about the occult sciences in general, but it wasn't easy, despite their best efforts, to persuade him to do so. With the same disconcerting spontaneity he would either talk very volubly or say hardly anything at all. When it suited him to talk – whether about himself, about the great book of nature, or about the secrets of the spirit – then everyone, even the most refractory, would listen captivated [51].

Cagliostro was severely critical of doctors, whom he thought of as superficial people for the most part, people who thought they'd examined a patient when all they'd really done was feel their pulse. At the school where he had studied [52] he'd been taught that nothing in nature is isolated, that every being has bonds that closely unite it to the centre, and that since a series of events forms an uninterrupted chain [53] then every action must be realised in the spiritual world before it can be carried out in the material one. 'As above, so below' was his maxim: the true expert of nature must therefore look upwards and downwards, and seek to penetrate the world of the spirit as well as that of matter. All medicine and all chemistry, with its 'dissolutions' and 'compositions' [54], must be based on this knowledge of life. This science gives us total power, but to possess it – and, indeed, even before we can possess it, to be considered worthy of it – one must be regenerated both physically and morally.

Already at this early stage therefore Cagliostro was making it clear that tests and a graduated initiation were an essential preparation if someone was to achieve the degree of evolution that it was necessary for them to reach. This was the task of Freemasonry, and the goal would surely be achieved if Freemasonry followed the pure and primitive Rite [55]. The doctor therefore prepared the way for the initiator: the goal of Egyptian Freemasonry was to train such people, now free, having recovered (as he himself had done, and he gave evidence of it) their original capabilities. Many of those who listened to him missed the point, at least in part, but others reflected upon the task and followed his advice.

If you arrived when Cagliostro was giving one of his famous 'audiences' [56], i.e. when he was welcoming to his huge drawing-room the many patients of the city and its environs, you would find yourself surrounded by the most incredible hubbub, where the only semblance of order and silence was preserved by respect for the Master and a desire to hear what he had to say. The hallway, the staircase, the courtyard, even the pavement by the front-door would be full of people pushing and shoving [57]. Through the middle of them Cagliostro would pass, alone or sometimes with an aide, chatting to everyone [58]: a glance, a word, a name was enough for him to acknowledge, help and sometimes even permanently cure a patient. His aide would note down any relevant addresses and, when the audience was finished, would rush hither and thither with drugs, prescriptions or on miscellaneous errands, or catch up on the latest news of those patients who were confined to bed [59].

Sometimes Cagliostro would spend more time than usual with patients, speaking to them either in front of everyone or privately, describing to them the symptoms of their disease or the deep-seated emotional problems which the patients thought that only they knew about. By making the necessary adjustments in their hearts and souls he also healed their bodies [60]. At other times, in response to something that someone had said to him, he would raise his voice and address everyone: on those occasions he would speak of the eternal verities with authority and exaltation. As a contemporary wrote:

I've just emerged from one of his audiences. Imagine Madam, if you will, an immense room filled with these poor wretches, almost all of them at the end of their tether, stretching heavenwards their faltering hands which they'd previously scarcely been able to raise in order to beg Count Cagliostro to help them. He listens to them, one after the other, doesn't forget a single word that they've said to him, leaves the room for a few moments, and then returns loaded down with a whole host of remedies which he dispenses to each one of these unfortunates, repeating to them as he does so what they have just told him of their illness, assuring them that they'll soon be cured if only they carry out his instructions to the letter. But the remedies alone would be insufficient: they need soup to give them the strength to carry on, and as few of these poor wretches have the means of acquiring any, Cagliostro – moved to pity – divides his seemingly inexhaustible purse amongst them. Happier to give than to receive, his joy in giving to others is palpable. These unhappy folk, full of gratitude, love and respect, hurl themselves at his feet, throw their arms around his knees, call him their saviour, their father, their god... The kind and gentle man becomes emotional, and tears start to well up in his eyes. He tries to hold back the tears, but he cannot. He starts to cry and then the whole assembly with him... delicious tears that express all the heart's joy, the delights of which cannot be understood by anyone who has not been happy enough to have poured out similar tears themselves! Well, that's an entirely inadequate sketch of the enchanting spectacle that I've just enjoyed, and which I'm told is repeated three times a week [61].

Much has been made of his secret medicines. The doctors, unable to deny his successes and wanting to attribute them only to actions within the scope of their art, claimed that all his 'miracles' were due to the use of either well-known drugs or, as some have alleged, secret ones which would have behaved in exactly the same way if anyone else has prescribed them.

Others accused him of using violent and 'incendiary' poisons [62] without discretion. Others still said that his remedies were just anodynes devoid of any qualities except that of letting nature take its course. In brief, his medical rivals provided the most ridiculous and often self-contradictory explanations [63].

In fact Cagliostro did not use just one therapeutic technique: he varied his procedures *ad infinitum*, being guided less by the disease in question than the spiritual, emotional and intellectual state of the patients and those they were surrounded by, and always taking into account the result – whether inevitable scandal or worthwhile encouragement – to which his actions were likely to lead. Sometimes, like any sensible doctor, he used standard everyday drugs, such as lead acetate [64], aloe and refreshing herbal teas, formulating according to the usual practices of the time a prescription that the pharmacist would then make up [65]. At other times he was completely at odds with the current procedures, e.g. with his miraculous Pink Powder [66] or his Balsam or Wine of Egypt [67]. If the attending doctor had ordered a water-diet then Cagliostro would get the patient eating again and give them a glass of red wine.

His profound understanding of the human mind and soul opened doors to him that remained closed to the ordinary run of doctors. He knew how to bandage the wounds of the heart and to restore energy and happiness to poor wretches crushed by unhappiness. The use of special powers, the existence of which was denied in his time and which is scarcely accepted in ours despite the labels they have been given of magnetism, hypnotism and suggestion, was very familiar to him. If he did not actually call them by these particular names then he knew something that was more important than what they should be called, which was their underlying laws, and he applied them according to his needs, but only rarely it is true [68] as he preferred other means of treatment. If he thought it was worth proving the existence of these forces to his disciples or some sceptic or other then he would make recourse to them, not because it was essential for the patient but because it was useful for the eye-witnesses.

Finally, beneath all these external processes, in each and very one of these treatments, there was the true and unique action which was his very own, something that could not be confused with any one of them, whether magnetism or pharmacotherapy, an action that is as wholly unknown nowadays as it was in his own time – I am talking about *spiritual* action. In Strasbourg, as in Lyons and in Paris, when Cagliostro said, 'It is our wish that such an evil immediately disappears' or 'Heaven grants you your request', whether this was at a public meeting, or in the Cardinal's chambers or in the Egyptian Lodge, then the spiritual world obeyed his command and the material action, whatever it was, would occur immediately. He used this power in his own distinctive way, but always discreetly, and if he wanted to apply it to physical medicine then the illness, even if terminal, would disappear with or without the use of pharmaceutical assistance such as lead acetate or the yellow drops [69]. This power, this right of command was his property and remained his secret [70]. A shortage of documents and the limitations of our intellect mean that all we can do is point to a few cases where he manifested his miraculous therapeutic abilities, but we cannot even dream of analysing them. To understand Cagliostro, a contemporary of his once said, you have to *be* him. To try to explain him, to analyse his ways of doing things, would be more absurd still. We shall therefore content ourselves, as his faithful disciples did, with respecting his name, admiring his works, and nourishing in ourselves the hope that he left to us that we ourselves one day would 'attain moral mastery by unceasing effort and by the grace of God' [71]. Even at this distance in time we can sense the excitement that surrounded him. The most

Chapter V

refined people in society hastened to his audiences without worrying about having to rub shoulders with tradesmen, patients with contagious diseases or paupers in rags. Going round to Cagliostro's place had become fashionable [72]. As his lodgings were near the Place d'Armes many of the local garrison came to see him, most around noon, others from five to eight, and others still when he was actually holding his audiences [73]. Even during the intervals between audiences Cagliostro's house remained full. Courtiers eager to please the Cardinal, or hoping to meet some important person, even a friend of the Master perhaps, could show up at any time. Cagliostro hardly had time to eat and often had a meal of bread and cheese, water and some coffee standing up or on his way out [74]. From early morning to noon he was rushing around seeing patients, on foot or by carriage, regardless of what the weather was doing [75]. People who recognised him in the street would sometimes stop him and throw themselves at his feet. Old women would tell their rosaries or cross themselves as he passed as a sign of veneration [76].

On his return he would find his house full of locals seeking his help, disciples, newcomers waiting to be presented to him or foreigners come from afar to consult him, and who danced attendance upon him, sometimes for several hours, before being able to join him [77]. So large was the crowd that, despite the very short time granted to each person, and despite the good manners of his friends, the audiences often extended late into the evening, which meant that Cagliostro slept as little and as badly as he ate [78].

Cagliostro was the man of the moment, the pride of Strasbourg. He made hoteliers rich, patients happy, and souls more enlightened. Everyone agreed that he should be encouraged to stay in Strasbourg: with his approval some friends even petitioned the King for a licence to practise medicine and to make up his own drugs in Strasbourg. Such a licence would have officially crowned his success [79]. But Cagliostro's fame as a healer was starting to get on the nerves of the local medical profession [80]. In the Temple of Aesculapius a storm was brewing, and the incident that we are about to describe caused the clouds to burst.

On 23rd May 1781 a poor woman of Leimengœssel called Catherine Grœbel, the wife of a stonemason, fell seriously ill. Her pregnancy, almost at term, was causing the most alarming symptoms. Madame de la Fage, a lady of quality who took an interest in the family, asked one of the most famous obstetricians in Strasbourg, a Dr. Ostertag, to visit her. He considered the case to be a very serious one. In his subsequent report on the matter he describes the patient's condition at great length and without, I'm afraid, very much clarity [81]:

Hippocratic face, infectious status, eclamptic seizures, uterus tipped to the right, neck of uterus very high and set to the left, semi-open but not dilated, frequent fainting fits.

At least I *think* that this is what we are meant to infer through the fog of imprecise and archaic terminology that he uses. Anyway, he added that the baby was almost certainly dead. Two other doctors, Wittel and Schuabé, were also in attendance, along with the midwife Madeleine Leidnerin. The case was obviously a serious one. Although Ostertag was able to offer the midwife some small amount of reassurance for the present, he told her that the situation could worsen, that he might perhaps be forced to consider an intervention, that she should not leave the patient under any circumstances, and that she should send someone to fetch him should an emergency arise [82].

Ostertag returned on each of the following days. The patient was still having seizures but her condition did not seem to be worsening. On the 28th, at 4 p.m., he was sent for again: there had been a sudden deterioration and the patient was having a fainting-fit. He arrived at 7 p.m. Due no doubt to his extreme haste he *did not examine the patient*, but simply chatted to the midwife and told her to come and and fetch him if anything untoward occurred.

Night fell, and on the following day, the 29th, at around 11 a.m., he returned and, on opening the door, saw Cagliostro and the parish-priest, a Father Zaegelins, near the patient's bed. He closed the door again, sent for the midwife and asked her whether it was she who had summoned Cagliostro. 'No Sir, it was Father Zaegelins that brought him. In any case, Count Cagliostro hasn't touched the patient at all'. She added that Cagliostro had not issued a prescription but had given the patient a six-franc piece. Ostertag was furious. He left, never to return.

In the interim Cagliostro had examined the patient. He then sent Father Zaegelins around to see her with a red powder to be administered to her in a little red wine that same evening at 5 p.m. He also gave permission for the patient to drink a little more wine and coffee and to eat some moist bread if she was hungry, and at around 8 p.m. she did so. At 10 p.m. – the patient now being up and about – her waters broke. Half an hour later she gave birth with just two contractions. The birth was spontaneous and very rapid – almost immediate in fact.

The following day at 2 p.m. Cagliostro visited her. We can only imagine the gratitude with which she received him. Cagliostro took a vial out of his pocket, opened it, poured some drops of the balsam that it contained into a spoonful of water and gave it to the patient to drink. Just a short while afterwards the mother was able to get up and have her child baptised, in the presence of Cagliostro, in the parish church of Saint-Pierre-le-Vieux.

This wonderful act of healing became widely known: both the grateful patient who couldn't stop talking about what had happened and the beneficent priest – the family's protector and an eye-witness to the events, who was so happy to have brought the woman's saviour to her in the hour of danger – were only too happy to spread the good news wherever they went in the parish. Cagliostro, for his part, was in no mood to spare Ostertag's feelings.

Meanwhile Ostertag's friends, whether true or false, went to see him with gloomy expressions to try to console him and give him their advice [83] Ostertag, increasingly upset, sent for the midwife and made her sign a statement purporting to show that the patient had never been in any danger, that the case was actually a very straightforward one, that he had never even mentioned performing a Caesarean or expressed the opinion that her child had died, and that Cagliostro had done nothing but harm. It was disgraceful, he said, that a medical expert of his standing was being discredited.

Was Cagliostro repelled by this act of bad faith on the part of Ostertag and the way the midwife was being forced to bear false witness, or did his friends apply pressure? We cannot say, but whatever the facts of the matter he certainly did not keep silent. The healing had been spectacular, something that would certainly cause people to reflect very carefully. To establish the truth he called upon the testimony of Father Zaegelins, who had witnessed the entire drama from beginning to end just as the midwife had and who, moreover, had been privy to Ostertag's confidences at the bedside of the dying woman. Here is Father Zaegelins' statement in its entirety:

I the undersigned, being curé of the Parish of Saint-Pierre-le-Vieux, certify that on 24th May I was summoned by one Catherine Noirot, wife of Nicolas Grœbel, a burgher and master-stonemason of this city, to receive her confession and, if necessary, to administer Holy Communion, a precaution recommended by Dr. Ostertag, doctor of medicine and obstetrician of this city (as her previous Communion had also been) as she was suffering a continuous fever with unrelenting pain and as her midwife had stated that both the obstetrician and she herself feared that the patient's child was no longer alive.

Chapter V

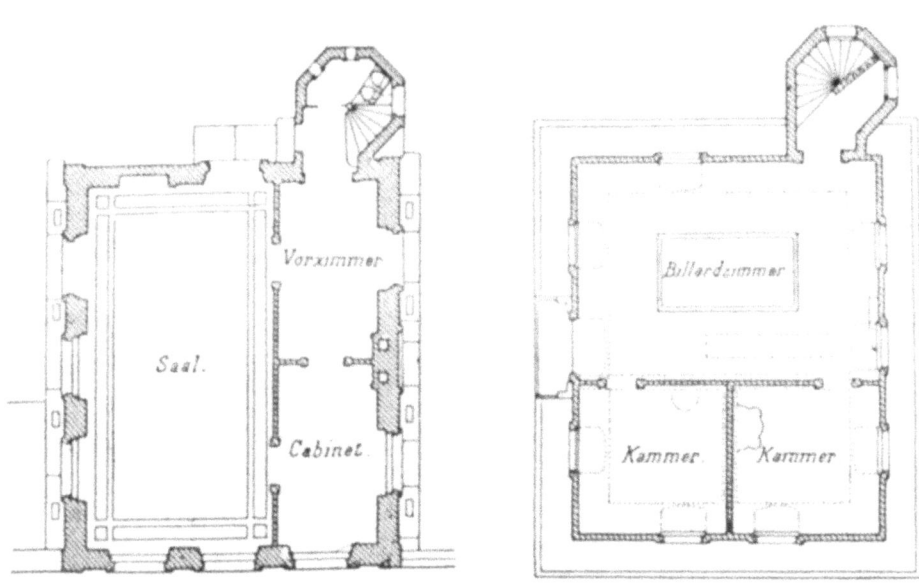

View and ground-plan as it was in 1912 of the 'Pavilion for Regeneration' built in Riehen in 1781 on the Sarrasin estate in accordance with Cagliostro's instructions.

Moved by compassion I mentioned the matter conversationally to Monsieur Milliaut, who did not think that he could offer any sort of remedy since he had not seen the patient. I then approached Count Cagliostro, whose sensitivity of heart is well known to me, as is his generosity and the help that he has already given in my parish since he came to live in this city. The Count promised me that he would provide immediate relief, and gave me a remedy for her: hardly had the patient swallowed it than she was seized with birth-pangs. The obstetrician, who had arrived unexpectedly, found the patient's condition sufficiently improved to be able to hand over the childbirth to the midwife, saying that the child would be born naturally.

The following day Count Cagliostro again administered a remedy and the birth-pangs again began immediately but without result. Finally, on 30th May, he administered the first remedy to her again. She gave birth extremely comfortably to a boy who was in such a good state of health that she dispensed with an emergency baptism. Indeed, her son was baptised in the church at 4 p.m. that same day.

In witness whereof I offer this statement, signed with my hand and provided with the parochial seal,
Zaegelins, curé.[84]

This affidavit, provided by a man known for his good works whose word was well respected, was a severe blow to Ostertag. In vain Ostertag tried in his lengthy report [85] to disparage the curé's testimony, to show that he could not have been deceived, that all Cagliostro had done was to harvest the fruits of medical care that he himself had provided, that Cagliostro's drugs were worthless and that the sequence of facts as reported by Zaegelins was inaccurate. In doing so he wrestled with the evidence, contradicted himself, fruitlessly invoked the authority of the local Medical Faculty, and piled unnecessary medical jargon on top of irrelevant quotes from the medical literature [86]. His report did not impress the city's governing council, the *Chambre des Quinze* [87], who sent for him and told him that the harangue that formed part of his submission to them was 'unbecoming a professional man' and must be deleted [88]. Several people, including Cagliostro, had considered that the permission that the magistrates had given Ostertag to print and distribute his submission was tantamount to an admission that the Royal Praetor actually agreed with Ostertag's libellous statements. Cardinal de Rohan [89] demanded that the submission be revised before publication, and the *Conseil de Quinze* agreed: this made it clear to everyone that Ostertag's report was simply the airing of a personal grievance rather than the sort of scientific statement of general protest that one had a right to expect from a member of the Medical Faculty [90]. Ostertag, now humiliated, and exasperated both by his failure and by the not very flattering comments made about him by the *Conseil de Quinze*, would not admit defeat. He decided to take vengeance on Cagliostro, and he had already found some allies.

Cagliostro's unpolished frankness and easygoing charm, his refusal to acknowledge any constraints, and his lack of patience with fashionable conventions [91] had already got on the nerves of several vain and conceited habitués of the local *salons*, including a cavalry colonel in the Queen's regiment, the Vicomte de Narbonne. One evening in August 1781 the Vicomte dined at Cardinal de Rohan's [92] in very brilliant company, which included the Cagliostros. Around this time rumours about Cagliostro had already begun circulating and there had also been some spiteful gossip about the Countess, who was all the more obvious a target for criticism because some were so eager to praise her good qualities and great charm. The Vicomte was only too happy to act as an echo-chamber for these malicious rumours, especially as Cagliostro had already wounded his pride on a previous occasion. He still viewed him with suspicion, and spent the evening at the Cardinal's looking for a suitable opportunity to vent his animosity [93].

When no natural opportunity presented itself he decided to create one: during dinner he up-ended a sauce-boat all over Countess Cagliostro's dress [94]. General chaos ensued, everyone except the Vicomte rushing to the side of the Countess. The Vicomte, under the guise of an apology, simply emphasised his poor manners and thus forced Cagliostro to intervene.

'Oh what a lot of fuss about a dress!' shouted the Vicomte. 'I'll pay for the damage, don't worry'.

'I thought I'd given you some sound advice when I told you *not* to seat yourself alongside this gentleman', Cagliostro said to the Countess with extreme calmness.

'You are an insolent fellow Sir, and you will give me satisfaction, sword in hand', yelled the Vicomte.

'I'm no swordsman Sir', answered Cagliostro. 'Fighting is your job not mine'.

'Very well, we shall use pistols'.

'I won't accept that challenge either', replied Cagliostro. 'My job is healing people not killing them'.

The Vicomte leapt to his feet and threw a plate at Cagliostro's head.

'This is what happens when you're forced to dine with so-called Counts and Countesses with self-inflicted titles who've fallen out of the sky like bombs!' [95]

By now everyone was on their feet and the dinner had ground to a halt. The Cardinal, his Vicar-General the Abbé d'Aymar, and the Maréchal de Contades all tried to intervene, entreating, threatening, doing whatever they could to stop the Vicomte in his tracks and to apologise to the Countess. Eventually, after a fashion, the evening came to an end.

These shenanigans created quite a stir in Strasbourg: the hatred that the Vicomte de Narbonne already felt for Cagliostro prior to this episode, and which had increased that evening, continued to haunt Cagliostro. The Vicomte was Ostertag's first ally – and by no means the least important – in the campaign that they jointly conducted against Cagliostro during 1781 [96].

A second acolyte joined them a few months later: Carlo Sachi was a former hospital-porter now passing himself off as a dentist who arrived in Strasbourg from Spain in November, right in the middle of the conflict between Cagliostro and his enemies. Ostertag needed information, but Cagliostro's own servants were loyal to their master. He had to have a spy in Cagliostro's immediate circle. Sachi was sufficiently short of money to accept the job and certainly possessed all the dubious qualities required to do justice to it [97]. Cagliostro recalled that he had spent some time in Valencia around 1771. That was enough to enable Sachi to insinuate himself. He was presented to the Count, claimed that he had known him in Spain, recalled his kindness towards him and now wanted, simply out of gratitude, to devote his life to his service. Cagliostro left for Saverne, promising to look after him.

On his return on 27th December he took Sachi into his service as a 'runner' [98], helping him in his work with patients. Sachi wasted no time: his job was to take drugs to the patients and hand them over free of charge, but unknown to Cagliostro he made the patients pay over the odds for them, stole the poorest patients' money and presented Cagliostro with apothecaries' bills for payment. This led to Cagliostro acquiring a reputation in the city as an astute dealer in drugs: consequently he lost the respect of his patients and laid himself open to criticism. That suited Sachi, who was able to fill his boots [99], and it suited Ostertag as well.

Sachi spread his poison in private homes, in cafés and in public places. To anyone who would listen, Cagliostro's surgical assistant would begin by referring to his Master in the most impressive terms, and then sprinkle some reservations into the conversation and make risky allusions to his past, which he claimed to know all about. Finally he would give the impression that he was ready to take people into his confidence and would pour out all the infamies that his enemies have since been happy to repeat.

'In Valencia', he would say, 'I nursed that rascal when he was suffering from a dreadful venereal disease which he'd picked up – and the little Countess as well – by visiting brothels [100]. There's your 'great man' for you! As for his famous medical formulas, they're not worth a penny. And all the funny faces that he pulls, and all these grand gestures, if I weren't an honourable man then I could imitate all of them for you. I've often felt like throwing everything I could at him when I've heard him talking to me as if I was a little boy and treating doctors like stupid asses'.

'Well why don't you then?' his gullible audience would ask, immediately shaken in their sympathies towards Cagliostro and already starting to come over to Sachi's camp.

'Why? Because he'd kill me that's why, the way he's already killed other people. Give me six Grenadiers to defend me and maybe I'd say to his face what I've just said to you'.

When he told this tale in a Strasbourg café on 2nd January 1781 [101] one of Cagliostro's patients was in the audience. The man was grateful for what Cagliostro had done for him but was very disturbed by what he had just heard. He rushed round to see Cagliostro and told him everything. He begged Cagliostro to try to extricate himself from the trouble that Sachi had just plunged him into. Cagliostro sent for Sachi, reprimanded him and then sacked him. Sachi, dismayed, excused himself and withdrew, but he had hardly left Cagliostro's presence than he ran back into the house, seething with anger and with pistol in hand, ready to kill him [102]. The matter was eventually submitted to Monsieur De La Salle who, after investigations, ordered Sachi to be expelled from Strasbourg, both for the threats he had made against the life of a citizen and for his calumnies against a man who was universally respected for his kindness and goodness. Sachi repeated his excuses, stated in vain that he had been misunderstood and was actually talking about someone else, that Cagliostro was and had always been his benefactor, and that he would always be happy to serve him [103], but the judgment was upheld and Sachi had to withdraw to Kehl. There he stopped all pretence and immediately combined his attacks on Cagliostro with those of the other members of the anti-Cagliostro faction, claiming by means of open letters, newspaper articles and posters the sum of 125 gold *louis* from Cagliostro for his services, and actually arraigning him before the courts for that amount [104].

One hundred and twenty-five *louis* for six days' work, during which he had probably extorted just as much from the poor wretches he was supposed to be helping, and had caused the greatest possible harm to the reputation of the man who was nourishing him! The judges refused to listen to him, but the general public, always malicious, was acquiring a taste for these debates. Ostertag and De Narbonne kept up the pressure. The rejected suitors of the pretty Countess, the many women who were jealous of her, the doctors who were hostile to Cagliostro [105], the many enemies of Cardinal de Rohan, the plain jealous – all joined forces with them. A faction was formed against a man whose goodness had become legendary, and the scandalmongers started to make progress.

Chapter V

Everything that had formerly been so much admired about Cagliostro was now deprecated. His numerous good deeds and virtues were distorted and used against him, with his critics claiming to find in them indications of just how dark and murky his soul really was [106]. Simplicity of life and frugality? Either play-acting to impress the imaginations of the vulgar [107] or proof of his avarice! Dressing simply, with no apparent interest in looking fashionable? Just scruffiness ('How impertinent to receive people – and good-class people at that – with his hair looking like that, blowing about all over the place!' [108]). Wearing expensive clothes when he took his wife out for a stroll? Ostentation, vanity and 'a sickening and scandalous level of self-indulgence!' [109].

Even his fondness for Cardinal de Rohan was considered suspect. Those who would have been quite happy to see him lose all his invaluable friendships wanted to know why he sought out the friendship of high aristocrats when he claimed not to need their support, and why, if his secret intrigues were not subversive, he felt the need to surround himself with powerful protectors.

Even his medical successes did not escape criticism. If he dealt, for a change, with a relatively straightforward case then people would say that he was only interested in cuts and grazes [110] or women with the 'vapours' – yes, a real challenge! But even if he was trying to help an incurable patient who'd been abandoned by their doctors then his critics would find something to disapprove of. As Bürkli, for example, expressed it so foolishly and so ponderously: 'I think I can state that in Cagliostro's case ambition is a substitute for egoism, as he's only really interested in patients whom their doctors have written off as incurable, while he *unworthily* ignores those who have ordinary illnesses of the nerves or digestion or who just feel a bit feverish' [111]. So you say that Count Cagliostro has cured fifty terminally ill patients? But that's not the point – my wife still has toothache, and Monsieur de Cambis is as dead a a doornail! [112].

This is all so absurd as to be actually quite amusing. Any accusations, even flatly self-contradictory ones, were good enough for Cagliostro's enemies: if it wasn't irreligion then it was Jesuitism, if it wasn't avarice it was profligacy [113]. Even his morals were considered fair game: he was attacked for his vigorous social life (even though we know that he hardly ever went out anywhere), for keeping a good table, for gambling, and so on and so on and so forth [114].

Soon all these malicious insinuations were being transferred to his wife: 'Oh you know she's on *very* good terms with the Vicomte. I mean, *very* good terms indeed. He gives her the most wonderful presents. She must be drowning in debt [115] but the Vicomte is rich and Cagliostro knows how to turn a blind eye to certain things!'

We may perhaps appear to have dwelt at excessive length on the current of opinion that was so skilfully created against Cagliostro in Strasbourg by his three implacable enemies but it is from this that there stemmed the entire campaign of blackmail and hatred that pursued him in Paris and London and which only ended with his death in Rome. What started with malevolent assumptions, mere jokes and discreet calumnies eventually became stubborn legend by way of some pretty unscrupulous lampoons and allegations, and the modern chronicles have taken this as the basis for their so-called 'biographies'. But what were the origins of all this? Nothing more the idle chatter of gossips in Alsace and the gratuitous insults of despicable rascals: this is a point that we simply had to make and forcibly, and we think we have succeeded.

In Strasbourg, therefore, opinion was strongly divided. Cagliostro was a subject of controversy, and some at least began to have doubts about him. But this was not enough for the three leaders of the anti-Cagliostro faction: he had to be destroyed, and traps had to be set for him.

In his *Mémoires d'un octogénaire* Baron de Lamothe-Langon tells the amusing tale of a visit to Cagliostro by two medical students, posing as a patient and his attendant, who were clearly out to bamboozle and discredit him. Cagliostro received them cordially, listened to what they had to say, then pointed to the bogus patient and said gravely to his equally bogus attendant, 'I'm afraid I'll have to keep your friend with me for a fortnight on an absolute fast. I'm sorry, but if he's to get well again then it's virtually no food for him from now on'. Unsurprisingly the unhappy 'patient' took fright, vigorously refused the suggested treatment and asked if he could just have a diagnosis. 'Nothing simpler old chap', answered Cagliostro, writing on a slip of paper, '*Superabundance of bile in young medical students*', and gave it to them. The disconcerted students stammered out an excuse of some kind. Cagliostro, good man that he was, put them at their ease, and invited them to lunch. Since then, I believe, they have become some of his most enthusiastic admirers' [116].

On another occasion the secret police of Paris, intrigued by certain libellous allegations, eventually decided to investigate, putting Cagliostro under close surveillance [117]. But there again the anti-Cagliostro gang was to be disappointed. Desbrugnières, the police-agent involved, visited Cagliostro *incognito* very much as an enemy but left him with enhanced respect, almost as a convert.

Now Sachi tried a new tactic: competing with Cagliostro. During his short period of employment with him he'd managed to form a collaboration with the apothecary that he visited with prescriptions. Since he'd been able to steal some of Cagliostro's drugs and formulations and had also managed to piece together some information on the probable composition of the Balsam or Wine of Egypt which Cagliostro administered to so many patients, he made a counterfeit version of it which sold like hot cakes at exorbitant prices under the name of *Gouttes jaunes* (Yellow Drops) or the *Balsam of Count Cagliostro* [118]. Cagliostro was completely nonplussed by the discredit that such a counterfeit medicine might bring upon him, but he could not ignore the danger that patients were running. He therefore had the following message posted at various places in the city:

WARNING
Count Cagliostro, having learned that certain drops called 'Gouttes du comte de Cagliostro' are being sold to the public feels obliged to state that the people producing them cannot possibly know the real composition of his Drops, and that he therefore cannot be held responsible for any harmful effects that a remedy thus falsified could produce. He therefore repudiates them, as well as all those that might be administered by persons other than him [119].

It was in February and March 1782, after the sacking of Sachi, that the anti-Cagliostro campaign reached its peak. Some hostile articles had already been published [120], and now Sachi's memoir and a new anonymous lampoon were added to them [121]. Cagliostro was not bothered: he never responded to insults [122], never asked for any kind of official intervention, and bore without anger this torrent of hatred against him, but he was nonetheless profoundly disheartened at the prospect of leaving a city that had shown itself to be so stupid and ungrateful after he had given it so much evidence of his kindness and had accomplished so many marvels. His true friends and his disciples begged him to stay, redoubling their efforts to defend their Master and friend. Throughout this odious campaign they had never ceased to support him. Despite the carefree scorn that Cagliostro always displayed they hated to see him insulted in this way. In the salons of the town they tried to stop the poison spreading. When the abusive placards were posted, Cardinal of Rohan, Maréchal de Contades and Monsieur de l'Ort intervened vigorously [123]. After Ostertag had submitted his infamous report Sarrasin had written an open letter to Straub testifying to the miraculous cure of his wife and the fond respect that he had for Cagliostro [124].

In response to the Sachi pamphlets, the anonymous lampoons and the article by Görge in *Variétés Haut-Rhinoises* (16th July 1781) another disciple of Cagliostro sent the latter newspaper, along with a formal request for inclusion, the following magnificent response:
To the editor of the Variétés Haut-Rhinoises,

I always thought your newspaper was intended to amuse your readership while at the same time instructing them, rather than attacking the honour and consideration of people who have not only never done you any harm but who, through their love of their neighbour and their sheer integrity, still compel the respect of every honest man.

This is however precisely what you did in Article VIII of July 16th in which Maître Görge, using the style of writing of a humble labourer in order to disguise his identity, maliciously and wrongfully attacked the noble philanthropist Cagliostro...

It would be easy to refute point by point all the calumnies contained in this piece, but I do not want to compromise myself by reproducing before the public all those sarcastic remarks which jealousy alone must have inspired. I will simply trace a portrait that is diametrically opposed to that one, so that everyone can see things in their true light.

Count Cagliostro must indeed be quite a novelty for anyone who is hearing of him for the first time. It is such an extraordinary thing nowadays to meet someone who does good just for the sake of it without selfishness or ulterior motive, someone who doesn't allow himself to be distracted either by envy or by malicious gossip, and who follows his own path in life because an inner force drives him to do so. That is precisely the case with Count Cagliostro.

This noble foreigner first came to Strasbourg as a temporary resident. He lived quietly without seeking – but without avoiding – opportunities to make friends. Chance or, to speak more exactly, Providence revealed his philanthropy: certain successful cures made him fashionable in a way that he'd certainly never sought to become. All the most respected citizens were eager to get to know a man who acted so nobly, and soon his house became the meeting-place of all the most distinguished people of the city. But being at the heart of such a circle did not compromise our Count's independence in any way. Every patient, no matter to which social class he or she belonged, was entitled to benefit from his help and activity. Not only did he never accept even the shadow of any remuneration, either from rich or poor, on any pretext, he even very discreetly distributed largesse from his own pockets to hundreds of people around him.

These actions and, moreover, his way of thought and his knowledge, won the friendship of the most distinguished people, especially the nobility. He has maintained all these friendships, and he has been here now for some nine months [125]...

It seems to me that a man like this can spend his money as he sees fit, does not have to tell you his real name, or where he comes from if he doesn't want to, and can speak only Arabic with some professor or other who came to see him out of mere curiosity if that's what he wants to do.

Even if this man did not do any good, who would have the right to insist that he do so? Who would have the right to force him to mix with doctors if he's an amateur neither of medicine nor of specifically European medicine? He claims to have knowledge from the East, but nobody is forced to believe that against his will.

This is not the place to defend the Count, otherwise it would be with joy and from the bottom of my heart that I would tell you all about the elevated, noble and beneficent deeds that I have seen him do every day. But in doing so I would be frightened of offending the modesty of this great man and of besmirching his dignity by saying everything that I think about him in response to a vulgar clutch of calumnies written by a man who is obviously plunged in spiritual darkness [126].

Cagliostro, touched by the zeal and affection that his disciples were displaying towards him, decided to remain in Strasbourg. But from this time onwards he limited the number of his 'audiences' [127], received only his loyal former patients (the number of which was still considerable) and devoted himself almost entirely to his friends, i.e. the Sarrasins, whom he accompanied several times to Basel, Cardinal de Rohan, with whom he spent fifteen days every month, the Straubs, and the De Barbiers [128]. But, in general, high society forsook him and went back to their footling distractions. The doctors, of course, were delighted.

Two events helped Cagliostro to make up his mind to leave Strasbourg: first, the departure of Cardinal de Rohan for Paris, and second, just a short while afterwards in August 1783, the serious illness of his friend and former protector, Chevalier Aquino who, *in extremis*, had summoned him to Naples to be near him. Cagliostro used these two events to explain to those who so much wanted him to stay why he had decided to leave them, and to moderate the pain that such sad news would inevitably cause them. But the real reason for him leaving Strasbourg was because he felt that his work there was done: he had sown precious seeds in the dry and dusty field of Strasbourg medicine and helped expose the heavy veil of prejudice, pride and selfishness that prevented the local medical profession from understanding nature and her laws; he had exercised, in the midst of much physical evil, the ministry of the Man-spirit and had demonstrated its reality; finally, he had done enough to awaken in human hearts the desire for regeneration. Now his mission called him towards other work [129].

Despite all the machinations of his enemies the people of Strasbourg had remained fundamentally loyal to him and a substantial crowd, truly sympathetic and sorry to see him go, followed his carriage as far as the outskirts of the city. Some of them were weeping. 'It's the good Lord himself who is leaving us', cried the poor, the sick and the lame, whom he loved so much.

NOTES

(1) During his first few weeks in Strasbourg, however, while staying at the hotel, he did not give any open displays of his medical knowledge. Cf. Blessig, *Lettre*, p. 7, in *Cagliostro à Strasbourg* (Laurent Blessig, philosopher and theologian, had been a Professor at the local University since 1778). Cf. also the article by G. Weisstein in *Elsaß-Lothringische Zeitung*, year IV, no. 37, Strasbourg, 1882, and H. Funk, *Cagliostro à Strasbourg*, in *Archiv. für Kulturgeschichte*, vol. III, pp. 223-234, Berlin, 1905. This study contains extracts of letters from J. Bürkli, poet and *chef de corporation* of Zurich, written to his friend Bodmer during a stay which he made in Strasbourg in January 1782 specifically for the purpose of getting to know Cagliostro.

(2) 'Hath not God chosen the poor of this world rich in faith, and heirs of the kingdom which he hath promised to them that love him?', *James*, II, 5.

(3) Cf. Chapter II of this book, 'Portrait'.

(4) *Letter from Bürkli*, in Funk, loc. cit., p. 14. This is even more impressive than the well-known

charitable propensities of Louis-Claude de Saint Martin.

(5) 'At the beginning of his stay Cagliostro was able to get someone released from debtor's prison by paying off the money he owed', Görge, Letter of 10th June 1781, *Variétés Haut-Rhinoises*, Basel, 1781, art. VIII, p. 120.

(6) Weisstein, loc. cit., p. 7, Funk, loc. cit., p. 7 & 12, Meiners, *Briefe über Schweiz*, Part II, quoted on p. 19 of the *Lettre de Mirabeau sur Cagliostro*, Berlin 1786.

(7) De Gleichen, *Souvenirs*, p. 136. See below for details of this affair which aroused great controversy.

(8) Spach, Works, vol. V, pp. 72-73.

(9) Funk, loc. cit., p. 7.

(10) Funk, loc. cit., p.7. Weisstein, loc. cit., p. 7. Georgel, *Mémoires*, p. 52

(11) Madame d'Oberkirch, *Mémoires*, p. 8.

(12) De Gleichen, *Souvenirs*, p. 136.

(13) The Marquis de la Salle. Cf. Letter from Bürkli in Funk, loc. cit., p. 5.

(14) Weisstein, *Letter from Blessig* in *Cagliostro à Strasbourg*, p. 8.

(15) De Gleichen, *Souvenirs*, p. 136.

(16) Funk, *Letter from Bürkli*, loc. cit., pp. 10 & 20. Cf. below: *Letter from Sarrasin*. Schlosser, Goethe's brother-in-law and a friend of the Sarrasins, who was furious about the lies that had been published about his case in 1787 – some had even said that Cagliostro had killed Madame Sarrasin – wrote a remarkable letter of protest to the *Deutsches Museum*. He testified that ever since Cagliostro's intervention Madame Sarrasin's health had been perfect and that when he saw her again later that year (1787) she even seemed to him to look younger and happier than she had ever been, no. 13, p. 388.

(17) Entry for 21st May 1781, *Archives Sarrasin*, Basel.

(18) *Letter from Bürkli* in Funk, loc. cit., p. 10.

(19) Ibid., p. 15.

(20) *Lettre à l'archéologue Séguier*, in Funck-Brentano, *L'Affaire du Collier*, p. 91.

(21) It was translated in *Ephemeriden der Freymaurerey*, but has remained virtually unknown.

(22) Letter from Langlois to Thilorier, *Archives Sarrasin*, Basel, Volume XXXIII, shelf-mark 13, folio 1, v°.

(23) Treasurer of the Republic of Basel.

(24) Letter from Wieland to an Infantry Colonel of the same surname, written from Saarwerden, in: supplement to issue 27 of the *Journal de Paris*, Monday 27th January 1783. This letter is as little known as Sarrasin's letter to Straub is famous.

(25) Cf. *Letter from Bürkli* in Funk, op. cit., p. 17.

(26) '...who would tell anyone who would listen about the miracles that Cagliostro had performed, and would present himself as living proof of them, having been miraculously cured by him of goodness knows how many diseases, the names of which alone were enough to make your hair stand on end', Beugnot, *Mémoires*.

(27) Note that the patient's condition improved as soon as the Cardinal told Cagliostro about him and deteriorated as soon as Cagliostro said that he would no longer be bothering with him and wanted to leave, cf. *Mémoire pour le comte Cagliostro contre le Procureur général*, 1786, p. 31.

(28) De Saint-Félix, *Aventures de Cagliostro*, Paris 1875, p. 99 (according to the *Correspondance de Grimm*).

(29) *Lettre au peuple anglais*, 1787, p. 62.

(30) *Mémoires de Madame d'Oberkirch*, vol. I, chapter VII, p. 9.

(31) The reader should note that we have quoted only authentic texts and some testimonies by contemporaries who were often hostile but who were forced to face up to facts. 'No reasonable and impartial person, having spent three months in Strasbourg, can deny that Cagliostro is a man of profound knowledge, however eager he might be *not* to be recognised for any achievement outside the scope of his art', *Letter from Bürkli*, loc. cit., p. 8. 'A number of sudden cures of diseases judged to

be terminal and incurable performed in Switzerland and Strasbourg were attributed to Cagliostro by word of mouth', Georgel, *Mémories*, p. 46. 'Cagliostro is here. He says he has the universal medicine. He has performed some amazing cures and won't take any money for them, saying that he is very rich', Letter from Salzmann to Willermoz, 22nd November 1780, *Collection Bréghot du Lut*. Professor Stark, who was Cagliostro's personal enemy and who deals with him extremely harshly in his *Über Krypto-Catholicismus*, p. 337, was forced to recognise that he surpassed all other 'swindlers' in his remarkable knowledge of psychology, medicine and chemistry. Nor should we see this as a mere fad confined to the people of Strasbourg. Cagliostro performed these extraordinary cures whenever and wherever he wanted, whether in London, Paris or elsewhere. The cure of Ivan Isleniev in St. Petersburg and that of the American in Lyons have passed into legend. In Bordeaux he was so successful that the police had to defend his house against swarms of grateful patients.

(32) He arrived in September 1780 (19th or 27th according to Sarrasin, d'Oberkirch and Salzmann) and stayed for a few days at the Hôtel de l'Esprit, 7 Quai Saint-Thomas. At the time of writing (1912) this house still bears a plaque inscribed: 'Herder and Goethe met here, September 1770'. It was obviously a highly-regarded hotel and a very old one too, part of it dating back to 1306. Until 1785 many associations, almost certainly including the local Freemasons, met in its vast rooms. Cagliostro then went to live for a few weeks in lodgings that Count von Medem, the brother of Countess von der Recke, had previously occupied at the house of a Monsieur Vogt in the little street known as Rue du Marché-aux-Vins (German: Alte Weinmarktstrasse), at no. 86 (no. 25 since 1785). This house, which adjoined the church of Saint-Pierre-le-Vieux, belonged to the maidservant of the Canon of the church. Even at this time the door of this small house was besieged by crowds of patients (Spach, Works, vol. V, p. 69). This was the reason for him having to move. He then rented a large apartment near the Place d'Armes (later Place Kléber). This was a town-house with high windows and extensive balconies which was long known as the 'House of the Blessed Virgin' because of the large statue of Her that decorated one corner of it. At the time of writing a bakery, with the sign of the Blessed Virgin hanging outside, occupies the ground floor, while the building forms 1 Rue des Veaux (German: Kalbsgasse). In 1782 it was 6 Rue des Écrivains (German: Schreiberstubgasse). It's also said that Cagliostro had a country-house called *Cagliostrano* some way outside the city. This is doubtful, and we can find no trace of it. It could have been the villa of one of his disciples named in honour of the Master, which would explain the confusion. Cf. Weisstein. *Letter from Blessig*, loc. cit., p. 7, Spach, *Strasbourg historique*, p. 69, Ad. Seyboth, *Der alte Strassburg*, Heitz, Strasbourg, p. 236, I.

(33) *Letter from Blessig* in Weisstein, loc. cit., p. 8. *Letter from Bürkli* in Funk, loc. cit., p. 9.

(34) *Letter from Blessig* in Weisstein, loc. cit., p. 10. Madame d'Oberkirch, Abbé Georgel, Lavater, De Gleichen, etc., have all left similar descriptions of him.

(35) Or Deslort, cf. Letter from Ammeister Lemp to the Royal Praetor, Manuscripts of the Library of Strasbourg, Bundle AA, 2110 and Hermann, *Notices historique sur Strasbourg*, Strasbourg, 1819, 2 vol.

(36) The *Intendant* Chaumont de la Galaizière.

(37) Cf. Madame d'Oberkirch, *Mémoires*, vol. I, chapter VII, p. 8, *Letter from Blessig* in Weisstein, loc. cit., pp. 8 & 11 and Funk, *Letter from Blessig*, loc. cit., p. 5.

(38) This is what the Swiss Bürkli reports in terms that are uncalled-for to say the very least: 'Madame Sarrasin played the principal role in this farce', loc. cit., pp. 9-10.

(39) Cagliostro was actually reproached for it! Bürkli (loc. cit., p. 9) writes: 'Madame de la Salle and Madame de la Galaizière held receptions only twice a week, whereas Countess Cagliostro had to hold one every day. With the other ladies people stayed for about half an hour, but in the case of the Countess they were there from 5 o'clock till 8 o'clock in the evening!' Poor woman! But instead of feeling sorry for her and admiring this self-sacrifice to help her husband in his work this self-denial is seen as a mark of vanity. There was yet another difference in the different salons that Bürkli omitted to mention in his comparison: whereas the receptions by the other two ladies, as in any worldly salon, were mere breeding-grounds for scandals, elegant mischief and intrigue, in the salon of Countess Cagliostro the talk was entirely about sufferings to be relieved, philanthropy and genuine acts of charity.

(40) *Lettre d'un Suisse* in Spach, Works, vol. V., p. 80 dated 1st April 1782.
(41) In Strasbourg, Paris and everywhere else Cagliostro showed his wife great tenderness and attended to her every need. He always insisted that his wife be received along with him if he was invited to people's homes. People's attitudes and their attacks on him often barely concealed impertinence, insinuation and innuendo aimed at the Countess, which angered him greatly.
(42) *Letter from Blessig* in Weisstein, loc. cit., p. 10. The author notes how much this contributed to a tendency on the part of those who had only seen Cagliostro under one or other of these aspects to judge him in widely varying, contradictory and incorrect ways, cf. idem., ibid., p. 5.
(43) 'He could always spot an atheist: their presence alone, without them even saying anything, was enough to cause him to feel 'quite distinctive shivers down his spine', as he used to say quite openly to those who questioned him about it', *Lettre de Mirabeau sur Cagliostro*, 1786, p. 17.
(44) Cagliostro, when speaking, almost always referred to himself in the third person, Spach, loc. cit., p. 75.
(45) *Lettre d'un Suisse* dated 27th October 1781, in Spach, loc. cit., p. 75.
(46) Cf. Spach, Works, vol. V, p. 75. The theologian Blessig reproached him for being over-optimistic in his prognoses, but as his promises were always fulfilled then criticism was uncalled-for. Dr. Martius quotes a good example: 'Cagliostro gave some medicine to a non-commissioned officer who had consulted him and assured him that he would be well again in fifteen days. He actually invited him to come and dine with him to celebrate the cure – and that's exactly what happened', cf. Dr. Martius, *Erinnerungen aus meinem...*, Leipzig, 1847, p. 74.
(47) *Letter from Blessig* in Weisstein, loc. cit., p. 7, quotes these words without really understanding them.
(48) He said this, sometimes in a quite brutal tone of voice, to people such as Cardinal de Rohan and Lavater, cf. Spach, loc. cit., p. 71 and Meiners, Letter, in *Lettre du comte Mirabeau sur Cagliostro*, 1786, p. 17.
(49) d'Oberkirch, *Mémoires*, vol. I, chapter VII, p. 2. 'He was simultaneously ice and flame'.
(50) *Letter from Bürkli* in Funk, loc. cit., p. 11.
(51) 'I was astonished by his answers', said a visitor who had been very prejudiced against him, 'and found him to be not just a competent doctor but an astute philosopher, a true judge of men and a fine physiognomist as well...', *Letter from Bürkli* in Funk, loc. cit., p. 15.
(52) He used to say that this was in Medina and that it had *very few pupils*. From there he had crossed the Red Sea and Egypt to reach Europe. He had taken a vow, like all those of his brotherhood, to travel for the good of humanity and to distribute freely whatever he had himself freely received, cf. *Letter from Blessig* in Weisstein, loc. cit., p. 6. The meaning of this statement will be clear to all those who have studied occult symbolism even a little: even the name Medina is significant. All these statements point to membership of the Rosicrucian Brotherhood.
(53) Cf. Spach, Works, vol. V, p. 70.
(54) This is the *Solve et Coagula* of the alchemists, cf. *Letter from Blessig* in Weisstein, loc. cit., pp. 5-6.
(55) 'Cagliostro said that a Freemason who needs a doctor when he is sick is not a Freemason at all, claiming that Masonic science is closely related to the art of healing', Letter from Salzmann to Willermoz written on 1st June 1781 after a visit to Cagliostro, *Collection Bréghot du Lut*.
(56) 'Cagliostro had posters printed to tell people when his audiences would be held', Letter from Salzmann to Willermoz, 1st June 1781, *Collection Bréghot du Lut*.
(57) *Letter from Blessig* in Weisstein, loc. cit., p 7.
(58) A man called Jaquaut, a former clerk in an auction-house, was the first of such aides. Cagliostro had several others, 'whom he paid extremely well' but whose names remain unknown to us. Sachi (see later in this Chapter) also fulfilled this role, cf. *Letter from Bürkli* in Funk, loc. cit., p. 12.
(59) Cf. *Letter from Bürkli* in Funk, loc. cit., p. 12.
(60) Cf. *Letter from Bürkli* in Funk, loc. cit., p. 15.
(61) Laborde, *Lettres sur la Suisse*, Geneva, 1783, 2 vol. In the letters recommending Cagliostro from

Monsieur de Vergennes and Cardinal de Rohan we find the same praise and same testimonies of the enormous number of patients who passed through his treatment-room and were healed by him, cf. *Lettre à Madame de Créqui, Brevet de De Vergennes*, in d'Alméras, loc. cit., pp. 200-201. Also, Letter to the Royal Praetor in: Manuscripts of Strasbourg, Bundle AA, 2110, document VII.

(62) *Letter from Bürkli* in Funk, loc. cit., pp. 19-20, Dr. Ostertag, *Mémoires*, p. 49, Library of Strasbourg, Bundle AA, 2110, *Oberrheinische Mannigfaltigkeiten*, 1781, 1st quarter, p. 114, Letter from Görge.

(63) *Letter from Bürkli* in Funk, loc. cit., pp. 16-17, D'Oberkirch, *Mémoires*, vol. I. chapter VII, p. 1. Madame de la Motte repeated all this in her *Réponse au mémoire du comte de Cagliostro*, Paris, 1786, pp. 21 et seq.

(64) *Letter from Blessig* in Weisstein, loc. cit, p. 9. Cf. also Spach, Works, vol. V, p. 70.

(65) Dr. E. W. Martius, former pharmacist to the Court and the University of Erlangen has left us some interesting comments on this subject in his *Mémoires*: 'Cagliostro had deposited several of his prescriptions at the pharmacy where I was working (the *Pharmacie Hecht*) and I had to make them up. These medicines, to which Cagliostro had given some very high-flown and expressive (*sehr viel versprechende*) names, were drawn from the General Pharmacopoeia, e.g. purgative herbal teas and pills, stomachic elixirs, a pectoral electuary and an ointment for the face'. The most original formula was for the *Oleum sacchari* which is similar to some Hermetic preparations. These recipes will be found in the Appendix to this book. Dr. Martius, like many people of his time, testifies to Cagliostro's great scientific knowledge, especially of chemistry, in two other passages, cf. Dr. E.W. Martius, *Erinnerungen aus meinem neunzigjährigen Leben*, Leipzig, Voss, 1847, pp. 74 et seq. Dr. Ostertag, in his memoirs, gives the complex formula for one of Cagliostro's fortifying powder with a special action on the uterus, which he claims to have obtained from a trustworthy source but which has a less certain origin. Cf. the Appendix to this book.

(66) A so-called *consolidante*, cf. Chapter III.

(67) Ostertag, *Mémoires*, p 49: 'His Balsam of Wine of Egypt cures everything'. It was administered in drops. Laborde, in his *Lettres de Suisse*, also refers to it enthusiastically. Cf. also Manuel, *Lettre d'un garde du roi*, p. 34.

(68) Cf. pages 63 & 77. We have indicated that Cagliostro used it only very occasionally. Even in Strasbourg he never resorted to magnetic healing. Dr. Martius, an expert on the subject as he was attending the experiments of Puységur who was in Strasbourg at that time, stated that Cagliostro did not get involved in animal magnetism, cf. Dr. Martius, loc. cit., pp. 74 et seq.

(69) The last phrase of his 'Warning' is quite telling for those who know how to read between the lines: he repudiates the yellow drops manufactured by Sachi in imitation of his own, 'as well as all those that might be administered by persons *other than him*', Cf. p. 56.

(70) 'It's the master-stroke, the secret that I keep within my breast', he said one day to a lady who held him in genuine esteem and to whom he had just explained many things… but, unfortunately, not *that* thing, *Letter from Blessig* in Weisstein, loc. cit., p. 5.

(71) *Rituel de la Maçonnerie Égyptienne*, Reception of an Entered Apprentice, Mss. Papus, page 5.

(72) *Letter from Blessig* in Weisstein, loc. cit., p. 7.

(73) *Letter from Blessig* in Weisstein, loc. cit., p. 3. Following some sensational cures he had many patients from amongst the officer-class, cf. Dr. Martius, loc. cit., p 74 et seq.

(74) *Letter from Blessig* in Weisstein, loc. cit. p. 14. Cf. also Letter from Labarthe to Séguier in Funck-Brentano, *L'Affaire du Collier*, p. 90 and D'Oberkirch, *Mémoires*, vol. 1. , chapter VII, p. 2.

(75) De Gleichen, *Mémoires*, Paris, 1868, p. 136.

(76) *Letter from Bürkli* in Funk, loc. cit. p. 7.

(77) *Letter from Blessig* in Weisstein, loc. cit., pp. 7 & 9.

(78) Often he would drowse, for just a few hours at a time, in an armchair. Cf. Chapter II of this book, 'Portrait'.

(79) This request, supported by a letter from Cardinal de Rohan dated 17th July 1781, will be found in the Library of Strasbourg, Manuscripts, Bundle AA, 2110.

(80) *Letter from Blessig* in Funk, loc. cit., p. 8.
(81) *Mémoire pour le sieur d'Ostertag...* 56 pp., Levrault (printer), Strasbourg, 1781 (stated at the end). Library of Strasbourg, Manuscripts, Bundle AA, 2110. It is from this report, which is hostile to Cagliostro, that we have extracted our summary of the affair.
(82) Did Ostertag write a prescription or not? He insists that he did, explaining why it was made orally (because no pen and paper were available). He says that he prescribed half a scruple of nitre in some veal broth. The precise medical treatment was obviously of no great interest, but Ostertag's statement is really quite incredible: it seems impossible to believe that, after consultations with three doctors, no written prescription was furnished and that a regime of half a scruple was prescribed simply by word of mouth.
(83) *Mémoire d'Ostertag*, p. 25.
(84) The curé's account of the matter differs in some minor but extremely interesting details from that of Dr. Ostertag, but it remains fundamentally the same, and in it the respective roles of Ostertag and Cagliostro are truthfully restored.
(85) The 56-page report appeared at this time.
(86) From the Professor's report we will quote these lapidary phrases: 'The patient no longer had a fever because the uterine pains had ceased and fever is always and solely connected with the contractions of the womb' (p. 31). 'The child was not dead because there was no foetidness or haemorrhage there and the woman did not experience any exceptional movements in her stomach' (p. 32). 'Childbirth is a purely mechanical operation and always proceeds without need for intervention, assuming a normal pelvis, if the baby presents head-first, but never proceeds if the baby presents otherwise' (pp. 38 & 39). Finally, this one to finish with: 'If Count Cagliostro believes that a drug can cause uterine contractions then it doesn't say much for his medical knowledge' (p. 36). Cagliostro certainly did believe that, and he believed it because it's true. Perhaps he made use of that knowledge. In any case Ostertag did not know this and, what's more, any doctor would agree that he made a complete mess of what he had to do in terms both of the knowledge he displayed and the duties of his profession. This is undoubtedly why Cagliostro, who was usually utterly indifferent to any attacks made by his detractors, reacted with such energy and severity towards Ostertag.
(87) The 'Chamber of Fifteen' (German: *Fünfzehnmeister*), one of the city's three advisory councils. The duty of this Chamber was to uphold the Constitution. Cf. E. Müller, *Le magistrat de la ville de Strasbourg*, Strasbourg, Solomon, 1882.
(88) Session of Monday 16th July 1781. A report of this official disapproval was inserted, at the request of a friend of Cagliostro, in the *Varieties Haut-Rhinoises* of 27th July 1781, p. 196.
(89) Letter from Cardinal de Rohan to the Royal Praetor of July 17th 1781, Library of Strasbourg, Manuscripts, Bundle AA, 2110, II.
(90) The Royal Praetor also wrote a letter to Monsieur Barbier de Tinan assuring him officially that 'all the members of the *Magistrat* (which is how the *Chambre des Quinze* styled itself) are far from being in agreement with the picture of Count Cagliostro that the document in question seeks to propagate', 27th July 1781, Library of Strasbourg, Bundle AA, 2110, document VII.
(91) D'Oberkirch, *Mémoires*, vol. I, chapter VII, p. 4. Cf. also *Ein paar Tröpflein...*, p. 2.
(92) Letter from Ammeister Lemp to the Royal Praetor, 7th August 1781, Library of Strasbourg, Manuscripts, Bundle AA, 2110, document XI, p. 1. The word *Ammeister* is untranslatable: the post blended supervisory and executive functions. Cf. E. Müller. *Le magistrat de la ville de Strasbourg*, Strasbourg, Solomon, 1882.
(93) De Narbonne may even have been a professional duellist who'd been given the task of starting a fatal quarrel with Cagliostro by people who wanted to get rid of him. Cagliostro's remarks to him that evening seem to confirm this.
(94) Lemp, Letter cited, folio 1 r°. *Lettre d'un Suisse*, in Spach, Works, vol. V, p. 76.
(95) Spach, ibid., *Lettre d'un Suisse*, 27th October 1781, p. 76.
(96) One night the following offensive poster was pasted up in the busiest parts of all the districts of the city:

Le comte Cagliostro.

Marchand d'orviétan en Malte, y étant arrivé en habit turque, charlatan à Toulouse et Rennes, fourbe et imposteur en Russie, menteur et aventurier à Strasbourg, impertinent et jean-foutre à Saverne.
Sera regardé partout de même.
5 août 1781.

i.e.

Count Cagliostro.

A snake-oil salesman in Malta, having arrived there in Turkish garb; a charlatan in Toulouse and Rennes; a cheat and impostor in Russia; a liar and adventurer in Strasbourg; an impertinent fellow and a scoundrel in Saverne.
Wherever he goes in the world he will be seen in the exactly same light.
5th August 1781.

A second followed, which was posted on the doors of the local inns:

Flachsland le faquin protège Cagliostro le coquin.
7 août 1781.

The wretch Flachsland protects Cagliostro the rascal.
7th August 1781.

These were followed by a third in which Cagliostro and Madame de Terche were odiously insulted.

The police were almost certain that these were the handiwork of the Vicomte de Narbonne. The Maréchal was outraged, and to keep him happy the police went through the motions of finding the culprit, without of course finding anybody, and contenting themselves with tearing down the posters and stifling any rumours. Cf. Letter from Lemp to the Royal Praetor dated 16th August 1781, same bundle, document XII, p. 2, and *Letter from Blessig* in Weisstein, loc. cit., p. 9, which also refer to these shenanigans.

(97) Letter from Barbier de Tinan, Muster-Master to the Royal Praetor, 18th January 1782, Library of Strasbourg, Bundle AA, 2120, III.
(98) Spach, ibid., *Lettre d'un Suisse*, p. 78, of 25th February 1782. Cf. also Letter from Barbier, p. 2.
(99) Letter from Barbier, p. 5.
(100) Sachi repeated these repugnant and wholly untrue stories in his pamphlet. We encounter them again in the *Réponse de Madame de la Motte au comte de Cagliostro*. Paris, 1786, p. 6.
(101) Letter from Barbier, p. 2, Spach, *Lettre d'un Suisse* of 21st January 1782, p. 78. A journalist writing in the *Berliner Monatsschrift* (December 1784) also echoed Sachi's insolence and threats.
(102) Letter from Barbier, p. 3.
(103) Letter from Barbier, p. 4.
(104) Letter from Barbier, p. 4. Poster of January 12th, 1782 in: Bibl. of Strasbourg, bundle AA, 2110, document V.
(105) 'The jealousy of the doctors, who stand together when they are persecuted every bit as much as priests tend to do, pursued him relentlessly everywhere he went. The hatred which was borne towards the Cardinal de Rohan, who had formed a close alliance with Cagliostro, also rebounded onto him. If we combine the calumny of so many definite enemies with the ill-will of the sort of people who in general prefer to believe in and repeat evil rather than good, we shall readily see that it was certainly possible that a stranger who aroused envy rather than pity could be the victim of scandalmongering', De Gleichen, *Souvenirs*, p. 137.
(106) D'Oberkirch, *Mémoires*, vol. I, chapter VII, p. 2.
(107) 'His virtue was only a vice in disguise', *Letter from Bürkli* in Funk, loc. cit., p. 13.
(108) *Letter from Bürkli* in Funk, loc. cit. p. 19.
(109) Madame de la Motte, *Réponse au comte Cagliostro*, Paris 1786, pp. 27 & 37. Cf. also *Letter*

Chapter V

from Bürkli, in Funk, loc. cit., p. 17.
(110) D'Oberkirch, *Mémoires*, vol. I, chapter VII, p. 1 and Letter from Görge, in *Oberrheinische Mannigfaltigkeiten*, 1781. p. 10.
(111) Which we should take to mean: 'He's neglecting Madame Bürkli'. That was his main complaint. Cf. *Letter from Bürkli* in Funk, loc. cit. p. 17.
(112) Faced with hundred of remarkable cures we can find reference to only two patients, abandoned by their doctors, who died in spite of the care that Cagliostro gave them. 'Two of his patients died. Although he had certainly not said that they would certainly be cured, the doctors took advantage of this to blacken his name even more', Letter from Salzmann to Willermoz of 1st June 1782, *Collection Bréghot du Lut*. One of those patients was a Monsieur de Cambis: 'In March 1782, a lieutenant-general, a Monsieur de Cambis, died in Strasbourg abandoned by his doctor, and with good reason, because it was the doctor who was responsible for him being in such a bad way in the first place. Cagliostro saw the patient, but he died nevertheless. This led to vicious abuse of Cagliostro by the patient's regular doctor. I must say in Cagliostro's favour that he reacted with great leniency, as he could well have made some very inconvenient revelations about him but was instead content to send him a certain amount of money to reward him for his generous actions', cf. Spach, Works, vol. V., *Lettre d'un Suisse*, p. 79. It is also not inconceivable that the ill-will of some of his enemies actually helped bring these events about. 'Cagliostro claims that some of his patients who should have recovered were poisoned', Letter from Görge, in *Oberrheinische Mannigfaltigkeiten*, 1781, p. 113 et seq.
(113) Spach accused Cagliostro of 'piling up money only to spend more than he has received', loc. cit., p. 68. What avarice, and what style!
(114) It is true that he sometimes gambled with the ladies *but almost always lost*, Borowski, *Cagliostro...*, p. 102, and Meiners, Letter, in Mirabeau, *Lettre sur Monsieur de Cagliostro et Lavater*, 1786, p. 20.
(115) 'The woman *they say is Cagliostro's* runs up debts and receives presents, only I haven't been able to verify this for myself personally', Letter from Görge in *Oberrheinische Mannigfaltigkeiten*, 1781, pp. 113 et seq. 'His wife? His mistress? God only knows!' Cf. *Letter from Bürkli* in Funk, op. cit., p. 4.
(116) Cited in D'Alméras, *Cagliostro*, p. 228.
(117) Blessig: 'The police certainly had their eye on him. They were spying on him from quite close quarters, but he affected an air of defiance', d'Oberkirch, *Mémoires*, vol. I, chapter VII, p. 1. Cf. also *Lettre au peuple anglais*, 1787, pp. 61-62.
(118) *Lettre au peuple anglais*, 1787, p. 52.
(119) Library of Strasbourg, Manuscripts, Bundle AA, 2110.
(120) Letter from Hans Görge of Colmar in *Oberrheinische Mannigfaltigkeiten*, 16th July 1781, p. 113.
(121) *Ein paar Tröpflein aus dem Brünnen... Am Vorgebürge* (May) 1781 (by J.- J. Bode).
(122) And yet, in return for these idiotic calumnies, what terrible truths he could have used his clairvoyance to reveal! We have already mentioned his generosity towards the doctor who attended Monsieur de Cambis, p. 121.
(123) Letters from Ammeister Lemp to the Royal Praetor, Monsieur de Gérard, of 7th and 16th August 1781, in Bundle AA, 2110, documents V and VI, Manuscripts of the Library of Strasbourg.
(124) This letter appeared in the *Journal de Paris*. There we can read, besides the technical details of Madame Sarrasin's cure, the following testimony: 'To give you all the details, Sir, of the care and attention that Count Cagliostro has bestowed upon her would be superfluous, for like me you are the eyewitness of all the trouble that this great friend of humanity goes to in order to relieve suffering, and because like me you know that the heady wine of flattery for which so many men crave has no attractions for him. To do good for good's sake is his motto, and his heart seeks its reward in its own inherent virtues. To express my gratitude would be beyond me. I simply cannot find the words to express the feelings in my heart...', supplement to no. 365 of the *Journal de Paris* of Monday 31st December 1781.
(125) At this point the author mentions several names which we have already encountered. Pastor J.F.

Cagliostro – The Unknown Master

Oberlin, from the Ban de la Roche, also welcomed Cagliostro to his home for a few days, cf. *Revue Alsac. Illustrée*, 1910, II, p. 55, article by Madame Witz.

(126) *Oberrheinische Mannigfaltigkeiten* dated 6th August 1781, instalment XI of the 1st quarter, Basel, Turneisen *fils*, vol. I, p. 161. This text, like many other invaluable documents relating to Cagliostro in Strasbourg, was obtained for us by our friend Monsieur Alfred Haehl, to whom we wish to publicly extend our gratitude for the considerable assistance he has been to us in our researches.

(127) 'They were held just three times per week (with one day, Friday, being reserved for the poorest patients), and always at specific times. He even refused to receive certain strangers', *Letter from Blessig*, in Weisstein, loc, cit., p. 9. No opportunity was lost to reproach him for this change.

(128) Cf. *Letter from Bürkli*, in Funk, loc. cit., pp. 11-12. 'We live very simply here in any case', Madame Sarrasin wrote to Madame Burckhardt on 19th June 1782. 'Count Cagliostro and his friends are virtually the only people we see, and we find their company very agreeable', *Archives Sarrasin*, Basel, vol. I, shelf-mark 105, folio 2.

(129) 'One might suppose that this man has very extensive plans and that Strasbourg is simply too small a stage for them', *Letter from Blessig*, in Weisstein, loc. cit., p. 10.

CHAPTER VI

—

'THE CHARLATAN'

CAGLIOSTRO IN LYONS

Cagliostro arrived in Lyons on 20th October 1784 [1] and moved into the Hôtel de la Reine [2] run by the Mesdames Forest. He'd been introduced to them by a local merchant called Alquier, whose name we find in the Lodge membership-lists of the time [3]. Indeed, the hotel welcomed many foreign Freemasons as guests. These facts point to the auspices under which Cagliostro first came to Lyons. Cagliostro had been initiated into the English Rite in London in 1777 at *Loge L'Espérance* where, as he later recalled, he had met some remarkable people [4]. He'd thoroughly enjoyed his contact with the lodge and been very happy with the cordial reception he'd received. After living amongst these Masonic friends he'd moved to Holland in 1779 where he'd been received with great honour by the Grand Lodge [5]. In Liège he aroused such interest at the *Parfaite Égalité* lodge that it immediately affiliated to his Egyptian Rite as soon as it became aware of it. In Germany also he visited lodges of all Rites [6]. Sometimes, on his travels, he would ensure that he was recognised by fellow-masons and would speak to them about Masonic matters with such knowledge and authority that they would assume he was the Unknown Grandmaster of Freemasonry [7]. At other times, at lodge meetings in Poland, Courland and Nuremberg, he would take issue with characteristic energy against the superstitious errors of sects that practised Low Magic or taught atheism. During his interrogation in Rome [8] he admitted to these activities, and what he had to say accorded with the facts as the accounts by Countess Von der Recke show. Cagliostro identified as the leaders of those revolutionaries who, under the guise of philanthropy, were working towards a secret political end a Portuguese called Ximenes and someone called Falk. We have not been able to identify Ximenes [9T], but the Falk is question is none other than Samuel Falk, the Ba'al Shem of London, a leading Rabbi and famous magician [10T]. Baron de Gleichen [11], Louis-Claude de Saint Martin and Saint-Martin's follower the Marquise de la Croix all knew him well. The Marquise claimed that, simply by the power of prayer, she'd been able to shatter, at a plenary session of the French Convention, a talisman that Falk had given to the Duc d'Orléans (known as 'Philippe Égalité') and which he wore on his chest, and that when it shattered the Duke immediately turned pale and fainted, an incident much talked about at the time. In Leipzig Cagliostro met the head of the Order of Strict Observance, Scieffort, and attended some of his workings. In Frankfurt-am-Main too he was welcomed to a meeting of the Strict Observance [12].

It's all these encounters and solemn receptions, with each lodge rushing to bestow honours and dignities on the famous and powerful stranger, that have given rise to the story that Cagliostro was initiated in Germany by the Adept Saint-Germain [13]. So tempting was this basic framework that lampoonists and fiction-writers seized upon it to produce heavily-embellished accounts that blend the obscene with the simply ridiculous. We have not been able to establish whether the Comte de Saint-Germain was even alive at this time and, if so, whether he ever met Cagliostro. In any case it matters little to us. What we have had to say about Cagliostro up to this point is, we feel, sufficient to give people a clear enough idea of exactly how we see him. In any case, any meeting between these two men, if it ever took place, would not have been an initiatory experience for either of them: it would certainly not have changed Cagliostro, any more than his reception into the *Loge L'Espérance* or the convent of the Bonfratelli in Palermo did. As for Saint-Germain, he was already a legend, rumoured to be a sorcerer and Grandmaster of all the various occult fraternities with which Germany was riddled. But Cagliostro was known to have passed through all the centres of Masonic influence in Central Europe, and that was enough for yet another new story to be spun which everyone, whether scandalmonger or simple storyteller, then rearranged to their liking.

On his return to Strasbourg Cagliostro was welcomed by the local Freemasons [14]. While he was there he imparted to them some basic principles of his Masonic teachings and left them with fond memories of him. When the Egyptian Rite was subsequently propagated, the members in each city dated the foundation of their Lodge to their personal initiation while Cagliostro was passing through: we can therefore say that the Egyptian Lodge was established in Strasbourg on 8th October 1779 [15]. From there he went to Naples, where he was welcomed at the Lodge of *Perfect Union*, and subsequently to Bordeaux, arriving on 8th November 1783 [16], There he remained for eleven months and became increasingly involved with Freemasonry. We should note that, before his initiation into Freemasonry in London, he saw himself – and indeed, worked – primarily as a healer. As soon as he started visiting lodges however he appeared in a new light. Of course, the Freemasons he met were struck as everyone was by his therapeutic gifts, but their greater inquisitiveness and open-mindedness meant that they were not content with a superficial view of this mysterious man. They fired questions at him, pressed him, and gradually drew him out of his shell of secrecy. In Bordeaux, while also helping him with his ambitions to practice medicine there [17], they gathered around him, issued constant invitations, and sought his assistance in bringing enlightenment to the Lodges which were such an important part of that city [18]. Cagliostro was able to relax and become more open amongst these courageous and tolerant men of good will, who sought the truth through tests and trials, somewhat maladroitly perhaps, but with all their might.

It was while he was in Bordeaux that Cagliostro had a strange vision that confirmed him in his resolve to develop Egyptian Freemasonry. He saw two people grab him by the neck and drag him off to a deep underground chamber. There a door opened and, passing through, he found himself in a most delightful and magnificently-illuminated room, which he compared to the salon of a royal palace. A great festival was being celebrated there. All those present were clad in white gowns which reached right down to their heels. Amongst them he recognised, as he later told his circle of Freemasons, several of his Sons in Freemasonry who had passed on. He felt he had been delivered from the evils of this world and that he had arrived in Paradise. He himself was given a long gown and a sword similar to the one that Abaddon the Destroyer traditionally holds [19T]. He walked on and, dazzled by a great light, threw himself on the ground and rendered homage to the Supreme Being for having enabled him to have achieved happiness. But then he heard an unknown voice say: 'This shall be your reward, but you still have work to do'. And there the vision ended [20].

Cagliostro had acquired a better knowledge and understanding of the various European nations than probably any diplomat or intellectual of the time. In his travels he'd lived in all sorts of environments, sometimes at the courts of kings and princes, sometimes rubbing shoulders with scientists, mystics and literary men, at other times with the common people, even in inns and taverns or in the attics of the poor, or assailed in his own home by strangers. In the process he became privy to many secret scandals and a confidential adviser to more than one important dignitary. In the process he had heard the rusty wheels of the machine of the Ancien Régime squeaking and rattling, and had seen how worn-out many of its individual parts had become and how close they were to complete collapse, however impressive they might look from the outside. The dismal state of France on the eve of the Revolution has been recounted too many times for us to have to recapitulate the decadence and decline of the nobility, clergy and upper middle class, and the mediocrity of literature and the arts. Paris was full of embittered satirists, blackmailers and finaglers while, a world apart, the common people were ignorant and starving. Everything was worn out, lacking in faith, devoid of energy, and dying of complacency and selfishness [21].

Everywhere in his wanderings through these largely somnolent cities, which were destined for a terrible awakening, whether it was Paris or St. Petersburg, Cagliostro encountered in the Masonic lodges, alongside an admittedly uneven clarity of vision regarding the goals to which they aspired, the same desire for truth, knowledge and justice and the same youthful aspirations that made Freemasonry the only viable organisation of its time, for European Freemasonry, still very much in its infancy and utterly obscure between 1717 and 1740, had advanced by leaps and bounds between 1773 and 1775.

In France the English Grand Lodge controlled almost all the lodges, but the Grand Orient, founded in 1775 by the merger of the *Loge Lacorne*, which had split from the English Rite, and the *Chevaliers d'Orient* (Chapter of Clermont), controlled the rest. This power-struggle had led to a blossoming of isolated Rites such as those of the *Illuminés* of Avignon [22], the *Philalèthes* [23], the *Elect Cohens* and others. In 1776 there were some 300 French lodges. In 1789 there were 629. All these lodges, where noblemen, priests and the petty bourgeoisie met on equal terms, were hives of activity despite disagreements over precedence, affiliation or outward forms. 'At a time when the form of government was an absolute monarchy, when the State was divided into quite distinct classes, when the advantages of birth were enshrined in law (even if they were starting to lose standing in everyday life), when inequality in circumstances and responsibilities formed part of the social contract, when the fanaticism of the priests could arm itself with the weapons of the supposedly secular power, the fact that there were 700 lodges on French soil where the bravest and most illustrious men of our time repeated each day the lessons of freedom, equality, fraternity and religious tolerance will help you understand the extent to which Freemasonry, while remaining largely theoretical, was able to assist in the great social changes that were suddenly afoot, and of which the first tremors were already being felt' [24]. In Paris it was in the Masonic temples that the new school of philosophers, literary men, artists and politicians coordinated their efforts: the *Encyclopédie*, which had been in preparation since 1740 when the Duc d'Antin was Grandmaster [25], had now finally appeared in 28 folio volumes, with five volumes of supplements, a colossal undertaking on which, under the direction of Diderot, a whole galaxy of scholars and savants had collaborated.

Apart from Paris the leading centres of French Freemasonry were Bordeaux, Lyons and Strasbourg. In Bordeaux the first lodge had been founded in 1723 and was the first of many. In 1783 the two leading lodges were the *Loge française* and *L'Amitié*, both of which had been visited and chaired in 1776 by the Grandmaster the Duc de Chartres, the future Duc d'Orléans. Martinez de Pasqually and Louis-Claude de Saint-Martin had also left memories and followers behind them in Bordeaux. In Lyons, thanks to the influence and inspiration of

Willermoz, lodges and chapters were flourishing. Strasbourg, as a staging-post on the way to Eastern Europe as well as an intellectual powerhouse, had enjoyed a close relationship with all the Masonic centres of Europe since 1742. Marseilles, Dunkirk and Arras also had their lodges, but there were of lesser importance.

We have already discussed the lodges in Russia and Courland and the work that they carried out [26]. In Poland Freemasonry had initially been tolerated but had then been prohibited by Augustus II the Strong. Despite the ban, it remained extremely vibrant as an underground organisation and re-emerged in 1780 when the Grand Orient was founded in Warsaw [27]. In Austria Emperor Joseph II himself – 'that bold and innovative ruler' – had been initiated into Freemasonry by Baron von Born. In Holland the Grand Lodge, directed since 1757 by Charles de Boetzelaer, was on terms of friendship and equality with the Grand Orient of France. In the part of Europe that is now Belgium there were 29 lodges. In Maastricht the lodge *La Constance* had been founded in 1761. In Switzerland Freemasonry was prohibited only in Bern. Everywhere therefore the Masonic idea was blossoming. In Prussia the Freemasons were protected by a king of a philosophical cast of mind, who had himself been initiated in Brunswick by Major Bielefeld [28]. Freemasonry had become well established in Berlin, and one of its lodges worked alternately in French and German. Freemasons could be found in all the major cities, including Hamburg and Prague. The hereditary Prince of Bayreuth had opened up his palace to Masonic meetings, and Dresden had a special Rite of its own. Baron von Hund, along with Kittlitz, had founded a Lodge for his Reformed Templar system; the Prince of Gotha gave asylum to Weishaupt; and Augustus of Saxony, the Prince of Neuwied and even the Coadjutor Bishop of the ecclesiastical principalities on the banks of the Rhine all showed enthusiasm for the mysterious doctrines of Freemasonry. In some areas – such as the Palatinate and Bavaria – there was persecution, the local political reactionaries seeking to dampen the enthusiasm of the free spirits, but the only effect of this was to spur the Freemasons on to further efforts. New Rites emerged, some mystical, some political. The power-hungry and the sectarian were also very much in evidence. Germany was truly the 'the natural home of Illuminism' [29].

It was around this time in particular that we see new orders being born, many of which included with higher degrees. They seemed to just spring out of the ground, and their motives were sometimes hard to fathom: the *Aufklärer* of Nicolai, the *Illuminés* of Pernety [30], the Rites of Schröpfer, Schröder, von Hund, Marschall, Weishaupt, Scieffort, Zinnendorf [31] and others suddenly appeared, causing trouble and arousing enmity. People of faith wondered where the truth was actually to be found, which school of thought would produce a new ethics and a new science, and which individual would prove to be the source of the illumination they had so long awaited.

Such therefore was the speed and vigour of Freemasonry's expansion. According to official statistics published at the beginning of the 19th century there were 137,675 active lodges in the whole world, comprising 21,300,000 masons. It might be argued that the order had developed too fast to be effectively directed and controlled by a central authority and that many schisms had developed as a result, but if lodges sometimes concerned themselves unnecessarily with trivial matters of form which they struggled to resolve, then underneath it all they were united by the same feeling of brotherhood. Only one thing was missing: a spiritual direction. In formulating its goal Freemasonry was indeed turning its back on its origins. Pulled leftwards by the Grand Orient, which was chiefly interested in intellectual and political reforms, and rightwards by the intrigues of the Jesuits, and not knowing in general what was in its own archives or what its symbols meant or which rough ashlar it should be working with [32], Freemasonry possessed great power but was only able to use it intermittently and, even then, solely out of a need to find an outlet for the strength in which it abounded.

In the midst of all these rivalries and uncertainties the more conciliatory went to great lengths to organise so-called *convents* or general assemblies in an attempt to group together and perhaps unify sects with diverse tendencies; to try to find out who actually directed Freemasonry and according to what principles; and, if such men and such principles did not in fact exist, which men would be worthy of being entrusted with such a task, and what ideal should form the spiritual goal of this universal order [33]. Despite the best intentions of those behind all these efforts, however, they remained sterile. After each general assembly Freemasonry remained just as disorientated and confused as it had been before.

Cagliostro's goal was to infuse the Christian spirit and a desire for wisdom and truth into this young and dynamic organisation that was destined to achieve such great things in the world. To achieve that he had to acquire control over the whole of the organisation, snatch it from the jaws of all the various human intrigues that were besetting it, and steer it towards the light. This was certainly a programme that he had pondered on several occasions before he arrived in Lyons. The fact that a man like Cagliostro, independent and individualistic as he was, had decided to become a Freemason in the first place, and the trouble to which he had gone to maintain relationships with the various lodges he had encountered in his travels, are proof enough that his project had been slowly gestating for some time, but it was to be in Lyons that his work as a Freemason was finally to blossom.

Certainly everything conspired to keep him there, as there was no town in France that was a better match for him. The spirit of the Lyonnais is a strange mixture. Behind the forbidding doors of its ancient houses, in the dark hallways and corridors and behind their narrow windows there lies concealed a profound mysticism that has survived all revolutions, all upheavals, for man's interior life seems to develop more quickly and more surely in those cities where mists and a glowering sky encourage him to leave the public places and hide away by the fireside, reading, meditating, praying. The Lyonnais keeps this inner life very much to himself: whether out of prudence, timidity or a simple respect for his beliefs or knowledge, he hides his psychic side beneath as forbidding an exterior as that of his house. Only after long scrutiny will he admit a stranger, and even to a fellow Lyonnais he will not reveal all his secrets or intimate feelings, even if he stands or works alongside those same people every day of his life, except perhaps after many years of reserve and dissemblance.

It is true that, once that stage is reached, friendship will blossom into a form of mutual devotion, and conversation will acquire a depth of sincerity that will cause each of them to rapidly forget the cold austerity of the early phases of their relationship. By nature of course a mystic is inclined to piously conserve his revelations and his graces, but in Lyons, more than anywhere else, that reserve is taken to extremes, and if you are fortunate enough to eventually pierce the veil of some of the social milieux of this great city then, even in our own times, you'll often be astonished to find that some humble artisan or clerk or shop-assistant, someone with simple ways and a self-effacing personality, someone who's only ever spoken to you to sell you some coal or give you a receipt for your rent, is actually someone with the most wonderful mystical propensities or depth of learning.

In a Lyonnais, cautiousness is in the blood. If he's a mystic by temperament then he also has pragmatism in his genes. He no more wants to be taken for a ride in his metaphysical speculations than he does in his business dealings, and that is the hallmark of his mysticism. He is not easily enthused: he needs evidence, facts. He will carefully observe a system or a person and will judge them fairly according to their tendencies, but he won't follow them unless they can offer him some tangible benefits. There's no falling in love with an idea at first sight, no response on the basis of first impressions; on the contrary, there is only mistrust. But if he encounters a new moral theory or the person who thought it up, whether it was today or ten days or ten years ago, whether the man or the idea is on the political right or the political left, then as long as they've benefited him in some way, by increasing the joys of his family-life perhaps, or helping his peace of mind or his health or his business, then he will become his disciple, and a more loyal and devoted disciple no one could wish for. Neither logical argument nor ridicule will ever shake his loyalty, and his enthusiasm, which more fickle minds might have had in abundance at the outset only to lose it thereafter will, in the Lyonnais, grow slowly but unceasingly.

It was amongst such people, at once mystical and practical, that Count Cagliostro found himself in 1784, basking in the fame of all the miracles that he had performed in Strasbourg [34] as well as the reputation of a man that even the most powerful in society welcomed and respected, and with all the prestige of a Grandmaster of Freemasonry.

In Lyons, as everywhere else, Freemasonry was in ferment [35]. The higher degrees were certainly a subject for discussion, but the locals were much less interested in arguments about precedence than they were in theurgy. The ideas of Martinèz de Pasqually (of whom Willermoz was a follower), Mesmer and Swedenborg were fighting for their attention. This was the time when Louis-Claude de Saint-Martin and the Abbé Fournié were working in Lyons, and when the works of the former, known as the *Philosophe Inconnu*, the Unknown Philosopher, were being published. The advertisements in Péricaud's *Éphémérides lyonnaises* which were published in Lyons at that time also include a considerable number of works on animal magnetism [36].

The local Freemasons were especially enthusiastic about these studies. When the lodges of Bordeaux and Strasbourg announced that Cagliostro would be arriving at the Hôtel de la Reine there was a mad rush to see him. Visits were paid, he was invited to lodges, celebrations were organised in his honour, and his wife was showered with presents [37]. Questions were put to him and his lectures carefully listened to, but the Lyonnais retained their characteristic caution.

But not for long: although he'd initially refused to accept any patients, wanting to make philanthropy rather than medicine his focal-point in Lyons, his hand was suddenly forced. A rich proprietor, a Monsieur J.-B. Delorme, known locally as 'the American', had been struck down with a terminal illness. In despair his doctor, Dr. de la Bruyère, persuaded his family to entrust him to Cagliostro. Thanks to some secret powder, as Péricaud tells us [38], the 'quack' cured him. Other cures followed. Then there were some miracles of clairvoyance, for Cagliostro could read people's hearts as well. In some of his experiments certain local children, awake and fully conscious, became 'lucid subjects' in response to his commands. They claimed to be able to actually see the beings about which Cagliostro spoke, and they testified to the respect that these spirits had for the Master. The cures, the useful advice, the secret knowledge – all were now common knowledge in the city. The facts were there, and no scrap of doubt remained: Cagliostro had conquered Lyons.

People begged him to continue with his work and to train some disciples. He agreed, and with twelve Freemasons selected from amongst the best-known members of the lodges *Parfait Silence* and *La Sagesse* he founded at the latter's premises [39] a new lodge which he called *La Sagesse triomphante*. Initially the aim of the lodge was to enable Cagliostro to speak privately to certain carefully-selected people and to have somewhere discreet and secluded where he could develop their abilities and demonstrate the reality and extent of his powers. But in this new lodge, though only just founded, in this melting-pot of enthusiasm, the miracles followed one after the other.

New treatments, lectures on every conceivable subject but especially the divine sciences [40] and experiments with 'doves' constituted the theoretical and practical work of all the lodge-meetings. Sometimes the phenomena became more widely manifested and more intense: on such occasions all those attending perceived them directly instead of through intermediaries. These events long remained in the memories of the Lyonnais [41].

The value and clarity of the revelations were remarkable. Take the story of the Duc de Richelieu, for example, who'd gone to see Cagliostro in disguise. Cagliostro 'showed him in a mirror everything that he already was and everything that he would become' [42]. Another of Cagliostro's prophecies became famous largely due to its prompt realisation. 'I predicted', he said in Rome, 'that just as amongst the twelve apostles there was one who would betray Jesus Christ, so there would be amongst the Freemasons someone who would betray the Order. They said that it could not possibly happen, but I repeated the prediction to them on two further occasions, adding that this traitor would be punished by the hand of God'. This prediction related to a certain Monsieur Finguerlin, a businessman who betrayed his vows, turned his back on Cagliostro and subsequently attacked him. On 30th December 1785, after Cagliostro had left Lyons, he lost his entire personal fortune when someone called Thévenet broke into his premises one night and stole 403,653 *livres*. Finguerlin was left penniless' [43].

But Cagliostro's popularity was raised to its apogee by the following marvellous event. Monsieur Prost de Royer, a former alderman of Lyons and Venerable Master of the lodge *La Bienfaisance*, had died on 21st September 1784. His lodge celebrated a service 'for the repose of his soul' on Wednesday 24th November 1784 at the church of the Recollects, a reformed branch of the Franciscans. Memories of him were still vivid in many people's minds, especially members of the lodge *La Sagesse triomphante*. Cagliostro, in conversation with his disciples, had often taught them that the light preserves a reflection of every being that has passed on, and that the spirit can – in exceptional circumstances and by the grace of God – perceive these images. This is what tradition has always taught, what certain people have affirmed, and what modern science has at last begun to study [44]. Cagliostro was often pressed by his disciples to provide evidence of this, and one day, during a secret session of his Lodge, he was able to oblige: the 'shade' of Prost de Royer suddenly appeared, clearly recognisable, before the eyes of his former friends [45]. This fact is indisputable: it was witnessed and certified by a large number of men worthy of our complete trust. Péricaud, who was one of the people to report it, heard it from the lips of some of his contemporaries who had witnessed these wonders. We also know about the dazzling apparitions associated with the dedication of the Temple of Les Brotteaux. We shall discuss these later in this chapter.

These two events – the inauguration of the lodge *La Sagesse* and the dedication of the temple at Les Brotteaux – were more than a year apart, and not a day passed it would seem without some new demonstration of Cagliostro's power to further increase his celebrity and revitalise the zeal of his disciples. Unfortunately no official reports or correspondence have survived to tell us about this extraordinary work [46].

We can well imagine how keen Cagliostro's disciples were to persuade him to stay with them in Lyons. Cagliostro was exactly what they had been looking for, someone they'd dared not hope to meet: he alone could teach them perfect doctrines, he alone could regenerate Freemasonry, ensure salvation, and achieve restoration of the world. They begged him to codify his teaching, to give to all those whom he judged worthy of receiving them a dogma, a ritual and a temple so that they could think, pray and act with him under his personal direction. What is more, it seemed disrespectful to hold meetings in his presence in a room that was used by other Lodges which were so different to his. Cagliostro accepted their invitation with gratitude. He promised that the resulting temple would have a consecration without equal, that he would give him the titles and powers of Mother-Lodge of the Egyptian Rite, and that he would entrust to his 'dear sons', in Ritual format, an account of the only pure Masonic doctrines. A subscription was organised to which many donated, all of them undertaking to make regular payments at various intervals. When the required sum had been raised a start was made at the material level with the initial building-works. The place chosen for the Temple was a secluded, almost rural spot in the district of Les Brotteaux, which had just been connected with Lyons by the Pont Morand.

Around the same time Cagliostro shared with some of his disciples his preliminary drafts of his Rite of Egyptian Freemasonry. Much nonsense has been talked about this Rite. The legal procedures launched by the Inquisition, who were able to examine these notebooks, have spread the legend that the Rite was just a copy of some manuscripts that Cagliostro had bought in England from someone called Cofton or Coston, and that the original of the Rite, signed G. Coston, was found in his papers during his arrest. There is no evidence to support this allegation. They also alleged that in Cagliostro's storage-boxes they had found magical objects, including a statuette of Isis, Apis bulls, talismans and so on. In their diatribe the Inquisitors exploited these finds to show how deeply immersed he must have been in black magic, and what an abomination his Egyptian Rite must therefore be. But do these statues really prove that Cagliostro was Egyptian, or that he worshipped Hermanubis? All this bric-à-brac, if it ever existed, was probably just a pile of unwanted presents of some kind for we know that, if he was always giving, he was always receiving as well. His storage-boxes could very well have been crammed with souvenirs of this kind, and certain books and manuscripts that were also found amongst them support this theory.

In any event, whether the Rite of Egyptian Freemasonry is truly of ancient origin and was merely adapted by Cagliostro or was entirely original, whether he dictated it to secretaries or whether it was a joint enterprise between him and some of his disciples well-versed in Masonic lore [47] is not especially important. We have only to study it to note the elevated religious feeling that inspired it, to confirm the identity of the principal ideas it contains with everything that Cagliostro taught and practised, and to rebut all the calumnies that the Inquisition's animosity heaped upon it.

This is what we propose to do by summarising as briefly as possible the main theoretical concepts about God, the world and man, the practices relating to double regeneration, and the moral instruction given to initiates that we find disseminated here and there in Cagliostro's drafts of the three degrees of Egyptian Freemasonry.

Egyptian Freemasonry
Masonic work is entirely spiritual. Its only goal is to be found worthy to enter the Temple of God. Man, created in the image and likeness of God, is the most perfect of His works.

As long as Man preserved his innocence he had authority over all living things, even the angels, who are intelligent forces, ministers of God, and intermediaries between the Creator and His creatures. After the Fall [48] however the harmony of the universe was disturbed and man was plunged into matter. His task – recovering the original purity and power that were his prerogatives – thus became a considerable one, and the goal of initiation is to help the fallen man to recover his lost dignity.

This regeneration must be seen as dual: moral and physical [49]. For a profane person to become a child of God again one must first awaken within him the desire to start orienting his life in this direction and to rectify his faults. If he is sincere in his efforts then God will assign one of his elect to help him on this path [50]. He will then learn from this Master that his work consists of glorifying God (spiritual regeneration), making himself into an apostle and the sacrificer of all his power, penetrating the sanctuary of nature (intellectual regeneration), and purifying the elements within himself (social and physical regeneration). To glorify God in oneself is to reform one's interior and to mortify oneself, not by external austerities [51] but by interior struggle. The work is long and much patience is required, and the goal is not achieved without a great deal of effort, known as the Ritual of the Apprentice.

The two virtues are the practice of charity and the vitalisation of pure faith within oneself without falling into superstition.

To penetrate the Sanctuary of Nature one must first acquire knowledge, but this is not the knowledge of the social sciences but a direct understanding of other beings, a complete comprehension of people, which goes hand in hand with the practice of charity.

Finally, the transformation of the old man into a new man can only be achieved by following a course of conduct entirely opposite to the one previously followed. One must live impenetrably and in concealment, and one must free oneself from the prejudices and the material things of this world. You must reach the stage of being able to say the password of the Fellow Craft: *Sum qui sum*, 'I am who I am'.

The physical regeneration of the body follows these preparations and is intended to provide the spirit with a vital force free of the tares, either inherited or acquired, that poor hygiene, bad habits, the passions and the influence of one's fellow-men and one's surroundings imprint deeply in each being. Cagliostro gave precise details for achieving this physiological cure. Many have made light of these, which have always been presented to readers as the Grandmaster's only secret. As we shall see, it was actually only the tiniest part of his work – the final piece of the jigsaw [52].

Portrait engraved by J.-B. Chapuy after Brion de la Tour.

This description of the various stages of physical regeneration, written so as to capture the imagination, also summarises the symbolism of the entire process of restoring one's being. Taking it literally, without making it clear that it is extracted from a Masonic rite, made it fair game for those who simply wanted to ridicule its details, but adopting such an approach would lead to exactly the same result if applied to all the rites or sacraments of any religion or belief that you care to name [53].

When man, thrice regenerated, has a healthy soul within a healthy body God bestows mastery upon him by the impulse of his grace [54]. He then becomes a Master, one of the Elect. He enjoys knowledge of all the powers that God, in principle, had accorded to man, and retains it for as long as he scrupulously obeys the laws implicit in his new duty. He no longer needs the protection or help of any other mortal. He can be recognised by his works [55]. He has the power of evoking the beatific vision and higher spirits (these are the two modes, the active and the passive, of the same faculty, i.e. the ability to comprehend the spiritual world.)

Just as the ordinary man living in the material world can perceive and act, so in the same way the regenerated man can perceive and act in the spiritual world in which he dwells. Whether that perception occurs via an intermediary, with or without apparatus, or directly with the spirit of the Elect, whether it is rendered perceptible to several people, whether it is perceptible simultaneously or successively, or stimulated in other people is of no great importance, for these are mere differences in procedure, action or detail.

An analogy would be an astronomer asking his assistant to observe the various phases of a celestial phenomenon and to describe them to him, as opposed to observing them himself with his eye pressed to the telescope and describing to his audience what he can see. Alternatively he can take a photograph of what his apparatus is recording, project the photograph onto a screen that is visible to all, and, in a single action, show an entire roomful of people the image of what he has perceived. The astronomer will thus do for the sidereal world what the Elect can do – and what Cagliostro did – for the spiritual world.

But we can take the analogy further. The astronomer could teach his assistant to stand in for him at some future time – tomorrow perhaps, or a year or two hence – when the phenomenon in question will reoccur, and can show him how, subject to certain caveats and following a certain method, he will be able to experience and share the same ideas, and other ideas even more precise perhaps, about some star or other or the state of the examined sky. If the observatory assistant is inadequately trained then, despite his best intentions, he will sometimes perform his task well but at other times produce useless or absurd results [56]. If the method and apparatus are entrusted to a properly-trained colleague then the scientist will be able to transfer his powers almost in their entirety, and any subsequent operations will be equivalent to those of the original master. In the case of the Elect this transmission of powers is performed in exactly the same way, but in the spiritual world. Of course, the relevant symbolism was already to be found in the forms and rites of installation of certain lodges and in the ceremonies of transmission of certain ecclesiastical or aristocratic dignities, but whereas in those cases it was nothing more than a dead letter and a sterile memory, Cagliostro in his Egyptian Freemasonry actually found a way of effectively transmitting these powers and enabling his Elect officials to transmit them also [57].

Just as the early Masters chose their followers according to their character and the abilities that they were able to awaken in them [58] so as to then develop these latent personalities to their maximum power, in the same way the Elect chooses and develops an initiate and, when his development has achieved the necessary level, transmits to him the necessary knowledge and powers that will open up and reveal to him a whole new world [59].

It should be noted however that in Cagliostro's ritual the degree of power possessed by an initiate who has been trained by an Elect is limited to his spiritual individuality. He is not yet an adept [60]. He has major pitfalls to avoid [61] and his powers can deteriorate and even be completely lost as we have mentioned above. Only the first level of the system has been climbed, yet it is from amongst these initiates of a lower degree that, 'by the grace of God' and depending on their progress, there will emerge the Elect, those who are capable of attaining absolute mastery.

He who lives in the spiritual world, who can see there, hear there and act there, has by the same token a power in the material world that is incomprehensible to the profane. This power can be used to heal the sick and to purify imperfect metals. It can penetrate the secrets of the human mind just as much as the hidden destinies of nations. Cagliostro demonstrated the reality of these powers so often that even his critical biographers, his enemies and his ecclesiastical judges could not rebut them. He provided evidence to support all his teachings. By what right therefore can we deny the spiritual concepts with which he explained his power?

These theories and their associated practice will be found preserved in the Ritual and Catechisms of Egyptian Freemasonry [62]. It is from there that we have drawn our information, quoting from them as literally as possible. In these rituals, however, the doctrines are enveloped in symbolism, decorated with allegories and disseminated in speeches of reception or formulas of initiation. This was obviously done to make the monitors of the Order as similar as possible, at least in outward appearance, to those which the Freemasons for whom they were intended were used to studying. We have therefore had to prune, amalgamate and summarise. What remains is however is certainly an interesting read: the abbreviated and symbolic history of Freemasonry and the choice of names, signs and numbers reveal the simplicity of the doctrines and their ancient and traditional truth. The prayers that accompany the opening of the workings and the speeches of reception are surrounded by a genuine and profoundly spiritual aura which it is certainly hard to find in the rituals of other orders.

Here, for example, is an extract from the speech of reception to the rank of Master :
My God have mercy on the man (NN) according to the greatness of Thy mercy.
And remove his iniquity according to the multitude of Thy tender mercies.
Cleanse him thoroughly of his sins and purify him of his transgression.
For he acknowledged his iniquity and his crime is ever before him.
He hath sinned before Thee alone, he hath done evil in Thy sight, so that Thou shalt be justified in Thy word, and victorious in Thy judgement.
Thou seest that he hath been begotten in iniquity and that his mother hath conceived him in sin.
Thou hast loved the truth, thou hast revealed to him uncertain things and the secrets of Thy wisdom.
Thou shalt purge him with hyssop and he shall be clean, Thou shalt wash him and he shall be whiter than the snow.
Thou shalt make him to hear a word of consolation and joy and his bones which Thou hast humiliated shall leap with joy.
Turn Thy face from his sin and blot out all his iniquities.
Create in him a pure heart, O God, and renew a right spirit within him.

Cast him not away from Thy presence and take not Thy holy spirit from him.
Restore unto him the joy of Thy salvation and uphold him with Thy free spirit.
He shall teach transgressors Thy ways and sinners shall be converted unto Thee.
Deliver him from bloodguiltiness O God, Thou God of his salvation and his tongue shall sing aloud of Thy righteousness.
O Lord, open Thou his lips and his mouth shall show forth Thy praise.
For Thou desirest not sacrifice; else would he give it; Thou delightest not in burnt offering.
The sacrifices of God are a broken spirit; a broken and contrite heart, O God, Thou wilt not despise.
Do good in Thy good pleasure unto Zion; build Thou the walls of Jerusalem.
Then shalt Thou be pleased with the sacrifices of righteousness, offerings and burnt sacrifices shall they offer on Thine altar.
We beseech Thee Great God to grant him the grace which Thou hast granted to the Grand Copht, first Minister of the Great Temple.

Is it possible to find doctrines more sublime, an initiation more genuine, and sentiments more respectfully religious than these?

This was the form of Freemasonry that Cagliostro brought to Lyons and which he taught in the lodge *La Sagesse*. He counted amongst his disciples a number of local dignitaries, including the banker Saint-Costar, President of the Provincial Grand Lodge in 1779 and a former Worshipful Master of *La Sagesse*; Aubergenois and Alquier, both merchants and high officials; Finguerlin, Philippon, Morin, Journet, Colonge, the two Magnevals, and Terrasson de Sénevas, a former officer. All were devoted, body and soul, to their initiator. Louis-Claude de Saint Martin, who met Gabriel Magneval in 1795, tells us [63] about the profound respect Magneval had for his Master and how he still maintained close relations at that time with Cagliostro's Swiss disciples. Péricaud [64] also reports that it was in Lyons that Cagliostro first met Louis-Marc-Antoine Rétaux de Villette, the son of a tax-farmer and later a victim of the intrigues of Madame de la Motte in the Diamond Necklace Affair.

The financial contributions made by these disciples along with those from grateful patients were more than enough to cover the sum necessary for the inauguration of the Mother-Lodge of the Egyptian Rite, and the Temple was built with much magnificence [65]. In the interim, Masonic workings continued at the former premises. Cagliostro's authority and reputation increased and the Egyptian Freemasons were now being lionised as vigorously as they had previously been shunned. A long time after the Diamond Necklace Affair, and even after Cagliostro's arrest in Rome, we can still find Saint-Costar, the Worshipful Master of *La Sagesse triomphante* and a loyal friend of the Grandmaster, being sent as a deputy to the Provincial Grand Lodge, and Alquier being promoted to the office of Keeper of the Seals in the same assembly [66].

In 1785 Cagliostro was surrounded, as few Masters have ever been, by adoring disciples whom he had chosen and was guiding step by step on the path to enlightenment. Such was his grandeur, his goodness and his power that the Lyonnais gave their hearts to him with the sort of abandon of which only they are capable. Despite his successes in Strasbourg and his triumph in Paris this was probably the happiest time of his life, a time when the spiritual light that he shed was at its most radiant.

Then suddenly, amidst all these achievements and successes, when all was finally going according to plan, when the new lodge was ready to open and conquer Freemasonry and Europe with Cagliostro at its head, the great man disappeared. When his critics see him leaving St. Petersburg or London in the wake of controversy and personal attacks they are quick to explain his departure as the 'flight' [67] of a crook and a charlatan. Isn't this proof, they say, of his falseness, isn't this testimony to this deceit and general crookedness? The charlatan suddenly finds the public turning against him and the ground beneath his feet starting to tremble, so he runs away. Isn't it obvious? But in this instance Cagliostro left at the moment of his greatest glory and greatest success, surrounded by tokens of esteem that would ensure his happiness and that of his wife until the end of their days. What is more, his departure was even more abrupt than usual. Yet, strangely, the biographers and historians are silent on the matter, apparently not noticing or wanting to notice what had happened, however significant it might have been [68].

Cagliostro left Lyons on 27th January 1785 [69]. His departure caused general consternation, although he did maintain contact with his intimates. He commended to them a few leaders whom he had specially trained and to whom, during the previous few months, he had imparted his teachings along with some general information. Through his Rite of Egyptian Freemasonry he'd also communicated to them some secret recommendations [70]. He promised to return to them one day. The love and respect they had for him was so great that they respected his decision, however incomprehensible it might be to them.

The opening workings of *La Sagesse triomphante* took place without him on Saturday 20th August 1785 [71]. Later, at the dedication of the Temple on 25th July 1786, First Commissioner 'R.' [72], representing the absent Grandmaster, made the following magnificent speech which reflected the feelings of everyone present:

Speech by Philippe R., First Commissioner and Grand Inspector, given in the Mother-Lodge at the Ceremony of Dedication on Tuesday 25th July 1786:
Brethren,

It is indeed with a heavy and regretful heart that Bro. V. [73] *and I must, on your behalf, say farewell to our founder, the Grand Copht. He has left France for ever and now lives in another country. Your pain and sorrow at this unhappy event must be all the keener in that, having foreseen his departure, he gave us fair warning, and because right up to the very last minute of his sojourn in our fatherland his sole concern was his Children of Lyons and their happiness.*

You will be aware of just how many times he formed the intention of coming in person to dedicate and inaugurate your Temple, this new Jerusalem which was so dear to his heart and which is destined to enjoy such an extensive and brilliant future. However, the decrees of Providence have constantly put barriers in his way. Men without faith or belief might complain about this, but privileged beings such as ourselves must know that our weakness prevents us from conceiving, let alone fathoming, the secrets of the Supreme Being. We must resign ourselves to them and we must submit to them. Once upon a time Abraham agreed to sacrifice his own son to Him: today we must sacrifice our Father. Let us not judge or torment ourselves about the future effects of a cause that is unknown to us, and instead say with Job, 'The Lord gave, and the Lord hath taken away; blessed be the name of the Lord' (Job I.21). Let the example of these two Elect, favourites of the Eternal, be our models and our consolations, because if they were happy during their lives they are even happier today, and if your confidence in the Eternal equals my own and that which I seek to inspire in you then you will be justly rewarded.

Until now, blind and undecided, you could at most form only conjectures, but reality will replace your doubt: you will become men and you will know a part of the infinite and supernatural favours with which the Supreme Being has blessed those He has adopted and cherishes, so arm yourselves with strength, vigour and wisdom!

Strength to prove the power of the true Egyptian Freemason who, having raised in his heart a sanctuary worthy of the Eternal, has acquired the courage necessary to firmly support and defend the precepts and laws prescribed by our Great Founder;

Vigour to courageously embark upon a new road unknown to all other mortals, to face all manner of dangers, and finally to bear patiently the happiness or misfortune that results from the various events of life;

Wisdom to acquire knowledge of the high, sublime and true Hermetic philosophy, so as to one day win the right to perform the marriage of the Sun and the Moon, thus attaining complete happiness, the greatest reward granted by God to man, true physical and moral perfection, which renders him His Elect and the possessor of the primary and universal matter.

Love and worship the Eternal therefore with all your heart, discourage evil and never engage in it, cherish and serve your neighbour by doing him all the good of which you are capable, and consult your conscience in all your actions, but fly from and drive out all scruples, for scruples lead to crimes, crimes lead to sins, and sins, as we know, are the curse of God [74].

The First Commissioner then asked everyone, including the Fellow Crafts and Entered Apprentices, to swear an oath of discretion, as during the ceremony of dedication some of the secrets of the Masters would be revealed to them. The ceremonies of purification and dedication ordered by the Ritual of the Grandmaster were then performed under the supervision of the acting Master in accordance with the powers granted to him. The results exceeded the hopes of all his disciples. Here is the proof, brought to us in an authentic letter from the Worshipful Master of *La Sagesse triomphante* and addressed to Cagliostro as a report of the meeting and as a token of thanks:

Master,

Nothing could ever equal the blessings that you have bestowed upon us except, perhaps, for the happiness that they bring us. Your delegates used the keys that you had entrusted to them. They opened the door of the Great Temple, and they gave us the strength we needed to cause your great power to radiate forth.

Europe has never seen a ceremony of greater majesty and holiness, but dare we say, Sir, that it could not have had witnesses who were more infused with the greatness of the God of gods and more grateful for your supreme goodness.

Your Masters have developed their ordinary zeal and this religious respect which they bring to bear every week in the internal workings of our lodge. Our Fellow Crafts have shown an enthusiasm and a noble and sustained piety, and have edified the two brothers who have had the honour of representing you. The worship and workings lasted three days, and, by a remarkable coincidence, there were 27 of us, and a total of 54 hours of worship.

Today our desire is to set before you what we realise is a wholly inadequate expression of our esteem. We shall not undertake to provide you with an account of the sacred ceremony of which you deigned to make us the instrument. We hope to forward those details to you soon via one of the Brethren, who will present them to you in person. We shall however say to you that at the very moment we requested a sign from the Eternal that our vows and our temple were pleasing to Him, while our Master was in mid-air, the First Philosopher of the New Testament [i.e. John the Baptist] appeared to us without being summoned. He blessed us after

Chapter VI

prostrating himself before the blue cloud, the apparition of which we had obtained, and then rose upwards on this cloud, the splendour of which was so great from the moment that it touched the ground that our young 'dove', a little girl, could no longer bear to look at it.

The two great prophets and the law-giver of Israel gave us signs expressive of their goodness and their obedience to your orders. All of them contributed to making the operation complete and perfect, insofar as our weakness can be a judge in such matters.

Your Sons will be happy if you deign always to protect them and cover them your wings. They are still infused with the words that you, floating high within the room, addressed to the dove who was beseeching you on her and our behalf: 'Tell them that I love them and that I shall always love them'.

They swear to you their eternal respect, love and recognition, and join us in asking you for your blessing. May it help fulfil the desires of your very humble and very respectful Sons and Disciples,

The Elder Brother Alexandre Ter…
1ˢᵗ August 5556.

This letter, which was discovered by the Inquisition, was published in the *Vie de Joseph Balsamo* [75] and it is from that source that we have taken it. Louis-Claude de Saint Martin also gave an abbreviated account of this meeting in his Letter XXI to Kirchberger [76]. The latter text is often quoted, but as it is not a personal testimony and as its information has been taken from this same source, the *Vie de Joseph Balsamo*, we have preferred to concentrate on the original document.

Cagliostro's promises relating to the majestic display that was to accompany the consecration of the Temple of the Mother-Lodge were therefore fulfilled, and more besides. His disciples had never doubted that they would be but, even so, their expectations had been exceeded and they were delighted. The two Worshipful Masters he had himself installed and the twelve Masters that the Deputy Commissioners confirmed in their degree on 25ᵗʰ September 1786 [77] continued to work enthusiastically in a Temple that had been made sacred by such marvels. The results of their work were communicated to their Master who remained in direct contact with them [78].

As always happens however, after the founder departed division and dissent gradually arose, and superstition, differences in interpretation and other factors led to schism. Financial problems added to the discord: some of the subscribers, after Cagliostro's departure, simply did not want to pay any more, and one even started a lawsuit [79].

The terrible days of the Revolution and the Siege of Lyons (9ᵗʰ August to 9ᵗʰ October 1793) followed: *La Sagesse triomphante* suspended its meetings and, when Freemasonry came out of the shadows once more, the surviving disciples of Cagliostro, now dispersed, no longer met in lodge [80]. But this decline in the Egyptian Rite in Lyons really only began in 1788. Until then *La Sagesse triomphante* did its best to help the Master with his Masonic work in Paris. The latter subject is too closely connected with the material discussed earlier in this chapter for us to pass over it here.

When Cagliostro arrived in Paris he found the same intellectual turmoil and general confusion he had found in Lyons. Paris offered much more scope, and it is true that Cagliostro arrived there with much greater personal authority, but the Parisians were also much more aloof and much less sincere.

The Convention of the *Philalèthes*, which brought together members from a wide range of Rites, sought to unify Freemasonry by clarifying its aims, principles and operations. It met for the first time on 13th November 1784 [81]. On 23rd November its President, Savalette de Langes, proposed that Cagliostro, to whom so many marvels had been attributed, should be summoned before the Convention along with Mesmer in the hope that these two Brothers could shed some rays of light into the darkness of the delegates' debates.

Regarding Cagliostro there was some hesitation, some of the Freemasons present thinking that his attendance might compromise them. They hesitated, and eventually only Mesmer, by far the less controversial of the two figures, was invited. We should remember that the majority never gets things wrong, as they always know how to pick the mediocrities!

After three months of deliberation, however, the Convention had made no progress. On 10th February 1785 Savalette de Langes once again suggested inviting Cagliostro, and this time the idea was accepted. Cagliostro had only just arrived in Paris [82]. He replied immediately, saying that he would be happy to correspond with them. He agreed in principle to the idea of shedding some light on the *Philalèthes*, provided that they welcomed him and some of his disciples, and especially Monsieur de L... [83]. When this reply was received some members of the Convention raised fresh formal objections, such as the fact that Monsieur de L... was not 12° and other complaints of the same level of triviality. Cagliostro's good will was being obstructed by vanity and bureaucratic rigidity or, more correctly, by certain personalities who were hostile towards the Grandmaster and who were using these as excuses to try and keep him away.

This hesitation, which was simply a repetition of the wariness that had greeted the original proposal to invite him, made it clear to Cagliostro just how little enthusiasm for the truth the *Philalèthes* really had. From that point onwards he became increasingly insistent, and the Freemasons increasingly oily and evasive. On 10th March 1785 the Convention received a letter [84] from Cagliostro stating that, since they showed so little passion for the truth and since they refused to take even a single step towards those who had come to them in the name of God, he would demand an even higher price for his collaboration. Here were his terms:

1. The *Philalèthes* must *burn* their entire archives and make a clean slate of a deluded past;
2. All of them would be received as Egyptian Freemasons.

Then, in full lodge, he would give them any proofs they might demand [85].

This letter baffled the Convention. Even so, Cagliostro's dynamic self-assurance began to impress these men who, up to that point, had floated around in a state of constant uncertainty. The matter was discussed, and eventually two of the Brothers – the Marquis Chefdebien (Secretary-General of the Convention) and Baron de Gleichen – were delegated to visit Cagliostro and ask him to reconsider what seemed a harsh decision and to make it clear to him that although the Convention had been convened by the *Philalèthes* it was not actually the *Lodge* of the *Philalèthes* [86] and therefore did not have any archives to burn and was not even able to enter into any undertakings on behalf of the *Philalèthes*, although it was happy for Cagliostro to share his enlightenment with them.

We can see the skilful diplomacy that was being deployed here: anxious to receive without giving anything in return or making any firm commitments, the Convention claimed not to understand that before you can sow you first have to till the soil, and that if they were serious about performing genuine Masonic work then bundles of parchments and a few routine and superficial gestures could in no way be compared with the promise of true celestial light and spiritual power [87].

Chapter VI

On 17th March 1785 de Gleichen reported back to the Convention on his visit to Cagliostro. Cagliostro agreed that the archives need not be destroyed, but he insisted that a delegation of three *Philalèthes* visit Lyons on behalf of their own Rite to request initiation into the Egyptian Rite. He also recommended to the *Philalèthes* that they send an 'honourable' letter to the Mother-Lodge of the Rite based in Lyons [88].

To facilitate this reconciliation the members of *La Sagesse triomphante* sent the Convention the following letter:

To the glory of God,
In the name and with the authority of the Grandmaster of the Order,
The lodge La Sagesse triomphante, Mother-Lodge of the Egyptian Rite with its seat at the Orient of Lyons,
To the Respectable Lodge of Amis réunis at the Orient of Paris,
Greetings, strength and happiness.
Very Dear Brethren,
There are Freemasons that no place on Earth has yet presented to your gaze. Their fraternal voice dares to say to you, 'Cease your searching. We have seen the immutable truth descending amidst us on the ruins of doubts and systems, and you yourselves, Very Dear Brethren, will see it descending into your own lodge as soon as you abandon those many things that have no use other than the motive that caused you to assemble them.
Yes, Very Dear Brethren, take care that you conform to the rules that the known Chief of true Freemasonry has laid down for us. Send us delegates with suitable authority and we shall hasten to fulfil our Master's desire by giving them the instruction that you lack, supported by the real and palpable evidence that he has deigned to share with us.
May we hope to see you soon being embraced by our fraternal arms which are always open to you! We shall certainly feel our happiness even more keenly if we are able to share it with you.
Such are the feelings and the wishes, Very Dear Brethren, of your affectionate Brethren,

S. Costar, Worshipful Master... [89].

On 12th April 1785 the Convention, instead of issuing a clear acceptance, once again tried to draw a fine distinction between the lodge of *Philalèthes* and the Convention, and instructed Beyerlé (standing in for the Secretary-General, who was absent) to write to Cagliostro to repeat the reservations that it had to his offers. The letter even went as far as to claim that the initiation of its delegates should be regarded as purely individual. On 13th April Cagliostro send the following indignant response:

In the name and to the glory of the Eternal,
We offered you the truth and you scorned it.
We offered you the truth for the love of it, and you have refused it out of a love of outward forms.
But what are these forms worth when there is no basis to them? Do you elevate yourselves towards God and divine knowledge solely with the help of a Secretary and a Convention? When hearts are truly ignited with a keen and pure desire then why should one need a Secretary to act neglectfully while the days pass by unheeded?
Don't bother to explain yourselves, for we are not offended. Suppose that, to raise you to a higher spiritual level we sent you forth in front of our own members? But if you cannot elevate yourselves spiritually by your own efforts then why should you expect to reach as

far, in a spiritual sense, as we can?
We want to give, and yet you want to tell us how and to whom we must give. You want to tell us where and how to walk on a path on which you have not yet even taken the first steps.
And just see how clumsy your own steps are!
You have taken six weeks to respond to our simple offer, whereas we have not even taken a day to respond to the work of six weeks.
We therefore withdraw our offer, and in doing so all the scruples and uncertainties that your own forms breed within you are thereby removed. Reflect upon this light of which you have caught a glimpse. May the great Lord, in whose name we work, guide your steps and govern your deliberations,
Given at the Orient of Paris, on [date]

This is followed by the hieroglyphic signature of Cagliostro (see Appendix) followed by those of Montmorency Prince of Luxembourg (Grandmaster Protector), Laborde (Grand Inspector) and Saint-James and De Vismes, secretaries [90].

The Convention was frankly annoyed. After the visit by their delegates they'd hoped to make some progress, but here was Cagliostro every bit as distant and aloof as before. They had to start all over again. A new delegation was chosen and sent to see him, consisting of Bros. de Paul (from Marseilles), de Marnézia (from Franche-Comté) and Ramond (from Besançon). Abbé de Laffrey, from Paris, who was originally chosen, was not free on the day appointed. The interview with Cagliostro took place on the 15th and 16th, and the delegates reported back to the Convention as follows:

From their communication it would seem that Count Cagliostro received the delegates with the greatest consideration; that he promised to fulfil the Brethren's wishes; that he then explained his doctrines in some detail; and that the delegates found these to be sublime and pure... The delegates have produced a written report which has been filed under Actes, shelf-mark C, document no. 4. Bro. de Paul has gone into the greatest detail about the delegation and was invited to put his interesting account into writing, which he has promised to do.'
(From: Minutes of the meeting of the Convention of Saturday 16th April 1785) [91].

We can see from this the very great impression that Cagliostro made upon everyone he met. Here are a group of Freemasons, prejudiced, their chests already swelling with pride thanks to their supposed dignities, who are no longer surprised or baffled by arcane formulas and symbols, and who have been given the task of investigating – and, indeed, almost unmasking – a man who could not throw any sand in their eyes – and these were people, don't forget, who were accustomed to being bedazzled by the smoke coming out of Lycopodium pipes or by the enchantments of allegorical speeches. What was their reaction to him? They came back from their meeting with him simply transformed. They had encountered a man who was straightforward, affable, the possessor of incredible secrets, someone who performed miracles of a kind that they would only ever think about with an ironic smile on their faces, in a word they had met – and I am sure they would have admitted it – a *divinely-inspired* Cagliostro, and their hearts were transformed by him.

Indeed, their impressions of him were so vivid and intense that they passed them on to the Convention, which then agreed to write to *La Sagesse triomphante* [92]. This time however the style of their letter is very different. It still sounds a little false, but this time the falseness

Chapter VI

is the product of embarrassment: the *Philalèthes*, clearly upset, seek to erase any memories of their former mistrust by indulging in excessive flattery. Even so, they didn't commit themselves to anything, they didn't meet any of Cagliostro's requirements, and they contented themselves with receiving the promised revelations either from the Mother-Lodge or from the Grandmaster.

The following day, 28th April 1785, Cagliostro answered simply and clearly that he maintained his offers but that all his requirements also held good. The bombastic letter from the Convention had obviously not beguiled him as it certainly would have done if he had really been the conceited adventurer of legend. He was certainly not interested in getting involved in tedious discussions about lodges, committees and personalities.

Portrait engraved by Bollinger, published by Schumann in Zwickau.

'You should know', he wrote to them, 'that we're not working on behalf of one man, but for all humanity; that we want to destroy error, and not one error alone but all error; and that this league of ours is directed not against an isolated falseness but against the whole arsenal of lies' [93].

The members of *La Sagesse triomphante*, who had hoped that this debate would kill two birds with one stone in that new adepts might be encouraged to join the Egyptian Rite while their Master's renown would be further increased, supported Cagliostro's sentiments in a new letter of their own:

Providence granted the desire of some of you by making the voice of truth resound amongst you, but you did not take a single step towards it. You ask for everything, everything is offered to you, and yet you insist on prevaricating and asking all sorts of tedious preliminary questions! You prefer words to deeds, and the vagueness of discussion to the certainty of facts.

The truth, in giving us the power to illuminate with its flame someone who truly seeks it and is prepared to grasp it, does not allow us the freedom to hold it up before the eyes of a person who neglects or scorns it.

(Letter from the lodge *La Sagesse triomphante* to the Convention of Paris of 29th April 1785.)

The *Philalèthes*, who had fondly believed that this time they had succeeded, through their superficial testimonies of respect, in winning Cagliostro to their cause, realised that they had actually lost ground, and hastily sent a new delegation to see him, but all these prevarications, hypocrisies and attempts at being clever eventually exhausted even Cagliostro's fund of good will. On 30th April 1785 he answered them definitively:

To the glory of God!

Why are lies always to be found on the lips of your delegates, and doubt constantly in your hearts? Do not apologise: as I have already told you, you have not offended me. God alone can decide which of us is right.

You say you're seeking the truth. I presented it to you and you scorned it. Since you prefer a pile of books and childish scribblings to the happiness that I had set aside for you and which you should be sharing with the Elect, and since you have no faith at all in the promises of Almighty God or his minister on Earth, then I simply abandon you to yourselves, and I say to you, in truth, that it is no longer my mission to instruct you. Oh unhappy Philalèthes, you sow in vain, for you shall reap only rye-grass! [94].

And from that moment onwards the Grandmaster concerned himself only with his own Rite, reserving his teachings for his Egyptian Lodges, ignoring Freemasonry entirely, and making no efforts to disguise his lack of regard for it.

Cagliostro brought back to the Temple the Lost Word of which an indifferent humanity had forgotten even the existence, and which Freemasonry alone still sought, albeit in the wrong places. He gave the most marvellous proofs not only of his own personal powers but also of his ability to transmit it to his disciples. He asked for just one thing in return: that man agree to lift up his head and walk with him with his eyes raised heavenwards.

The self-styled initiates scorned him, abandoned him, disowned him. These are irreparable faults which have weighed upon and will continue to weigh upon Freemasonry until its dying day, not as the result of the vengeance of some cruel divinity but because a person who voluntarily turns his back on the light sinks more and more into the darkness as he walks on and the clock implacably measures out the passing of time.

NOTES

(1) *Mémoire pour le comte de Cagliostro contre le Procureur général*, Paris 1786, p. 37.
(2) Also known as *L'Hôtel du Parc*. This hotel made the corner of Rue d'Algérie and Rue Sainte-Catherine. Cf. Péricaud, *Cagliostro à Lyons*, 8 pp. Cf. also the end of the *Pièce justificative*: *Requête à joindre*, 1786, p. 10.
(3) Worshipful Master of *La Sagesse* since 1763, *Archives de Maçonnerie lyonnaise* (Author's private collection).
(4) *Lettre au peuple anglais*, 1787, p. 70. We should note that this was not one of the 'aristocratic' lodges that were then so numerous in London but a lodge composed of people of modest means drawn from the increasingly influential 'Third Estate' (Lodge no. 369, meeting at the Royal Tavern, cf. *Monist*, July 1903, p. 528).
(5) *Vie de Joseph Balsamo*, p. 117. We have no hesitation in quoting extensively from this work. The author tried to find out everything he could about Cagliostro's links with Freemasonry simply to embarrass him, and in telling us everything he knew on that subject he proved an excellent biographer in spite of himself.
(6) *Vie de Joseph Balsamo*, pp. 124, 126, 149.
(7) *Vie de Joseph Balsamo*, p. 118.
(8) *Vie de Joseph Balsamo*, p. 119.
(9T) But see Salvador de Madariaga, *The Fall of the Spanish American Empire*, Greenwood Press, 1947, p. 256: 'In his travels over Europe, he [Cagliostro] met everywhere with a mysterious leader of Freemasonry, a Spaniard [sic] Tomás Ximenes',
(10T) For Samuel Falk, see the forthcoming English translation of *Rabbi, Mystic, or Impostor? The Eighteenth-Century Ba'al Shem of London* by Michal Oron (Littman 2014).
(11) *Souvenirs du baron de Gleichen*, Paris, 1868, p. 176.
(12) *Vie de Joseph Balsamo*, p. 130.
(13) *Mémoires authentiques*, Paris, 1786, p. 6 et seq.
(14) *Letter from Bürkli* in Funk, loc. cit., p. 4. Cf. also *Letter from Salzmann to Willermoz* of 22nd

September 1780, *Collection Bréghot du Lut*.
(15) *Acta Latomorum*, Paris, 1815, vol. I, p. 141.
(16) *Mémoire pour le comte de Cagliostro contre le Procureur général*, Paris, 1786, pp. 36-37.
(17) So great was his success that his house had to be defended from the huge crowds of patients. Sachi had come to the city to continue his campaign of calumny against him: the local magistrates suggested to Cagliostro that they throw Sachi into jail, but this 'Quack of Quacks' (as the ridiculous Thomas Carlyle termed him) nobly refused and asked for him to be released.
(18) Cf. Kauffmann & Cherpin, *Histoire de la Franc-Maçonnerie*, Lyons, 1851, p. 295. See also later in this chapter.
(19T) Cf. Revelation 9:11: 'And they had a king over them, which is the angel of the bottomless pit, whose name in the Hebrew tongue is Abaddon, but in the Greek tongue hath his name Apollyon'.
(20) *Vie de Joseph Balsamo*, p. 52. Cagliostro told several of his disciples about this vision. He acknowledged it and repeated it during his interrogations in Rome.
(21) In the *Mémoires de M. le prince de Montabarey*, Paris, 1827, 3 vols., we find (vol. III, pp. 94-97) a striking description, one of best I know, of the state of people's minds at the end of the 18th century.
(22) Founded by Pernety, 1766.
(23) Founded in 1773.
(24) Kauffmann & Cherpin, *Histoire de la Franc-Maçonnerie*, Lyons, 1851, p. 280. 'The *Philosophes* sensed that the French Revolution was on its way, and Freemasonry was the bellwether', *Mémoires de M. le prince de Montabarey*, Paris, 1827, 3 vols., vol. III, p. 94.
(25) Cf: Papus, *Martinisme et Franc-Maçonnerie*, Paris, 1899, p. 64 et seq.
(26) See Chapter IV of this book and Friedrich, *La Franc-Maçonnerie en Russie*, Paris, Dorbon-aîné, 1908.
(27) Kauffmann & Cherpin, op. cit., p. 269.
(28) Lamartine, *Histoire des Girondins*, 1st edition, vol. I, pp. 251 et seq.
(29) Caro, *Essai sur la vie et la doctrine de Saint-Martin*, Paris, 1852, p. 13.
(30) First established in Berlin.
(31) Cf. Bulau, *Personnages énigmatiques*, Paris, 1861, vol. I, p. 355.
(32) *Circulaire préparatoire au Convent des Gaules*, 1778.
(33) In the *Notes à soumettre au Convent de Wilhelmsbad* (1782) we find the following questions:
'Does Freemasonry have Unknown Superiors and, if so, who they are?'
'Can we have authentic documents relating to the Chiefs or Masters who have laid claim to the possession of true occult knowledge, such as Martinez de Pasqually, Kukumus (sic, for Von Gugomos), John Jonston, Hunt (sic, presumably for Von Hund), Weeler (sic), Srœpher (sic, for Schröpfer)?'
'If, despite the efforts of the Convention, true Masonic science remained unknown, do you think it would be possible to reform Freemasonry in such a way as to make it known?'
This last article (Article X) was certainly the most sensible.
(34) The Masonic links between Lyons and Strasbourg (thanks in particular to Salzmann) and with Russia were continual. In fact it was a Lyonnais, a Monsieur Mioche of the lodge *Le Parfait Silence*, who founded in 1765 one of the Warsaw lodges, and in the *Tableaux* (i.e. membership-lists) of the Lyons lodges in 1775 and 1785 we still find *garants d'amitié* (official representatives) of the lodges residing in Russia and Poland (Author's Personal Archives).
(35) Although Freemasonry made its first appearance there in 1725 it only really started developing from 1755 onwards. In 1781 there were twelve lodges, the most important of which were *Le Parfait Silence*, *La Bienfaisance*, *L'Amitié* and *La Sagesse*. There were also some chapters of other orders, such as the Grand Lodge of the *Maîtres de Lyons* (1750) and the chapter of the *Chevaliers de l'Aigle Noir* where Willermoz and Sellonf organised the Grand Conventions. A lodge of Elect Cohens had operated since 1765. These lodges were in contact with those of Saint-Étienne, Bourg, Grenoble and Avignon. Cf. *Éphémérides des loges maçonniques lyonnaises*, Lyons, 1875, and my personal archives.

(36) *Discours sur le magnétisme animal lu dans une assemblée du Collège des médecins: résultat des observations faites à Lyons* by J.-E. Gilibert, 1784. *Détail des cures opérées à Lyons* by Monsieur Orelut, Lyons, Faucheux, 1784, *Mémoire de Pététin sur les phénomènes de la catalepsie et du somnambulisme*, 52 pages, *Expérience faite le 9 août 1784 à l'école vétérinaire sous les yeux du comte de Monspey, du comte d'Oels* (i.e. Prince Henry of Prussia), *du chevalier Barberin, de M. Millanois sur un cheval*. A diagnosis by a trance-medium, II ff.
(37) *Vie de Joseph Balsamo*, p. 137, Péricaud, *Cagliostro à Lyons*, p. 2.
(38) Péricaud, *Cagliostro à Lyons*, p. 1.
(39) *La Sagesse*, founded in 1725, met at the Maison Puylata, 33 Chemin Neuf. Its Worshipful Master was Willermoz the Elder. In this chapter we reproduce its seal taken from the *Éphémérides des loges maçonniques lyonnaises*, p. 21.
(40) *Vie de Joseph Balsamo*, p. 137.
(41) Péricaud, loc. cit., p. 2. Here is what one of his disciples wrote about it: 'I would like to add just one more thing, and that is to wish you as much satisfaction from it as I myself have experienced, as well as all the other Brethren who, like me, were witnesses to these wonders. I swear to you in the name of Almighty God that what I have just told you is the whole truth', *Rituel de la Maçonnerie Égyptienne*, Mss. Papus, p. 31.
(42) *Notes sur les travaux de Cagliostro à Lyons*, in *Initiation*, March 1906, p. 256.
(43) *Vie de Joseph Balsamo*, p. 138, *Journal de Lyons*, 4th January 1786.
(44) Phantasms of the living, Exteriorisation of motricity, Materialisations, Psychometry.
(45) Péricaud, *Cagliostro à Lyons*, p. 2. Prost de Royer devoted most of his life and personal fortune to those around him but died, friendless and alone, in the direst poverty.
(46) If such minutes or official reports ever existed then perhaps they disappeared along with Cagliostro's papers in the auto-da-fé in Rome on 20th June 1791.
(47) On this subject we have the following theory to offer: Saint-Costar, Cagliostro's disciple and Worshipful Master of *La Sagesse* must have been one of the drafters (or, at least, one of the copyists) of the Ritual. Hence the signature S. COSTAR.

S. Cofton.

In the cursive writing of the 18th century this could have been read, if the letters were badly formed, as G. Cofton or G. Coston, as well as S. Costar. Could it have simply been a copy of the Ritual, signed by the Worshipful Master, which had led to the misunderstanding and the subsequent calumny? G. Coston is a name otherwise unknown in Hermeticism and Freemasonry.
(48) 'Man having degenerated by abusing this great power, God deprived him of that superiority; He made him mortal and deprived him of knowledge of these intermediary beings', *Rituel de la Maçonnerie Égyptienne*, Mss. Papus, p. 23. [This and other extracts from the Ritual are taken, with gratitude, from Faulks and Cooper, *The Masonic Magician: the life and death of Count Cagliostro and his Egyptian Rite*, Watkins 2008, Chapter 9. However, the text quoted here does sometimes differ from the Morison copy from which the translation was made and adaptations have therefore sometimes been necessary.]
(49) 'To undergo a second birth is what the Saviour requires of those who wish to be part of his Kingdom, Jews as well as pagan, cf. *St. John*, II.23 & III.21. The Rabbis also designated the change of nature required of the Proselytes by the words הירב השדח (literally 'new creatures', 'new beings'). Jesus says that this new birth must be dual: initially of the spirit and subsequently in water (i.e. in the vital principle). Cf. H. Olshausen, *Commentaire à l'Évangile de Saint-Jean*, Neuchâtel, 1844, p. 100 et seq.
(50) *Rituel de la Maçonnerie Égyptienne*, Mss. Papus, p. 23.
(51) 'Redouble your efforts to purify yourself, but not by external deprivations or penitences, for it is not a question of mortifying the body and causing it to suffer, but rather of rendering the heart and soul good and pure', *Rituel de la Maçonnerie Égyptienne*, Mss. Papus, p. 47. Some have relied on distortions of this phrase to argue that Cagliostro taught Epicureanism and encouraged depravity!

Chapter VI

(52) The Catechism of Master says that this follows (and must follow) the candidate's moral regeneration. It is achieved by a forty-day retreat under the supervision of a friend and with the help of certain medicines, purifying ones to begin with, and then vitalising ones. Cagliostro prepared some of these medicines in the form of powders (known as *rafraîchissantes*, 'refreshers') and a fortifying liquid in the form of white drops, the Grandmaster's Balsam, *Notes sur les travaux de Cagliostro*, in *Initiation*, 1906, p. 261.

(53) If we reflect carefully and objectively on all the various medical theories and practices we can see that, for example, the cells of the intestine are renewed within forty-eight hours, others less quickly but quite regularly. From this we must conclude that within seven years an organism will no longer be constituted of anything it contained just seven years before; that, in certain diseases, the organic destruction and regeneration occurs in a mass, within a few days; and that this is why fasting has always been used in medicine and religion as the most powerful means of purification. In the light of this we must undoubtedly conclude that Cagliostro's charlatanism is less deserving of mockery than is the ignorance of his detractors. A paper by Dr. Guelpa read on 7th January 1909 at the Neurological Society of Paris tells us that tissues can and must be repaired, and bodily functions renewed, by a prolonged absolute fast, and that if this technique, which he himself has used with success, has not yet found the place in therapeutic practice that it deserves then that is because it must be accompanied by repeated purgation to ensure the evacuation of organic waste. Cf. *Gazette des Hôpitaux*, no. 2, 1909. This is precisely what Cagliostro taught, although he improved on the treatment by subsequently revitalising the patient. Are we to assume that the learned members of the Neurological Society greeted Dr. Guelpa's paper with peals of laughter?

(54) 'Grace is acquired above all by actions: by living the same life as one's neighbours in the society in which Heaven has placed you, by respecting its laws, and, in particular, by dedicating yourself to the happiness and solace of your neighbours – that is the first duty of a philosopher, and work that is pleasing to God', *Rituel de la Maçonnerie Égyptienne*, Mss. Papus, p. 13.

(55) 'One will recognise by his patience, his frankness, the reality of his actions, his success and his manner of working which must only be that of entreating the Great God, and by commanding the seven primitive angels without ever having recourse to any superstitious or idolatrous way', *Rituel de la Maçonnerie Égyptienne*, Mss. Papus, p. 28. We can see that the form of initiation described and offered by Cagliostro differs from all the others. It involves neither weakness nor superstition. He proclaims the great dignity of man and his right to command. Nor do pride or temerity form a part, because he teaches his disciples that retention of the powers received is closely related to the continual practice of holiness.

(56) Cf. *Vie de Joseph Balsamo*, p. 151. One day, it seems, some disciples' work resulted in monkeys appearing instead of angels! Louis-Claude de Saint-Martin repeated this story but we haven't found confirmation of it anywhere.

(57) 'I found out through their conversations that their Master, *despite his abject moral state* (!), had used the spoken word in his operations and that he had even taught his disciples to operate in the same way during his absence', Saint-Martin's, 73rd letter to Kirchberger, *Correspondance*, p. 205. Saint Martin was judging Cagliostro's moral state from the *Vie de Joseph Balsamo* which he misguidedly considered to be a book worthy of his confidence.

(58) By means of a pentagon appropriate to each individual which could put him in contact with the sole angel corresponding to that pentagon, *Rituel de la Maçonnerie Égyptienne*, Mss. Papus, p. 79. 'Through regeneration man does not receive a character that is opposed to his nature: it transforms and glorifies our personal nature, and raises us to a higher power of life and existence', H. Olshausen, *Commentaire à l'Évangile de Saint-Jean*, Neuchâtel, 1844, p. 100 et seq.

(59) Here are the true keys of the Temple, the passwords, the rooms or apartments into which the initiate alone can penetrate 'without hat and cane' (*Discipline pour les maîtres*, p. 56 of the Mss., Catechism of the Fellow Craft, commandment VII), nothing of which he must reveal. Religions and Freemasonry have allowed all this to be buried under a mountain of forgetfulness through ignorance and under a mountain of ridicule through their indiscretions, but the Children of God preserve the spirit

and reality of the initiations. They are imperishable, and God would cause certain beings to keep the lamp burning in the sanctuary if it were not for the fact in each generation He is able to find people who will take upon themselves this mysterious task of preserving the life-force through which the world subsists.

(60) He can only communicate with the angel whose seal and sigil appear on the pentagon. He possesses his power only from his Master, cf. Opening of the workings for the degree of Master, Mss. Papus, p. 79; and note 58 above.

(61) Cagliostro was very insistent about these dangers and how to avoid them, *Catechism of the Entered Apprentice*, Mss. Papus, p. 30.

(62) The original manuscript is in quarto and bears at the beginning and the end the emblem, sigil or seal of Cagliostro on green wax, namely a snake pierced by an arrow and holding an apple in its mouth. It is illustrated with coloured drawings depicting the symbolic costumes of the various degrees. This manuscript is lost. Cagliostro gave it to *La Sagesse triomphante*. Monsieur Romand, of Lyons, was once privileged to inspect this manuscript and copied some passages from it. Two other copies of the original were made and given away, the first to the 1st Deputy Worshipful Master. This is known as version *Alexandre II*. Monsieur Dubreuil, a member of *La Sagesse triomphante*, owned it at one stage and bequeathed it to an unknown person who bequeathed it in his turn to Bro. Bacot, Worshipful Master of the lodge *Le Parfait Silence* in 1844, who left it to the Orator of that lodge. The scholar Mr. Morison made a copy of it, and Monsieur Guillermet (Standard-Bearer of *Le Parfait Silence* in 1845), copied the Morison version. It is this latter copy which we have had the opportunity of studying. Some fragments of it have appeared in *Initiation* (1906-1908) but the text of that article contains many errors. The third original copy, which was given to the 2nd Deputy Worshipful Master (known as version *Alexandre III*) has also disappeared. Cf. Notes on the flyleaf of the Guillermet Mss. In collaboration with Dr. Papus we shall shortly be publishing a complete edition, with commentary, of this important manuscript by Cagliostro [Apparently this edition was never published].

(63) Correspondance between Saint-Martin and Kirchberger, p. 305.

(64) Op. cit., p. 2.

(65) *Vie de Joseph Balsamo*, p. 139. There were three main rooms: one on the left for the Apprentices, one on the right for the Fellow Crafts, and one in the middle for the Masters with a bust of Cagliostro placed in the centre of it.

(66) *Éphémérides des loges maçonniques lyonnaises*, p. 98. In 1790.

(67) This was the name that Carlyle gave to each of Cagliostro's moves around Europe.

(68) If there are beings who are frightened by happiness and who believe themselves to have been abandoned by God when destiny is actually smiling at them then those other beings who seem to have been born to live in the middle of storms (and can even cause them sometimes if they are taking a while to start thundering) will understand Cagliostro's action and recognise it as of their own.

(69) *Pièce justificative*, end of document: *Requête à joindre*, Paris, 1785, p. 10.

(70) 'If you practice what these statutes and regulations that I am giving you contain then you will come to know the truth, my spirit will not abandon you, and Almighty God will be always with you... If you do not obey these regulations then in truth I say to you that confusion, discord and misfortune will arise amongst you', *Rituel de la Maçonnerie Égyptienne*, Mss. Papus, p. 91.

(71) 'Count Cagliostro was due to arrive in Lyons on 19th August with De Luxembourg and eight to ten other leading figures. The grand ceremony of consecration of *La Sagesse triomphante* was due to take place on Saturday the 20th. Cagliostro was to wear a magnificent uniform of green cloth with gold braid which was the usual country-dress of the Lodge's Grandmaster, but the plan never went ahead. Cagliostro was arrested and thrown into the Bastille on the 24th, cf. unpublished letter from Willermoz to Chevalier de Savaron dated 30th August 1785, *Collection of Bréghot du Lut*.

(72) Undoubtedly Rigollet, a former member of *La Sagesse*. Cf. *Éphémérides des loges maçonniques lyonnaises*, p. 8..

(73) Undoubtedly De Vismes, Grand-Secretary of the Egyptian Rite.

(74) *Rituel de la Maçonnerie Égyptienne*, Mss. Papus, p. 127-128.

(75) Op. cit. pp. 198-199.
(76) Correspondence of Saint-Martin and Kirchberger, p. 1862.
(77) *Patente de la Sagesse triomphante.* See Appendix, part II, document 4.
(78) Letter from Cagliostro at the time of the Congress of the Philalèthes. Cf. later in this chapter and *Vie de Joseph Balsamo,* pp. 199-200.
(79) Péricaud, *Cagliostro à Lyons,* p. 3.
(80) The archives of *La Sagesse triomphante,* entrusted in 1821 to the lodge of Memphis (Rite of Misraïm) by Worshipful Master Dubreuil, passed to *Le Parfait Silence* at his death. In 1845 the Orator of this latter lodge was the last owner of whom we have any record. No trace of the archives of the Egyptian Rite can any longer be found amongst the rare documents preserved by the lodges of Lyons. The Temple, which was on the right-hand side of Allée des Brotteaux (later Cours Morand), some way beyond the Place du Bassin (later Place St.-Pothin), which was occupied for a very short time by *Le Parfait Silence* (1824), was eventually abandoned. In 1843 the house was being used as lodgings by the teaching-brothers from the local Christian schools.
(81) Cf. Acta Latomorum, Paris, 1815, 2 vols., vol. II, pp. 92 et seq. *Initiation,* 1904, Nos. 1-7, reproduced these documents in part. A good study of the Convention of *Philalèthes* will also be found in the preface to the *Enseignements secrets de Martinès de Pasqually,* Paris, 1900, pp. 40-151.
(82) 30th January 1785.
(83) Undoubtedly De Laborde.
(84) Letter dated 1, I, 5555.
(85) Cagliostro's power was incomparable and indisputable: those who had wanted to follow him had reached their long-sought goal in only a short time and had seen all their Master's promises fulfilled. Could the disciples of Martinez de Pasqually, of Schröpfer, the *Philalèthes,* the *Illuminés* and the disciples of Mesmer say the same? When Cagliostro demanded that the Freemasons destroy their files and adhere purely and simply to his Rite, was this not simply an attempt to set their feet on the right path? Was it not an act of charity which, both in his time and ours, has been mistakenly portrayed as bragging and boastfulness? The Masonic archives that he wanted to destroy contained only errors and fantasies and, if we are to believe recent polemics (see, for example, Teder's articles and pamphlets on the origins and irregularities of Freemasonry), perhaps even carefully substantiated falsifications of the historical record. Moreover, as we shall see later on, Cagliostro did not actually require the material sacrifice of this pile of paper and later conceded that the *Philalèthes* should be allowed to retain their archives.
(86) *Les Amis réunis,* at the Orient of Paris.
(87) In Ephesus, in response to the words of St. Paul, books were burned that were of much greater value than the Rituals of Adonhiramite Freemasonry or some Masonic song-books. He was inspired by the words of Christ. Cf. *Acts of the Apostles,* XIX.19.
(88) The concessions made by Cagliostro and the fact that agreement was almost obtained are largely due to the lodge's choice of representative: Baron de Gleichen. He was a highly-educated man whose spiritual development set him well above his colleagues in the Convention.
(89) Acta Latomorum, vol. II, pp. 104-105.
(90) Acta Latomorum, vol. II, pp. 108-109.
(91) Acta Latomorum, vol. II, p. 115.
(92) Acta Latomorum, vol. II, p. 121-123.
(93) Acta Latomorum, vol. II, p. 128.
(94) Acta Latomorum, vol. II, p. 126. This prophecy, which came true for the *Philalèthes,* who broke up after three months of fruitless meetings, then gathered together again with even less success, was intended to be general in scope. Cagliostro, in addressing himself to the Convention, was actually speaking to all Freemasons, and his prediction extended to all Masonic work.

CHAPTER VII

—

'THE FALSE PROPHET'

CAGLIOSTRO IN PARIS

Cagliostro arrived in Paris on 30th January 1785 and moved into one of the city's best hotels, the Palais-Royal, at 15 *louis* per month [1]. He therefore made his first appearance on the Parisian scene as a rich traveller rather than as someone in financial need. In any case he had to choose a suitably plush residence because no sooner had he turned up than the Cardinal de Rohan and several other friends, delighted by his arrival, rushed round to see him. They were not at all happy to see him living in a hotel. The increasing number of visitors that he was receiving also necessitated a house-move. Everyone urged him to rent a private house in a quiet area, but they could hardly expect someone as important as Cagliostro to walk the streets looking for lodgings. This task was therefore delegated to the young Ramond de Carbonnières [2], a friend and protégé of the Cardinal, and to the Cardinal's business-manager, Monsieur de Planta. The town-house of the Marquise d'Orvillers was finally chosen. Cagliostro made all the necessary payments, including a down-payment, furnishing-costs and even carriage-expenses [3], and after just a few days was able to leave his hotel and move to the beautiful house at 30 Rue Sainte-Claude in the Marais.

'It's still there', writes Lenotre [4], 'and we have no difficulty in imagining the effect it must have made in the night-time upon those who walked along the deserted rampart with its corner-pavilions, in those days partially hidden by ancient trees, or strolled across its immense courtyards and wide terraces, with the vivid gleams of the alchemist's crucibles filtering through the tall shutters. The house, which retains its noble lines beneath the parasitic structures added during the 19th century, still has an indefinable atmosphere of the Baroque but also a mildly macabre air. The carriage-gates open onto Rue Saint-Claude at the corner of Boulevard Beaumarchais and the courtyard, squeezed in between the surrounding structures, is morose and solemn in aspect. In the depths of the courtyard a stone staircase which time has forgotten and which still has its ancient iron handrail rises from a flagstone portico. Some secret stairs, now walled up, which duplicate the main staircase, originally rose as far as the first floor, and traces of them can still be seen there. A third staircase, narrow and tortuous, still survives at the other end of the building alongside the boulevard. It winds along the wall in full view but is shrouded in the deepest darkness. It serves the former salons, huge when they were originally built but now partitioned, with the French-windows opening onto a terrace that retains its old iron balconies. Below we find the carriage-shed and the stables with their worm-eaten doors. But where the alchemical laboratory was, about which everyone's tongues wagged in those far-off days, nobody except the Cardinal could say. All anybody knew was that the apartments were decorated and furnished very luxuriously and that 'in the anteroom was a slab of black marble bearing, in gold letters, Alexander Pope's universal prayer, 'Father of all! in every age', etc., a paraphrase of which Paris would be singing some ten years later in the form of the Hymn to the Supreme Being" [5].

In no time at all the mansion was full of cheerful chatter and animation. From morning to night there was a constant to-and-fro of people of every stamp in their brightly-coloured liveries. The courtyard was full of lacquered coaches, neighing horses, shouting coachmen and a steady stream of elegant young women going up and down the stone steps, dirtying their stylish and immaculate gloves on the wrought-iron banister, their noses in the air, their expressions eager, moved, alarmed, fearful... [6].

Cagliostro entertained lavishly. He had plenty of guests and he kept a good table [7]. The Cardinal came three to four times a week to dine, but always simply. His place was always laid, and sometimes he would unexpectedly bring dining-companions but on those occasions, not wanting to put Cagliostro to the expense of these unplanned receptions or to inconvenience the Countess, he would always send some food round prepared in his own household [8]. In the salon after dinner there would gather a throng of great lords, friends of the Cardinal, Courtiers of the Prince de Soubise (who felt they owed Cagliostro an enormous debt of gratitude [9]), the merely inquisitive attracted by the Grand Copht's great fame, seekers after truth investigating the occult and, of course, patients seeking a cure.

Although Cagliostro didn't really want to practise medicine any longer [10], preferring to spend his time amongst a few carefully-chosen friends whom he could teach at his leisure, this was a freedom that was obviously going to be denied him. The whole of Paris was talking about the miraculous cure of the Prince de Soubise as well as the case of Madame Augeard [11]. The newspapers also carried stories of his successes both abroad and in the provinces, and about the tokens of esteem he'd received from the most illustrious of men. Hadn't Monsieur de Vergennes himself and the Keeper of the Seals Monsieur de Miromesnil not officially intervened in his favour in Strasbourg and Bordeaux [12]? The torrent of patients of high birth and others seeking his advice grew larger and larger.

Cagliostro did nothing to encourage them. He showed the same side of his personality he had shown in Lyons, then in Strasbourg, and then in Russia: very reserved, independent, brusque in manner, making no attempts at flattery. We've already heard about his haughty response to the initial approaches of Cardinal de Rohan in Strasbourg [13]. In Paris he went one better: when the Comte d'Artois, the King's brother, and the duke of Chartres invited him to dine with them he simply refused [14]! And it was not out of timidity: at his new lodgings, in the middle of this same high-flown world, his manners and behaviour were more aristocratic than any of them as he lorded it over his guests, displaying an innate nobility and an indisputable and irresistible dignity and spiritual refinement [15]. When he replied, in a grave voice, to those great men who promised him their favour and protection that he was deeply honoured and, in return, would be taking *them* under *his* protection, their natural reaction was not to smile or to argue with him: instead they were filled with respect and, indeed, would have fallen to their knees if he had not called them back to their senses with a jest or a sharp word.

The evenings were spent questioning him and trying to prise some answers out of him. What people particularly wanted to hear about of course, and what especially attracted them to him, were the secrets of his clairvoyance and his marvellous knowledge of both objective and spiritual reality. Face to face, indeed, he told people things, in the minutest detail, which they thought only they knew [16], and this baffled everyone. In larger groups or surrounded by an attentive circle he would talk about anything and everything, following the flow of other people's conversations but without any apparent order and without heavy pedantry, moving swiftly from one subject to another. He would always adjust his conversational style to suit the pace of his audience, realising that none of his light-headed listeners was capable of much in the way of uninterrupted effort and seriousness, and yet his digressions always touched the heart of the matter and helped them form a sound general conclusion [17].

Most of the people who frequented Cagliostro's mansion – men and women of the world for the most part – simply didn't understand him, and declared as they left that he talked pure gibberish. Others, especially the Freemasons, caught a few shafts of illumination but were disappointed that these were lost in what they considered to be a flurry of obscurities and trivialities, everything they had not understood, of course, falling into this category. Finally there were some, whose names we do not know – for the best people are always the most humble and inconspicuous – who listened with their whole being, sensed the hidden relationships between the spirit of the answers given and the questions that had been asked, and remained silent, not finding within themselves – being so close to him as they were – either the need to ask further questions or to say anything else, for their sole desire was to continue enjoying his presence [18] and to bask the light shed by this human Sun that warmed and dazzled them at the same time. Such people were certainly quite rare, and for three-quarters of his visitors his revelations remained a dead letter. But the indifferent, the sceptics even, could not entirely avoid the impression left by his words when, as a true prophet who was seldom listened to, he would suddenly wind the clock forward and give his questioners a glimpse of something that was about to happen the following day or, piercing the veils of the future to an even greater extent, uncover the broad horizons of the future for a person, a nation, or even the whole of humanity [19]. All this was done without any apparatus amid the simple chatter of the dinner-table or during intimate receptions on these evenings when people left his presence much later than intended [20] and much more deeply moved than they would have liked to admit. Their hearts, suffused with the breath of his spirit, felt within them an energy that made even the highest peaks seem accessible to them and even the hardest roads easy to follow. In such a mood they would have happily taken on any ordeal, even martyrdom, if it meant arriving more quickly at this knowledge, this all-powerful freedom that overflowed within the Master and which he promised could be acquired by all those who were willing to follow him.

And so, whether he liked it or not, Cagliostro was surrounded on all sides and assailed with daily requests for guidance and encouragement. He couldn't very well close upon these people the same doors that he had only recently half-opened to them, or refuse to Parisians of good will what he had so freely granted to those of Lyons. He therefore opened an Egyptian Lodge at his mansion [21] and, within this temple, instructed them in his Rite. We are already familiar with the nature of that Rite [22]. We have seen the atmosphere of religious gravity that prevailed at those meetings and the series of workings and meditations with which he led the Egyptian Freemasons to first comprehend and then progressively achieve the putting-off of the old man and the regeneration of their being. The Egyptian Lodge in Paris witnessed the most extraordinary experiments and occurrences, similar to those that had filled with enthusiasm both the Cardinal de Rohan in Strasbourg and Cagliostro's disciples in Lyons, in an atmosphere of the greatest and most religious secrecy. Men of the very greatest ability, of the very highest birth, most of whom had already passed through lodge after lodge and had studied all the systems, were eye-witnesses to them and were filled with wonder. Their faith in Cagliostro became unshakeable [23].

If, at regular meetings of his Lodge, it was mostly the privileged that Cagliostro initiated into true masonry, then in his everyday encounters he was perfectly happy, as we have seen, to speak to anyone, rich or poor, male or female. His female followers in particular were both more numerous and more socially-select that they had ever been before: in Strasbourg and Lyons they had been mostly petty bourgeois, women of great spirituality no doubt but relatively uneducated, with minds that were largely closed to scientific or metaphysical speculation. In the Paris of 1785 in contrast Cagliostro found a large group of women who were highly cultivated, had a thirst for knowledge and were full of dynamism [24], but with whom no one else could really be bothered. Women were still shut out from discussion of the majority of serious issues. Even within Freemasonry, an organisation that embodied the most egalitarian and progressive ideals of the time, women were regarded as little more than ornaments, as one of the attractions of the Order's social events [25]. The rituals and songs intended for Open Days and the mixed lodges show just how widespread within Freemasonry this polite disdain for women really was. Cagliostro sought to eliminate this social iniquity, this false and repugnant *galanterie* which, under the guise of refinement and respect, actually masked a brutal contempt of man for woman, a hypocritical procedure designed to make it all the easier for men to prevail over women [26]. Why, he asked, shouldn't women also aspire to an understanding of truth and goodness and take an active part in the work of regeneration? [27] Was it not a woman who was the first to place her foot on the head of the Serpent? [28] Was it not in the crystal-clear mirror of her heart that the first rays of Wisdom were reflected? [29]

We can well imagine the joy with which Cagliostro's female audience greeted his words. Cagliostro was opening up a path that all these female souls could follow. In doing so he had won their devotion to his work, an enterprise that defended their rights and proclaimed the importance of their mission. The Comtesses de Brienne, Dessalles, de Polignac, de Brissac, de Choiseul and d'Espinchal; Mesdames de Boursenne, de Trévières, de la Blache, de Montchenin, d'Ailly, d'Auret, d'Évreux and d'Erlach de la Fare; and the Marquises de Genlis, de Loménie, de Bercy and de Baussan [30] all beseeched him to initiate them and open to them also the doors of the sanctuary.

A Lodge of Adoption, called *Isis*, was therefore constituted and, out of simple respect, the shy and unassuming Countess Cagliostro was appointed the first Grandmistress. The ritual was drafted, and it was as a regular Lodge of Adoption that the instruction continued. The inauguration, on 7th August 1785, was an imposing affair and was the talk of the town [31]. The Rites were the same as for masculine Freemasonry and so were the workings, the instruction alone being slightly different, with more of an emphasis on the development of physical energy and the intellectual faculties, as it was assumed that the emotions, the imagination and the heart, being naturally more developed in women, required less cultivation. [32]

The success of these courses exceeded even those of the Masonic Lodges [33]. The air of mystery with which the disciples, both male and female, were surrounded, the theurgic operations to which the witnesses alone were privy but which were widely discussed in the outside world, the curiosity of the non-Freemasons, and the jealousy of other sects all contributed to the creation of the most amazing and incredible rumours about Cagliostro's activities. Romanticised accounts proliferated, and gossip spread from *salon* to *salon* and from newspaper to newspaper. And so there were born the two legends that we find everywhere today: that of the 'Magical meeting in the Ladies' Temple' [34] and that of the 'Banquet of the Ghosts' [35].

These two stories have seen their fair share of variants. Here is another anecdote of the same kind and with roughly the same degree of credibility. A very sensible young fellow

Chapter VII

who suspected that one of his girlfriends had become mixed up in Cagliostro's daydreams went to see her and found her completely besotted both with the man and with his system. The young man sat down and ate his soup. After the plate was removed however he could still see four extra table-settings and four extra chairs too, as if other people were expected. He asked who the other guests were but didn't get a reply. He asked again, more insistently this time, and his girlfriend told him that all the seats were filled and that he was lucky to have been given the chance to dine with certain Higher Beings. The man just shrugged his shoulders, not wanting to contradict her as she was displaying an unusual degree of charm and interest in what she was doing: never before had he seen her taking so much trouble over entertaining her friends or looking as happy in the process as she did that day making sure that her invisible guests were enjoying their dinner.

Then the man and his girlfriend left the dining-room to walk through the garden. She told him that every tree had its own hamadryad, that every plant was being cultivated by a genie, and that even the individual jets of water had their own nymphs. Naturally the young man didn't want to fall out with his lady-friend, so he was happy to let her go on talking, and indeed he finally left the house without trying to destroy an illusion that was obviously bringing her great happiness.

It is said that Cagliostro, at the time he was arrested, had forty students of this kind with this sort of ability [36], and the editor of the *Gazette de Leyde* assures us that 'two days before Cagliostro's arrest he had persuaded the Cardinal that he had just dined with King Henri IV of France' [37].

These were obviously ridiculous exaggerations, mere superstitious legends intended to harm Cagliostro, and harm him they did. They might also have intoxicated him with a fatal pride if he had not possessed, as he himself sometimes said [38], the antidote to every poison. They are also, however, irrefutable testimonies of his mysterious powers, of the boundless devotion that he inspired, and of the triumphant success that he enjoyed in Paris within just a few months.

Welcomed by and indeed surrounded by the elite of Parisian society, Cagliostro inevitably found himself right in the middle of a world of intrigue and conspiracy [39], and the biggest scandal of the entire 18th century, the Diamond Necklace Affair, was about to engulf him. And as his opponent he had one of the most dangerous adventuresses of all, a woman of unparalleled daring: Jeanne de la Motte.

The daughter of a drunkard father and a debauched mother Jeanne de Saint-Rémy [40] had a difficult early life full of moral pitfalls. By turns a cowherd and a professional beggar she was then locked up in a convent from which she managed to escape. Adopted by some kind people whom she repaid by playing the cruellest tricks upon them [41] she then fell back into poverty and vagrancy before again being rescued, this time by the Marquise de Boulainvilliers, who was intrigued by the fact that a girl of apparently aristocratic origins had ended up in such misery.

Frantz Funck-Brentano, who has devoted several chapters of his excellent book on the Diamond Necklace Affair to Madame de la Motte, provides the following portrait of her [42]: 'Madame de la Motte was a petite lady with a lithe, slender body, and was graceful in a fluttery but vivacious kind of way. She had chestnut hair, blue eyes and a mouth that was perhaps a little too large for her face, but a smile that 'went straight to your heart' as Beugnot puts it, and he was speaking from experience. Her bosom would have been everything you could have wished for if there had been more of it, but as Monsieur Beugnot (again) observes, 'Nature had stopped half way through her task, but this half was enough to make you regret that she had not completed it'. Finally there was her voice – gentle, insinuating, easy on the ear, caressing. Despite her lack of education she had a quick, natural intelligence. She also spoke well and with great fluency. 'Nature', as Bette d'Étienville puts it, 'had blessed her with a considerable gift – that of persuasion' [43], or, as another contemporary put it, 'an air of good faith in what she had to say brought persuasiveness to her lips' [44]. As for the laws both of moral conduct and those of the State, for Madame de la Motte these were quite simply – and in the most natural possible way – unknown territory. As a result she always went straight to her goal, never seeing any obstacles in her way. 'And that', concludes Beugnot, 'made her alarming to see in action, and winningly attractive for the vast majority of men'.'

After her marriage in 1780 to a fat and stupid policeman nicknamed Momotte she started styling herself the *Countess* de la Motte, although her husband had never been a Count. It was this pretty unpleasant couple that the Marquise de Boulainvilliers light-headedly introduced and indeed recommended to Cardinal de Rohan [45]. The Cardinal's protection enabled the couple to leave for Paris with a little money, some letters of introduction, and their papers in order (indeed a little bit *too much* in order, as the warrant that the Cardinal gave her husband incorrectly referred to him as Count de la Motte, and he was to use this document to justify his use of this bogus title thereafter. The couple moved into a small town-house at 13 Rue Neuve-Saint-Gilles in the Marais. By dropping the Cardinal's name here and there and maintaining a morally easygoing *salon* with luxurious furnishings purchased with loans, Madame de la Motte soon attracted a circle in which everyone who was anybody was to be found: middle-aged financiers; abbés; lawyers like Maîtres Laporte and Beugnot; aristocrats such as the Comte d'Olomier and the Marquis de Saisseval [46], the latter a heavy gambler very well-known at Court; and Freemasons like Lecoulteux de la Novaye [47] and Father Loth [48]. Rubbing shoulders with them were proven scoundrels, who came in handy on those frequent occasions when life in the De la Motte household became especially difficult. These included Rétaux de la Villette, a great favourite (to say no more!) of Madame de la Motte [49]; Bette d'Étienville [50]; bogus Marquises; so-called 'officers'; and the 'other Madame de la Motte' (Marie-Josephe-Françoise Waldburg Frohberg), whose own moral example and advice were in no way alien to the enterprises of our pseudo-Countess [51].

'Many gentlemen, in keeping with etiquette, came alternately to visit the Countess while the Count went to warm himself in the apartments of the château. Military men and lawyers had the pleasure of visiting her and leaving signs of their

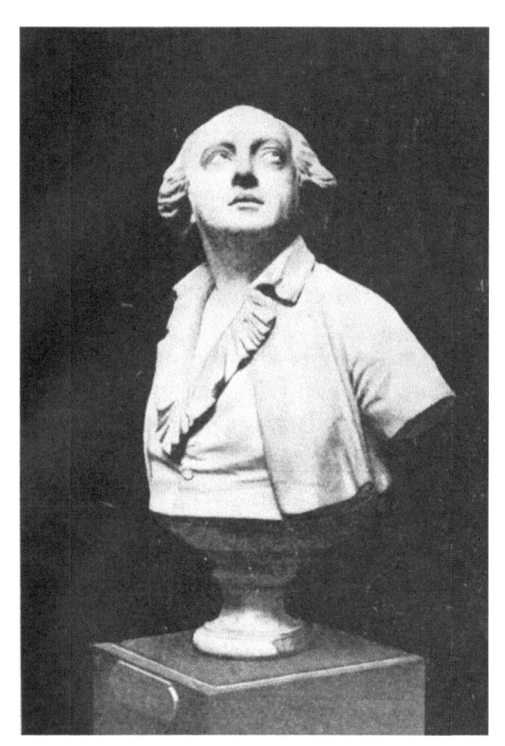

Bust by Houdon, Museum of Aix-en-Provence

Chapter VII

generosity' ⁽⁵²⁾. But whether people visited her to see her, to see her maidservant, to enjoy the wine-cellar or play at the gaming-tables was of no real significance. The important thing was that Madame de la Motte had a plan, and the aim of it was for everyone to be made aware of the fact that Madame de la Motte-Valois, a lady of royal blood, was well regarded and well treated at Court. She would tell people that her family misfortunes and the low status in which she had previously vegetated made it impossible for the Queen to publicly bestow any favours upon her but that, in secret, the she was entrusting her with some of her most delicate commissions. An occasional influential position which she was able to obtain through the mediation of the financiers who frequented her *salon* helped persuade the gullible that this was indeed the case. To make things look even more convincing she actually rented a room at an inn in Versailles where she would go and shut herself up a couple of times a week, often going without food in the process. 'Where's the Countess? Why she's at Court of course', her entourage would mutter mysteriously on those special days.

From this time onwards her reputation was made and the royal blood of the Valois was the bait on the hook. She became an influential 'go-between in the Ministerial Offices and at Court', as the Lieutenancy of Police was told ⁽⁵³⁾, and began running a protection-racket. She had already extorted 1000 *écus* from a Monsieur de Ganges by promising to influence the Queen in his favour to obtain an influential position for one of his relatives. Messrs. Perrin, merchants of Lyons, had also sent her, in exchange for influencing the King in an important commercial matter, a box of superb fabrics estimated to be worth more than 10,000 *livres*. But her first really brilliant coup involved swindling 150,000 *livres* from the Cardinal de Rohan. The story is well known ⁽⁵⁴ᵀ⁾. Having found out what was eating away at the Cardinal's peace of mind she had no difficulty in persuading him of her influence with the Queen ⁽⁵⁵⁾ and offered her services as an intermediary to ensure that the Queen would allow the Cardinal to present the formal justification of his conduct that he was so eager to submit. 'But will she accept it?' he asked Madame de la Motte anxiously. Imagine his delight when he heard the incredible news that the Queen had granted him a special night-time rendezvous in the gardens of Versailles! Madame de la Motte had been daring enough to find someone who called herself Nicole Leguay d'Oliva – a milliner by profession ⁽⁵⁶ᵀ⁾ – who looked just like Marie-Antoinette to play the part of the Queen, accompanied by Rétaux kitted out as a manservant, in the *Bosquet de Vénus* in the gardens of Versailles. The poor deluded Cardinal returned from the meeting all excited, beside himself with happiness, hoping that all would be resolved, and telling Madame de la Motte that there was no way he would ever be able to adequately show his gratitude. Madame de la Motte knew it was time to strike: she asked, on the Queen's behalf, for 50,000 *livres* for a family that had fallen on hard times, and later for a further 100,000 *livres*, which the Cardinal seemed only to happy to hand over. The Cardinal, on her advice, then left for Strasbourg, but not before ordering his faithful business-manager De Planta to give the Countess *everything that she might ask for* to pass on to the Queen, even if it meant auctioning off some of the treasures in his much-loved collections ⁽⁵⁷⁾. Madame de la Motte used the money to pay off some restless creditors and to do up her mansion. As her receptions became even more dazzling, so the number and enthusiasm of her visitors increased even further.

One day, on 29ᵗʰ November 1784 the Court Jeweller Bœhmer, who had heard a great deal about Madame de la Motte's alleged influence at Court, asked the lawyer Laporte ⁽⁵⁸⁾ to tell her that he would be happy to pay 1000 *louis* to anyone who could persuade the Queen to take a superb diamond necklace valued at 1,600,000 *livres* which had been expressly made for her but which she vigorously refused to buy. Madame de la Motte's thoughts turned to the gullible Cardinal and she formulated a plan. De Rohan was in Alsace at that time, so she dictated a letter to him:

An important lady who is well-known to you is simply dying to own this necklace. She wants to buy it, but secretly. What she needs is for a friend that she can utterly rely upon to make the purchase for her and to provide the necessary guarantees in anticipation of 1st August, the date on which she will re-pay him.

How could the Cardinal *not* accept this token of confidence? He rushed back from Alsace and reached Paris with his mind already made up. Any misgivings that he might have had evaporated when he read a letter purportedly from the Queen herself which Madame de la Motte showed him. The jeweller Bœhmer was anxious to draw up a contract [59] regulating the terms of payment by instalments and Rohan was happy to commit himself to this as long as the Queen herself signed it. Since one forgery more or less was not going to matter very much to the Madame de la Motte, Rétaux de la Villette, who had already manufactured all the Queen's letters in this little affair, countersigned the contract in the name of Marie-Antoinette *de France* [60]. By 21st January everything was in place. On the 24th the Cardinal went to Bœhmer's to see the necklace and conclude the final arrangements. On 1st February Bœhmer delivered the necklace and, that same evening, 'at the Queen's insistence' said Madame de la Motte, who was anxious to conclude the matter, the Cardinal rushed round with the necklace to Madame de la Motte's lodgings in Versailles. Through a glazed door he then saw her handing over the box containing the priceless item to a young man whom he clearly recognized, even in the dim light of the alcove, as the same manservant who had accompanied the 'Queen' in the *Bosquet de Vénus*. It was indeed the same person: Rétaux de la Villette.

That same evening, while Bœhmer and the Cardinal were basking in their illusory success, the cutting-up of the necklace began. The accomplices spent the week deciding how best to benefit from it: eventually Rétaux sold some of the diamonds in Paris while Monsieur de la Motte was to take the remainder to London a few weeks later [61].

The Countess had played the Cardinal and the Royal Jeweller like a violin. She felt safe from any consequences: nobody knew anything about what had happened and she herself had remained on the sidelines throughout, for everything that had taken place had involved only the Cardinal (who himself was too heavily compromised to speak out about it, whatever might happen), the Royal Jeweller, and the unknown and unknowable character who had received the necklace on behalf of the Queen. She was quite calm and yet felt a sense of triumph.

And what had Cagliostro been doing all this time? What part had he played in all these events? In September 1780 Cagliostro arrived in Strasbourg. He left there in August 1783 and, until 30th January 1785, travelled through Italy and France, passing through Bordeaux and spending some time in Lyons, totally absorbed in his Egyptian Freemasonry [62]. When he returned to Paris on 30th January 1785 Madame de la Motte was still very much in the Cardinal's favour. Cagliostro knew his disciple's dangerous friend only too well: he had met her for the first time in Saverne and had dined with her several times at the Château there. Beugnot, who attended one of these dinners, tells us that Cagliostro often interrupted his more serious conversation to pay Madame de la Motte 'extremely tender compliments and amusing favours, calling her his little doe, his gazelle, his swan or his dove – in other words comparing her to all the sweetest and cutest things in the animal kingdom' [63]. The Countess therefore felt that, in her very first encounters with Cagliostro, she had won the regard of a great man whose least gestures were under close scrutiny. That satisfied her vanity, but in her heart she really just mocked the utterances of 'the divine Cagliostro' and the stupidity of his entourage. She saw him as nothing more than a happy-go-lucky adventurer, someone who was easily seduced with a little flirtation. 'Although he seems to disdain material wealth he claims to have coffers full of it', she thought to herself, 'and the likelihood is that money is really all he's interested in – just like me! And he enjoys a very special kind of prestige of a kind that I shall never have. That's certainly not something to be sneezed at. I shall make him my ally'.

The Cardinal, for his part, was happy: on the one hand he had the friendship of Madame de la Motte who, he believed, would persuade the Queen to look favourably upon him, on the other he had Cagliostro ready to open the doors to the celestial mysteries. What more could anyone ask for? He got the impression that his guests were on terms of the frankest cordiality: Madame de la Motte seemed to please Cagliostro, and in her turn she seemed to understand and admire him. The Cardinal obviously did not sense, amid the pleasant and unembarrassed good-naturedness with which Cagliostro would suddenly stop talking about serious and elevated subjects and start engaging in lively banter with the bogus Countess, the secret contempt that she felt for Cagliostro. Cagliostro's personal contact with Madame de la Motte was intimate but dignified and full of good humour. He saw her essentially as the Cardinal's protégée. He never displayed any hostility towards her, but not did he show her much respect either. Cagliostro was certainly not her ally: he remained aloof from her personal secrets, just as he was quite happy to leave her in ignorance of his esoteric ones. Only once did he get closely involved: it was in 1784, during the d'Oliva affair, when the Cardinal, totally in thrall to her, had allowed himself to commit the most foolish indiscretions. Cagliostro offered some gentle advice to try to moderate the Cardinal's behaviour and help him to, at least, avoid leaving a leg or a wing in Madame de la Motte's sticky and complex spider's web.

For Madame de la Motte the penny had finally dropped: she realised that she had been guilty of a misjudgement in thinking of Cagliostro as a buffoon, that he had a clear view of the situation, and that he would never allow her to manipulate him. Since Cagliostro was obviously not for sale he would have to be destroyed, and Madame de la Motte decided to busy herself with this task. 'Countess de la Motte did not find the benefits that she was able to extract from the Cardinal de Rohan to be in any way sufficient, and she felt they would have been more considerable if Cagliostro had not told him to set limits to the generosity that he was displaying towards her. She did everything in her power to turn the Cardinal against Cagliostro, but when she failed in that task she started nurturing secret plans for revenge and waited for an opportune moment to strike' [64]. Madame de la Motte's silent animosity and Cagliostro's attempt at intervention which had displeased the Cardinal were the two factors that disrupted the disciple's relations with his Master. The Cardinal, out of sheer funk, was frightened of incurring reproaches and of seeing Cagliostro thwarting Madame de la Motte's clever tactics. He began concealing from Cagliostro the joint enterprises in which he was engaging with the Madame de la Motte, started listening to her advice, her flattery, and her calumnies against Cagliostro, and abandoned himself to the dazzling ambitions she was setting before him. Cagliostro, busy with other matters, did nothing to halt this increasing estrangement.

In November 1784, when the Diamond Necklace Affair was being organised [65], Cagliostro was in Lyons, utterly absorbed in his Masonic work. By January 1785 the affair had come to a head. The Cardinal, Bœhmer and the Countess met every day, while Cagliostro was still at a distance. The Countess applied pressure on the Cardinal to bring things to a conclusion. There was an air of urgency, of a need to rush things, as if they expected an intruder to suddenly arrive. The Cardinal fell into the trap and, on the eve of Cagliostro's arrival in Paris, signed the agreement. The deed was done, the necklace bought, the Queen compromised, and the Cardinal lost, unless a Saviour came along to help him. But not only had every detail of the affair been planned and executed while Cagliostro was far away in the provinces, even after he'd come back strenuous efforts were made to carefully conceal from him the final episodes of the drama. The Cardinal rushed round to Versailles with the necklace, handed it over, and returned, beaming, convinced that his fortune had been made.

It was only then, in early February [66], that he spoke to Cagliostro in veiled terms about his astute speculation, this master-stroke that he'd pulled off which he expected to produce the most spectacular results. Cagliostro was unimpressed and expressed some misgivings. The Cardinal responded vehemently that he was sure that all was well: secretly he was delighted that he hadn't told Cagliostro about the matter earlier, as he would probably have done his best to discourage him. 'In any case', said the Cardinal curtly, 'it's a done deal'. 'Well if it's a done deal then there's no point in talking to me about it is there?', replied Cagliostro, with the very obvious meaning of 'Well, you allowed your imagination instead of your brain to do your thinking for you, and you didn't want – and you still don't want – my advice on the matter. So much the worse for you' [67]. And that's where conversation on this subject ended.

The Cardinal was shocked. He had hoped for some words of congratulation or at least encouragement but instead seemed to be facing something that was bordering on reproof. His pride was hurt, but his hopes prevailed over his confidence in Cagliostro. 'Maybe the clairvoyant is no longer seeing things so clearly. Anyway, he knows nothing about business matters', he thought to himself, and this judgement alone was enough to remove the last hope of seeing the light that Cagliostro had offered him. If he had only listened or at least asked for advice then things could still have been sorted out. The diamonds could still perhaps be recovered, payment made, measures taken, or, at least, the whole business hushed up before the Court found out about it. But, sadly, it was only when it was too late that the Cardinal would realise where he had gone wrong.

Despite his apparent insouciance the Cardinal's breezy self-confidence had actually been undermined by his conversations with Cagliostro. He was starting to worry. The Countess perceived this and knew exactly what the cause was. She was also secretly pleased that she'd been able to hurry things along to achieve completion of the matter before the 'Sorcerer' arrived. She reassured the Cardinal [68] and, although very busy selling the diamonds, she took immediate steps to get her adversary out of striking-distance. She explained to De Rohan that he must go and question Cagliostro not as a source of good advice but as an expert on the occult: 'Get him to perform a ritual, or submit questions to a 'dove'. We won't tell him what it's all about. You will tell him about an important lady, in a very difficult situation, who wants to know something about her future, and you will think of the Queen. The subject will clearly see who it really is, and that will reassure you. It will also enlighten Cagliostro as to who is in error. As it happens I have my niece, Mademoiselle de la Tour, at home with me at the moment. She's an innocent little girl, and if the Grand Copht is happy to use her as a dove then it should be easy'.

Her plan was certainly a clever one: either the dove would announce all sorts of marvels and Cagliostro would be forced to agree with them and so join the conspiracy, or Cagliostro would challenge the dove's statements and accuse her of lying, in which case the Cardinal

Chapter VII

would develop very understandable doubts about Cagliostro's clairvoyant abilities and, indeed, about the integrity of any of his previous activities: De Rohan would be turned against him.

The trap had certainly been well laid, and if Cagliostro had really been a charlatan then he would undoubtedly have been caught in it. Where the Countess went wrong was to mistake Cagliostro for a sham. Absolutely nothing went according to plan: young Mademoiselle de la Tour, half-asleep, acting under some unforeseen influence, didn't say any of the things that she'd previously agreed with the Countess, but nor did she see anything that was best left concealed, and if the Cardinal did form any doubts then it was only about the clairvoyant abilities of Mademoiselle de la Tour [69].

The months passed, the Cardinal hoping from day to day for some sign of recognition from the Queen and for the first payment that she was due to make, but he did not breathe a word of all this to Cagliostro. Bœhmer, astonished not to have seen the Queen wearing the necklace, became suspicious and started firing questions at the Cardinal, whose answers were confident but not sufficiently so to allay Bœhmer's concerns. Finally, in July, with both the Cardinal and Bœhmer no longer sure about what was happening, they both made efforts, unknown to each other, to find out what was going on. Bœhmer arranged for the Queen to receive a letter of thanks. She glanced at it, could make no sense of it, and threw it into the waste-paper basket. Bœhmer interpreted the resulting silence as a sign of consent and was somewhat reassured. The Cardinal, overcoming any feelings of embarrassment, finally decided to speak to Cagliostro. He told him everything, showing him for the first time the letters and the contract with the jeweller countersigned by the queen, and asking him for advice and protection. This time Cagliostro was categorical: time was pressing, and Bœhmer had already written to the Queen. Even if the cardinal wasn't aware of that fact then Cagliostro was. They had to act fast so that the matter could be settled between the King, the Queen and the Cardinal. 'You have been most wickedly deceived', Cagliostro told the Cardinal. 'There's nothing for it but for you to throw yourself at the King's feet and tell him exactly what has happened' [70]. The Cardinal was terrified and refused to comply. 'Then one of your friends will have to go on your behalf', said Cagliostro [71]. The Cardinal still refused, even more stubbornly this time, restrained by fear and by pride in his name. What Cagliostro had suggested was, however, the only way of avoiding the terrible scandal that was rapidly unfolding.

The Cardinal, dismayed, did nothing. Madame de la Motte, who had learned of Bœhmer's course of action and of Cagliostro's advice, felt her cause was lost. The Cardinal was either going to confess or be arrested: whatever happened he would denounce her. There was therefore only one possible chance of saving herself: she had to incriminate Cagliostro. After all, a mysterious magician, someone who was always throwing money around yet didn't seem to have any known financial resources, who was a close friend of the Cardinal (indeed, his spiritual director), someone whom Madame de la Motte had, with some degree of skill, managed to implicate in the matter in such a way that he couldn't deny at least some knowledge of the events, was certainly the person at whom the finger was going to be pointed. 'And what's more', Madame de la Motte said to herself, 'this Italian fellow is simply ridiculous, useless and fragile. He'll quickly alienate the judges, the witnesses and the spectators'.

Somewhat reassured by this idea she still had to face up to an immediate threat, which was the falling-due of the first instalment on 1st August. She arranged for the Cardinal to receive yet another forged letter from the Queen saying that the 400,000 *livres* that had been promised would not be paid until 1st October, that appropriate arrangements were being made with Bœhmer, and that on 1st October 700,000 *livres* would be paid. In the interim she was sending, to cover the interest, 30,000 *livres* which she'd borrowed using some of the diamonds from the necklace as collateral [72].

The Cardinal felt a little bit better as there was no way, in his view, that Madame de la Motte could have got her hands on such a large sum of money except from the Queen: the Queen must therefore have the necklace, so all was well. He then went to Bœhmer, who was furious when he heard the news, refusing to accept the 30,000 *livres* as interest and accepting it only as a down-payment against the sum that was immediately due and to which he laid claim. And he didn't leave the matter there. On 3rd August he had a meeting with the Queen's Reader, Madame de Campan, who told him that the Queen had never received the necklace – it was all a swindle. He then went back to the Cardinal who, in good faith, swore that he was sure that the Queen *did* have the necklace and that she would pay the principal sum just as she had paid the interest. In any case, he had her guarantee [73].

Madame de la Motte saw that the game was finally up. She sent away to Italy the only really dangerous witness, Rétaux, and that same day went to see the Cardinal with her husband, requesting his hospitality for some forty-eight hours. 'They're spreading rumours about me, they're watching me, following me around', she explained. 'If I've compromised myself then it's only been on your behalf. I have done nothing except follow your orders. I want to flee to the provinces, just disappear, but until then it's up to you to protect me'. Through this last manoeuvre, as Funck-Brentano writes [74], the Countess thought she had definitively bound her fate to that of the Cardinal de Rohan and so established her innocence. After all, if she had not acted in good faith then would she really have gone to the Cardinal and given herself up?

The Cardinal took urgent steps to lodge her at his mansion [75], where she remained until 6th August, when she left for Bar-sur-Aube with the money and what was left of the necklace. Hardly had she left than on 9th August the Royal Jeweller was summoned to the Trianon to provide the Queen with an explanation. The King was informed and a private session of his Ministers was convened in his rooms. De Breteuil of course was delighted, revealing all his subdued animosity towards the Cardinal and demanding his immediate arrest. The King still hesitated, but on 15th August, on the day of the Feast of the Assumption, he cross-examined the Cardinal in front of all his courtiers and had him immediately arrested. On 18th August Madame de la Motte was captured at Bar-sur-Aube and brought back to Paris. On 21st August Baron de Breteuil signed a *lettre de cachet* for the arrest of Cagliostro [76].

On 23rd August at 7 a.m. Chesnon, the Police Commissary at Le Châtelet, accompanied by a posse of eight or ten men, including a man called Desbrugnières [77], broke down the door of Cagliostro's apartment. In his presence and despite his protests Chesnon emptied his chest-of-drawers, quickly rifled through his writing-desk, took whatever suited him and ordered him to be taken away. But where to? He wasn't told. Cagliostro was worried – he had an inkling as to what had happened. And what would happen to his wife and his home? But they told Cagliostro that no warrants had been issued against his wife and that she would be allowed to remain at home to look after her interests. Then Desbrugnières suddenly hurled himself at Cagliostro and dragged him 'by the scruff of the neck and between four armed warders' [78], on foot, along the boulevards to the Bastille. Meanwhile Police Commissary Chesnon remained in Cagliostro's quarters and continued his ransacking, forcing locks, snaffling everything he liked the look of, pocketing some things, shovelling other things into a cardboard box, snapping bad-temperedly at Cagliostro's wife, and frightening the servants

Chapter VII

[79]. Then, when he'd finished his plundering, he took Countess Cagliostro off to the Bastille and, without explanation, had her locked up separately from her husband [80].

On the 24th August Countess Cagliostro was interrogated. The Governor of the Bastille De Launay and Chesnon made this terrified woman sign (with a cross) and add her seal to a statement containing everything that they wanted her to say. As a favour her maid Françoise was allowed to join her to keep her company [81]. The purpose of this apparent act of kindness was actually to enable the Police Commissary to install a lady-friend in Cagliostro's now empty apartment in Rue Saint-Claude and enjoy the exclusive use of it.

On 26th and 27th August Cagliostro was summarily interrogated. He recounted the facts that we have reported above insofar as they related to him. This basic account should have been sufficient to exclude him from enquiries, but it did nothing of the sort: on the contrary his interrogators tried to catch him out and lay traps for him. De Launay solemnly swore (the second act of perjury) that his wife had not been arrested and that she was still at Rue Saint-Claude. They suggested that he write to her. They would make sure that she received all his letters and that he received all her replies. In this way they hoped to catch him out in some indiscretions. The letters that Cagliostro wrote – after being thoroughly scrutinised by De Launay [82] – did reach his wife, but were of course delivered to her in her cell. She was then told what to write in reply. A police-officer was sent to Saint-Claude to collect any clothing and linen that Cagliostro needed and the whole lot – both the parcel and the letter – was then given to him as if it had been sent by his wife. Any person other than Cagliostro would have been reassured by all this that everything was in order back home, but he found these procedures very far from convincing. So sure was he that he had been deceived, that his wife was suffering, and that his apartment had been plundered, that he showed signs of the most terrible agitation and despair. Delorme, the Deputy Governor of the Bastille, became frightened that Cagliostro would commit suicide, and on the evening of the 29th he assigned a guard to keep watch over him [83].

The months went by without any further developments. What torture it must have been for Cagliostro! The inquiries were proceeding slowly and it was not until that winter [84] that the first official interrogations were carried out. It was only on 27th February 1786 that Cagliostro finally received permission to see his lawyer and learned from him that he had been deceived, that his darling wife had been in the Bastille for some seven months, that she was ill [85], that she was complaining in vain about the way she was being treated, and that her life might even be in danger. Along with his lawyer, the faithful Thilorier, Cagliostro immediately drafted a formal request that Countess Cagliostro be released and that he be granted the right to see her. D'Éprémesnil, touched by the weakness and gentleness of the innocent Countess Cagliostro, intervened on her behalf and supported the request [86]. Countess Cagliostro left the Bastille on 26th March 1786 and finally returned to the Rue Saint-Claude to find the writing-desk empty and the house ransacked.

A series of interrogations followed: the Cardinal, Madame de la Motte, her niece Mademoiselle de la Tour, and some other suspects were all questioned. The more Cagliostro showed himself to be calm, dignified and actually solicitous towards the culprits, and precise and consistent in his answers, the more Madame de la Motte became spiteful and frenzied [87], constantly changing her story in a desperate attempt to save her head. She then played her last cards: to implicate Cagliostro she piled lies upon lies, but these lacked the necessary astuteness [88]. Her lawyer, Maître Doillot, who had taken on the wretched Sachi as his assistant, published the latter's *Mémoire*, repeated his calumnies and had huge quantities of anonymous lampoons printed containing everything that was too obviously untrue, odious or obscene to be signed off and published in the official record. Paris was flooded with these pamphlets, and the populace fell over themselves to get their hands on them. They were of course only the most disgusting kind of libel but, as Beaumarchais put it, *il en restait toujours quelque chose* – some of the dirt always sticks and simply cannot be removed [89].

As the judges continued to examine the witnesses, so their opinion changed somewhat: Madame de la Motte was increasingly under suspicion, and Cagliostro decreasingly so. The judges were quite sure that it was Rétaux de la Villette who had forged the Queen's signatures and that it was he also who had pretended to be her manservant. His confessions, if they could have been obtained, would have shed all the light that was required, but he stubbornly denied everything.

Lettre de Cachet ordering the arrest of Count Cagliostro.

Chapter VII

He was then made to face Cagliostro, who spoke directly to his heart and obtained in one hour what the judges had failed to obtain in eight months: a full confession. 'It was then', wrote Cagliostro, 'that I delivered to him a sermon lasting all of one and a half hours in which I told him about the duty of an honourable man, the power of Providence, and the need to love one's neighbour. I then told him to place his hope in the mercy of God and that of the French government. My sermon was so long and so impassioned that eventually I actually lost the power of speech. So touched and mollified was the *Rapporteur*, the judge that prepares reports and summaries of the evidence for the other judges, that he told De la Villette that he would have to be a monster not to be affected by my words because I had spoken to him as his fellow-man and as someone full of religious faith and moral sensibility. He told him that what I had just said to him was a speech made in Heaven' [90].

We can see from this just how much energy and high-flown sentiment Cagliostro would have manifested in Court. Did he really look and sound like a guilty man? It was Cagliostro who did all the talking, the persuading, and who clarified points of justice to the extent of winning the admiration of the judges. He was the same man in the Bastille as he had been in his mansion in Strasbourg or amongst his beloved 'children' at *La Sagesse triomphante*. He was filled with truth, light and strength, and nothing human could stifle them. His calmness failed him only once – and that was entirely intentional. After eight months of captivity, of struggle, separation from his wife, after eight whole months of concern for her welfare, during which his work had been forcibly suspended and his disciples and patients forsaken [91], he finally came face to face again with Madame de la Motte, the person who was the root-cause of all this trouble and who continued, in an odious campaign, to drag the reputations of the Cardinal, Countess Cagliostro and Cagliostro himself through the mud. It was on that one occasion only that Cagliostro allowed his indignation free rein [92].

The next day it was the Cardinal's turn to face Madame de la Motte. 'Tomorrow I'm coming face to face with that wretch', he told his lawyer. 'Today she made a scene with Count Cagliostro. She actually threw a candlestick at him which hit him in the stomach, but she was instantly punished because the candle flew into her eye' [93]. But it was all over anyway: thanks to Cagliostro, Rétaux had confessed. Eventually Madame de la Motte confessed also following a dreadful attack of nerves. All that remained for the Cardinal to do was to harvest the fruits of Cagliostro's devotion and wisdom – and he knew it.

In any case, ever since the day of his arrest the Cardinal had never ceased to show a genuine interest in and a marked respect for Cagliostro: was this really a fit of remorse, or was it just that, in these days of trial, he placed his hopes in him alone? His confidential correspondence shows him to be genuinely concerned about Cagliostro's circumstances, and eager for his lawyers and his entourage to show him every possible respect and to render to him all the services that were within their scope [94].

On 30th May, the investigatory phase concluded, the Court sat and the defendants were questioned publicly [95]. The Cardinal was dignified but cowed, whereas Cagliostro appeared firm, even domineering.

'Who are you?' asked the judge.

'A noble traveller', answered Cagliostro in a powerful and brilliant voice which contrasted strongly with the stammering and snivelling of the previous defendants [96]. Then, without waiting for the next question, and with his head held high, he began to speak impressively, soulfully, about his life, the mystery that surrounded him, his powers, his personal trials, about God, Whose soldier he was and Who protected him, and about everything that the spirit inspired within him [97]. He improvised, not having prepared any of his answers in advance, sometimes smiling, sometimes terrifying in appearance, amusing and impressive by turns, his words penetrating deeply in the hearts of his listeners. His cheerfulness, his powerful gestures and the sheer authority of what he had to say had the audience eating out of his hand. When he had finished the President of the Court started to congratulate him but his words were drowned out by thunderous applause from the public gallery.

Around 6 p.m. the defendants were taken back to the Bastille, the crowds forcing the coaches to leave via the Cour Lamoignon. The air was filled with the names of De Rohan and Cagliostro as the crowds cheered them on and sent them their best wishes for their early release. Cagliostro acknowledged everyone, greeting those he knew, thanking those he didn't, raising his arms aloft and throwing into the crowd his hat which 'a thousand hands fought for', as Funck-Brentano writes [98]. That is perhaps an accurate picture, for Cagliostro knew how to speak to a crowd as he knew how to speak to an individual – in their own language.

On 31st May 1786 at 9 p.m. judgment was given, with the Cardinal and Cagliostro being found not guilty and leaving Court without a stain upon their characters. The Court ordered that they be set free immediately, that the verdict be printed and posted, and that the various pamphlets and lampoons written against them should be destroyed. The Cardinal's dreadful nightmare was at an end: now he could emerge from Hell along with his liberator. Should the King not find some way of helping Cagliostro forget about these painful moments? And, in particular, should he not set aside for Cagliostro some compensation for the persecution he had undergone, some tokens of his benevolence to remedy the abuses of power that had been inflicted on his behalf upon an innocent subject, a man who had devoted his life to love of his fellow man? And should the general public have any emotions at all except pity for the Cardinal and admiration for Cagliostro?

Unfortunately, as we shall see, this was in no way the case: the King wanted to forget about the whole thing; the Queen, for her part, was certainly aware of Cagliostro's role as the Cardinal's saviour, but for her this was only an excuse to cause him even further harm; as for the general public, they went back to their other amusements. And quite quickly, forgetting Cagliostro's complete innocence, his courage in adversity and his noble self-control, despite the evidence, the confessions, the judgment of the Court, as soon as the historians had reason to start discussing Cagliostro again they immediately started surrounding his name with an aura of suspicion [99]. Their ridiculous insinuations, their vague terminology and their *double entendres* all helped to destroy the torrent of exculpation and left his memory tarnished with a 'probable' involvement in the whole business, even though he had less to do with it than the King himself! Isn't this an iniquitous, repugnant and terrible thing to have to admit?

Many people will wonder why, if Cagliostro was genuinely clairvoyant and must therefore have known about the criminal schemes of Madame de la Motte, if he had seen through the secret plans of Cardinal de Rohan, and if he could see the abyss towards which everyone was rushing headlong then why, if he knew what was going to happen, did he allow these dreadful events to unfold? This is a perfectly logical question, but if you care to reflect upon Cagliostro, if you have watched this great figure gradually emerge in these pages, if we have had any success at all in describing him as he actually was as opposed to the distorted picture of him that the bad faith of the chroniclers have handed down to us, then it should prove quite an easy question to answer.

With regard to Madame de la Motte, as we have already explained, there was no reason for Cagliostro, who was not by nature a person who went around denouncing other people,

Chapter VII

to try to stop these developments in their tracks. Everything must progress, and if one cannot grow in goodness then it is better to manifest the evil immediately rather than harbour within oneself a seed of wickedness that will sprout more terribly later on. That is not our own opinion, nor that of Cagliostro alone: the Son of David, many centuries ago, said very much the same thing.

Should he perhaps have intervened on behalf of his friend Cardinal de Rohan? What exactly did he want from the Cardinal? He'd often said to him, as he had to his other disciples, that the role of every initiation and the goal of human life itself was spiritual renewal – the acquisition, by daily effort, of that light that shines within every man who comes into this world and which, in our profane lives, we repress and obscure through our selfish desires and personal actions. Cagliostro recognised that the Cardinal had a spirit that was capable of attaining a higher degree of knowledge [100]. He had therefore wasted no opportunity in providing him with exemplars, encouragement and life-lessons. A respectful affection united the Cardinal with his Master, and Cagliostro had high hopes of him achieving spiritual heights, promising him that he would take him further – much further – than any of the others if he remained faithful to him and his teachings. But the Cardinal was a weak character, impatient and ambitious. His excellent and lively mind saw in the acquisition of supernatural powers and Cagliostro's protection only a means to satisfy his worldly ambitions. He wanted wealth, power and success at Court – with the best of intentions no doubt – but on the basis of emotions that were entirely personal. Interpreting his Master's promises in the light of his desires and not seeing those promises realised he began to doubt his Master's sincerity and sought to acquire *by his own efforts* the treasures that he coveted the most, namely the favour of the Queen and influence over the King. Initially he acted without Cagliostro, then behind his back. When his conscience enabled him to realise that the conquest of human glory was not the same as the conquest of immortality he tried to calm his scruples by, as it were, dividing his life in two, leaving the care of his soul to Cagliostro and the realisation of his ambitions to intrigue. So well did he understand that his Master would stand in the way of his plans that he learned to carefully conceal from him even his most trivial actions. Matters were therefore planned and executed hastily, behind Cagliostro's back. By acting in this way the Cardinal paralysed Cagliostro's ability to protect him, closed off the paths of Providence, and headed straight for the rock on which pride is always shattered. Cagliostro simply let him get on with it, as one might leave a stubborn and conceited child to burn his fingers so that he learns the effects of fire.

When a creature of light comes to you with undeniable proofs of enormous power and unparalleled goodness then should an otherwise intelligent man really allow some petty feelings of mistrust to lead him astray and cause him to try to outsmart the messenger of God, seek wealth and glory without his knowledge, mislead him in his words and flee from him in his heart, while preserving an outward appearance of devotion? But that is precisely what De Rohan did.

And yet heaven is always on the side of the passionate and the determined. Heaven has no time for the tepid and the mediocre, and even less does it grant its power to the recalcitrant. For heaven to take root within a man it needs, not an appearance of inner peace and genuine goodness, but the reality. There is no room for division: he who wishes to serve God but who turns back after initially putting his hand to the plough is not worthy of his wages. The Cardinal wanted to adore Cagliostro's God but at the same time, unknown to him, he wanted to worship at the altar of Mammon. By rights Cagliostro should have been saddened by this, but he respected his disciple's right to be enveloped in an aura of illusion.

He allowed him free rein to mistrust his advice and puff himself up with what he fondly believed to be success. Time caught up with De Rohan rather faster than he would have liked or anticipated, and he learned a hard lesson when he finally fell. What remorse must have eaten away at him, what sense of humility and contrition towards Cagliostro must have arisen within him when, from hour to hour during the trial, he was forced to concede that Cagliostro had been the only one out of all of them to see things with any clarity, that he alone had proved a true friend, and that he had freely, in spite of everything, shouldered one part of the cross to help him to carry it and so ultimately save him. And while De Rohan – both a prince and a Cardinal, and a cousin of the King to boot – was blanching and trembling in front of a handful of petty 'limbs of the law', Cagliostro was speaking to the judges with this same serious assurance and grandeur that formerly, in Saverne, had impressed De Rohan with such a sense of nobility and something bordering on mastery [101]. What lessons he must have learned, how his interior blasphemies must have returned to haunt him along with the proud words of his Master: 'You are offering to take me under your wing? I am deeply touched, Your Eminence. And in return, I shall take you under mine!'

There were also less personal reasons of a more general order which dictated Cagliostro's conduct. Himself an innocent party, the support that he gave, on behalf of the truth, justice and human dignity, for the palpable injustice of an arbitrary arrest, the violence of the police, the plundering of his property, the physical and moral torture of the false imprisonment, and the wounds inflicted by libel and gossip simply increased the liability of the culprits, forcing them to the utmost limits in their abusive behaviour and so eventually bringing about the end of their criminal careers. One thing that is particularly striking in the life of Cagliostro is that whenever he had to endure some injustice at the hands of a fellow human-being or the legal system we see those human-beings or those unjust laws coming to immediate destruction, as if the cup of iniquity was filled to overflowing when the persecution of Cagliostro had added the last drop to it [102]. Not that he had ever rebelled against any of these abuses: on the contrary, in a way he supported them, always showing respect for the government and institutions of the country that had welcomed him. But it is written in the laws of Heaven that there are limits to evil, and that when its teeth, having torn to shreds both the petty and the mighty, turn upon a friend of God and cause him harm then they are shattered for all eternity [103].

Historians and philosophers have written that the Diamond Necklace Affair was the immediate prelude to the French Revolution [104], but it should not be understood by this that it was the sole cause of the Revolution, any more than Cagliostro's imprisonment in the Bastille was the sole reason why it was stormed on 14th July. That would display a lack of judgement. For many years the ground had been prepared for the events of 1789, and the necessary preconditions had gradually accumulated. People had sown the seeds, toiled in the fields, and now it was time to reap the harvest. But the harvest only begins when the Master, entering his field, administers the first blow of the sickle to the ripened corn. At the very moment when Desbrugnières, *in the name of the King*, placed his hands upon Cagliostro, when the doors of his cell clanged shut behind the Being of Light, the spirit of France left Versailles and the foundations of the Bastille began to tremble: the conventional image of the Revolution had come to pass, and now the people would do the rest.

On 1st June, at 11.30 p.m. (the late hour being the result of a deliberate attempt to wear out the patience of those people in the public gallery who had hoped that Cagliostro would make a speech [105]) De Launay opened the gates of the Bastille and released his prisoner. Despite the lateness of the hour the demonstration in Cagliostro's favour was impressive:

eight to ten thousand people thronged around his mansion [106], there were cries of joy, the beating of drums [107], the lighting of flares – it was almost a revolution in miniature!

'My door had been battered down', wrote Cagliostro. 'The courtyard, the staircases, the apartments, all were full of people. I was carried along by the crowd into the arms of my dear wife. My heart was unable to contain all the various feelings that fought for its control. My knees were buckling beneath me. I fell onto the wooden floor, senseless. Then my wife uttered a piercing cry and fainted'.

There was alarm, panic... the Cagliostros finally came to, dissolved into tears and then experienced the most infinite joy, 'this first sweet moment of happiness after ten months of torment' [108]. The next morning the crowd was still thronging in front of their mansion and that of the Cardinal who appeared on his terrace to greet the crowd [109]. These demonstrations of loyalty and fervour were much remarked upon at Court [110].

But Cagliostro's joy was to be short-lived: as a reward for his services and as compensation for his unmerited sufferings he was offered... exile! The hatred of De Breteuil [111] continued to pursue its victim. The Queen's wounded pride was also avenged by this arbitrary act. Twelve hours after Cagliostro's release Desbrugnières, whom we have already met, served upon him an expulsion order in the name of the King: he must leave Paris within twenty-four hours and the kingdom within three weeks, and was forbidden to return on any pretext. Cagliostro obeyed without demur [112]. On the morning of 3rd June, leaving his wife in Paris to gather together those few belongings of theirs that had not been plundered, he left for Passy in the company of some devoted friends, and spent nine days [113] there.

The fury of the people of Versailles, which had been increased by the popular expressions of sympathy that Cagliostro had received, was such to make his friends fear for his life. A sudden assassination attempt was thought likely, and so he hid himself away in his room [114]. His friends, working in pairs, swords in hand, took it in turns to stand guard outside his door day and night. Many of his disciples, both men and women, came to Passy, lodging at the inns and private houses, just to be near their Master. Thilorier, his faithful lawyer, would not leave his side. It was also on Thilorier's advice that Cagliostro decided to sue Chesnon and De Launay jointly for damages, for was it not their fault that Cagliostro had been unjustly implicated in this whole sorry affair and had lost most of his personal fortune as a result? At the time of his arrest a horde of plunderers had laid their thieving hands on his most invaluable possessions: Chesnon had rummaged in his private papers, taking deeds, share-certificates and securities, without performing an inventory [115], and Desbrugnières had surreptitiously pocketed some of his rare elixirs and balsams [116]. After his imprisonment the house had remained unguarded and vulnerable to crooks, police-agents and others. To prevent him from taking the least precaution to safeguard his interests, false oaths were sworn on two occasions (21st and 26th August) to the effect that his wife was still living there. There was also the nonsense of the letters allegedly sent to and from Countess Cagliostro. Furthermore, upon the return of the Countess there was a further breach of trust by which a pretence was made of giving her discharge of all her precious belongings, whereas they had not in fact been returned her at all. Upon Cagliostro's own departure from the Bastille exactly the same swindle was attempted all over again [117]. Then there were the ill-treatments they had undergone and the deceptions they had to put up with during their imprisonment. All these abuses of power and all these exactions, all of them against the spirit of the law if not indeed the letter of it, were surely more than enough to justify Cagliostro's protests and his demands that the culprits be punished and that, in future, the necessary surveillance be undertaken to ensure that nothing like it could ever happen again.

In a petition drafted by Maître Thilorier, the *Mémoire contre Chesnon*, Cagliostro asked for restitution of 100,000 *livres*, which he estimated to be the approximate value of his stolen goods and securities [118], plus 50,000 *livres* in damages for the loss of priceless documents and papers [119] which had disappeared during the searches of his premises. To make it clear that this was not a speculative venture on his part but a matter of principle, he also made it clear that these 50,000 *livres* 'would be used to provide better food for the unfortunate prisoners in Le Châtelet' [120].

The procedures followed by Police Commissary Chesnon and the conduct of the Governor of the Bastille were obviously similar to those inflicted upon the majority of people arrested in Paris around that time. Chesnon was not perhaps strictly *obliged* [121] to draw up an inventory of goods or to affix seals to prevent unlawful entry as the *lettre de cachet*, the legal instrument which had been used to arrest Cagliostro, fell outside the scope of the law. But that, of course, is exactly what Cagliostro was protesting against: what he was fighting for was legality, justice for all, respect for the individual and the suppression of everything that was 'outside the law'. He had appointed himself a people's advocate and a champion of the weak, a role that he continued to play throughout his life whatever the circumstances.

The petition against Chesnon that he drew up with Thilorier is an therefore important social document: it is not simply a personal claim for justice but a plea for human rights [122]. As we have seen Cagliostro always respected authority and never rebelled against any laws. Indeed he bore all their rigours without complaint or protest, but when the law falls short, when self-indulgence reigns, it is there that iniquity rears its head. It was against the abuses by the police-force, the arbitrary behaviour and discretionary powers of De Launay the Governor of the Bastille, and against the illegal and unfair processes which were used against the prisoners [123] that he raised his voice. Above all, Cagliostro knew that we need to respect justice in spirit as well as in truth: he could not allow her to be harmed with impunity. His memorandum also gives us a foretaste [124] of what he would make more explicit later on [125]: that a time would come when *lettres de cachet* and the dreadful sufferings behind the walls of the Bastille would become things of the past.

Cagliostro's petition against Chesnon was taken into consideration [126], as it could hardly fail to be, but that was all. Despite a second petition, the *Requête en exécution de l'arrêt* [127], no further action was taken: the culprits kept their jobs along with the money and other things they had stolen. De Launay and Chesnon defended themselves, after a fashion, in pretty incoherent responses [128] which sought to rebut the plaintiff's claims only on certain points of detail. The matter ground to halt [129]. Apart from Thilorier and some of Cagliostro's friends there was perhaps nobody who really understood the significance of his humane actions.

But now it was time for Cagliostro to leave Paris. It had been hoped that intercession by powerful friends or a simple turn of events would have caused the expulsion order to be rescinded or at least postponed, but this did not happen. His enemies were still in power and he had no alternative but to obey. On Tuesday 13th June at 5.00 p.m., to the sorrow of his whole entourage, Cagliostro left Saint-Denis. On 15th June he was in Boulogne, and on the 16th he embarked for England [130]. Many disciples had followed him or had even gone ahead of him to await him on this final stage of his journey through France. If he had had bitter enemies in France we must also say, in praise of the French, that it was in their country that he also encountered the deepest affection and had the largest number of devotees, and that these were the most faithful he had ever had. Apart from Cardinal de Rohan he had also enjoyed the support of Thilorier, Ramond de Carbonnières and D'Éprémesnil [131], whose loyalty to him had increased day by day. In his Paris Lodges the respect and devotion shown towards him actually increased in those days of struggle and trials, which had been initially crowned with success only to be followed by renewed persecution. Some of his disciples had joined him in Passy, and everyone rushed to Boulogne [132] to share with him his last few hours on French soil.

Then it was finally time for him to go, and both men and women fell to their knees along the sea-front, weeping and asking him for one last blessing. Cagliostro, standing aboard the ship that was to take him away, stretched out his hands towards them. He was unable to contain his emotions: 'What memories, oh what cherished memories, but oh what cruel ones as well!' he wrote in his *Lettre au peuple français*. In his *Mémoire contre Chesnon*, as he remembered with emotion those tokens of sincere affection that he had received in Paris after his acquittal and in Boulogne at his departure, he could still write the following:

Oh people of France, citizens of a nation so truly generous and so truly hospitable, I shall never forget either the touching interest which you took in my fate or the sweet tears that your rapturous farewells made me shed... A single day of glory and happiness was compensation enough for my long sufferings... Citizens of this happy clime, so friendly and so sensitive, receive the farewells of this poor unfortunate, who is perhaps worthy of both your esteem and your regrets. He has gone, accustomed as he is to submitting himself without demur to the will of Kings. He may have left, but his heart has remained amongst you. Wherever he might live now, rest assured that he will always remain a true friend of the French people [133].

Nor was Cagliostro embellishing these touching expressions of feeling with rhetorical devices. On the contrary, if anything they probably fell short of the reality, for the veneration that everyone showed their Master was simply beyond belief.

Cagliostro had fervent disciples in places other than Paris. Those who were prevented by distance from fighting alongside him longed to be of use to him and always tried to do their best for him. From Strasbourg, Barbier de Tinan had sent the *Correspondance secrète de Neuwied* a letter setting the record straight and testifying to his affection and devotion to Cagliostro [134]. Around the same time the Chevalier de Langlois wrote to Thilorier as follows:

How happy I would be if I could give him proof of the tender and respectful attachment for him which I feel in my bones, that spiritual affection which I do not know to reciprocate but which I feel so vividly. My entire physical and moral existence belong to him: they are things of which he rightfully enjoys the usufruct... My wife, my brothers, my parents, Maître du Picquet and his family, who also feel a great sense of obligation towards him, want Count Cagliostro to understand that we are affected beyond our powers of expression by everything that unforeseen events are causing him to undergo, and that our ambition and our glory would be satisfied if we could find opportunities be of some use to him. That is the simple and unadorned homage to be found within our hearts.
Signed, Chevalier de Langlois, Captain of Dragoons, Regiment of Montmorency [135].

Sarrasin also poured out his feelings about his Master to the man that he loved and respected the most after Cagliostro himself, Lavater:

Help me to thank God and his so grievously misunderstood servant Cagliostro for everything that I have received. It seems to me that these seventeen hectic months have been nothing more than a most beautiful and splendid dream which, if God wishes it, must render me a better person for the remainder of my life, and I am counting on taking something of it with me when I awaken on the Other Side. Cagliostro has never seemed so great to me as he has during these last few days and at the time of my departure.

And when he learned about the ordeals that Cagliostro was undergoing in Paris he wrote:
We are quite calm here, and are more than ever attached to our father and benefactor. Even if he shares the destiny of Socrates we shall always be honoured to have been his pupils and his apostles [136].

These proofs of devotion are plain and sincere, but however beautiful they might be they are nothing besides the rare – and indeed extraordinary – tokens of filial love that united some of his disciples to their Master, some glimpses of which we can find in the letters written to Cagliostro from Boulogne on the day of his departure from France, and happily preserved [137]. Here is the first of them:

My eternal Master, my Everything, it seemed that the sea itself was opposed to the separation that I was being forced to endure. We spent eighteen hours at sea and arrived at eleven in the morning. My son suffered so much. But, Master, I had the happiness of seeing you tonight. The Eternal had brought to fulfilment the blessing that I received yesterday. Ah! my Master, after God Himself you have been the architect of my happiness. The youngsters X and Y commend themselves always to your kindness. They are honourable young people and, with the help of your power, they will one day be worthy to be your Sons.

Oh Master, how I wish it was already September! How happy I shall be when I can see and hear you again, and can assure you once more of my happiness and respect. We leave tomorrow. What a pleasure our Brothers shall enjoy! ...

Is it really possible that I shall no longer find in Paris the person who made me so very happy there? But I am resigned to it, and I prostrate myself before God and before you.

I wrote to Monsieur X to tell him what you have told me to do. Ah my Master, how hard it is for me to no longer be able to assure you of my feelings except by letter!

September will come, that happy time when I shall be able, at your feet and those of Mistress Cagliostro, to assure you of the submission, respect and obedience that will always inspire those who dare to call themselves the humblest and most unworthy Sons of their Master, their Everything...

Dare I ask you, Master, to allow me to kneel at the feet of the Mistress?
Boulogne-sur-Mer, 20th June 1786.

The second letter is no less touching:
My dear Master,
Monsieur X told me how I might forward to you some tokens of my esteem. The first use that I am making of that is to throw myself at your feet, to give you my heart, and to ask you to help me to raise my soul towards the Eternal. I will not tell you, oh my Master, of the pain that I suffered when the floods of the ocean took away from France the best of all the Masters and the most powerful of men: you will know that better than I.

My heart and my soul are always open to you. Your inspiration and your blessings and yours alone have the right to fill them for all eternity. Deign, oh my Sovereign Master, to remember me, to remind yourself that I remain isolated amidst my friends now that I have lost you, and that the unique desire of my heart is to reunite myself to the all-good, all-powerful Master, who alone can communicate to my heart this power, this belief and this energy which will render me capable of carrying out his will.

Chapter VII

Deign only, my Master, to promise not to abandon me, to grant me your blessing and to enfold me in your spirit, for then I feel that I shall be everything that you would want me to be.

My pen is unequal to the many promptings of my heart, but my heart is filled with feelings of the utmost respect. Decide my fate therefore; do not let me languish far from you for too long. The happiness of my life is all that I ask from you. You inspired the need in me, oh my Master, and you alone can satisfy it.

With all the feelings of a resigned and submissive heart I throw myself at your feet and those of our Mistress,

I am, Sir and Master, with the deepest respect, etc.
Boulogne-sur-Mer, 20th June 1786 [138].

In all these letters we can sense the same faith, the same afflatus that motivated Sarrasin in his letter to Lavater, or Cardinal de Rohan when he was talking to Abbé Georgel and Baroness d'Oberkirch. What sort of Master is it whose disciples express themselves like that, and what sort of man would you need to be to inspire enthusiasm of that kind?

NOTES
(1) *Interrogatoire à la Bastille*, Arch. Nat., X² 2676, and Campardon, *Marie-Antoinette et le procès du Collier*, Paris, Plon, 1863, p. 340.
(2) Born in Strasbourg in 1753, known specifically as a man of letters and naturalist. He began a political career rather too late in life. Died 1829.
(3) *Interrogatoire à la Bastille*, Arch. Nat., X² 2676 and Campardon, loc. cit., p. 341. If we have drawn attention to these details and to the fact that when he first arrived in Paris he lived quite luxuriously and did not count his pennies then that is because some have exploited the claim that he arrived penniless in Paris to support the calumny that he got rich by blackmailing the Cardinal.
(4) *Vieilles maisons, vieux papiers*, 1st series, Paris, Perrin, 1910, p. 161.
(5) Lenotre, ibid. p. 166. 'His apartment remained closed for as long as the Revolution lasted. It was only in 1805 that its doors were opened again after some 18 years, when the new owner sold off the furniture that Cagliostro had used for just 18 months'. Lenotre quotes this as fact but without references, but he was undoubtedly led astray by the auction of Cagliostro's furniture in London in 1787. 'Since that time', continues Lenotre, 'this serene house in Rue Saint-Claude has faded from history – but wait a moment, I stand corrected: around 1855 some repairs were undertaken there and the two leaves of the old carriage-gate were replaced with wooden doors from the ruins of the Palais du Temple, and they were still there, with their huge bolts and enormous locks, in 1910. So a door from Louis XVI's prison was used as an entrance to the house of Cagliostro... Hmm, life is full of its little ironies is it not!', Lenotre, p. 171.
(6) Funck-Brentano, *L'Affaire du Collier*, p. 102, following the memoirs of Madame de la Motte, I, 39-40.
(7) Cf. Chapter II of this book, 'Portrait', and S. Laroche, *Tagebuch einer Reise*..., Offenbach, 1788, p. 314.
(8) *Interrogatoire à la Bastille*, Arch. Nat., X², 2676. Campardon, loc. cit., p. 341.
(9) Source: Monsieur d'Hannibal.
(10) *Mémoire pour le comte de Cagliostro*, Paris, 1786, p. 37.
(11) Cf. Chapter V of this book.
(12) *Mémoire contre le Procureur*, 1786, pp. 33-35.
(13) 'If His Eminence is sick then let him come here and I will cure him. If he's feeling alright then he doesn't need me, nor I him', Cagliostro replied to the Cardinal's hunt-master, the Baron de Millinens, who had requested an audience. Cagliostro explained in his *Mémoire contre le Procureur*, Paris, 1786, p. 30, that he wasn't interested in satisfying people's idle curiosity. However, when he learned one day

that the Cardinal was having an asthma attack he rushed to be at his side.

(14) Funck-Brentano, *L'Affaire du Collier*, p. 102. Was the invitation made with bad grace perhaps, or did Cagliostro think that he simply had too many people sick in mind or body on his hands to waste his evening entertaining some princes? Whatever the case may be he declined this 'honour'.

(15) D'Oberkirch, *Mémoires*, vol. I, chapter XII. 'In his presence the Cardinal felt his body shaken by a strong spiritual sensation, and his first words to Cagliostro were charged with a very special form of respect', Georgel, *Mémoires*, vol. II, p. 49.

(16) Von der Recke, *Nachricht von des berüchtigten...*, 1787, p. 87.

(17) 'He spoke a sort of patois, half-French and half-Italian, sprinkled with quotations in what was supposed to be Arabic. He delivered monologues, and always had time to cover about twenty different subjects because he only dwelt on each of them for as long as it suited him. He would always stop and ask at appropriate moments if he was being understood, and would peer around at his circle of listeners, looking at each person in turn, to make sure that this was the case. When he launched into a particular topic he seemed to be transported, and both his mannerisms and his voice would have an especially elevated character, but then he would suddenly come back down to earth again and pay the lady of the house some very tender compliments or make some amusing remark to her. He followed the same procedure all the way through supper. I must admit that I didn't gather very much of what he had to say, but I do remember that our hero spoke in turn about the heavens, the stars, the Great Arcana, Memphis, the hierophant, transcendental chemistry, giants, gigantic animals, a town in the African interior ten times the size of Paris where he had some correspondents and, of course, our own lamentable ignorance of all these wonderful subjects which he himself knew inside-out...', Beugnot, *Mémoires*, Paris, 1889, p.46.

(18) *Lettre d'un disciple à Cagliostro*, in *Vie de Joseph Balsamo*, p. 196.

(19) *Vie de Joseph Balsamo*, pp. 68, 120, 123, 124, 127, 128, 137 to 139, 147, 216. The prediction about the Bastille, in particular, was made, and even committed to writing, a long time before it was printed.

(20) Lenotre, loc. cit. p. 163.

(21) A lodge under the obedience of the Mother-Lodge of Lyons.

(22) Cf. Chapter VI of this book, *Cagliostro in Lyons*.

(23) The Egyptian Rite was developed in Paris. A Supreme Council was established, with the Duc de Montmorency as Grandmaster Protector; Monsieur de Laborde, tax-farmer, as Grand Inspector; Baudard de Saint-James, a very wealthy banker, as Grand Chancellor; and Monsieur de Vismes as Secretary. It was this Supreme Council which had to put up with the struggle with the *Philalèthes* to which we referred in the later pages of Chapter VI.

(24) Philanthropic activities and serious discussions on social or moral subjects were fashionable in Parisian *salons* at this time, especially amongst women.

(25) 'In all the lodges', he told me, 'there are special celebrations to which the ladies are invited. There are waltzes and charming concerts, followed by banquets which are certainly not worthy of disdain', *Mémoires inédits du comte de Lamotte*, Paris, Poulet-Malassis, 1858, p. 382. 'The women admitted to the celebrations were in no way involved with the teachings and secret knowledge of the Lodge', Prince de Montbarey, *Mémoires*, Paris, 1827, 3 vols., vol. II, p. 100.

(26) 'This servitude to which women are condemned is carefully veiled under a sort of cult, namely the laws of chivalry. Alongside this hypocritical devotion which is essentially a counterfeit piety modern nations have developed *galanterie*, which is essentially counterfeit love. The woman, surrounded by fawning courtiers who flatter her and yet look down on her at the same time, bestows her smiles upon all except the man she has sworn to love... By turns despotic mistress and degraded slave, the woman humiliates the man with her caprices until the day when he finally crushes her with his contempt', L. Ménard, *Lettre d'un mort*, Paris, 1890, p. 32.

(27) *Rituel de la Maçonnerie Égyptienne*, Adoption: Degree of Mistress.

(28) *Rituel de la Maçonnerie Égyptienne*, Adoption: Degree of Mistress, Mss. Papus, p. 195.

(29) The truly enlightened have always understood the true role of woman and her spiritual superiority,

Chapter VII

which is portrayed for us in the symbol of the Annunciation: isn't it the Archangel Gabriel who bows first to the Virgin? Guillaume Postel wrote eloquently about it, and Swedenborg also glimpsed the truth of it.

(30) Funck-Brentano, *L'Affaire du Collier*, p. 104.

(31) *Das Graue Ungeheuer*, 1785. Vol. V, No. 15, pp. 338-345, and Thory, *Histoire de la fondation du Grand-Orient*, p. 212.

(32) All the Rituals and Catechisms of the three degrees of female Egyptian Freemasonry contain the following:

'The purpose of initiation is to strengthen in the woman the spiritual part of her being', Reception of Apprentice, p. 154.

'Strength, power, patience, this is the motto inscribed upon the apron', Reception to the degree of Fellow Craft, p. 169.

'The sign that you see here, *Ego sum homo*, means that the spiritual power that dwells within you is not female, that it is active, male, or, to speak more accurately, that it has no gender... This spiritual power will be raised to a new state where it will possess wisdom, intelligence, the ability to understand and speak all languages, and the joy of becoming the intermediary between God and those made in his likeness', Catechism of the degree of Mistress, pp. 204-208.

'Purify your heart, raise your spirit ceaselessly to the Eternal; finally, acquire wisdom, which is the perfection of the supernatural philosophy; you will then be admitted to the interior of the temple', Catechism of the Fellow Craft, p. 182.

'Love your neighbour as you love yourself, be kind to the unfortunate, give continual tokens of your discretion and your wisdom... seek to gradually enlighten yourself by an attentive reading of the Scriptures (the Old Testament), for no book will be able to give you greater illumination regarding all the principles of the Egyptian Hermetic School', Catechism of the degree of Mistress, p. 189.

(Pagination refers to the Mss. Papus.)

(33) 'You will never', said Baroness d'Oberkirch, 'be able to conceive the fury and passion with which everyone threw themselves at Cagliostro', *Mémoires*, vol. I, chapter VII. His bust, as sculpted by Houdon, decorated the living rooms, his portrait was everywhere – on rings, on fans, on snuffboxes, and engravings of him and his wife decorated booksellers' windows.

(34) This story, drawn from De Luchet's *Mémoires authentiques*, depicts the women's Egyptian lodge-meetings as Bacchanalian orgies with Cagliostro playing a particularly ludicrous and obscene part. The scandal-sheets spread this story, especially abroad (*Das Graue Ungeheuer*, 1787, No. 15, pp. 331-345). It was also repeated by Gérard de Nerval in his *Illuminés*, Paris, 1868 and by J. de Saint-Félix in his *Aventures de Cagliostro*, Paris, 1855, pp. 104 et seq. We have already acquired a clear idea of just how dignified Cagliostro's life was. Regarding the irreproachable morality of the Egyptian Order we would suggest that the reader examine the Ritual of Egyptian Freemasonry and, in particular, the Ritual of the Lodge of Adoption. There they will see the scrupulous precautions taken for mixed meetings; the oath that was required (p. 153); the seven points; the symbols (gloves and the *habit talare* (a soutane, an ankle-length robe) p. 173; the recommendations to the Initiates; and their duties, pp. 204-208. Thory, *Histoire de la Fondation du Grand Orient*, p. 213, provides a serious and impartial study of Cagliostro's Freemasonry of Adoption which, it would seem, has done nothing to stop the spread of malicious rumours.

(35) This second fantasy, of the same origin, which puts sour jokes about various 18th century personalities and habits into the mouths of ghosts and spectres is a satire of no interest, but at least it is free of obscenities and is sometimes actually quite spiritual. Like the previous fantasy and the account of the pseudo-initiation of Cagliostro by the Comte de Saint-Germain we find it taken literally and quoted by chroniclers, just like so many other 'facts' about the life of Cagliostro.

(36) *Ma Correspondance*, 1785, No. 73.

(37) *Gazette de Leyde* of 9th November 1785.

(38) In Russia to Rogerson and in England to Morande, cf. Chapter IV of this book.

(39) On Paris at that epoch see Taine, *Les origines de la France contemporaine: L'ancien régime*,

Loménie, *Beaumarchais et son temps*, Paris, 1858, and P. de Nolhac, *Marie-Antoinette*, Paris, 1890.
(40) The Saint-Rémy family were descended from Henri de Saint-Rémy, a bastard acknowledged by his father, Henri II. Cf. Funck-Brentano, *L'affaire du Collier*, Paris, 1902, p. 60.
(41) Monsieur and Madame de Surmont, cf. Funck-Brentano, loc. cit., p. 73.
(42) Funck-Brentano, loc. cit., p. 83.
(43) *Second Mémoire*, Collection, II, 32.
(44) Abbé Georgel, *Mémoires*, II, 36.
(45) She was introduced to him in 1781 *en route* from Saverne to Strasbourg. Cf. Campardon, *Marie-Antoinette et le Procès du Collier*, Paris, Plon, 1863, p. 207.
(46) Worshipful Master of the lodge *La Candeur* in 1776.
(47) Cf. Deschamps, *Sociétés secrètes*, 2 vols., II, 139.
(48) A worldly abbé, a member of the lodge *Les Amis réunis*, a man of affairs and Procurator-General of the Minims, who insinuated himself effortlessly just about everywhere, especially in and around the Palace of Versailles. The protection of Cardinal de Rohan enabled him to preach before the King. The *salon* of Madame de la Motte was his centre of operations, cf. *Mémoires du comte de la Motte*, Paris, Poulet-Malassis, 1858, p. 282.
(49) Funck-Brentano, loc. cit., p. 126.
(50) A Jack-of-all-Trades, general swindler and go-between, who quickly became the associate of Madame de la Motte.
(51) Cf. Funck-Brentano, loc. cit., pp. 128-129.
(52) *Notes de Target*, Bibliothèque de la ville de Paris, Manuscrit de la réserve, cited in Funck-Brentano, op. cit. p. 117.
(53) Funck-Brentano, loc. cit., p. 123.
(54T) Marie-Antoinette was, of course, the daughter of the Empress Maria Theresa. De Rohan had got on the wrong side of the Empress during his days as a special envoy in Vienna, partly as a result of his opposition to an alliance between France and Austria, and partly also because of his generally venal and self-indulgent lifestyle. Maria Theresa's loathing for the Cardinal seems to have transferred itself to her daughter.
(55) Funck-Brentano, loc. cit., p. 124.
(56T) Actually she was a prostitute.
(57) Funck-Brentano, loc. cit., p. 161, based on to Georgel's *Mémoires*. The Château de Saverne contained, in addition to the *Bibliotheca Tabernensis* with its fabulous collection of morocco armorial bindings, 'cabinets' of medicine and natural history considered remarkable for the time. The budget allocated to these collections was in line with that spent on the remainder of the Château. Since the house had no fewer than 14 Stewards and since, on feast-days, the Cardinal wore a cassock of Brussels-point worth 100,000 *livres*, we must assume that it was these collections that he preferred to anything else, but that he felt they were well worth the sacrifice, cf. Le Roy de Sainte-Croix, *Les quatre cardinaux de Rohan*, Strasbourg, 1880, pp. 89 et seq. The events described occurred between March and August 1784.
(58) He was the son-in-law of Achet and associate of Bœhmer.
(59) Dated 3rd January 1785.
(60) It was this gross error that subsequently caught the eye of the investigators and judges, exonerated the Queen, and made it possible to find out what had really happened.
(61) On 10th April he was in England for this purpose. In May he sold or swapped some of the diamonds. Ramond de Carbonnières who, out of affection for the Cardinal, undertook a private investigation in London in October 1785, was able to identify the role played by Monsieur de la Motte in the cutting-up of the necklace. Target, the Cardinal's lawyer, published the results of his investigation and the official documents relating to it in a booklet entitled *Pièces justificatives pour le Cardinal de Rohan*, Paris, Flon, 1787.
(62) At the end of 1781, when Madame de la Motte first settled in Paris and began her swindling, Cagliostro was still in Strasbourg. In March 1784, when she acted out the little comedy of the *Bosquet*

Chapter VII

de Vénus and during the whole of the d'Oliva affair and the theft of 150,000 *livres* from the Cardinal, Cagliostro was in Bordeaux, a very long way from the Cardinal and these intrigues.

(63) Beugnot, *Mémoires*, vol. I, p. 46.

(64) *Mémoires de l'abbé Georgel*, vol. II, p. 46.

(65) Funck-Brentano, loc. cit., p. 175. Abbé Georgel also points out the extent to which Cagliostro was kept away from all this intrigue, *Mémoires*, vol. II, pp. 45-53.

(66) *Interrogatoire du Cardinal à la Bastille*, Archives Nationales, X^2 B., 1417.

(67) *Interrogatoire de Cagliostro*, in Campardon, loc. cit., p. 342. We can see from this accurate account of the events that Abbé Georgel was entirely mistaken in supposing that Cagliostro was ultimately obliged to encourage the Cardinal in his plans. On the contrary, everything happened without Cagliostro's knowledge, in defiance of his own views on the subject, and without the knowledge of Abbé Georgel, to whom the Cardinal would not entrust, in such a serious matter, either his secrets or his doubts, or pass on to him anything that Cagliostro had had to say.

(68) Cf. Funck-Brentano, *L'affaire du Collier*, Paris, 1902, p. 107.

(69) Cagliostro was however compromised by performing this experiment with Madame de la Motte and her niece in order to fulfil the Cardinal's wishes. Madame de la Motte was able to put this fact to dangerous use later on, arguing that the 'wizard' Cagliostro had used magic spells to bewitch the Cardinal and push him into buying the Diamond Necklace, *Mémoires de Madame de la Motte*, and *Réponse au mémoire de Cagliostro*, 1786, p. 29. Fortunately the testimony of Mademoiselle de la Tour destroyed this calumny. She swore on oath that neither before nor after this magical demonstration, during which she herself had only spoken in jest, there had not been any form of understanding with Cagliostro, *Interrogatoire de Mademoiselle de la Tour*. And here is how Cagliostro himself recalled the incident during his examination (Arch. Nat., X^2 B., 1417): 'At the Cardinal's request, in order to try to reassure someone he was fond of, I agreed to perform the experiment that Madame de la Motte had requested, but I gave her the following warning: 'Madam, my expertise is in the medical field. Although I don't have much faith in animal magnetism I do believe that it can be used quite effectively with children, where it might be possible to discover something by inducing catalepsy'.' We notice that the language that Cagliostro uses here is very different from his usual discourse: he doesn't talk about the Beatific or Angelic Vision or divine grace as he usually did when he was working with doves, but simply in terms of animal magnetism, and even then with a great deal of reserve. That was because he was dealing with two women who wanted to ruin him, and with the Cardinal who had been immature enough to try to deceive him. He was not going to allow his divine powers to be misused on their behalf. They were playing him for a fool: it was as a hypnotist and, what is more, a hypnotist with little faith in what he was doing, that he acted in this case. The answers given to him by his hypnotic 'subject' were what one usually gets in such cases: a mixture of influences, suggestions, errors and pure imagination. Mademoiselle de la Tour's sceptical reminiscences are further evidence that our interpretation is the correct one.

(70) *Interrogatoire de Cagliostro*, in Campardon, loc. cit. p. 373. The advice that Cagliostro gave, i.e. to own up completely to the King, is obvious proof of his absolute innocence in the matter. If he had been involved, even to the smallest extent, in this dark intrigue, then would he really have urged the Cardinal to make a clean breast of it?

(71) He was actually putting himself forward as an ambassador, and no other intercessor, despite appearances, could have done a better job.

(72) Loan made by Madame de la Motte to the notary Minguet on 27th July, cf. Funck-Brentano, *L'Affaire du Collier*, Paris, 1902, p. 222.

(73) Arch. Nat., *Déclaration de Bœhmer*, F^7 445, B.

(74) *L'Affaire du Collier*, Paris, 1902, p. 229.

(75) Funck-Brentano, *L'Affaire du Collier*, Paris, 1902, p. 229.

(76) We reproduce this in the Appendix (Bibliothèque *de l'Arsenal*, Ms. no. 12457.). 'It was the allegations made by Madame de la Motte pointing to Cagliostro as being the sole culprit and someone who was totally *au fait* with the whole matter that led to his arrest', *Ma correspondance*, 1785, no. 70.

Cf. also Bachaumont, *Mémoires*, Paris, 1808, vol. II, p. 217.
(77) Or 'Des Brunières': the name is found in different spellings. This was the same person that went to Strasbourg to spy on Cagliostro.
(78) *Mémoire contre Chesnon*, Paris, 1786, p. 5.
(79) This took place in the presence of G... (an Augustinian Father), Madame de B... (Françoise), another Madame de B... and Baronne de B..., cf. *Requête au Roi contre Chesnon*, Paris 1787, p. 42.
(80) The Countess was locked up in the Bastille at 10 a.m. that same day, 23rd August. Both Cagliostro and the Countess were unaware of the other's fate.
(81) She arrived at 9 a.m. on 25th August.
(82) 'We also recognise in these papers five original letters written by the famous Cagliostro and given to Monsieur De Launay to be taken to his wife, as this *illustrious defender* of the Bastille who had been assigned the task of guarding him had taken care to confiscate them (i.e. some letters translated into French) but then neglected to use them for the purpose that their author had intended', cf. *Révolutions de Paris*, documents found in the Bastille, London, 1789, p. 75 (dated 27th July 1789).
(83) Letter from Thiroux de Crosne to De Launay, Bibliothèque de l'Arsenal, Manuscripts of the Bastille, 12457, fol. 12.
(84) The *Interrogatoire de Cagliostro* dated from 30th January 1786, Arch. Nat., X^2 2676.
(85) *Requête au Parlement par le comte de Cagliostro*, of 24th February 1786, Lottin, 8pp. 'This was a moving account of the critical and dangerous condition in which Madame Cagliostro currently found herself, something that required the beneficent talents of her husband who had had the pleasure of snatching thousands of French people from the jaws of death', *Journal de Hardy*, 25th February 1786. 'When the Countess Cagliostro left the Bastille she was utterly exhausted. Hundreds of well-intentioned people came to see her, but they had to content themselves with registering with the caretaker. She could personally receive only a very few people. Those whom she was able to receive testified that she had cried so much during her time in the Bastille that her eyes were red', *Ma Correspondance*, no. 29 of 1786.
(86) This request was fully justified: Mademoiselle de la Tour had been freed on 7th February. However the bailiff and the solicitor who presented the request were very nearly struck off for having dared to do it, cf. *Ma correspondance*, no. 19 of 15th March 1786). Intervention by Messrs. d'Ormesson and d'Éprémesnil secured acceptance of the request.
(87) 'Madame de la Motte made the most terrible fuss when the time came for her to be escorted to court for her examination. She tore off her clothes, feigned insanity... then tried to hide under the bed. They had difficulty dragging her out from underneath it. Finally they grabbed one of her legs and managed to pull her out, wrapped her up in a blanket, and took her away. When she finally arrived at her place of interrogation, in front of the Cardinal, she showered him with insults and recriminations', cf. Letter from Chevalier de Pujol of 7th April 1786 in P. Audibert, *L'affaire du Collier*, Rouen, 1901, 31 pp. On the same day, after her confrontation, 'she bit the warder who had been given the job of taking her back, drawing blood', *Ma correspondance*, no. 31 of 9th April 1786.
(88) 'The necklace was bought on the advice of Cagliostro. The Cardinal gave the necklace to her in the presence of Cagliostro, on the orders of Cagliostro, to be sold for Cagliostro's financial benefit. Countess Cagliostro was the person who was boasting about secretly having the Queen's ear, and she was the person who transmitted her husband's orders to her. And it was Countess Cagliostro to whom the Cardinal gave the most beautiful diamonds from the necklace', etc., etc., *Interrogatoire de Madame de la Motte*, Arch. Nat. X^2., 2576. *Mémoire de Madame de la Motte*, passim.
(89) Several of these pamphlets were condemned by the court and subsequently destroyed as libellous and abusive, cf. *Courrier de l'Europe*, no. 48 of 1787, p. 402, 1st column.
(90) Funck-Brentano, op. cit., p. 268.
(91) 'Since Cagliostro's imprisonment all his friends have become desolate and desperate. Nothing exists for them anymore. They have lost their most cherished possession', *Ma correspondance*, 5th December 1785, no. 101.
(92) 'Madame de la Motte could only answer him by treating him as if he was a paid impostor',

Mémoires de l'abbé Georgel, vol. II, p. 186. Her aggression towards her co-defendants and the warders increased as the enquiry stage of the legal proceedings proceeded, cf. *Gazette de Leyde*, 14th April 1780. See also *Journal de Hardy*, Bibl. Nat. Mss. français 6685, p. 316.

(93) *Lettre du cardinal à Target, Dossier Target*, Bibliothèque de la ville de Paris, Ms. in the Reserve.

(94) Cf. Funck-Brentano, *L'Affaire du Collier*, pp. 102 and 275, following the Target correspondence. When the Cardinal was seriously ill in the Bastille he took some powders that Cagliostro had once given him and which he always had with him to medicate himself before seeing a doctor. It was only at the instance of his family that he then sent for Dr. Portail, *Gazette de Leyde*, 13th December 1785, no. 99.

(95) Cagliostro was transferred to the *Conciergerie*, to a cell in the *Cour des hommes*, while the Cardinal was sent to the office of the Chief Clerk of the Court, *Mémoires de Bachaumont*, 2 vols., Paris, 1808, vol. II, p. 268.

(96) *Gazette de Leyde*, no. 96, 9th June 1786.

(97) 'But when they shall lead you, and deliver you up, take no thought beforehand what ye shall speak, neither do ye premeditate: but whatsoever shall be given you in that hour, that speak ye: for it is not ye that speak, but the Holy Ghost', *Gospel according to St. Mark*, XIII.11.

(98) *L'affaire du Collier*, p. 310.

(99) See, for example, Spach, the historian of Alsace: 'So that was the scandalous and irrefutable history of the Diamond Necklace then', he writes foolishly. 'Cagliostro was certainly mixed up in it. This involvement alone would have been enough to cast his previous career in a sinister light, even if it had been otherwise irreproachable', *Biographies alsaciennes*, Works, vol. V, p. 61.

(100) Cf. Funck-Brentano, *L'affaire du Collier*, p. 97. But even if he had intimated to the Cardinal that he held him in special esteem 'he had never told him that he would help him to succeed in everything that he desired', Statements by Cagliostro during his examination, cf. Campardon. loc. cit., p. 349. On the contrary he had always advised the Cardinal 'to stay on his estate, far from Court, and live a quiet life in Saverne', (ibid., p. 18). Cagliostro could fairly say – because it was the truth – that his powers were unlimited, but he couldn't use them to make some people successful at the expense of others.

(101) At that terrible moment when the whole intrigue started to unravel, the Cardinal, in a panic, rushed around to Cagliostro who was the only person who could find the words to lift his spirits and strengthen his resolve. The Cardinal left the conversation '*transformed*', said the Abbé Georgel, 'and never again perhaps did the Cardinal display the sort of dignity and courage that he showed in the moments that followed', *Mémoires de l'abbé Georgel*, vol. I, p. 99.

(102) Cf. *Lettre au peuple anglais*, p. 74.

(103) Doesn't the *Lettre au peuple anglais* predict the abolition of *lettres de cachet*, the fall of the Bastille and the summoning of the States-General?

(104) Goethe, Mirabeau, the Comte de Lamarck, etc. In 1786 *La Gazette de Leyde* (no. 2) pointed out that the lawsuit raised the question of *lèse-majesté* and that this is what the general public was really concerned about and which led to a spate of pamphlets.

(105) An order from De Breteuil to De Launay (Bibliothèque de l'Arsenal, Ms. 12457, folio 69) fixed this late time for Cagliostro's departure and specified that it was the will of the King that Cagliostro and the Cardinal remain on their respective premises and only receive relatives and people on business.

(106) Hardy, *Journal*, 1st June 1786 and Bachaumont, *Mémoires*, vol. II, p. 261.

(107) *Mémoire de Cagliostro contre Chesnon*, 1786, p. 16.

(108) *Mémoire de Cagliostro contre Chesnon*, 1786, p. 16, and *Vie de Joseph Balsamo*, pp. 63-64.

(109) Bachaumont, *Mémoires*, Paris, 1808, vol. II. p. 271. The entrance to the Cardinal's mansion, which was right next door to that of Soubise (later the home of the Archives Nationales), was in Rue Vieille-du-Temple. For many years it was the home of the *Imprimerie Nationale*, the French equivalent of Her Majesty's Stationery Office.

(110) The newspapers, the *Gazette de Leyde* in particular, joined in the general chorus and offered their noisy congratulations to the accused on their release.

(111) Manuscripts of the Bastille, Bibliothèque de l'Arsenal, no. 12457, folio 69.

(112) 'Eager to show my obedience to the will of a sovereign who had allowed me for six whole years to perform acts of philanthropy in his kingdom, I hastened to obey', etc., *Mémoire de Cagliostro contre Chesnon*, Paris, 1786, p. 18.

(113) From there he moved, on 12th June, to the *Auberge de l'Épée* in Saint-Denis, where his wife joined him (Bachaumont, *Mémoires*, II, p. 274). The *Gazette de Leyde* (no. XLIX) of 20th June 1786 says that he went to the Essonne and that it was there that the Countess joined him, but this is undoubtedly wrong because the other newspapers, and Cagliostro himself, indicate Passy and Saint-Denis as the stages in this short journey, cf. *Mémoire de Cagliostro contre Chesnon*, Paris, 1786, p. 18.

(114) 'He did not want to re-ignite the anger of the Government by stoking up strong emotions in the public at his departure', *Mémoire de Cagliostro contre Chesnon*, Paris, 1786, p. 18.

(115) 'Even if I had foreseen that I was going to be arrested', wrote Cagliostro, 'I would still have seen this precaution (i.e. having an inventory of his possessions drawn up by a bailiff) as a useless and abusive course of action in a nation that had offered me its hospitality', *Mémoire de Cagliostro contre Chesnon*, Paris, 1786, p. 23.

(116) *Mémoire de Cagliostro contre Chesnon*, Paris, 1786, p. 5.

(117) 'A poor prisoner who is only too eager to run away will sign whatever people want him to sign, whether it's accurate or not... and the savage mastiffs of the Bastille had no difficulty at all in getting their hands on his property', *Remarques historiques sur la Bastille*, London, 1789, p. 78.

(118) 'My fortune is the inheritance of the unfortunate, and when I strive to preserve it then it is their rights that I am defending', *Mémoire de Cagliostro contre Chesnon*, Paris, 1786, p. 4. The rich man, he taught, is the poor man's banker: 'You should only use this transient wealth (which the knowledge and power that you will acquire can certainly one day obtain for you) for the relief of your neighbour, for you are only the guardians of it and must share it with the poor', *Rituel de la Maçonnerie Égyptienne*, Ms. Papus, p. 201.

(119) 'All I can say is that for me these papers are of inestimable value. For special reasons I am unable, at this moment, to go into precise details about their nature, but their importance is such that I would give everything that I have in the world to have them in my hands once more, and Providence alone can compensate me for having lost them...' *Mémoire de Cagliostro contre Chesnon*, Paris, 1786, p. 34.

(120) *Mémoire de Cagliostro contre Chesnon*, Paris, 1786, p. 34. During his stay in the Bastille Cagliostro often helped his fellow-prisoners, his companions in misery, out of his own pocket.

(121) That is what he said in his defence.

(122) 'The sacred idea of justice, forgotten or ignored for fifteen centuries, asserted itself in the face of the world of 1789 and created an unbridgeable chasm between the night of yesterday and the dawn of today... The *Assemblée* destroyed what was referred to as 'royal abuses of authority' and abolished the *lettres de cachets* which had led to the exile or imprisonment without trial of 150,000 people during the last reign, and 14,000 since', L. Ménard, *Lettres d'un mort*, Paris, 1895, pp. 74-75.

(123) 'The loss of freedom, the uncertainty surrounding one's fate, the continuous exposure to the most hideous sights, and the repeated ill-treatment at the hands of savages who turn increasing the miseries of already wretched people into a sort of barbaric game... are the least of the evils that one suffers in the Bastille. Contempt for all human laws seems to be the rule there. The severest form of incarceration and the most meticulous and humiliating precautions are combined with the most disgusting parsimony in the prison regime, the blackest hypocrisy in offers of service, the most malignant duplicity in the art of trickery, the most unforgivable indifference to the diseases that the foetid air of this hole inevitably gives rise to, the bitterest irony towards complaints long stifled by fear – in a word, everything that one can conceive that is most corrosive to the human spirit is here gathered together for the torment of what are often the least guilty of men and women (pp. 10-11).

The present Governor, Monsieur De Launay, is, of all those persons who have occupied this post until now, the most miserly and the most insensitive to the evils of humanity as well as being, above all, the most insolent of upstarts. He bought his post by prostituting his daughter and by paying the Prince de

Chapter VII

Conti a fortune for his personal recommendation (p. 74). His job pays, in addition to court-fees, more than 60,000 *livres*, which he earns, or rather steals, on the backs of the prisoners, whom he amusingly refers to as his *pigeonneaux* ('little pigeons') (p. 77). When he isn't renting out the Prisoners' Garden (p. 65) he's selling the prisoners' wine to an inn-keeper (p. 55) in exchange for an undrinkable vinegary substance (p. 57)', *Remarques historiques sur la Bastille*, written in 1774, republished in London in 1789. The final chapter in De Launay's life was a tragic one: when the Bastille was attacked De Launay pretended to surrender, hoisted a white flag, opened the gates, and let 600 of the assailants enter the fortress. Then, raising the drawbridge, he had them gunned down inside the courtyard at point-blank range. The people, infuriated by this betrayal, rushed the gates, broke them down, and within a few hours had gained control of the fortress. Then they seized De Launay who, trembling and weeping, begged for mercy: 'Have pity on me', he sobbed, full of remorse, 'I fully confess that I've betrayed my fatherland!' This late confession and final act of cowardice did nothing to mollify those who had come to avenge their murdered brothers and the martyrs of the Bastille. De Launay's head was the *very first* to fall into the executioner's basket amongst the many that shared a similar fate in the bloody days of the Revolution, and those who had conquered the Bastille took pleasure in parading it through the streets of Paris. The second head to fall was that of the *Major* (second-in-command) of the Bastille, *Révolutions de Paris*, London, 1789, pp. 10, 11 & 12.

(124) *Mémoire de Cagliostro contre Chesnon*, Paris, 1786, pp. 16, 21, 37.
(125) In the *Lettre au peuple français*. Cf. also Chapter VIII of this book.
(126) *Arrêt du roi pour faire examiner le cas*: 10th July 1786.
(127) Of 11th August 1786. In this request Cagliostro also protested against the new satirical pamphlets making fun of him which De Launay and De Breteuil had had printed *using Cagliostro's own money*.
(128) *Mémoires. Pièce importante dans l'affaire Cagliostro-De Launay*, September 1786.
(129) The King-in-Council mentioned the matter and filed it on an unsigned *Requête* (Document O^1 598 C^1 of the *Archives Nationales*) but since this emanated from De Launay that was the end of the matter. Later on Sarrasin, in response to a complaint from Cagliostro, asked d'Éprémesnil to find out what judgment had actually been given, but for obvious reasons did not get an answer.
(130) Cf. preliminary note to *Mémoire de Cagliostro contre Chesnon*, Paris, 1786, folio 1, v°.
(131) Duval d'Éprémesnil, adviser to the Court, had an interest in animal magnetism. He had approached Cagliostro regarding it, but undoubtedly failed to recognise Cagliostro's greatness. He did however think he was an honest man and an innocent victim, and did everything he could to protect him from the ignorance and spite of those who were persecuting him. That earned him the dubious honour of being singled out for satirical treatment by the lampoonists who were in the pay of Madame de la Motte and De Launay. Ramond de Carbonnières 'did his best during the lawsuit to thwart the machinations of Madame de la Motte. He even travelled to England to undertake a personal investigation, and managed to find out who Madame de la Motte's accomplices were and who had received the diamonds', *Mémoires de l'abbé Georgel*, vol. II, pp. 176 sqq.
(132) People even came from as far away as Lyons, 'Thousands' of people came to Boulogne, a newspaper of the time tells us.
(133) *Mémoire de Cagliostro contre Chesnon*, Paris, 1786, p. 37.
(134) This letter is reproduced *in extenso* in the Appendix of this book.
(135) *Archives Sarrasin*, Basel, vol. XXXIII, shelf-mark 13, folio IV, v°.
(136) Letters in the *Archives Sarrasin*, Basel. According to Langmesser, *Jacob Sarrasin*, pp. 41-50, the last letter is dated 1st March 1786.
(137) They have come down to us thanks to the fear that they engendered in the Court of the Inquisition. A man capable of provoking such intense feelings and inspiring such devotion must have struck them as a terrifying figure who was capable of anything. Rome's official historian published these letters as proof of the dangerous fanaticism that Cagliostro inspired in those around him, but at least this has enabled us to make their acquaintance.
(138) *Vie de Joseph Balsamo*, Paris, 1790, pp. 194-195. See also the letter from a Lyons Freemason in Chapter VI of this book.

CHAPTER VIII

—

'THE EXPLOITER OF PUBLIC GULLIBILITY'

CAGLIOSTRO IN LONDON - SECOND VISIT

Marie-Antoinette was infuriated by the acquittals of Cardinal de Rohan and Cagliostro. Her pride had also been wounded by the obvious enthusiasm that the populace had shown for the two accused: indeed, she saw it as a personal insult [1]. She demanded that the Cardinal also be exiled, if only so that his presence at Court would not constantly remind her of the recent unhappy events. The Cardinal, now back in the Auvergne [2], sensibly kept his head down and, from that point of view, her aim was achieved. She had also got rid of Cagliostro: he was known to be in England, and one could readily believe that this would be the end of the matter.

But if the unhappy Cardinal, crushed by his recent legal struggles and by illness [3], had gone to ground and was largely invisible, the same could certainly not be said of Cagliostro. Released and rehabilitated, the defendant became a plaintiff and, as we have seen, through his defence advocate Maître Thilorier he filed complaints with the Paris Courts and writs against Chesnon and De Launay. These signs of vitality in someone they'd thought they'd seen the last of naturally worried the interested parties. Baron de Breteuil – the Queen's factotum and Minister of Police, who is said to have hated Cagliostro so much that he couldn't even look at a sculpture of him without gnashing his teeth [4] – was asked for his advice. He proposed enticing Cagliostro back to France under a pretence of generosity: there, back in the King's territory, he could be re-arrested and shoved back into the Bastille. François Barthélemy, France's Minister in London, accepted the appropriate orders from Paris and sent for Cagliostro. Here's what happened next.

On 21st August, between 11.00 p.m. and noon, Cagliostro went to see Barthélemy accompanied by Lord George Gordon and Monsieur Bergeret de Frouville, a cavalry officer in the French army. After some insistence (because only Cagliostro had been formally invited to the meeting) Lord George Gordon and Monsieur de Frouville won the right to be present at the discussions, which proceeded as follows:

Barthélemy: 'Count Cagliostro, I have orders to grant you your freedom to return to France'.

Cagliostro: 'I've come here willingly to receive the orders of His Majesty'.

Barthélemy then drew from his pocket not an order of the King, as Cagliostro had been expecting, but just an ordinary letter from Baron de Breteuil.

Cagliostro: 'Do you really expect me to respond to an order like this? When they threw me into the Bastille, when they let me out of it again, and when they threw me out of Paris, I got a *lettre de cachet* signed by the King in person. How can a simple letter from Baron de Breteuil revoke clear instructions from His Majesty? I tell you, Monsieur, I am able to recognise neither Baron de Breteuil nor his orders. The only French sovereign that I recognise is the King. I shall address you with my usual frankness. I didn't come here today to see you in your capacity as a Minister but as a Frenchman of whom everyone speaks highly. Please let me have the letter from Baron de Breteuil, or a copy of it at least'.

Barthélemy: 'Count Cagliostro, I'm afraid that that is quite impossible. I understand what you're trying to say, but I've carried out my orders and I cannot go into any further details'.

That is a *verbatim* account of what occurred between Cagliostro and the Minister of France in the presence of Lord George Gordon and Bergeret de Frouville. Cagliostro had sprung the trap that had been set for him. As we wrote later in his *Lettre au peuple anglais* [5]:

Any innocent man who has spent nine months groaning in the Bastille and who, after being acquitted by a unanimous judgment, has received by way of compensation only an order expelling him from the country is fully justified in mistrusting everything and everybody, and seeing traps all around him. The King's intentions are undoubtedly pure, but the way in which the letter was written has caused me justified alarm. It did not specify any time-limit for my stay in France. My lawsuit could be judged from one day to the next and, on the day when judgment was delivered, they would be free to arrest me again, without me being able to use my letter of recall as a safeguard. I want to save my enemies the trouble of committing new atrocities, and I want to spare Europe from yet another scandal. So I will NOT be going to France.

Cagliostro knew only too well from which direction the blow would come. Almost immediately he published his *Lettre au peuple français* (Letter to the French people), which is both a spiritually inspired criticism of French justice and a lively response to Baron de Breteuil and his murky intrigues. This document [6] is now very scarce, and is far too interesting not to reproduce *in extenso*:

LETTER FROM COUNT CAGLIOSTRO TO MONSIEUR X [7].
London, 20th June 1786.

My dear X, I'm writing to you from London. My health is good, as is my wife's. You'll have heard of course all about my journey here. Oh, how touching those scenes were! It seemed as if my friends from just about everywhere in Europe had preceded me. And the scenes in Boulogne put the finishing touches to it all. All those good people on the shoreline, their arms outstretched towards the boat, calling my name, crying out, heaping blessings upon me, and asking me for mine!... What memories I shall always have! Memories that are both so dear and so cruel! They had thrown me out of France! The King had been deceived! Kings are certainly to be pitied for having ministers like that.

I heard people talking about Baron de Breteuil, my persecutor. What did I ever do to this man? What exactly is he accusing me of? Of being liked by the Cardinal? Or liking the Cardinal in return? Of never having betrayed the Cardinal? Of having good friends everywhere I went? Of seeking the truth, speaking it, defending it, when God ordered me to do so, when He gave me the opportunity to do so? An opportunity to help, to succour, to comfort suffering humanity with my alms, my remedies, my advice? So are those all my crimes! Is he trying to say perhaps that my plea for mitigation was also a crime? That certainly comes to mind. It was a rare defeat for him certainly. But I hadn't even submitted it when he saw that bust of me at the Cardinal's house and said, angrily, between his teeth: 'We see this bust all over the place. It's time that a stop was put to it, and believe me a stop will be put to it!'

It's been said that it was actually my courage that got on his nerves. He simply couldn't come to terms with the fact that a man who'd been clapped in irons, a foreigner under lock and key in the Bastille, someone within his power, had the temerity to raise his voice to him. To him, him! the worthy Minister of this ghastly prison! Just because I wanted to make clear to the French courts, to the French nation, to the French King, to all of Europe, just what I thought about him, about his principles, his cats-paws, his creatures. I'm willing to admit that my behaviour must have astonished him but, ultimately, I adopted the tone that suited me best. I am well persuaded that, in his natural environment back at the Bastille, this man would not have adopted the same tone towards me.

But, my friend, please clear up a doubt for me. The King drove out me of his kingdom but he didn't even listen to what I had to say. Is that how all lettres de cachet are expedited in France? If that's the case then I feel truly sorry for your fellow-citizens, especially as long as Baron de Breteuil is in charge of this dangerous government department. What, my friend, are your people and your property really worth at the mercy of this man? Can he really lie to the King with impunity? Can he – simply on the basis of libellous gossip that is never contradicted – obtain by undue means, expedite, and then have the pleasure of implementing – or get people who closely resemble him to implement for him – orders that are so inflexible that they result in an innocent man being thrown into a dungeon and his house being plundered?

All I can say is that this deplorable abuse deserves the King's undivided attention. Was I simply mistaken about the French people perhaps? Is the common sense of the French people, whom I love so much, really that different from that of all other peoples of the Earth? Forget my own specific cause for a moment: let's speak in general terms. When the King signs a letter of expulsion or imprisonment, presumably that means that he has issued a judgment regarding the unfortunate person upon whom his omnipotence will fall. But precisely on what basis has he judged him? 'On the report of his minister'. Yes, but what has this minister based his report on? Anonymous complaints, murky information, which we never get a chance to see, simple rumour too sometimes, or someone's libellous mutterings, sown by hatred and reaped by envy. The victims are struck down without knowing from where the blow comes. Happy is he indeed if the Minister who's sacrificing him is not his sworn enemy! Are these, I ask, really the characteristics of a true legal judgment? And if your lettres de cachet are not simply private judgments then what are they?

I believe that the above reflections, if presented to the king, would certainly give him cause for thought. And what would his reaction be if he took a closer look at the evils that his legal rigour leads to? Are all French prisons really like the Bastille? You simply have no idea of the horrors of that place: the cynical impudence, the odious lies, the false pity, the bitter irony, the boundless cruelty, the injustice, and death itself of course – they all hold sway there. A barbaric silence is the least of all the crimes committed there: I was there for six months just fifteen feet away from my wife, and I didn't even know she was there. Others have been buried away there for thirty years! Their families thought they were dead, and indeed they were unlucky not to be, since they didn't even have, like John Milton's Damned, any daylight in their abyss except what they needed to see just how impenetrable was the darkness that enveloped them. Indeed, they would be alone in the whole universe if the

Eternal did not exist, this beneficent and truly Almighty God, who will render justice to them one day just as their fellow-men have not.

Yes, my friend, I said it when I was a prisoner there and I shall say it again now as a free man: there is no crime upon this Earth, however ghastly, that cannot be expiated by spending just six months in the Bastille. People also say that the cruellest forms of interrogation and torture abound there, and I can well believe it.

Somebody asked me whether I would ever return to France if the ban placed upon me were to be lifted. Of course I would, I replied, provided that the Bastille had been turned into a public promenade! For that is surely the will of God! You Frenchmen have everything you need to be happy: a fertile soil, a gentle climate, a good heart, a charming gaiety, genius, graces for every occasion – a people unequalled in the art of giving pleasure, and matchless in every other. You lack only one little thing my good friends, and that is the knowledge that you can sleep soundly in your beds when you have done absolutely nothing wrong. But, I hear you cry, we need to protect the honour of the great families! The lettres de cachet are evil, but a necessary evil! How simple-minded you are! They just rock you to sleep with their tall stories. Well-informed people have assured me that a complaint by someone's family was often a less effective way of obtaining a lettre de cachet than the hatred of some insignificant clerk or the 'reputation' of some adventuress! But what about the family's honour! What? Don't you think that an entire family is dishonoured by its members being tortured? What a shame you should think like that! My new hosts think rather differently. They believe that all you have to do is change the way you think and you will earn your freedom simply through the application of reason.

This most happy revolution would certainly be a worthy task for your Law Courts. Only the weak in mind and spirit would find it a difficult task. The secret I think is to be well prepared. They mustn't rush things. They must have the best interests of the people, the King and the royal family at heart of course. But they need Time on their side also: Time, the Prime Minister of Truth! Time, around which the roots of good as well as of evil slowly entwine and consolidate! You will need courage also, patience, the strength of the lion, the cautiousness of the elephant, the gentle simplicity of the dove. And this revolution, so very necessary, must be peaceful, for that is a precondition without which it should not even be contemplated. In that way you will owe your magistracy a happiness that no other people have ever enjoyed, that of recovering your freedom without opposition, and receiving it from the hands of your kings.

Yes, my friend, I predict that there will reign over you a prince who will owe his glory to the abolition of lettres de cachet, to the summoning of your Estates-General and, especially, to the re-establishment of the true religion. This prince, beloved by Heaven, will understand that, in the long term, the abuse of power is destructive of power itself. He won't be content to be the first amongst his Ministers, he will want to be the first amongst the French. Happy the king who will make this famous proclamation, happy the chancellor who will sign it, and happy the Parliament that will approve it!

What I am saying, my friend, is that perhaps the times are ripe for such a revolution. There's no doubt that your King is suited to this great task. I know that he would set to work on it if he would only listen to his heart, for his rigidity towards me does not blind me to his virtues.

So farewell, my friend. What are they saying about the Mémoire? I must say that when Thilorier last read it to me in Saint-Denis it gave me a lot of pleasure. Did he get to hear the details about what happened in Boulogne in good time to include a section about it? Has the Mémoire been published yet? It certainly should have been.

Chapter VIII

A very good evening to you anyway! Tell all our friends the news about us. Tell them that they will always be here for us, wherever we might be. And ask d'Éprémesnil if he really has forgotten all about me – I haven't had heard from him for ages.

Farewell my very good friend, or should I say friends, for it is to you all that I address myself. Think of us. May this letter be common to all of you for, indeed, we love you all with all our heart.

This letter, prophesying the summoning of the Estates-General, the abolition of *lettres de cachet* and the demolition of the Bastille, and denouncing in bald and biting terms the abusive behaviour of the all-powerful De Breteuil simply increased the Queen's wrath and De Breteuil's animosity to unprecedented levels. Cagliostro became a public enemy, and all his adversaries got together to act against him. A council of war was held.

Meanwhile, back in London, Cagliostro seemed invulnerable. His enemies hadn't been able to trick him into returning. They'd certainly considered forcibly dragging him back to France [8], but that would have caused a major scandal and, in any case, Cagliostro was constantly alert to any dangers. Then they found a better way of destroying him: they launched against him 'the sort of literary ruffian that people always resort to in embarrassing situations, and who suited everyone's needs provided that one wasn't too concerned about the price' [9].

We have already mentioned the journalist Morande. A captain of dragoons called De Saint-Hilaire, a relative of De Launay of Bastille infamy, visited London with a former musketeer, a Monsieur de J., and met up with Morande to discuss how to destroy Cagliostro [10]. Morande's immediate reaction to their proposals seemed noble enough: he turned them down. He went to see Cagliostro on his own account and learned, on the basis of certain definitive statements, that he wouldn't yield any further, or indeed yield at all [11]. Morande went back to his clients, where his second gesture, rather less noble but more practical, was to accept their offer (12). And so he became the mouthpiece for Cagliostro's enemies and the organiser of a man-hunt [13] that was to lead to the dungeons of Rome.

Morande was ideally suited to this task [14]. His real name was Charles Théveneau – he was never actually Morande or de la Morande, and he certainly was never a Chevalier. The son of a notary in Arnay-le-Duc, who died of the grief that his son caused him, he began his career in the Parisian brothels exploiting both men and women and earning a reputation as a 'dishonest gambler, a detestable creature, a dangerous swindler, a go-between for the wealthy lords that he frequented, and someone who was also strongly suspected of being the object of these villains' unnatural lusts' [15]. Arrested for theft and attempted murder and imprisoned in For-l'Évêque in 1768, he fled to England immediately upon his release where he successfully continued his vile trade of blackmail, threatening with violence anyone who couldn't or wouldn't pay up and selling his pen to the highest bidder. He was no respecter of persons, and even kings were not safe from him: his attacks on Louis XV and Madame du Barry were especially vicious. After he published *Le Gazetier cuirassé* [16] a price was put on his head, but De Sartines and his police-force admitted there was nothing they could really do about him: the only solution was to compromise and do a deal. Beaumarchais was sent to London to buy Morande's silence at the best possible price, but Morande simply had some fun with him [17].

Morande's reputation was now established. He was held in such scorn that his name actually passed into the language as an insult [18], and an anonymous lampoon of the period has a French police-officer, scorned and returning empty-handed to Paris, yelling at the

English people in anger, 'Well, cruel English, I've taken sufficient revenge upon you. I've left you Morande!' [19]. But he was genuinely feared: his cynicism had no bounds and he scoffed at people with such cruelty, bit so hard and insulted so violently that lovers of scandal loved him regardless, and everyone he had in his sights trembled before him.

The newspaper he directed, the *Courrier de l'Europe*, was thinly disguised as a purveyor of general information but was actually a dispensary of blackmail. Morande had gathered around him the dregs of London's French refugee community: crooked cashiers, bankrupts, unfrocked priests, officers who'd deserted their regiments and a fair sprinkling of gangsters. The newspaper and occasional lampoons were printed by Boissière, a former lackey of the Pole Matousky, a famous swindler who'd set up as a bookseller in London after stealing from his boss the money he needed to establish a business [20]. When Morande had finally been bought off by the secret police and the poacher had become gamekeeper [21], i.e. around the time that particularly interests us, the *Courrier de l'Europe* had become almost an official newspaper, and Morande played with ease his dual role in all this, duping – depending on the circumstances – either the French police for the benefit of his clandestine force of literary hacks, or *vice versa* [22]. Even so, he was constantly in debt and always on the look-out for money-making schemes. When the anti-Cagliostro campaign was first proposed to him his financial situation was at its lowest ebb. 'Without money, without credit, disappearing under a mountain of debt, surrounded by bailiffs and duns, he dared to leave his house only on Sundays. But suddenly he was paying off all his debts, paying cash for clothes and furniture, waving a wallet around stuffed with banknotes' [23].

Morande fired the first salvo on 25th August by publishing in the *Courrier* a report, inaccurate and hostile to Cagliostro, of the latter's interview with Barthélemy. Once he'd published this first article he cynically sought out Cagliostro and suggested that they do a deal. Cagliostro, for his part, was certainly not unaware of just how terrible an adversary he was confronted with. On his arrival in London he'd been put in touch with a certain Swinton, joint owner of the *Courrier* and a close friend of Morande [24]. It was through him that Cagliostro first got to know Morande. He had been told just how resourceful and powerful this man was, 'who'd made the King of France tremble, made the cleverest secret-policemen sweat, made a fool out of even an intelligent man like Beaumarchais, and who had brought to the negotiating-table the favourite of Louis XV, the all-powerful Madame du Barry, and even the King himself' [25]. Morande had told Cagliostro what he could fear if he were his enemy, and what he needed to do to win his friendship. Cagliostro didn't attach much importance to this advice and yet, having already been attacked by pamphleteers and suffered vexation at the hands of police-officers, he understood only too well the power of the press and that of the police – and here, in the person of Morande, they were combined in one and the same person! Cagliostro was quite happy to join the struggle against this new-born power, already as terrifying as Hercules in his cradle, and which, just a century later, under the name of journalism, would grow to such enormous proportions amid the ruins of all the powerful foes against which it had struggled.

Cagliostro therefore had no hesitation in joining battle and refusing the slightest compromise with the crooked Morande, sending the *Public Advertiser* [26] a note correcting the errors of the article in the *Courrier de l'Europe* and questioning the sincerity of its author. Morande, not used to being defied, simply went berserk: on 1st September a chronicle appeared covering several columns and stuffed with all the tittle-tattle, scandalous stories and ridiculous allegations that the memoirs of Madame de la Motte had already made known to the French people [27]. From that point on every issue of the

Chapter VIII

Courrier [28] contained an article or, at least, a paragraph, that was hostile to Cagliostro. The insults and personal attacks upon him, his wife and their friends become increasingly violent and repellent [29]. Morande was seeking to force his victim's hand and to secure from him either an offer of money to simply shut up, or a response that would make the exchange even more poisonous. It was the latter that actually occurred: Cagliostro, his pride wounded, finally caved in and wrote personally to Morande. In this letter Cagliostro sought to explain some of the things that had been said about him which Morande had foolishly ridiculed [30] and concluded by inviting Morande to come to see for himself whether his statements were anything more than jokes and his abilities simply those of a charlatan. Here is the text of this challenge:

3rd September 1786

Unfortunately, Sir, I am not sufficiently familiar with the finer points of the French language to pay you all the compliments that the excellent jokes in nos. 16, 17 and 18 of the 'Courrier de l'Europe' undoubtedly deserve, but as all those who have spoken to me about it have assured me that they combine grace with finesse, and decency of tone with elegance of style, I have come to the conclusion that you are indeed good company and I have therefore developed a fervent desire to make your acquaintance.

However, as certain malicious people have allowed themselves to unburden themselves of some very unpleasant stories which are to your discredit, I thought I should clear these up before yielding completely to the feelings that I have for you.

It gave me great satisfaction to see that everything that people had said about you was pure scandalmongering, and that you were most certainly not one of those slanderers who come along from time to time and who sell their skills with the pen to the highest bidder and make people pay up until they agree to fall silent, and that the secret proposals that you made to me via your worthy friend Mr. Swinton had startled me inappropriately, it being as natural to ask an Adept for gold as it is to draw water from the Thames.

Of all the good stories that you told about me, the best without question is the one about the pig fattened on arsenic which is used to poison lions, tigers and leopards in the forests of Medina. Now, Mr. Scoffer, let me put you in a position to be able to make jokes about it with full knowledge of the facts. From the point of view of physics and chemistry, reasoning proves little and mockery proves nothing at all: experimentation is all that matters. Allow me therefore to propose to you a little experiment, the results of which will entertain the public either at your expense or mine.

I invite you to dine with me, on 9th November next, at 9 a.m. You will provide the wine and all the cutlery, tableware and so on, and I shall provide you with just one dish cooked how I like it. It will be a small suckling pig, fattened according to my own method. Two hours before the meal I shall show it to you alive, chubby and healthy, and you will then arrange to have it slaughtered and dressed. I myself will go nowhere near it until it is time to serve it. You yourself will cut it into four equal parts. You will choose those parts that will best suit your appetite, and you will serve me whatever you consider appropriate.

Shortly after this meal one of four things will have happened: 1. We will both have died, 2. Neither of us will have died, 3. I will have died and you won't have, or 4. You will have died and I won't have. I am therefore offering you a three-out-of-four chance, and yet I will bet you 5,000 guineas that the following day you will be dead and I will be as right as rain. You must agree that I could not be more sporting, and that it is absolutely essential that you either accept the wager or agree that you foolishly jested about something that was outside your competence.

> *... I am, Sir, with the feelings that all those who have had the pleasure of dealing with you must universally feel,*
> *Your most obedient servant,*
> *Count Cagliostro.*

Morande delivered a riposte in the form of a rather ponderous letter in which he refused Cagliostro's invitation to take part in the experiment. Instead he retreated behind his *persona* as a man of letters – he said that he didn't want to be responsible for someone's death. If Cagliostro wanted to experiment on a cat or dog then he would accept, but his own life was too precious to place in the scales opposite that of Cagliostro. The following day Cagliostro sent him another letter. This time he certainly had people laughing with him rather than at him:

Second letter of Cagliostro to Monsieur Morande

Many thanks for having included my letter in today's edition of the Courrier. Your response is refined, honest and moderate, and richly deserves a response of equal merit, which I am hastening to send you so it can be included in the next edition.

A knowledge of the art of conservation is primarily dependant on a knowledge of the art of destruction. Remedies and poisons in the hands of a friend to mankind can also serve for the happiness of mankind: the former by preserving useful creatures, and the latter by getting rid of nasty ones. Such is the use to which I have always put them, and it was only thanks to you, Sir, that my suckling pig of London was not as useful or even more useful in Europe than the suckling pig of Medina was in Arabia.

I had, I will admit, the keenest desire to go ahead with the wager. You were good enough to inform me what kind of lure was most likely to attract you. The wager of 5,000 guineas was just the bait with which I hoped to ensnare you. The extreme cautiousness you displayed at more than one meeting prevented you from biting. But, as the 5,000 guineas held a keen fascination for you, you accepted the bet, subject to a condition that destroyed all the interest in it and with which I could not agree.

It is of no importance to me to win 5,000 guineas, but it is very important to society to be rid of a regular plague. You refused the lunch to which I invited you and you suggested to me that your place could be taken by a carnivorous animal. That's not quite what I had in mind. A dining-companion of that kind would only represent you very imperfectly. I mean, where would you find a carnivorous animal that was to his species what you are to the human race?

In any case, this matter concerns you and you alone. I'm not interested in dealing with your representative, but with you. Using champions to fight on your behalf went out of fashion a long time ago, but even if someone rendered you the service of reviving such a procedure, honour would still prevent me from fighting against any champion that you offered me. A champion should not be dragged into the arena: he must enter it voluntarily, and you will agree, as you admit that animals possess some reasoning ability, that not a single one of them, either carnivorous or herbivorous, would agree to become your champion under any circumstances. So stop making me proposals that I cannot agree to. Your conditional acceptance is a genuine refusal, and my dilemma remains.

What's more, it is with genuine satisfaction, Sir, that I see that it is you who have been instructed to defend Messieurs Chesnon and De Launay [31]. A cause of that kind and clients of that kind are lacking just one thing, and that is a comparable defence and a comparable defender.

Chapter VIII

Carry on as you are doing, Sir, and make yourself even worthier than ever of the esteem and praise of the general public. I shall certainly not interrupt your eloquent pleading. When you have completed the honourable course of action upon which you have embarked then I shall see what side I must take,

I am, Sir, etc.

Morande, having failed to make Cagliostro look a fool, lose his temper or take fright at his newspaper articles, now decided to choose a different terrain upon which to give battle. He collected all the nasty rumours about Cagliostro that he could find, scouring both London and abroad for people willing and able to make some sort of allegation, complaint or claim that could form the basis for a legal action [32]. Indeed, the English legal system at that time gave succour to bogus creditors and blackmailers: an alleged debtor could be instantly arrested just on the say-so of a self-proclaimed debtor. Cagliostro had to undergo vexations such as these on several occasions.

The *Courrier de l'Europe* went to great lengths to keep its readership abreast of Morande's so-called 'news'. One day it announced the arrival of a Monsieur Sylvestre who was complaining that Cagliostro had swindled him in some way about twenty years before. The following day it was the turn of a Monsieur B., who was claiming that Cagliostro had extorted £60,000 from the Lodges in Lyons. Anyone who has read the previous chapters of this book will be convinced of the absurdity of these claims, but even so they made a bad impression, and Cagliostro had to give up some time to defending himself against them [33]. Sometimes the *Courrier* would publish correspondence from abroad, like the Bracconieri report, which attracted so much publicity and did so much harm, accompanied by 'authentic' documents that Morande somehow managed to get his hands on [34]. Morande even went as far as asking for a writ to be issued against Cagliostro as an impostor just because, in Paris, he had allegedly claimed to be the Prince of Trebizond. The self-styles 'Chevalier de la Morande' obviously didn't see the irony in this situation.

But despite Morande's use of paid spies and informers all these attacks failed. Morande then found a better way of dealing with Cagliostro. Thanks to his connections in the French police he was able to track down Sachi, whom he invited him to London (at the French Minister's expense of course). Morande made use of him as an instrument of persecution and a means of blackmailing Cagliostro. Sachi, having been thrown out of Strasbourg and then out of Bordeaux, having been arrested and twice convicted in France, asked only for a chance to be avenged and to have a new platform, in a new jurisdiction, for his various moans, threats, lies, and complaints [35]. He proved to be an admirable accomplice for Morande.

As soon as Morande had things in hand and had finally managed to convince the solicitor Priddle [36], he surreptitiously had a warrant issued for Cagliostro's arrest. If Cagliostro had not been tipped off about it then he would certainly have been snatched from his home and locked up in Newgate Prison. Scandals, lawsuits – all were grist to Morande's mill. However, Cagliostro had found out about the warrant and the danger he was in, and hastily secured two guarantees which he presented in person to the bailiff before the warrant was served: the plot was thwarted [37] and Morande's parting shot had missed by a mile.

The educated and cultivated people of Europe knew all about Morande and how little credibility could be attached to his various insults and calumnies. The well-informed also saw right through the French's Minister's machinations, which were designed to save the skins of Chesnon and De Launay and to avenge De Breteuil [38]. Cagliostro had amused this elite with his brilliant and witty responses, but even so many of the less astute were misled and looked no further than the heinous slanders and calumnies spread by the hired gun Morande. Isn't this the mistake that many historians have also made?

In the light of this Cagliostro decided, on the advice of devoted friends, to rebut all the inaccurate and hostile statements published in the *Courrier de l'Europe* under the names of Ricciarelli, Pergolezzi, Sachi, Jackson and others, and to inform public opinion before the lawsuits that Sachi and Priddle had threatened him with came to court by writing his *Lettre au peuple anglais*, *the* Letter to the English People [39]. This letter, which is very well documented and written in a very dignified style, proved crushing for his enemies. We have already quoted the most important parts of it as events have unfolded. It ends with these words, addressed specifically to Morande:

Neither I nor my friends will ever trust Monsieur Morande [40] *for a quite simple reason, which I am sure my readers will agree with. Monsieur Morande knows perfectly well what that reason is, and it is the certainty of our refusal to trust him which gives him the courage to ask us to do so.*

Cagliostro is referring here to Morande's disgraceful conduct in respect of the Comte de Lauraguais, whom he tried to compromise by passing him off as the author of one of his more odious lampoons [41], and whom he also personally insulted and defamed. De Lauraguais actually beat up Morande in the street and then had him arraigned before the Queen's Bench. Morande sent his wife and children around to see De Lauraguais to beg forgiveness and subsequently went to see him in person to grovel at his feet. Morande was subsequently ordered to insert in a public newspaper [42] a retraction acknowledging that he was a forger and slanderer. However, when the legal action against him was halted Morande declared himself ready to start all over again. As Cagliostro continued:

Here is the man that our enemies have taken into their pay. Here is the 'worthy defender' that they have chosen. And this man has the audacity to challenge my friends and myself to a duel! And he even impertinently offers us a choice of weapons, without thinking that there is only one kind of weapon that can honestly be used against him.

I shall abandon to his own turpitude this journalistic has-been whom France has rejected, England has repudiated, and all Europe has known the true value of for a long time. He can continue to insult me all he likes.

I have no intention of summoning him before the courts. This unfortunate man has a wife and six children. His inevitable ruin, if I chose to attack him, would also harm his large family. I place my vengeance between the hands of Him who does not visit upon the children the sins of the father [43].

And with these words summoning Morande before the Court not of man but of God, and reminding him of the fate that awaits those who have defamed and persecuted the envoys of Heaven, Cagliostro concludes his comments on Morande. Indeed, this was the very last word in his rejoinder [44]. Did Morande, apparently an irresistible force, appreciate that at long last he had encountered an immovable object? As an astute journalist, did he not sense that the mockers were no longer on his side [45], that he had finally been unmasked, and that people could hear too many French coins jangling in his pockets when he patted his chest in some grand oratorical gesture? Or did the Minister pull the rug from under him perhaps? Whatever happened, Morande halted his campaign against Cagliostro at this point.

Chapter VIII

Cagliostro had triumphed over journalism, this force which was to overthrow monarchies and remain the sole reigning power, indeed the only one nowadays that can still make the last princes of the Earth, by which I means the Kings of Iron, the Kings of Copper and the Kings of Gold, blanch and tremble in their fortresses.

Now that he had won this battle, the most terrible he had ever fought, and was master of the terrain, he continued to live in London amidst his friends both old and new, continuing his teaching and philanthropy in all the milieux in which he found himself, but especially in the world of Freemasonry. Cagliostro was a close friend of Lord George Gordon [46] and the person who inspired the latter's work in the *Theological Society*. Invited to visit several of the oldest and most prestigious Lodges in London he was welcomed with the greatest possible respect [47]. It has been said that Freemasons put on fancy-dress and made fun of him to his face, but this is simply a misinterpretation of a caricature of the time, printed and published by the usual enemies, and which is without documentary value [48]. After all, will the scholars, intellectuals and statesmen of the early 20th century be judged on the basis of the drawings of Jean-Louis Forain or Emmanuel Poiré?

In his Masonic work in London Cagliostro tried, as he had in Lyons and Paris, to impart some sort of moral direction to the lodges and to infuse the Order with a sense of spiritual reality. Here is an announcement published in the *Morning Herald* of 2nd November 1786. It is not signed, so we don't know for certain if he actually wrote it, but it was certainly published on his behalf and under his inspiration [49]:

To all true Freemasons in the name of 9,5,8,14,20,1,8, 9,5,18,20,18 [50].

The time has come to begin the construction of the new temple or the new 3,8, 20,17,8 [51] *of Jerusalem. This notice is issued to invite all true Freemasons in London to meet in the name of 9,5,18,20,18* [52] *(the only one in whom there is a divine 19,17,9,13,9,19,23)* [53]*, to be held tomorrow evening on the 3rd day of the present month 1786 or 5790 at nine o'clock at O'Reilly's tavern* [54]*, Great Queen Street, there to form the plan and to lay the first foundation stone of the true 3,8,20,17,8* [55] *in this visible world, which is the material temple of the spiritual 9,5,17,20,18,1,11,5,12* [56]*. A Freemason is a member of the new 3,8,20,17,8* [57].

By this summons he sought to convene a general assembly not just of the higher degrees but of all Freemasons who wished to receive instruction so as then in this most excellent soil sow good seeds, revive the ancient rites, and inspire a brethren that had become sluggish and demotivated.

But in England, more so even than France, he ran up against petty rivalries and general indifference. Sensing that his efforts were wasted and yielding to the insistence of Sarrasin, who had always missed him and who retained a profound devotion towards him [58], he left England on 30th

Portrait of Cagliostro by Bartolozzi

March 1787. He left alone. The Countess remained in London in the care of her friend, Miss Howard, to complete the preparations for her own departure and, in particular, to sell any furniture that they could not take with them on their long voyage. This sale took place on 13th April in Pall Mall under the auspices of Christie's auction-house.

Learning of his departure, Morande again began a violent campaign of insults, this time on his own behalf, in the *Courrier de l'Europe*: initially it was a fanfare of triumph, with the journalist claiming the glory for having put his enemy to flight. Then he switched to a sudden commiseration for the Countess, talking about this unhappy woman, forsaken by her husband who had run away to save himself without paying even their maid, taking all her jewellery with him, abandoning her for ever after having made her undergo the most painful existence imaginable. He also gave the impression that the perfectly straightforward auction at Christie's was actually a distraint-sale. He even listed all the auction-lots, adding for enhanced pungency a few of his own creation, such as athanors, crucibles and other alchemical paraphernalia and 'thousands of remaindered copies of Cagliostro's *Lettre au peuple anglais* which were to be sold by weight'. In several consecutive issues he also published a detailed description of Cagliostro so that people could identify him and inform him of his whereabouts wherever he might appear.

Now that we have told you all about Morande it would be almost superfluous to attempt to rebut all these lies. And yet these last-minute calumnies, since they remained unanswered, had their effect. Historians [59] have attached some importance to them and, unfortunately, have also acted as something of an echo-chamber for them. Just one observation will be enough to establish the utter falseness of Morande's final allegations: Cagliostro, after a rapid crossing, stayed for just a few days in Belgium to visit certain Lodges that had asked to see him. Hardly had he settled down in Basel amongst his former friends than he was immediately joined there by Countess Cagliostro, who had now concluded the final matters that had kept her in London. We can see the impudence and offhandedness with which Morande mocked the truth and his audience, but we must also note how blasé the critics have been in blindly assimilating the most fantastic stories as long as they were suitably scandalous in character. The charge against Cagliostro of having robbed and abandoned his wife, and the legend that depicts him as a tyrannical husband and the Countess as a terrorised victim, were adopted and odiously amplified in the all-too-famous *Vie de Joseph Balsamo* by the anonymous Secretary to the Inquisition. Morande can therefore be said to have prepared the ground for the later work of Rome.

NOTES

(1) *Mémoires secrets*, vol. XXXII, p. 91. Both in Paris and abroad the newspapers were moved to pity by the Cardinal's sufferings, and congratulated him volubly when he was acquitted. Everywhere people were rejoicing. In the town of Mutzig, where the Cardinal had a château rivalling that of Saverne, a brilliant festival was organised to celebrate his return. The Cardinal, greatly moved, made a tour of the whole town. 'Before ending his tour he did not disdain to enter the local Synagogue, which was magnificently illuminated for the occasion. For half an hour he remained there, listening to hymns of thanksgiving as well as a Hebrew canticle specially composed for His Eminence, which he liked so much that he expressed all his gratitude to the townspeople all over again', Le Roy de Sainte-Croix, *Les quatre cardinaux de Rohan*, Strasbourg, 1880, p. 149.

(2) The Cardinal left for La Chaise-Dieu in the Auvergne on Monday 4th June 1786, cf. *Gazette de Leyde* no. XLIX of 20th June 1786.

(3) In the Bastille he had suffered from suppurative arthritis of the left knee, *Gazette de Leyde*, no. IX, 31st January 1786. 'The cardinal is visibly deteriorating', *Ma Correspondance*, no. 24, 1786.

(4) Cf. his Letter to the French people later in this chapter.
(5) p. 39.
(6) The letter is dated 20th June. It was passed from hand to hand in manuscript, and was only printed later on. We find it reproduced almost in its entirety in the memoirs of Bachaumont, op. cit., under the entry for 10th August 1786, vol. II, p. 279.
(7) Bibliothèque de l'Arsenal, Mss. 12457, folio 21, 3 p. The letter is known as the *Lettre au peuple français*.
(8) 'Hardly had this letter appeared than I noticed that Mr. Swinton was redoubling his efforts to be kind and solicitous. He seemed to have a burning desire to familiarise me with my surroundings in London... A boat-trip on the Thames was, he said, 'so delightful a pleasure that I couldn't even imagine it'. Well, as you know, by nature I'm essentially a thinker and a person of sedentary habits. This enthusiasm on the part of Mr. Swinton to get me out onto the water... aroused certain suspicions in me. I made some enquiries – a little late in the day I shall admit – about my walking-companion. And thereafter I was very much on my guard', *Lettre au peuple anglais*, 1787, p. 34. The idea of a boat-trip from which you didn't come back was not a new one: Morande himself almost became a victim in 1773, cf. Robiquet, *Théveneau de Morande*, Paris, Quantin, 1887, p. 39.
(9) Robiquet, *op. cit.*, p. 198.
(10) Morande admits that the meeting took place and, indeed, wrote about the encounter in his diary as an entry for 27th February 1787.
(11) The interview took place at Swinton's: 'Monsieur Morande wanted to sound things out for himself. He therefore came round to Swinton's one day when he knew I'd be there. His appearance didn't predispose me favourably towards him at all. I found his questions impertinent, his tone objectionable, and his threats ridiculous. I told him this to his face and added that I would be inconvenienced to only a very small extent by anything he could write about me', *Lettre au peuple anglais*, p. 32.
(12) *Lettre au peuple anglais*, p. 46, note.
(13) Morande twice gave a detailed description of Cagliostro in his newspaper so that his correspondents all over Europe could identify him and report his presence to him, cf. Chapter III of this book.
(14) Anne-Gédéon La Fite de Pellepore, the author of *Le Diable dans un bénitier*, referring to Morande's suitability for his role as a police-officer, wrote: 'They sent for the *Gazetier cuirassé*. Few people were more suited to provide agreeable company for the Baron de Livermont (the pseudonym of the police-officer Receveur), as Godard himself (another police-officer) had too much nobility of soul. A soul as dark as Morande's (although he could shed plenty of tears when it suited him), accompanied by such a vulgar turn of mind, and a turn of phrase of equal vulgarity (namely a prison-slang he'd learned in Bicêtre jail which the 'Baron', who'd spent half his life there, spoke fluently) all conspired to ensure that our *Gazetier* would be sharing the pleasures of the 'recruiter of Bicêtre'', Robiquet, *Théveneau de Morande*, p. 63.
(15) Report of Inspector Marais, vol. XII of the *Archives de la Bastille*, published by Monsieur Ravaisson, Paris, 1881. We have drawn most of the material on Morande from Robiquet's excellent book, *Théveneau de Morande*.
(16) *Le Gazetier cuirassé* was subtitled 'Scandalous anecdotes from the royal court of France printed a hundred miles from the Bastille', 1771. Voltaire described this lampoon as follows: 'There has just appeared one of those works of darkness in which, from the monarch himself down to the humblest citizen, everyone is furiously insulted, and in which the most atrocious and absurd calumnies drip a dreadful poison over everything and everyone that one loves and respects. The author concealed his identity out of fear of public execration', Voltaire, *Questions sur l'Encyclopédie*, 1772 edition, vol. IX, p. 224.
(17) Beaumarchais, upon his return, reproached him naively: 'I work day and night for six weeks, travel nearly 700 miles, and spend nearly 500 *louis* of my own money to prevent countless evils, whilst you, as a result of these labours, receive 100,000 *francs* and peace of mind, whereas I no longer know whether I'll even be refunded my travelling expenses', Letter to Morande quoted in Robiquet, op. cit.,

p. 51.

(18) 'His name should be treated the way the criminal justice system would treat his ashes', said Linguet in his *Annales*. 'Beaumarchais earned the abomination and hatred of Mademoiselle d'Éon because he went so low as to appoint as his confidant and deputy an even viler and more degenerate man, the author of the *Gazetier cuirassé* – namely Morande', *Observateur Anglais*, vol. IX, p. 14. Mirabeau had a similar opinion of him (cf. Robiquet, p. 263) and Voltaire said of him: 'This escapee from Bicêtre prison exploits to excess the contempt that everyone has for him', *Questions sur l'Encyclopédie*, 1772 edition, vol. VIII, p. 261.

(19) Robiquet, op. cit., p. 88.

(20) Robiquet, op. cit., p. 61.

(21) In March 1774 (Robiquet, op. cit., p. 90). The *Gazetier cuirassé* has been transformed into a policy-spy' says a lampoon of the time.

(22) Goëzman (Baron de Thurne), Robert de Paradès, Bouchardat (Belson) and even Meaupou (a former member of the *Parlement*) all plied a trade as 'licenced' police-officers in London around this time and all had a financial interest in the *Courrier de l'Europe* (Robiquet, p. 63). Irrefutable proof that the *Courrier* had been 'bought' by the French police is that, uniquely amongst printed material from England, it did not have to go through the censors. This was no secret: the newspaper was used as a means of reprisal against anyone who was hostile to the Ministry. The continuator of the *Mémoires secrets* (entry for 3rd April 1785) is quite explicit about this. Three years later nothing had changed: 'The *Courrier de l'Europe* is a mass-circulation newspaper sold to people like Lenoir, Beaumarchais, Albert and all the other rascals of France... Thanks to the vigilance of the Comte de Montmorin (Foreign Minister in 1788, replacing Monsieur de Vergennes) it is in this newspaper that the reputations of the most respectable people are periodically assassinated', *Lettre à Monsieur de Beaumarchais*, written from Aix in 1788.

(23) *Lettre au peuple anglais*, p. 47.

(24) Swinton acted as his guide and interpreter during the first few weeks of his stay in London. Swinton made sure that he was well remunerated for his services, resorting to some pretty unsubtle practices to increase his fees, *Lettre au peuple anglais*, p. 35.

(25) Robiquet, op. cit., p. 6.

(26) No. 16306 (1786).

(27) This interminable republication of the same baseless stories, even ones that had been refuted ten times, nevertheless had the effect of imprinting them in the public mind. Robiquet, who was an author who did not focus specifically on Cagliostro, tells us all about his this plagiarism in his excellent book (p. 108), displaying, as he does throughout that work, conscientious accuracy and a perfectly-judged critical sense.

(28) Cf. the Bibliography to this book.

(29) Republished and disseminated by Morande throughout the European press which, even though it had not yet been syndicated, still spoke pretty much with one voice, with virtually the same articles and official statements appearing in Namur, Leiden, Hamburg, Berlin, Florence, Schaffhouse, Amsterdam and Paris almost simultaneously with their appearance in London. It was in the face of this press campaign, which angered Cagliostro's loyal supporters in their home territories, that reinforced some of the traditional loyalties: Barbier de Tinan, Langlois, Schlosser, Sarrasin and Lavater all defended their friend against the allegations. Open letters of rectification were sent to editors; Schlosser protested against the libellous allegations of Meiners, who had judged and condemned Cagliostro on the basis of hearsay despite the fact that his sole contact with him was having seen him passing one day in his carriage (cf. article by Schlosser in Deutsch. Museum, April 1787); Barbier de Tinan publicly professed his 'respectful fondness' for Cagliostro and made clear his absolute impartiality (see the letter from Barbier de Thinan in the Appendix of this book); and Cardinal de Rohan wrote several letters of introduction and recommendation for him, cf. Letter to Monsieur de Créquy, Letter to the Praetor (Strasbourg Library, Ms. AA, 2110) and Letter to the Archbishop of Lyons (private collection of Monsieur Alfred Sensier), the last of which is all the more interesting as it dates from

Chapter VIII

December 1789.

(30) Cagliostro had spoken within his small circle of friends 'about an experiment known to all chemists which consists in imperceptibly accustoming an animal to a food poisoned with arsenic, and so turning its flesh into a most subtle poison', *Lettre au peuple anglais*, p. 40. This is what would later be terms the preparation of arsenical toxins.

(31) Morande had been unwise enough to have made this claim.

(32) 'Morande was seen crossing the city and its environs in his carriage, going wallet in hand from door to door, from pub to pub, from prison to prison, canvassing for people to speak ill of me. This is well known to any Londoner. Monsieur Dubourg, the notary at the France Embassy, who sometimes accompanied Morande in these murky researches, is understood to have received 50 guineas in fees from Morande. Morande offered up to 100 guineas to O'Reilly, the owner of the hotel frequented by the Freemasons and which was where I was lodging at that time, simply to state that I had left without paying at the time of my departure from England in 1777', *Lettre au peuple anglais*, p. 47.

(33) He did this in his *Lettre au peuple anglais*, p. 70, in respect of the allegation by a Monsieur B., but 'since Monsieur B. was in Paris when this calumny appeared, he formally contradicted it in a statement sworn before Maître Piquais, a notary in Le Châtelet, and I have a certified copy of it in my hands'... 'As for this 'Monsieur Silvestre', of whom we cannot find any trace except in the writings of Morande, apparently he's not the only creditor I have to fear. Morande assures me that the Paris Diligence will shortly be arriving in London with four Portuguese from the Faubourg Saint-Antoine and no fewer than six Germans from the Marais, all of whom will swear, one after the other, that I owe them considerable sums of money', ibid, p. 65.

(34) Brissot, an old friend of Morande who later became his enemy, testifies to it, depicting him '...tearing to shreds in the newspaper he directed the most estimable men... *fabricating or getting people to fabricate documents that were specifically designed to ruin those whom he feared*', Brissot, *Réponse à tous les libellistes des pièces pour perdre ceux qu'il redoutait*, Paris, 1791.

(35) Sachi was the main instrument of Cagliostro's misfortunes: his greed and jealousy pursued Cagliostro everywhere he went in Strasbourg, neutralising the gratitude that was felt towards him by the whole city. We then find him in Bordeaux preventing Cagliostro from enjoying his successes there. At the time of the Diamond Necklace Affair he was the mainstay of and a supplier of documents to Madame de la Motte. In London Morande made use of him again, and later the Inquisition in Rome republished his scandalous allegations. Always turning up like a bad penny, ceaselessly undermining Cagliostro's efforts, he was the slanderer with the hushed voice, the enemy lurking in in Cagliostro's shadow. It was only at the end of Cagliostro's career that Morande took over the role of Cagliostro's public persecutor when he prepared the case that he was to face in Rome. We can fairly say that, without Sachi, Cagliostro – loved in Strasbourg, in his glory in Bordeaux and Lyons, unassailable in Paris – would have enjoyed a degree of happiness equal to the level of persecution he eventually suffered. But Sachi was an unavoidable figure on the road that Cagliostro had to travel. Cagliostro had been so generous towards him: money, knowledge, jobs, secret formulas, he'd given Sachi all of them, willingly or not. And didn't Cagliostro, far from getting rid of him, actually protect him when some of his over-enthusiastic friends offered to get rid of him for him?

(36) Priddle submitted a claim of his own which was joined to that of Sachi.

(37) *Lettre au peuple anglais*, 1787, p. 48.

(38) 'The public noted that Morande's prose was riddled with Ministerial formulas and maxims', *Mémoires secrets*, 9th October 1786.

(39) In one volume, no place of publication given, 1787, 78 pp. + I.

(40) In Morande's challenge a further trap was concealed: the English duelling laws were quite explicit, and Cagliostro would been arrested on the field of honour even if he had not been assassinated.

(41) 'This is a scoundrel who dares to say something favourable about me in a lampoon in which he savages everything that I love and respect', Grimm, Correspondence, vol. X, p. 222.

(42) *London Evening Post*, no. 8062, 'APOLOGY: since the Comte de Lauraguais, after the humble submissions I have made to him, has agreed to halt the legal action instituted against me for having

defamed him by publishing injurious verses full of falsehoods which I caused to be inserted... etc... I beg you to publish in this same periodical my sincere apologies for having defamed so injuriously the said Comte de Lauraguais and to convey my very humble thanks to him for having accepted my submissions and halted his legal action against me, Signed: Morande'.

(43) *Lettre au peuple anglais*, p. 74.

(44) Morande's success began to wane from this day onwards. Forced to leave London and the *Courrier* in 1791 he returned to Paris to try to fish in the very troubled waters of the time, establishing the *Argus patriotique* 'with the task of defending patriotism, morals and the Monarchy' as he boldly stated on the masthead. The *Argus* changed its political complexion like a chameleon in its very short life of just a few months. Morande abandoned it at the moment of greatest danger and fled to Arnay-le-Duc. He cheated the guillotine but it was in this village that he was destined to die, quite miserably and completely ignored, in July 1805.

(45) Cf. *Mémoires secrets*, quoted by Robiquet, op. cit. p. 204.

(46) The *Courrier de l'Europe* mentions, as some of the friends and defenders of Cagliostro in London, a Mr. Cr...f..d., Monsieur du T..., Lord G... (Gordon), a Monsieur le Mi...re and a Monsieur Ag...sis, *Courrier*, 1787, p. 152.

(47) *Lettre au peuple anglais*, p. 74.

(48) *Monist*, 1903. This caricature, which the author of this article says is rare and preciously preserved in the Library of the Scottish Rite in Washington, is actually a very well-known engraving which is frequently encountered at auction. Cagliostro rebuts the calumny in his *Lettre au peuple anglais*, p.70.

(49) It was Bonneville who, in the *Berliner Monatsschrift* for March 1786, revealed Cagliostro to be the author of this anonymous manifesto.

(50) Jehovah-Jesus.

(51) Churh (for Church).

(52) Jesus.

(53) Trinity.

(54) The Freemasons' hotel in London.

(55) Churh (for Church).

(56) Jerusalem.

(57) Churh (for Church).

(58) Cagliostro, before his final departure, initially spent a few weeks in the countryside with Loutherbourg (born 1740 in Strasbourg, died 1812 in Chiswick, painter to the King and a very keen amateur alchemist) working with him in his laboratory. It was this same Loutherbourg and his wife who welcomed and housed Countess Cagliostro after her husband's departure and after she herself had finishing moving out of 4 Sloane Street, Knightsbridge.

(59) Including, somewhat surprisingly, Robiquet, even though he is very impartial and well-informed about the value of Morande's statements, cf. *Vie de Théveneau de Morande*, note 2, p. 205.

CHAPTER IX

—

'THE PROFANER OF THE ONE TRUE CHURCH'

CAGLIOSTRO IN SWITZERLAND AND ROME

Switzerland: Basel and Bienne
Since Cagliostro was an English Freemason he might have expected a sympathetic reception in England but, as we have seen, that was far from being the case. Nor was he given much opportunity to relax after all his trials and tribulations. Cagliostro, ever a victim of other people's arbitrary behaviour, had encountered in London only hatred and mockery. Wearied by these arguments, disheartened by the attitudes of both people and institutions, including unfortunately Freemasonry, he found his contact with the English more and more annoying with every day that went by. There were only two people he could be bothered to entertain, and those were Lord George Gordon and Loutherbourg. When Sophie Laroche [1] visited him and revived his best memories of Sarrasin she noted how he longed to leave England and how embittered he was. 'If it wasn't for my dear wife I would have gone into the desert, amongst the wild beasts, and I'm sure I would have found it easier to have made friends there', he told her [2]. Sophie, with as much delicacy as she could muster, reminded him that he had still had good friends in Basel, that the Sarrasins were devoted to him body and soul, and that they were always hoping that one day he would return to them.

Cagliostro was genuinely moved: he loved Sarrasin for his loyalty and fondly recalled certain proofs that he had given of it, including opening his purse to him as liberally as his heart [3]. Cagliostro was unable to conceal from Sophie the sweet emotions that this new assurance of Sarrasin's affection had revived within him [4] and when, shortly after her visit in December 1786, he decided to leave London, he wrote to Sarrasin, asking him to find him a little nest in some quiet corner of Switzerland where he could get way from his enemies [5]. Sarrasin dealt with his request immediately: in his opinion either Neuchâtel or Bienne (Biel) would be the most appropriate, but he favoured Neuchâtel as being the more important of the two towns. Also, Neuchâtel was a Prussian principality at that time, and Sarrasin thought that his protégé Prince Henry of Prussia, who'd honoured him with a visit some two years before [6], might be able to assist him in his task of helping Cagliostro. Sarrasin therefore wrote to the Prince about it, contacting at the same time the Governor of Neuchâtel, a Monsieur de Belleville. On 15th March 1787 the Prince answered him in person, writing in French. This letter will be found in the Sarrasin archives. The passage relating to his request reads as follows:

... As for Count Cagliostro, whom you would like to persuade to settle in Neuchâtel, allow me to make a few observations. A man whose morals are pure, who makes it an item of duty to obey the laws of the country that he wishes to live in and who only wishes to live

peaceably amongst his friends, does not need, it seems to me, permission to take up residence in that country, even less so under some form of special protection. Also, if he has had some legal problems with some foreign power, and this power is entitled to seize his person as a result, then no form of special protection could be granted to him.

You will readily draw the necessary conclusions from these reflections. Even so, I naturally hope that all your wishes are fulfilled. I shall continue to keep an eye on the matter in accordance with the concern that I have for you as well as my very considerable esteem, with which I remain, Sir, your affectionate friend,
Henry.
Berlin, 15th March 1787 [7].

Prince Henry's reply was cordial enough but also very reserved. Of course, Sarrasin fully appreciated that, although the Prussian Court might not actually place any obstacles in the way of Cagliostro relocating to Neuchâtel, it wouldn't be doing anything to protect him either. He therefore abandoned the idea of involving Prince Henry and turned to the banneret [8] Sigismund Wildermett, of Bienne, to whom he had been introduced by their mutual friend Pfeffel [9]. Wildermett made serious efforts to help, since he had been assured that the French Consul in Bern [10] would not object to Cagliostro settling in Bienne. He therefore launched an active campaign on his behalf with the local authorities and the citizens. In March 1787 Sarrasin went to Bienne in person to ask the city council, the *Conseil*, to allow Cagliostro to take up residence. He also rented, on Cagliostro's behalf, a beautiful property called Rockhalt [11].

Sarrasin told Cagliostro that everything was ready. Cagliostro left for Basel at once, arriving there on 5th April 1787. Sarrasin encouraged him to visit his new home [12], and also introduced him to the city worthies. They then returned to Basel. Everyone was glad to see him again. Apart from the Sarrasin family he also found there the Hazenbachs, the French pastor Touchon [13], Haas, Professor Breitinger, De Gingin and Burckhardt [14], all serious liberal-minded people, and all respectfully devoted to Cagliostro. Cagliostro had got to know them and had become fond of them during his first trip to Basel in October 1781. It was with them that he had examined the plans of the pavilion that he intended to be used for the secret workings of his Rite, the construction of which Sarrasin had himself supervised [15]. Since then his Swiss disciples had discussed his doctrines and generally cultivated his memory. The ground was therefore fully prepared for some new teachings, and Cagliostro was fully prepared to provide them.

Following his stay in Paris, where he had seen the conventions of Freemasons engage in such fruitless agitations, his disagreements with the *Philalèthes*, and his disappointments with the English Freemasons Cagliostro had rejected any ambitions to revitalise the Masonic body through the Egyptian Rite. He was now relying more on the creation of new men than on the transformation of minds that were already deeply impregnated with erroneous traditions, and if, up till that time, he had carefully cultivated the traditional usages and symbolism of the accepted Rites to make the transition to the Egyptian Rite easier for devotees of the Scottish Rite or the Grand Orient, he could no longer see any advantage at all in such an approach, now that the mistrust and presumptuous ignorance of the Freemasons had reversed all the advances that he had made. It was along these lines that he spoke to his friends in Basel and also to Lavater [16], encouraging them to think in terms of a simpler and more purely spiritual idea of the Egyptian Rite which would entirely replace and not merely remediate the existing Masonic Rites [17].

Chapter IX

A 'Mother-Lodge of the Swiss Nations', the members of which had been individually initiated in 1781, began its activities for the first time in regular session on 2nd May 1787 at Sarrasin's house [18]. The Lodge was arranged on a similar model to the Lodge of Lyons but was simpler: there were fewer ornaments and hardly any symbols. In the middle of the room was a marble bust of Cagliostro [19]. It was more a meeting-room and a mystical oratory than a Masonic temple. There were no symbols on the licence and diplomas, which were framed with a simple arabesque, and with just the name of God engraved at the top [20].

Apart from the temple, intimate *soirées* were held for those who had not actually been initiated into the Rite. Sarrasin in particular did a lot of entertaining on Cagliostro's behalf. Pastor Schmidt [21], who dined with Cagliostro, a French general and some ladies at Sarrasin's house on 8th May 1787, recorded his account of the evening in his diary [22]. He heard Cagliostro speak vehemently against the English character and against French society. He told the other guests that these receptions and his Masonic work took up all his time, and that he didn't bother with medicine any more, unlike his first stay there in 1781, when the Sarrasin mansion had not been big enough to accommodate all his patients [23].

At the end of May, Sarrasin took Cagliostro with him to Olten to attend the 27th annual meeting of the Société Helvétique where Cagliostro made a great impression. Matthaei [24], who was also present and who reported the event, announced this sensational news to his mistress and friend, the Marquise de Branconi [25] who, intrigued to learn that Cagliostro was in Switzerland and impressed by Matthaei's account, immediately sent Sarrasin the following letter:

Neuchâtel, 9th June 1787

I would be grateful Sir if you would inform Count Cagliostro of how great a pleasure it is for me to learn that I am now his neighbour [26], *and how eager I am to meet him again. I am similarly very grateful to him for having let me have a copy of the satire against him, which I shall read with as much indignation as everything else that seeks to attack his well-known benevolence, which surely even the worst-intentioned of men will never be able to question. I congratulate the people of Bienne and its environs on the fact that the Count has made his home there. Without in any way seeking to make apologies on his behalf I have spoken my mind to everyone who has asked me about him during my journey from Bern to Soleure, which I fortunately completed yesterday evening* [27].

She was indeed an old acquaintance of Cagliostro's. She had met him in Strasbourg at Sarrasin's house, had brought Lavater [28] to meet him, and had made overtures towards Cagliostro, whom she liked: 'I really like the Count. He simply *must* become my friend', she wrote [29] to Sarrasin, who remarks that she 'rashly threw herself at him'. This was a strategy that might have worked with other people, as indeed it seems to have done with Lavater and Goethe, the latter reportedly going weak at the knees in the presence of this 'siren' [30]. Cagliostro, in contrast, was not one of her conquests. This sultry temptress, used to being adulated and found irresistible, refused to accept that a man to whom she had shown some liking would not fall, hopelessly in love, at her feet. She was frankly outraged, and immediately became one of Cagliostro's sworn enemies [31]. She scandalised Sarrasin with her attempts to turn him against Cagliostro. '*Your* Cagliostro simply doesn't exist. He is less than nothing', she shouted at Madame Sarrasin, her friends [32], and indeed everyone she bumped into. Sarrasin was not especially impressed by this sudden resentment, and complained about it to Lavater: 'This pretty little doll can think and say what she likes. Let her buzz off if she wants. I would give you a thousand Branconis for one Cagliostro' [33].

Others however were more affected by the contretemps. Lavater himself was in two minds, oscillating between loyalty to his beautiful friend and to Cagliostro, and was even prepared to throw the latter to the wolves. In one of his letters to Madame Sarrasin he actually tried to turn her against his Master and saviour [34].

Such had been the estrangement during their previous encounter, but a lot of water had gone under the bridge since then, and after returning to her house at Chanet the Marquise de

Rockhalt, Cagliostro's country-house in Bienne.

Chapter IX

Branconi no longer thought any more of it: she was happy to meet once again this extraordinary and indeed unique man who had so intrigued her in Strasbourg.

Sarrasin passed on her request to Cagliostro, who did not refuse, insisting only that they meet on neutral territory. A few days later the Countess Cagliostro arrived in Basel [35] and, on 29th June, accompanied by Sarrasin and Loutherbourg, she left Bienne with her husband. They lunched at the banneret's where the Marquise Branconi was a guest [36]. The reconciliation was easy: at that time the Marquise was smitten with Franz Michael Leuchsenring, a counsellor at the Court of Darmstadt [37], a relationship that upset Matthaei and caused some jealous scenes [38]. Entirely absorbed in this recent passion the Marquise forgot all about her previous resentments and concentrated on her new flirtations. She was attentive and pleasant to Countess Cagliostro and found in Cagliostro himself the doctor and devoted spiritual director whom she had only herself to blame for originally alienating. Her visits to Rockhalt during the summer of 1787 were both frequent and cordial.

Cagliostro's life in Bienne was proceeding peacefully, alternating between entertaining and the practice of medicine [39], when an unforeseen event came along to spoil everything. Loutherbourg, influenced by someone or something unknown to us, suddenly decided to pick a fight with Cagliostro, involving some of other leading personalities in Bienne in the process [40]. The Loutherbourg affair is hard to explain, even though it gave rise to legal proceedings before the city's Grand Council, the records of which are listed as being held in the city archives [41], including Cagliostro's defence. Unfortunately they seem to have disappeared. In 1900 Dr. Türler of Bern published a book about this period which also notes their absence from the archives. They seem to have gone missing in 1792 or 1793, whether stolen or burned we do not know [42]. In the relevant correspondence and in Sarrasin's diary we find some references to that gentleman's involvement in the affair, but regarding the original reason for the rupture between Cagliostro and Loutherbourg we find either absolute silence or comments that are too vague [43] to allow for any hard and fast conclusions.

The likeliest explanation is that the Loutherbourg affair was the continuation of attempts in London, when Countess Cagliostro had remained alone with the Loutherbourgs, to obtain from her some confidences or some secret revelations about her husband, his adventures or his mysteries. Attempts were subsequently made to estrange her from her husband. But what exactly were people hoping to gain from such a separation? *Cui bono*? The whole thing's a mystery, but it seems that Cagliostro's former lawyer Thilorier was involved in the conspiracy: an indignant letter from Sarrasin to D'Éprémesnil written from Bienne on 5th July 1787 contains the following passage:

The people with whom Maître Thilorier has been collaborating, according to his own admission, have been flattering themselves that they will benefit personally from the various insinuations that they have put to the Countess. However, everything has now been disclosed, established from original sources, and set down in the best form in a voluntary legal statement [44].

Would you kindly inform Count Cagliostro without delay of the success of his lawsuit and also tell your relative Maître Thilorier that it is neither Monsieur Rey de Morande, nor Monsieur de Vismes nor Monsieur de Lansègre that he should be representing and advising but Count Cagliostro, and that it is not the job of a lawyer to tell his client's wife that she should separate her interests from his [45].

Loutherbourg and his wife had been working along the same lines as Thilorier. Suddenly the intrigue was unmasked. Cagliostro changed his attitude towards Loutherbourg, who no longer made any effort to conceal what he was up to. The animosity increased and two factions formed. On the one hand were the Loutherbourgs and their close friend the Mayor of Bienne, over whom Madame Loutherbourg had great influence [46], along with the Mayor's children – utterly brainless youngsters making common cause with Loutherbourg purely out of self-interest, though once again we don't know the precise details [47]. The other party consisted of Cagliostro and the Countess, De Gingin, Sarrasin, the Burgomaster and the banneret. Matters became increasingly tense [48] and open hostilities began. On 11th December 1787, when the Council met, Cagliostro filed a complaint against Loutherbourg claiming that, the day before, one of Loutherbourg's servants, one Abraham Ritter, had, on his master's orders, bought from a gunsmith some powder and bullets with which to load his pistols with a view to, it is alleged, murdering Cagliostro [49]. Consequently Cagliostro requested the protection of the Magistrates and the expulsion of Loutherbourg and his entourage from the city.

The matter created quite a scandal in Bienne. Enquiries confirmed the correctness of the allegations, but the Mayor hesitated and vacillated. The anti-Cagliostro party responded, made allegations of its own, and called the bailiffs in [50]. The affair became even more unpleasant. The little town, usually so tranquil, was suddenly tormented by scandal, and even outside the town there were repercussions [51]. Sarrasin felt pressurised to 'snatch Cagliostro from the jaws of his enemies' [52]. He rushed to Bienne [53] and gave the Mayor a two-hour talking-to at the banneret's house to try to persuade him to separate the cause of his own children from Loutherbourg's. He also asked for this embarrassing couple to be thrown out of the town [54]. Violent rows and lengthy discussions ensued. Finally, on 4th January, Sarrasin, 'using all his eloquence' [55] and, ironically, assisted by Loutherbourg himself, managed to find a way through the impasse and had two texts drafted: 1. an arrangement for the Mayor's family and son; 2. an arrangement for the Loutherbourgs. These documents were signed the following day at the Town Hall and certified by the Grand Council.

Cagliostro however was certainly not happy with the solution offered and with the text of the compromise: perhaps he thought that Sarrasin had not displayed as much energy in the matter as he should have done and had ended up having to buy something he should have insisted on automatically receiving [56]. Perhaps he was also strongly affected by the repeated defections and hostilities within his own circle. Whatever the case, Cagliostro seriously considered leaving Switzerland. After a short visit to his friends in Basel (from 17th January to 1st February 1783) he returned to Bienne. He accompanied Sarrasin to the 28th annual meeting of the *Société Helvétique* in Olten in June. Sarrasin took him back to Rockhalt and then said goodbye to him on 19th July [57]. He would never see him again: on 23rd July Cagliostro left Rockhalt.

Roveredo – Trento

After spending a season at Aix-les-Bains [58] for the benefit of his wife's health, Cagliostro passed rapidly through Turin [59], arriving in Roveredo on 24th September 1788. His life in this town would have remained as unknown to us as his time in Turin or Trento were it not for the fact that he met there, for the first time in his life, a truly impartial observer. A disinterested critic, neither disciple nor enemy, this prototype 'reporter' assumed the task of observing and writing up, on a daily basis, everything that he saw, heard or learned about Cagliostro in the few weeks that the Count spent in the town. Subsequently he worked the notes up into a book, and as it was fashionable in the 18th century to mix the sacred with the profane and to adopt a light-hearted approach to something that should have been treated

Chapter IX

very seriously, he published it in Latin under the title, *Liber memorialis de Caleostro [sic] cum esset Roboreti* in a style that was a pastiche of the Gospels.

The book came to be known as *L'Évangile de Cagliostro*, the Gospel of Cagliostro, and it is the most invaluable document that we have about him. It enables us to travel back in time and to spend a while in his company learning about what he was, listening to what he said, and finding out what those who came into contact with him might have thought of him. But this is not the only reason why this account of Cagliostro's brief sojourn in Roveredo is of such value, it's also because almost every copy of this book, along with Cagliostro's private papers, was burned by the Inquisition in the auto-da-fé in the Piazza della Minerva in Rome on 4th May 1791 that followed the Pope's judgment. Some copies that had already found their way into private hands escaped the inferno, but most of those too have since disappeared, either destroyed or lost. No copies are to be found in public libraries or at auctions of rare books, and even the work's contemporaries only knew its title. We were fortunate to find a copy of it in Italy. From this book, of which we have published an accurate translation with annotations [60], we can see that in Roveredo, as in Strasbourg and Paris, Cagliostro's house was besieged by patients [61] and that his medical philanthropy and successes won the enthusiastic recognition of the people. Several leading citizens also became his friends [62].

For six weeks, with boundless kindness, he welcomed and cared for the unfortunate. He also taught, speaking even more freely and openly than he had anywhere else about his mission and activities [63]. There too, unfortunately, cabals of doctors and the animosity of the local clergy made life impossible for him [64]. He left on 10th November for Trento. A grateful patient who had urged him to go there introduced him to the leading citizens [65]. Borowski cites 22nd October as the date of this departure, but without a reference. The date given in the *Liber memorialis* seems to us to be more authoritative. Borowski also refers to a visit by Cagliostro to Venice where, reduced to poverty, he had to sell his jewellery to survive. His beautiful watch, surrounded by diamonds, was bought by a jeweller from Mainz called Chardon. We should not however forget that this information is taken from the pages of the *Courrier de l'Europe*! We also know that, a short time afterwards, Cagliostro had a cash-box and a bill of exchange for 10,000 thalers. He then moved to Trento on 3rd April 1789 [66]. The story of Cagliostro's financial embarrassment in Venice is therefore scarcely credible. It is probable that in Trento things went pretty much the way they did everywhere with Cagliostro: warm greetings to start with, jealousy and hostilities to end with. It was the usual parade of feelings from those to whom Cagliostro had offered material succour and spiritual benefit. Cagliostro's excellent relations with the Prince-Bishop of the city would certainly have persuaded him to remain longer if the animosity of his enemies had not followed him to his new retreat. They even obtained from the Emperor Joseph II a comminatory letter to the Bishop of Trento, in which the Emperor expressed his displeasure at the town harbouring 'a dangerous *Illuminé* and a Grandmaster of a proscribed Rite'. To bring peace of mind to the town's protector Cagliostro was required to leave. Upon his departure the Prince-Bishop gave him letters of warm recommendation to show Cardinals Albani, Colonna and Buoncompagni, which proves just how warm relations between him and Bishop had actually been [67].

The *Vie de Joseph Balsamo* [68] tells us that the real reason why Cagliostro left for Rome was his wife's desire to return to her family and to be closer to her religion [69]. We have seen one of the reasons for his departure, but his wife's feelings may also have influenced his decision. But with Cagliostro becoming more and more estranged from mainstream

Freemasonry and increasingly eager to propagate, in the face of it, his own true, spiritual and Christian Masonic Rite, he conceived the idea of winning approval for it from both the Pope and the Order of Malta, to enable it to acquire a truly global reach. His arrival in Rome was therefore the next logical step in his work. But there was a more tangible and irresistible reason than his wife's preferences or his plans for Freemasonry which propelled Cagliostro towards the Vatican: an inner voice was summoning him there. When he entered the gates of Rome he had reached the last of his Stations of the Cross. He was heading for martyrdom.

Rome

In May 1789 Cagliostro and his wife moved into La Scalinata, a small hotel on the Piazza di Spagna in Rome [70]. He arrived with new letters of introduction in a country that he already knew and where many of his old companions from 1773 were still living. He found there, in particular, *Bailli* Le Tonnelier de Breteuil, the Order of Malta's Ambassador in Rome. Very soon he was feeling very much at home and was much sought after by those who were intrigued by his reputation and powers. Soon he had to change his initial residence for a beautiful apartment in the Piazza Farnese [71].

In his memoirs, Abbé Luca Antonio Benedetti, a lawyer of the Papal Curia, in an account of a magical session that Cagliostro organised in Rome and which was attended by many leading French and Italian aristocrats, names several of the people who entertained Cagliostro and formed bonds with him. Here is the relevant text. We shall discuss it later in this chapter.

Since I was unable to resist the entreaties of the Marquise M. P., who insisted that I accompany her as her 'gallant', I was obliged to attend a meeting presided over by Cagliostro at the Villa Malta [72]. We arrived at approximately 2.00 a.m. [sic]. A splendidly liveried lackey, after taking our cards, led us into a magnificently illuminated room, the walls of which were covered with drawings and emblems, including the triangle, the plumb rule, the level, and other symbols. There were also statues of Assyrian, Egyptian and Chinese deities. On the back-wall in large characters was written:

Sum quidquid fuit, est et erit,
Nemoque mortalium mihi adhuc
Velum detraxit [73T].

(That is to say, 'I am all that hath been, and is, and shall be; and my veil no mortal has hitherto raised').

The room was filled with all sorts of distinguished people, including some of very high rank. Imagine my amazement when I recognised, in the middle of the whole gathering, His Excellency François-Joachim de Pierre de Bernis, the French Ambassador in Rome, with, at his side, Princess Santa Croce. A little further along were seated Prince Federico Cesi, Abbé Quirino Visconti, the Ambassador of the Order of Malta Baron de Breteuil, and a host of other important characters and great ladies, in particular Princess Rezzonico della Torre with her cousin Countess Soderini, the Marquis Vivaldi with his secretary Father Tanganelli (notorious for all kinds of deceit and treachery), the Bailiff of Malta Antinori, Marquis Massini, and a French Capuchin.

At the very end of the room, on an altar, you could see arranged lines of skulls and crossbones, stuffed monkeys, live snakes sealed in glass cylinders, owls rolling their phosphorescent eyes [74], *parchments, crucibles, bell-jars, amulets, packets of mysterious powders and other devilries* [75].

Chapter IX

Cagliostro, having sat down on a tripod, began a long discourse: he spoke about himself, his knowledge [76] *and his mysteries, proclaiming himself to be immortal, 'antediluvian' and all-powerful. To demonstrate his abilities he led onto the platform a little girl whom he ordered to gaze into a crystal carafe filled with water. The 'dove', leaning forward, said that she could see, on a road leading from a big city to a neighbouring one, a huge crowd of men and, more particularly, women who were shouting as they walked, 'Down with the king!' Cagliostro asked the little girl what country they were in, and she answered that could hear the people shouting 'To Versailles!', and then she saw, at their head, a great lord.*

'My dove speaks the truth', exclaimed Cagliostro. 'Not much time shall elapse before Louis XVI is attacked by the people in his Palace of Versailles… A duke will lead the crowd… The monarchy will be overthrown… The Bastille will be razed to the ground… And freedom shall succeed tyranny!!!' [77].

'Oh!' exclaimed De Bernis, 'what a sad prediction about my king!'

'It saddens me to say this', answered Cagliostro in a serious tone, 'but it <u>will</u> happen'.

'I don't know… We shall see…', His Excellency muttered nervously as he sat down again'.

But according to the Abbé that was not all. Cagliostro performed even more miracles, proving the truth during the course of this one evening of everything that people had said about him in various places: he changed pure water into Orvieto wine, enlarged a diamond in front of the spectators, instantaneously rejuvenated elderly men by getting them to drink some drops of his Elixir of Life, and so on [78]. Enthused by these impressive deeds, two of the guests rose and asked to be initiated into the Egyptian Rite. The Abbé tells us that they were the French Capuchin San Maurizio and Marquis Vivaldi. After a brief Masonic interrogation Cagliostro accepted them on the spot, publicly, as Egyptian Freemasons [79].

Whatever the moral standing of the Abbé who penned this account [80] we cannot accept uncritically all the details of this interesting narration. To go with the personal reminiscences he has obviously spiced up his story with existing stories and various whimsical descriptions which, in our view, prove that he wrote this account at a later date, after Cagliostro's trial. How otherwise can we explain that he picked out of this huge and gaudy assembly an obscure French Capuchin alongside Cardinal de Bernis? As for Cagliostro sitting on a tripod like the Sibyls, the stuffed monkeys, the Egyptian and Assyrian deities, the mysterious flasks and bottles, the crucibles, the snakes decorating the room – all this is taken from the notorious *Vie de Joseph Balsamo* [81]. The rejuvenation, the enlargement of diamonds (a long and delicate operation which Cagliostro performed only for the Cardinal de Rohan when he was in Strasbourg), the story of Christ at the wedding in Cana, the motto *Ego sum qui sum* – all these are anecdotes taken from elsewhere [82] and joined together to give an overall impression. How also can we explain how, half-way through a posh soirée of his kind, two of the guests – both of whom were later suspected of belonging to Egyptian Freemasonry – and these two only, suddenly stood up to ask for initiation, which was done on the spot and in public? The improbability of all this is striking, especially for anyone who knows anything at all about Masonic customs and, in particular, those of the Egyptian Rite. The ideas and style imputed to Cagliostro in this narrative hardly resemble what we know about him, and the author, out of ignorance, puts in his mouth errors of fact [83] which serve to underline the imaginative and whimsical character of the story. We can therefore only accept points of detail with reserve. There is certainly some truth in the account: the author undoubtedly attended the evening where the famous prophecy of the fall of Louis XVI was made, and the subsequent emotional reaction of Cardinal de Bernis and the anxiety of the guests when they were confronted with this daring utterance are certainly true and original. The remainder of the account however is banal and comes from second-hand sources.

The same author assures us that other meetings 'in accordance with the Egyptian Rite' also took place in the same room. It is probable that Baron de Breteuil welcomed Cagliostro and his friends there several times [84] but – and this is another mistake by Benedetti – these were in no way Masonic gatherings. Cagliostro received and made visits, looked after patients [85], and had friends and disciples. He most certainly tried to get them interested in studying his doctrines and in the Egyptian Rite, but no Egyptian Lodge was ever opened in Rome. To open a lodge, as is well known, one needs *seven* people who are already members of the order. Such people were not however to be found amongst his entourage, and here is the proof: when Cagliostro was arrested only three registered members of the Egyptian Rite could be found, i.e. 1. Cagliostro himself; 2. Countess Cagliostro; and 3. a Capuchin, Father Francesco da San Maurizio, to whom we shall return. Cagliostro had not hidden or destroyed any of his papers (*Vie de Joseph Balsamo*, p. 76), as the letters of Donato and Damiano confirm. His friends Vivaldi and Tanganelli were only *suspected* of belonging to Freemasonry, but their membership could not be proved, nor had Cagliostro ever attended meetings in Rome of other Rites. Cagliostro was ostracised after his dealings with the *Philalèthes* [86], he had been poorly received by Lubel and the other Freemasons in Rome and, as we know, he was extremely hostile towards mainstream Freemasonry in any case.

The situation in the Papal States at this time was not easy for the French, and even less so for those who were suspected of being mixed up with secret societies. The news from Paris was terrifying. The Pope was worried, the police increased their surveillance operations, and denunciations flowed. The edicts against Freemasonry were renewed, the struggle against the Lodges' philosophical spirit increased in energy and Cagliostro, already under suspicion, came under increasing pressure. Traps were set for him, and although he was given fair warning [87] he walked into them with his eyes open. Far from hiding away, he spoke quite openly. Up till then, says the *Vie de Joseph Balsamo* [88], he had behaved with circumspection, but now he openly expressed his love of France and his approval of the movement for freedom that was taking shape there. He even addressed a petition to the French Estates-General, asking that they grant him permission to return to France, given that he had originally been banished only as the result of an arbitrary action by the King [89]. In his conversations he also promoted his Egyptian Freemasonry more emphatically [90].

At that time Cagliostro's circle included a man who professed the greatest respect for him and who considered himself to be his disciple: this was the French Capuchin Francesco de San Maurizio, who was, it is said, his active collaborator and who enjoyed his confidence during the eventful year of 1789. What role did this man play? The fact that the sole result of his zeal was actually to compromise Cagliostro and to trigger the meeting of the Inquisition which led to the issue of a warrant for Cagliostro's arrest; that he was the sole witness for the prosecution, whose confessions made it possible to establish that Cagliostro had initiated a Freemason into his rite in Rome (cf. the 'Letters of Donato'); and that he was shown special leniency, being sentenced to a 'mere' ten years imprisonment in Aracoeli prison, are all very suggestive. The most obvious explanation is that he was a secret agent of the Inquisition and that he did his job very well.

A man as trusting and as daring as Cagliostro was obviously easy meat for the Inquisitorial police. A final report was submitted and, on the morning of Sunday 27th December 1789, the Congregation of the Four Cardinals of the Holy Office [91] met at the apartments of Cardinal Zelada. 'The congregation was composed of the Secretary of State, Zelada (the Cardinal Vicario's vicegerent), and Cardinals Campanella, Antonelli and Fallotta. His Holiness also wanted to take part, something that was unparalleled in recent history' [92]. That same evening Cagliostro was arrested, as were his wife and the Capuchin San Maurizio. His apartment was searched and all his possessions seized [93].

This news terrified all those who knew Cagliostro and had attended his meetings. Vivaldi and Tanganelli fled immediately [94]. Marchesa Vivaldi, who was at Cagliostro's apartment on the evening of his arrest, was able to flee a few days later on the Venice mail-coach disguised as, of all things, an officer in the Hungarian hussars. De Loras, a Freemason and friend of Cagliostro and an important member of the Order of Malta, asked for help, received none, and so returned post-haste to Malta without doing anything for Cagliostro. Lubel, an artist at the Académie de France and a member of a French Masonic lodge [95], who was accused of complicity with Cagliostro because of his relationship with De Loras, did his best to defend himself by alleging that Cagliostro was 'just an adventurer who had never been received into any French lodge'. Cardinal de Bernis didn't intervene at all: on the contrary he didn't hesitate to give official approval for the proceedings against the Freemasons and Cagliostro [96].

But the Vatican was no less afraid. The Pope and Cardinals panicked, thinking themselves surrounded by a network of plots and cabals. They saw conspiracies in every nook and cranny. Everywhere they saw the hand of the Illuminati [97]. 'Even locked in his cell, Cagliostro seemed to the Pope and the Governor of the Castel Sant'Angelo to be an absolutely terrifying figure, and admission to the castle was restricted to those holding a special pass. Many French people hung around the prison and tried to communicate with him through his window in an unknown language' [98]. 'I can assure you', wrote Astorri [99], 'that Rome is currently repressed by the most atrocious inquisitorial machinery. Everyone feels utterly insecure. No one dare trust anybody else'. And the Tuscan Agent, for his part, wrote: 'The arrests continue, and always amidst the greatest secrecy. It's like Fairyland here' [100]. Every day new conspiracies were announced, and panic seized even those who had nothing to fear. The hammer of denunciation could fall at any moment. 'An edict of the government of Rome has banned the illuminations and celebrations which were customary during the last evening of Mardi Gras, measures which were greeted with some very bad language by the populace, who used to really enjoy the pleasures of the Carnival' [101]. The people, aware that all these prohibitions and the general police-terror were down to Cagliostro, joined the police in their persecution of anything remotely French.

This panic was not confined to Rome. The Queen of Naples, when consulted by the Pope, answered him via her Minister, Acton, that she had had Cagliostro put under personal surveillance because of correspondence he had maintained with certain disquieting characters, and that it was necessary to vigorously repress all dangerous political innovators [102]. She herself took rigorous action: 'I understand', wrote the Sardinian Minister, 'that she has had the Duke of San Demetrio locked up in Sant'Elmo because of some secret goings-on between him and Cagliostro. The Margrave of Anspach has left Naples precipitately... They say that the Cagliostro affair is very much an issue there as well' [103]. We can see what excitement the arrest of the Grandmaster of Egyptian Freemasonry had caused, and the great importance that was attached to it.

Initially Cagliostro was kept in strict solitary confinement in the Castel Sant'Angelo [104] in a dreadful cell on the staircase that connected the top of the central balustrade with the Cortile delle Palle, so called because of the cannon-balls that were stored there [105]. He remained there throughout the trial, constantly at the disposal of the Inquisitors. On 21st April 1791, on the orders of Cardinal Francesco Saderio Zelada, he was transferred, between four soldiers and under the watchful eye of Adjutant Grilloni of the Corsican Guard, to the fortress of San Leo [106], where he was locked in a dungeon called *Il Tesoro*.

We shall not describe the details of this captivity, which was under the overall control of the Governor, Sempronio Semproni. We can however say that, in general, Cagliostro suffered terribly in prison. Subjected to the continual surveillance of the warders, who were actually stationed inside his cell for fear that he might escape justice by committing suicide, he was regarded quite differently from all the other prisoners in the fortress. Everything to do with him was a matter for suspicion. Was he acting calmly? Bah, he's just pretending! Was he going all religious? He's putting on an act! Was he living off bread and water and fasting three days a week? That was for hygienic reasons, said the newspapers, because he ate too much on all the other days. If piercing cries and howling fit to cause the fortress to collapse were suddenly heard [107] then there was nothing to worry about – according to the gossips that was just Cagliostro in a drunken rage. Then everyone would rush to his cell but, as Governor Semproni said in a letter of 30th July 1793, even the systematic application of the bastinado wasn't enough to shut him up. Cagliostro's requests were always rejected. One day, when he was contorted in agony with dreadful colics he was even refused an enema which he had asked the doctor to administer [108]. Although this account is necessarily based exclusively upon reports produced by the clergy or the police charged with the surveillance of Cagliostro, and is therefore written from a hostile point of view, it is still full of interest.

From 24th December 1789 to 7th April 1791 the usual procedures of the Inquisition were followed methodically. As soon as he was arrested Cagliostro appeared before his judges. First he was interrogated to obtain compromising statements that would enable a clear-cut charge of heresy to be formulated. The interrogators knew that the most effective way of doing this was to put on a pretence of kindness and to show an apparent respect for his knowledge. They tried to get him talking [109] as much as possible while expressing nothing but curiosity, and avoided reacting to anything that might strike them as strange. Of course, Cagliostro was not unaware that his interrogators were playing games with him, but he pretended not to let it show: they were letting him talk, that was the important thing. It was essential that God's messenger make his voice heard before the highest court of religious orthodoxy, before these four Cardinals, before the immediate representatives of the Sovereign Pontiff, so that Rome would not one day in the future be able to deny ever having heard it.

But as always the subtle calculations of men led unintentionally to a providential outcome [110]. Addressing himself to his judges more gravely and more seriously than he ever had to his disciples, ignoring their smiles because he knew he was speaking directly to their hearts, he explained to them, without fear and without undue secrecy, the principles of his doctrines, and told them about Egyptian masonry and why it was important. 'Ordinary Freemasonry is a dangerous road that leads to atheism. I wanted to save Freemasons from this danger and to bring them back, while there was still time, by means of a new rite, to a belief in God and the immortality of the soul' [111]. Impressed with his eloquence his judges asked him where he acquired his knowledge and powers of persuasion. Cagliostro replied that, by special grace, God had inspired him [112] and given him a power that, by himself, he certainly would not have. He explained to them how he prayed, revitalising his faith before acting [113] and then, using young innocent subjects as intermediaries, received the revelations and directions that he had sought from God in the form of visions or else directly, *in propria persona*, in the form of interior impulses [114].

Chapter IX

I believe that man, created in the likeness of God can, by His special protection [115], *arrive at a knowledge of and control over the spirits. These spirits come from another form of creation, because Jesus, before His death, left us and gave us the beatific vision, as His own words testify: 'et ego claritatem quam dedisti mihi dedi eis'* (John XVII.22, 'And the glory which thou gavest me I have given them'). *But nothing like this can be achieved except by the grace of God* [116], *a grace that He dispenses to whomsoever seems good to Him, and which is something that only men of faith, good will and charity can ever hope to obtain* [117]. *Such are the goals, principles and Rites of Egyptian Freemasonry. Priests and prelates have approved it, and you also will recognise its purity and goodness, and will help me to present it to the Pope. He will listen to me, he will give me back my freedom and he will even offer me his protection for my Order, which is already so widespread* [118]

Thus did he speak frankly and eloquently [119] in front of judges who allowed him to raise all his hopes and who even encouraged him with their murmurs of approval. Then when, throwing caution to the winds, he had finished his account of his social achievements and theurgic works – statements recorded by the court-scribes – and when the Inquisitors felt that he had nothing more to say about himself, the appearance and the language of the actors suddenly changed. There was no more gentleness, there were no more promises, there was no more feigned pretence: the kindly advisers became pitiless inquisitors, and the real interrogation began [118].

An interrogation can always be specially *steered* in a way that suits the judges, and the judges of the Inquisition knew exactly how to go about it [120]. They skilfully intermingled questions so that the answer to one particular point could be transferred to another [121], and they played with words, set him traps, even lied to him outright [122], doing everything they could to defeat him. Sometimes, on the pretext of giving him an opportunity to prove that he was a Christian he would be ordered to recite something from the Catholic ritual [123] or asked to define theological terms in a sort of mini-catechism [124]. Word-games were not at all Cagliostro's thing: he would always answer according to the spirit rather than the letter, and with a philosophical breadth and symbolic richness that far exceeded the scope of the Inquisitors' narrowly-focused questions. But they carefully and pitilessly recorded his 'criminal ignorance of the number of cardinal sins' and 'his heretical opinions on the Ember Days' [125].

The denunciations of Cagliostro, whether purchased [126] or volunteered, also piled up. Those who had been close to Cagliostro, now trembling before the Inquisition, were only too happy to buy some peace of mind by supplying incriminating evidence against him [127]. When the voluntary statements proved insufficient, others were obtained by inducement.

Countess Cagliostro was also questioned: timid by nature, physically weak, broken down by an unusually challenging life, fearful of what was likely to happen to her husband, she was putty in the hands of the cunning priests who surrounded her. The intimidation, the false promises and the threats which had no impact on Cagliostro always had the desired effect on her. Depending on what the Inquisitors wanted they would make it clear to her that she could save her husband by responding along certain lines, and the poor woman – naive and intensely loyal as she was – would give them exactly the answers they wanted. Sometimes she would vouch for her husband's astonishing theurgic powers [128], and at other times admit that there were perfectly simple and logical explanations for his apparent ability to foretell the future [129]. Sometimes she would speak of his powers in terms of trickery and ignorance, and yet at other times praise his miraculous powers – all in accordance with whatever the Inquisitors required to build their case [130]. When Cagliostro called his wife to appear for the defence he had the dreadful experience of learning that her testimony flatly contradicted his own statements.

Almost always the Inquisition was able, through these procedures, to obtain the evidential detail it required to compile its case. Sometimes however, despite everything, Cagliostro did not want to provide them with the information they wanted, refused to admit to a crime of which he was innocent, or would not sign documents containing blasphemous or fictitious statements that he was alleged to have made [131]: in such circumstances there was a last resort - torture. And it was certainly used in this case [132].

Physical strength has its limitations: at a certain point, when courage and tenacity are confronted with the impossible they become mere irrational revolts and exhausting illusions. Cagliostro saw the uselessness of his efforts and the falseness and immutable prejudice of his judges. Tired of being alternately toyed with and tortured he eventually surrendered to the Inquisitors' demands, certain of the outcome and therefore seeking only to avoid the worst possible result for both himself and his torturers. The Inquisitors, masters of the situation, holding all the weapons necessary to crush Cagliostro and convinced of his heresy, now passed to the second act of their destructive task.

For the Inquisitors it was not enough for Cagliostro to simply disappear: he had to be discredited in the eyes of his disciples and turned into an object of ridicule for all mankind. To undermine his work, annihilate his sect, and shake Freemasonry to its foundations, the world had to be shown a humiliated and remorseful Cagliostro, someone who had returned to the bosom of the Catholic Church, disavowed his work and abjured his past errors. By the same procedures – deprivation, suffering, violence – Cagliostro was forced to accept confessor after confessor, Capuchin after Jesuit. These spiritual advisers entered his cell under guard and would only leave it when they had wrested out of him yet another retraction, another general confession, another humble petition [133]. It was, in any case, an easy task: Cagliostro, exhausted and now free of illusions, was showing less and less resistance [134]. Some books were sent to him, some monks visited him, all with the aim of encouraging him to ask for more – that was exactly what they wanted. We are then told with what confusion and baseness he acknowledged his heresy, with what a contrite heart he asked for forgiveness from the Church, for the Holy Father, had, for this pious work, *'deigned to dispense with the law of inviolable secrecy which always accompanies, with as much justice as caution, the procedures of the Holy Inquisition'* [135]. His resigned attitude was depicted as cowardice, his submission to the cruel requirements of Rome as nothing more than a contemptible hypocrisy [136]. To these allegations were added all the calumnies to be found in the denunciations and all the lies told by interested parties about his life and morals. Published in the press, disseminated by lampoons and pasquinades, spread yet further by conversation and correspondence, this news quickly reached the ears of his friends and disciples and wounded them deeply [137].

To obtain an official abjuration he was sent, in the guise of an adviser, not one religious advocate [138], which alone would have been contrary to the customs of the Inquisition [139], but two, namely Count Gaëtano Bernardini and a *pro bono* lawyer called Monsignor Charles-Louis Constantini. They used all their eloquence to convince him that the matter was clear-cut and that burning at the stake awaited him, if not something even worse [140], and that there was just one way that he could avoid this terrible death: he must sign a solemn abjuration, the text of which was written for him. That would spare him new torments, 'the guarantee of such mercy being sure and formal' ⁽¹⁴¹⁾. They obtained it and, at that moment, the legal proceedings were concluded.

On 7th April 1791 Cagliostro appeared before the Congregation in the presence of the Pope ⁽¹⁴²⁾ to hear, on his knees and with his head covered in a black veil, the reading of the following sentence:

Joseph Balsamo, arraigned and convicted of several offences, has incurred the censures and penalties pronounced against formal heretics, dogmatists, heresiarchs and both the masters and disciples of superstitious magic, and the censures and penalties laid down both by the apostolic laws of Clement XII and Benedict XIV ⁽¹⁴³⁾ *against those who, in whatever manner, support and form societies and conventicles of Freemasons, and by the Edict of the Council of State against those guilty of this crime in Rome or in any other place within the Pontiff's jurisdiction. However, by special clemency, the penalty relaxing the offender to the secular arm* [i.e. 'exemplary death'] *is hereby commuted to imprisonment for life in a fortress, where he shall be kept under close guard, without hope of amnesty, and, after he has made abjuration as a formal heretic within the current place of his detention he shall be exonerated from all censures and shall have salutary penitences prescribed to him to which he must submit* ⁽¹⁴⁴⁾.

This sentence, 'as absurd as it was cruel' said the *Feuille villageoise* ⁽¹⁴⁵⁾ aroused the indignation of all reasonable Europeans. The French translator of the *Vie de Joseph Balsamo*, although himself extremely hostile to Cagliostro, was unable to resist joining in with the chorus of disapproval protesting against the actions of the Inquisition ⁽¹⁴⁶⁾.

Thirteen days later, on 20th June, came the odious ceremony of public abjuration and the auto-da-fé of Cagliostro's writings. 'The Inquisition wanted to make an exhibition of the 'miracle-worker' in front of the rabble to show to them this heretical Freemason in all the abjection of repentance. Cagliostro, dressed as a penitent, barefoot, candle in hand, was made to walk between two files of monks from Castel Sant'Angelo to the Church of Santa Maria. There, kneeling before the altar, he asked for the pardon of God and the Holy Church and abjured his errors. Thus was the comedy played out' ⁽¹⁴⁷⁾. What depths of imagination one would need to comprehend the sorrows of Cagliostro at that moment! While all this was going on, in the neighbouring square the public executioner was solemnly burning all Cagliostro's papers, books, manuscripts and rituals, together with the ornaments of Egyptian Freemasonry, just as the sentence had ordered ⁽¹⁴⁸⁾.

'On the following day, while it was still dark, the prisoner was shaken awake and led under substantial escort to San Leo. While he was asleep his usual clothes had been replaced by new ones which he was told to put on. All these precautions had been ordered by the Cardinal Secretary of State, who perhaps hoped to find in them traces of a correspondence between Cagliostro and the outside world. Whatever the case, after Cagliostro had left, Cardinal Zelada immediately enjoined the Governor of Castel Sant'Angelo to lend all possible assistance to the two ministers of the Inquisition charged with the task of implementing the orders of the Sovereign Pontiff, namely a meticulous search both in the dungeon where Joseph Balsamo had been kept and amongst such of his clothes, rags and books as remained there' ⁽¹⁴⁹⁾.

In his dark dungeon in San Leo, which was even pokier than the one in Sant'Angelo, the torments began all over again. The letters of Semproni, some passages from which we quoted above are only too explicit on this subject: the object of his captivity was martyrdom, and even after he'd been sentenced the Inquisition continued to subject him to useless torments.

On 11th September, after Cardinal Doria had received an anonymous letter informing him of an alleged French conspiracy to attempt a daring aerial rescue of Cagliostro using 'these new-fangled flying-machines called balloons', Cagliostro was transferred from his dungeon to another called *Il Pozzetto* (the Italian word for a shaft that leads down to a sewer), no doubt to muffle his cries of agony. It was there that his sufferings found their final resolution.

The remarks by the Marchese San Picenardi on Cagliostro's detention in San Leo contain many details about these long and horrible months of anguish. This Italian author tries in vain to depict these in an attenuated, bureaucratic sort of way, and is similarly unconvincing in his attempts to use the prison's budgetary figures to explain why it should have had a relatively soft regime [150]. At the beginning he tries and fails to explain everything in terms of Cagliostro's deceit and determination to act out a part, and at the end in terms of his insanity caused by the indulgence in alcohol (!) of a naturally violent and crazy man. The general impression it gives of Cagliostro is atrocious. And if we bear in mind that it was just 100 years before this present book was written (1912) that this man who, whatever opinions he might have held, was in no way a criminal, was persecuted only for his ideas and not for his deeds [151] then one wonders if it would be too far-fetched to believe that, in the near future, we might not see similar horrors, and whether the bonfires have really been finally extinguished?

When the French troops made inroads into Italian territory and looked as if they were going to invade Rome the Inquisitors became extremely anxious, and the order was given to finally get rid of Cagliostro. It was then announced that he had died of apoplexy, and his death-certificate was drawn up on this basis [152]. But the Papal Secretary confessed to the antiquarian Hirt that Cagliostro was indeed murdered in his cell after, the Secretary claimed, he had gone for the throat of a priest who had come to see him' [153]. According to his death-certificate Cagliostro died in San Leo on 26th August 1795 at 3 a.m. [154]. He was buried in some waste-ground within the fortress, as a religious burial had been refused to him [155].

The arch-priest of San Leo, when drawing up the death-certificate, acknowledged that Cagliostro must have possessed extraordinary 'stubbornness' to withstand the torments of his prison-cell for more than four years [156]. Signor Picenardi should perhaps reflect upon the following passage: 'You didn't live more than ten years in an Inquisition dungeon: Death, who was more lenient than the Pope, would come to deliver you', says Gagnière in his extremely conscientious study of the Inquisition in Rome at the end of the 18th century [157]. He also points out that the last days of Cagliostro, a man usually so brimful of energy, must have been simply atrocious [158].

The French battalions arrived at the gates of Rome on 19th February 1797. Officers made immediate enquiries about Cagliostro but were told that he had died. General D☐browski seized San Leo and freed from its dungeons all the Inquisition prisoners to be found there. 'My friends', said the General in his official announcement to the prisoners, 'now you are free. The Cisalpine Republic, by destroying one of the Bastilles of Pontifical government, has restored all your rights to you'. Then he ordered the Fortress of San Leo to be blown up [159].

Countess Cagliostro had also disappeared. Initially locked up in the convent of Santa Apollonia in Trastevere [160] she was no longer to be found there in 1799. Had she been transferred secretly elsewhere? Had she died of sorrow a few months after her husband, as the nuns told her friends who went looking for her [161], or had she died of ill-treatment? We do not know. All we do know is that salvation came too late for her as it did for her husband.

Cagliostro, faithful to his task, showing nothing but contempt for suffering and for the

Chapter IX

danger of losing his life, had brought a torch of enlightenment to the foot of the Vatican, which had rejected it and then extinguished it in the apostle's blood. There too the cup of iniquity was full. These were the very last acts and the very last days of the Inquisition [162] and, for Rome, it was the start of its decline. San Leo was blown up in 1797 and in that same year [163] Napoleon dealt the fatal blow to Papal authority. Over the succeeding century the idol with feet of clay, which for fifteen centuries had kept people in ignorance and terror, fell with alarming speed.

NOTES
(1) German authoress, died 1807, author of the *Histoire sentimentale de Mademoiselle de Sternheim*, and editor-in-chief of *Pomona für Teutschlands Töchter*.
(2) S. Laroche, *Tagebuch einer Reise*..., Offenbach, 1788, p. 297.
(3) Schmidt, *Reise Journal, Biogr. Blätter*, vol. I., p. 217. Cf. also *Ma Correspondance*, no. 55, for 30th June 1786. Before Cagliostro's departure for London Sarrasin gave an order to an English banker to place at his disposal all the sums that he might require.
(4) 'Countess Cagliostro also never tired of questioning me, speaking affectionately about her friends in Basel', S. Laroche, op. cit., p. 296.
(5) A. Langmesser, *Jacob Sarrasin, der Freund Lavaters*, Zurich, 1899, p. 53.
(6) *Journal de Sarrasin, Archives Sarrasin*, Basel, for 21st July 1784.
(7) Langmesser, op. cit., p. 53.
(8) 'Banneret', not to be confused with the English 'baronet', was an old aristocratic title which had disappeared in France but which still existed in Switzerland.
(9) Goethe's brother-in-law. Undertook the defence of Cagliostro in 1787.
(10) Biel was administered from Bern.
(11) Actually 'Rocaille', which the Swiss turned into 'Rockhall' or 'Rockhalt'. It is located at the start of the Promenade du Pasquart at the gates of Bienne, cf. Langmesser, op. cit., p. 54. This house was still standing when this book was written (1912). See engraving in this book which is based on a photograph taken in 1911.
(12) Madame Sarrasin accompanied them. Cf. Langmesser, op. cit., p. 54.
(13) A patient he had cured in Strasbourg.
(14) Cf. H. Funk, *Die Wanderjahre der Frau von Branconi*, in Westermann's *Deutsche Monatsschrift*, 1896, pp. 172 et seq. and *Letter from Bürkli*, in Funk, op. cit., p. 20.
(15) This pavilion, built in Riehen 6 kilometres from Basel at Glögglihof on the estate of Sarrasin-Bischoff, was still in existence when this book was written (1912). At that time it was the property of Fritz Lindemeier. In this book we reproduce a ground-plan and a photograph of it. It was still called 'Cagliostro', and the legend is well established that it contains Cagliostro's funeral monument.
(16) Lavater was finally persuaded by this change and became his active collaborator. The *Mercure de France* (1787) tells us of Cagliostro and Lavater meeting and 'working together in Basel and with the Lodge of *Amis réunis* in Strasbourg, Mannheim and Bremen on the creation of the celestial Jerusalem'. Borowski, who reported this event, says that the local intellectuals found this joint enterprise, steeped as it was in Catholic mysticism and what they saw as superstition, very disorienting, Borowski, *Cagliostro einer der merkwürdigsten...* p. 130.
(17) 'During his interrogation he said he had conceived many doubts about Freemasonry since his stay in London and did not want to hear any more about it', *Vie de Joseph Balsamo*, p. 188. It was this comment that enabled the author of that book to claim, by juggling words, that Cagliostro had repudiated his own Egyptian Rite.
(18) Langmesser, op. cit., p. 55.
(19) The bust by Houdon, two photographs of which will be found in this book. At the time of writing (1912) it was in the Museum in Aix-en-Provence.
(20) *Life of Joseph Balsamo*, pp. 151-152.

(21) Christian Gottlieb Schmidt, author of *Reise Journal eines sächsischer Geistlichen*.
(22) An account similar to those that we already know. Like Beugnot, Cagliostro's dining-companion was surprised by the eccentricity of his manners and by the contrast between his total silence at some times and his exuberance of expression at others. 'His gaze dominates you, destroys you, and yet eludes you', the pastor wrote. 'Physiognomically he is the ideal type of the Magus. The shape of his cranium alone is enough to tell you that he's an extraordinary man… but he fools around and jokes too much. He lacks gravity', cf. Langmesser, op. cit., p. 55.
(23) Langmesser, op. cit., p. 55; and *Frankfürter Zeitung, Staats-Ristretto*, 1783. The extract will be found in the *Archives Sarrasin*, vol. XXXIII, shelf-mark 12. 'During his stay in Basel he dictated to Madame Sarrasin and her mother a large number of formulas for all the patients who came to see him, because he never writes his own prescriptions'.
(24) German writer, a friend of Goethe, born in Nuremberg.
(25) Madame de Branconi, born De Elsner, was widowed at fifteen following the death of her husband Francesco Pessina di Branconi, and became the mistress of Crown Prince Charles-Guillaume-Ferdinand von Brunswick, by whom she had a son, the Count of Fürstenberg, in 1767. She was ennobled by Emperor Joseph II in 1774. She was a woman of exceptional beauty and intelligence. After her breach with the Crown Prince in 1776 she travelled widely and ensnared all the eminent men she encountered: Lessing and Goethe were her admirers, and her intimate relations with Lavater are well known, cf. Zenker, *La marquise de Branconi*, in *Allgemeine Zeitung*, no. 199, of 20th July 1889, and Heinrich Funk, *Die Wanderjahre der Frau von Branconi* in Westermann's *Illustrierte Deutsche Monatsschrift*, vol. LXXIX, Oct. 1895, p. 172 et seq.
(26) Madame de Branconi lived at Chanet near Neuchâtel.
(27) *Archives Sarrasin*, Basel, a letter written in French.
(28) Funk, *Die Wanderjahre*, pp. 5 & 7. Countess von der Recke had already written to Lavater about Cagliostro in 1779, cf. Von der Recke, *Nachricht von des berüchtigten...* p. 115.
(29) From Strasbourg, in 1780.
(30) 'She was kind enough to inform me that I interested her and that my person was pleasing to her, which is easy to believe with Sirens like her. I'm glad I'm not in Matthaei's shoes, because it must be devilishly difficult to be like a pat of butter in the sun, all the year round and out of a sense of duty', Letter from Goethe to Lavater, in Funk, *Die Wanderjahre*, p. 174. Cf. also Langmesser, op. cit., p. 38.
(31) Langmesser, op. cit., p. 40.
(32) H. Funk, *Die Wanderjahre*, p. 7.
(33) Langmesser, loc. cit., p. 80.
(34) Langmesser, loc. cit., Letter of 17th August 1781, p. 38. Not long afterwards, when he was his old self again and had managed to disentangle himself from the charms of the sorceress La Branconi, he resumed his friendship with Cagliostro, and his letters to Sarrasin in July and October 1782 and later testify to his affectionate regard for the man. In 1793, after the trial of Cagliostro, he gave no credence to the rumours that were circulating. Living with the memory of a man he had held in high regard he declared that all the infamies that had been attributed to Cagliostro (or Joseph Balsamo) in Rome could not possibly be true of the great man he had known and loved. 'The Cagliostro who performed miracles, the Cagliostro that I knew, was a saintly character', he wrote to Goethe, cf. Heinrich Duntzer, *Neue Goethestudien*, Nuremberg, Bauer & Raspe, 1867, p. 143.
(35) Cagliostro had sent a German gentleman to London to find his wife and bring her back along with the Loutherbourgs. This gentleman 'had travelled in the Indies where, it seems, he had found buried treasure'. He arrived in Basel with Cagliostro, who had brought him with him, cf. Borowski, *Cagliostro, einer der merkwürdigsten...* p. 129.
(36) As well as Madame von der Lippe, in the presence of whom Cagliostro received the Marquise de Branconi, cf. H. Funk, *Die Wanderjahre...* p. 11.
(37) Langmesser, op. cit., p. 55.
(38) This new affair, the last of his life, ended in 1789. Madame de Branconi disappeared, travelled,

and returned shortly afterwards with a young child whom she had, so she said, adopted and whom she brought up. Falling ill, she went to Albano to recuperate but died there on 7th July 1793. Matthaei, still faithful to her after her death, wrote to Lavater: 'Everything is emptiness for me now', cf. H. Funk, *Die Wanderjahre*, p. 184.

(39) 'At the moment', Sarrasin wrote, 'I'm here to accompany Count and Countess Cagliostro to their new residence, which they seem very happy with and where they are being fêted as they deserve. Doing good in his own quiet way and taking his revenge on the envious by leaving them only good causes to make a mockery of, Cagliostro hopes to ultimately find here the peace for which he has been searching fruitlessly elsewhere', Letter from Sarrasin to Monsieur d'Éprémesnil written from Bienne, 5th July 1787, *Archives Sarrasin*, Basel, vol. XXXIII, shelf-mark 18, folio I, v°.

(40) 'Loutherbourg's honest physiognomy deceived us all. I thought he was a pleasant and gallant gentleman, but his actions towards Cagliostro prove the opposite. The only thing he desires is his ruin but he could well find his own ruin there', Letter from De Gingin to his brother-in-law Sarrasin, written from Bienne, January 1788, *Archives Sarrasin*, Basel, vol. III (1788), shelf-mark 20, folio 3.

(41) Cf. Raths-Kartabel, 1787.

(42) This finds an echo in the disappearance from the Vatican Archives of *all* the documents relating to the Cagliostro trial in Rome (see later in this chapter).

(43) 'This infamous business, at least as far as the laws are concerned', vol. III, shelf-mark 20, folio I. 'This accursed story', vol. III, shelf-mark 20, folio 3. Dr. Türler (*Neues Berner Taschenbuch*, 1901, Bern, Wys, 1900, pp. 110-118) has published, from the archives of the Heilmann family of Bienne, a humorous account of this quarrel. In this undated and extremely-badly written narrative the author, Niklaus Heilmann, has Cagliostro speaking in a half-Negro half-German patois, which was certainly not the way Cagliostro actually spoke! He also has the banneret Wildermett addressing Cagliostro as 'Signor Joseph Balsamo...', which nobody would have thought of doing in 1788, when he was still known to everyone (and especially to the banneret, who was his friend and protector) as Count Cagliostro. This text, although old (circa 1790 perhaps?) cannot therefore be considered a historical document: it is a work of pure imagination and Dr. Türler does not pretend otherwise (cf. ibid., p. 110).

(44) Countess Cagliostro did indeed make a statement before the magistrates in Bienne which was wholly in favour of her husband and which rebutted Loutherbourg's abusive allegations. It is this voluntary deposition to which the *Vie de Joseph Balsamo* refers, with the usual deceit, in the following terms: 'Cagliostro forced his wife to make a statement in his favour in which she retracted certain confidences which she had made in London in his absence… stating in particular that, in contrast to what she had previously deposed, Cagliostro had always been an honest man and a good Catholic', *Vie de Joseph Balsamo*, p. 70. This passage once again enables us to assess the concern for historical truth exhibited by Father Marcello.

(45) Archives Sarrasin, Basel, vol. XXXIII, shelf-mark 18, folio 3 v°.

(46) The strikingly beautiful Madame Loutherbourg had entirely ensnared the Mayor who, according to Sarrasin, was very much a womaniser (Letter of 12th January 1788, *Archives Sarrasin*, vol. XXXIII, shelf-mark 20). She had also enthused De Gingin who described her as 'the most beautiful of women'. During the discussions which took place to settle the matter, Madame Loutherbourg protested in front of the unofficial investigators, who were meeting at the banneret's house, that 'the rumours that were circulating were entirely without foundation, and that her relationship with the Mayor had never been anything other than one of very reserved friendship' (!). This singular protest, reported by Sarrasin (see *Archives Sarrasin*) in franker terms, remains one of the enigmas of the case: what did the private conduct of Madame Loutherbourg have to do with Cagliostro's lawsuit?

(47) *Archives Sarrasin*, Basel, vol. XXXIII, shelf-mark 20, folio 1 v°, and folio 4.

(48) There were other influences at work which further poisoned the atmosphere: echoes of Morande's press campaign in Europe resounded in Basel and Bienne. Loutherbourg, who was an alchemist, may have found that Cagliostro's experiments were slow to produce the promised results, cf. *Deutsches Museum*, 1787, vol. 1, p. 388, *Berliner Monatsschrift*, November 1787, pp. 449 et seq., Langmesser, op. cit., p. 57.

(49) *Registre des procès-verbaux du Tribunal de Bienne*, volume running 1782 to 1796, pp. 104 and 105.
(50) 'They have seized Cagliostro's possessions and he has to reclaim them... that is going to give rise to a lawsuit in all its forms... you can imagine how upsetting all these procedures are for Cagliostro who is proud and quick-tempered by nature and doesn't brook contradiction... It is filling up almost all his diary, which means that he doesn't have the time or leisure to deal with his patients', Letter from De Gingin to Sarrasin, January 1788, *Archives Sarrasin*, vol. III, shelf-mark 20, folio 2.
(51) An article about these scandals which appeared in the *Schaffhauser Zeitung* in March 1788 greatly displeased the magistrates of Bienne, *Registre des procès-verbaux du Tribunal de Bienne*, vol. cit., p. 139.
(52) Langmesser, op. cit., p. 57, according to a letter from Sarrasin to Lavater of 19th January 1783. However necessary this new intervention might have been it certainly cost him dearly: after so much effort to get Cagliostro some peace and so many attempts to get the intelligentsia on his side this new scandal must have affected him greatly.
(53) 12th January 1788.
(54) Sarrasin tells us that the Mayor, although he had links with Loutherbourg, started to become tired of the whole business. That was good news for Cagliostro, but the Mayor was also frightened of alienating Madame Loutherbourg. He also had the great misfortune to be stupid, which caused the matter to drag on longer than it should have done. Loutherbourg, who was more business-like, was ready to conclude an arrangement.
(55) Sarrasin tells his correspondent that he cannot put this irresistible oratory into writing but he agrees to tell them to him orally when they meet: 'Cagliostro had come out of all this with his honour intact, but he's lost a bit on the costs and expenses side', said the saintly Sarrasin, who certainly paid the difference out of his own pocket. 'I believe', he continued, 'that one was well worth the other', *Archives Sarrasin*, Basel, *Rapport de Sarrasin sur ses négociants à Bienne*, vol. XXXIII, shelf-mark 20, folios 3 & 4.
(56) Even if Cagliostro did show some dissatisfaction, the difficulties of the previous few days had not in any way harmed the affectionate regard that Sarrasin and his friends felt for their Master. In 1790, while the Inquisition was acting ruthlessly against Cagliostro, Sarrasin wrote to Lavater: 'Cagliostro's sufferings cause me pain, but I feel that if things are the way they are then that's because he wants them to be like that. The world understands nothing of such things, but I myself know, from experience, what his inner worth really is', Langmesser, op. cit., p. 57. De Gingin writes in the same spirit: 'I hope that Cagliostro will not be held in custody very long and that he will manage to get out of the Bastille as well' (cf. *Archives Sarrasin*, vol. III, shelf-mark 38 folio 3). In 1793 also, with everything pointing to Cagliostro being in the wrong and his reputation itself defamed, Sarrasin could still write to Lavater: 'We forge an ideal for ourselves, then get upset if the beautiful and the good turns out to be other than what we thought it was. Marist [sic] the physiognomist would not recognise Christ if he went for a walk with him!', cf. Langmesser, loc. cit., p. 68. These words are eloquent of the struggle that Sarrasin must have had to explain to himself Cagliostro's end and the circumstances surrounding it. But his faith in Cagliostro never failed, and neither did that of Lavater, cf. Chapter VII of this book, Cagliostro in Paris.
(57) These detailed extracts from Sarrasin's diary lead us to reject as inaccurate the account of a visit by Cagliostro to Vienna which, according to Borowski, would have taken place in June 1788. Borowski quotes as reference the *Archiv für der Schwärmerey*, folio II, part II, p. 79. He tells that Cagliostro enjoyed great success there, which included bringing someone back from the dead, before fleeing the city because Emperor Marie Theresa was trying to force him to sell her his secret of immortality. The details seem whimsical and the dates are in any case wrong (Maria Theresa died in 1780!) and we can therefore discount it.
(58) Casanova met him there, cf. Casanova, *Mémoires*, vol. VIII, p. 13 et seq.
(59) *Vie de Joseph Balsamo*, p. 153 says that he also stayed in Genoa and Verona but provides no evidence. There is such a short interval between his departure from Aix in early August and his arrival

in Roveredo on 24th September that, even if we omit the stay in Turin, the alleged stops in Genoa and Verona, if they took place at all, could only be coaching-stations *en route*, and are therefore without interest for the history of Cagliostro.

(60) *L'Évangile de Cagliostro*, rediscovered, translated for the first time from Latin and published with an introduction by Dr. Marc Haven, Paris, Libr. Des Sciences hermétiques, 1910, 1 vol., with Cagliostro's portrait and seal. We didn't want to duplicate our efforts by publishing this document as an appendix to the present book, but we urge everyone who is interested in Cagliostro to read this memoir. There they will find a series of 'snap-shots' taken at every hour of his day which provide a better picture of what he was really like than all other similar works about him.

(61) *L'Évangile de Cagliostro*, pp. 28, 36, 47, 51.

(62) 'The voice of the people rose on his behalf and thundered within the assembly', *L'Évangile de Cagliostro*, p. 38. The testimony of this impartial author rebuts completely the calumnies published around this time by an anonymous writer in the *Journal von und für Deutschland*, Dec. 1788, pp. 516-520 about Cagliostro's so-called failure in Roveredo.

(63) *L'Évangile de Cagliostro*, pp. 26, 50.

(64) *L'Évangile de Cagliostro*, pp. 54, 37. Joseph II, yielding to petitions submitted by doctors and other people hostile to Cagliostro, forbade him to practise medicine, *L'Évangile de Cagliostro*, p. 71, and *Vie de Joseph Balsamo*, p. 70.

(65) 'Festus, from whom he had rented the apartment in Roveredo, was originally from Trento and often stayed there. When he fell ill in Trento he sent for Cagliostro, *L'Évangile de Cagliostro*, p. 59.

(66) Borowski, loc. cit., p. 133.

(67) *Ist Cagliostro Chef...*, Gotha, 1790, p. 216. This mutual regard and amiable contact did not stop them from engaging in intense but courteous discussions: Cagliostro often talked about Freemasonry and theology with the Bishop or his entourage, and it is this stay in Trento which gave rise to the following anecdote, which his wife was unwise enough to recount and which was subsequently used against him. One day, after Cagliostro had got back from a face-to-face encounter with a theologian, he said to his wife in the course of the conversation, 'Ah! I really caught that priest in my trap!' (*Vie de Joseph Balsamo*, p. 74). No doubt he said this in Italian, so we don't know for certain what words were used. Is the French translation in the *Vie de Joseph Balsamo*, 'Ah! J'ai bien attrapé ce prêtre', correct? We don't know. This phrase, pejoratively interpreted by the author, would mean, according to him, that Cagliostro, through a pretence of religiosity, acted the fool with the priest and misled him, whereas this same sentence could also mean – and is more likely to mean: 'We discussed various things. He sought to dominate me with his theological arguments but I put him firmly in his place. I beat him at his own game, and he remained firmly caught in my trap'. Even though it's only a point of detail we thought it necessary to rebut this attribution here, as it has been heavily relied upon to illustrate Cagliostro's hypocrisy.

(68) *Vie de Joseph Balsamo*, p. 73.

(69) It's true that in Roveredo (*L'Évangile de Cagliostro*, p. 72), as in Trento later on at the Bishop's Palace, priests thronged around Countess Cagliostro. They had noticed that she was weak and timid and tried to bring her back to the beliefs and, especially, to the practices of the Catholic faith in which she had been raised.

(70) Gagnière, *Cagliostro et les Francs-Maçons*, p. 25. Article in *Nouvelle Revue*, pp. 25-56.

(71) Gagnière, loc. cit., p. 28.

(72) The Villa Malta at the Porta Pinciana was the summer residence of the Ambassadors of the Order of Malta.

(73T) According to Plutarch these words were engraved on the Temple of Minerva (Athena/Isis) in Saïs, cf. Plutarch, *On Isis and Osiris*, I.9.

(74) This is certainly a phenomenon which, in full light, only occurs in Italy!

(75) *Mémoires de Benedetti*, under the entry for 15th September 1789, cf. Gagnière, loc. cit, p. 33.

(76) When one of his guests asked him what this knowledge consisted of he replied, 'The scientist Lavater came expressly from Basel to Paris to ask me that, and I answered him with these exact

words: *in herbis et verbis*' ('in herbs and words'), Gagnière, loc. cit., p. 36.

(77) Something that came to pass on the following 5th October when the people, under the command of the Duc d'Aiguillon, marched on Versailles. The first Liberty festival was celebrated on 15th April 1792, the Bastille having been razed on 21st May 1791.

(78) Id. ibid. in Gagnière, loc. cit., pp. 34-35.

(79) Id. ibid. in Gagnière, loc. cit, p. 36.

(80) Gagnière, loc. cit., p. 32, praises him.

(81) Cf. pp. l5l, 159.

(82) We have already explained their origin.

(83) For example, Lavater knew Cagliostro in Strasbourg and never visited Paris.

(84) Gagnière, loc. cit., p. 32.

(85) 'Without success', says the *Vie de Joseph Balsamo*, p. 75. If that was the case then it was something unique to Rome, a bit like the phosphorescence of an owl's eyes in full light (see Note 74 above).

(86) Gagnière, loc. cit., pp. 27, 32.

(87) On two separate occasions his friends warned him of the dangers he was running. He thanked them but carried on as usual (*Vie de Joseph Balsamo*, p. 77.) 'I'm quite inclined to believe', wrote De Gingin to Sarrasin on learning of Cagliostro's arrest, 'that this is a continuation of French intrigues, given that the Polignacs and their entourage were there', *Archives Sarrasin*, 1790, vol. IV, shelf-mark 38, p 3.

(88) p. 65.

(89) *Vie de Joseph Balsamo*, p. 77.

(90) *Vie de Joseph Balsamo*, p. 155 et seq. The Sardinian Minister to Rome wrote to one of his correspondents on this date: 'These past few days Monsieur Mazin (the secret-agent of Maria Carolina of Austria), who is able, though exactly how I don't know, to intercept the letters arriving from Naples, managed to get his hands on one that a lady had written to Cagliostro. This unknown lady writes to this man in a style of fanatical admiration and blind obedience. She addresses herself to him as she would to her spiritual father, and finishes with these exact words: 'The order has been given... Everything is ready... The elected officials have been tested... They are people who enjoy all my confidence, ready to undertake anything', Gagnière, loc. cit, p. 42.

(91) 'The most important Congregation of all, and the only one that was nominally chaired by the Pope, was the *Sacra Romana e Universale Inquisizione* against the heretics. Even people in the highest ranks of society quaked in their boots at the thought of this congregation, which was composed of just four Cardinals, the Pope intervening only in exceptionally serious cases', Gagnière, loc. cit., p. 39, note.

(92) Letter from Chevalier Damiano de Priocca, Sardinia's Minister to the Court of Rome, Gagnière, loc. cit., p. 38.

(93) In Cagliostro's apartment they found a wide range of expensive clothes, only a small amount of money and some jewellery, cf. Borowski, *Cagliostro einer der merkwürdigsten...*, p. 134.

(94) Gagnière, loc. cit., p. 44.

(95) Chapter IV of the *Vie de Joseph Balsamo* goes on about this at some length in an attempt to confuse it in the reader's mind with the Egyptian Rite.

(96) We should note that the Cardinal's abandoning of Cagliostro (whereas he did intervene on behalf of Lubel) did not bring him much happiness. Just a few months later he lost his entire fortune and his job as well. The Princess, whose loyal and reliable affection should have brought him some comfort, immediately abandoned him. This string of disappointments undermined his health and he died soon afterwards, Gagnière, loc. cit., p 38.

(97) *Das politische Journal*, 1789, vol. I, p. 111. Borowski, op. cit., p. 134.

(98) Borowski, op. cit., p. 134.

(99) Dispatch by Minister Astorri to the Government of Siena.

(100) *Corrispondenze di Diplomatici della Republica e del Regno d'Italia*, quoted in Gagnière, loc. cit., p. 46.

Chapter IX

(101) Gagnière, loc. cit., p. 45.
(102) Gagnière, loc. cit., p. 47.
(103) Gagnière, loc. cit., p. 34. The Margrave d'Anspach was interested in Cagliostro and had both received and visited him in Trento in April 1789, cf. Borowski, op. cit, p. 133, and remained on good terms with him ever since, cf. *Mémoires de la margrave d'Anspach*, Paris, 1816, 2 vols., vol. II, p. 28.
(104) *Vie de Joseph Balsamo*, pp. 103 & 203. This is no doubt what the author means by being in the '*mains douces*', the 'gentle hands', of the ecclesiastical judges. 'The whole business is being carried out in great secrecy... Cagliostro, who has fallen into a state of great melancholy, refused to eat for the first few days. He asked for some heating for his cell, but this was refused to him. On 16th January he was subjected to an interrogation lasting five and a half hours following which, on the 17th, the Pope ordered him to be put into an iron collar and shackles. Cagliostro has prophesied the fall of the Pope and the destruction of the Sant'Angelo fortress. As he correctly predicted the fall of the Bastille, his latest prediction has naturally made a great impression', Borowski, op. cit., p. 155.
(105) E. Rodocanachi, *Le château Saint-Ange*, Paris, Hatchet, 1909, p. 238.
(106) Near Urbino. Rodocanachi says 25th April.
(107) Letter by Semproni dated 23rd October 1792. Whether it was under the blows of the jailers and the interrogations of the Inquisition that these piercing cries were suddenly produced we cannot be sure. Even so, the following passages can really only be explained by such assumptions:
I. 'When he was asked why he was shouting like that he replied that it was in their interests to kill him. The Police Commissary Stefani didn't think it necessary to search for some mysterious meaning in these words and came to the logical conclusion that Cagliostro was mad. He therefore felt obliged to resort to the use of the bastinado', cf. Letters by Semproni dated 4th July and 30th October 1792.
II. 'Cagliostro was locked up with his Confessor, Father Passi, a Dominican, when suddenly they heard Cagliostro crying out and saying, 'Stop, Father, stop! I don't want that! That serves no purpose!... I admit that I am a schismatic!', Letter from Semproni of 1st November 1791.
(109) Cf. *Initiation*, December 1905, *Quelques documents nouveaux sur le comte de Cagliostr*o, by Dr. Marc Haven. These new documents come from a study by the Marchese Sommi Picenardi based on letters by Donato and documents in the State Archives of Pesaro (*Carteggio sulla persona di Giuseppe Balsamo denominato il Conte Cagliostro, relegato nella fortezza di S. Leo per ordine della Santità di Nostro Signore Papa Pio VI*). These documents form two volumes of respectively 137 and 43 pages (nos. 8718-8719). Two other boxes, numbered 8721 and 8720, contain letters from officers, chaplains and various VIPs relating to the administration of the fortress, to Cagliostro himself, and replies to these letters. There are riches to be found there certainly, and it would be an excellent idea if some Italian scholar would publish these files from the Pesaro State Archives in their entirety, and if they could then be translated into other languages.
(108) *Vie de Joseph Balsamo*, p. 203.
(109) 'When the Child of Love came in person to introduce it to us by teaching us the way of eternal life we showed as much understanding of what He had to say as if He had been speaking a foreign language. He spoke *love*, and it was for that very reason that we put Him to death, but by a mystery otherwise unknown to the Ages we have still accomplished His work', *Triomphe de l'Amour*, Paris, 1828. vol. III, p. 118.
(110) *Vie de Joseph Balsamo*, pp. 165 & 167.
(111) *Vie de Joseph Balsamo*, p. 117.
(112) *Vie de Joseph Balsamo*, p. 177.
(113) *Vie de Joseph Balsamo*, pp. 174 & 190.
(114) *Vie de Joseph Balsamo*, p. 177.
(115) Ritual, Ms. Papus, p. 151; and *Vie de Joseph Balsamo*, p. 198.
(116) *Vie de Joseph Balsamo*, p. 192.
(117) *Vie de Joseph Balsamo*, p. 209. Jacques de Molay also believed in the divine wisdom and inspiration of the Pope, and therefore asked to be heard directly by him.
(118) *Vie de Joseph Balsamo*, p. 117.

(119) The documentary evidence available to us to help us follow this interrogation is pretty thin: the original minutes kept by the Clerk of the Court (which, in any case, have disappeared, cf. Gagnière, loc. cit., p. 47) would presumably have been drafted in a distorted manner, and the choice of a clearly hostile author (Father Marcello) for the official report of the trial means that we have only an unreliable account of what Cagliostro actually said to his judges.

(120) The judge used insinuation to try to suggest to Cagliostro how he should respond to questions (*Vie de Joseph Balsamo*, p. 189). 'The judge used hand-gestures to direct him in his testimony in certain ways' (ibid., p. 171). 'You would need a whole volume to set out in detail everything that was done to extract the truth from him' (ibid., p. 190). They cut him off in the middle of sentences or even half way through a word (ibid., pp. 171 & 207), and they disrupted his flow by taking him back over the same material again and again, asking him twenty times about the same point of detail until he compromised himself by saying what they wanted him to say (ibid., 163, 168, 169). The interrogation would stop, and he would be told that it was all over, that his answers were satisfactory and that his worries were at an end, only for them to then go back to some previous question and try to trap him again (ibid, p. 207). Even if we actually had the texts which were so prudently removed from the Vatican Archives therefore we could draw upon them successfully only by ceaselessly reminding ourselves that this was a hearing in front of the Inquisition. The trial of the Templars, to name just one, can be regarded as being very similar to that of Cagliostro, and those who have studied the legal proceedings of that trial will be better prepared to understand certain obscurities in the trial of Cagliostro.

(121) p. 3l5. They tried to get him to issue a blanket acceptance of an anonymous allegation that Cagliostro often spoke against the Christ, the sacraments, or other established verities.

(122) pp. 189-190. One day he acknowledged that he had recently been having doubts about the aims and character of Freemasonry. Some time afterwards it was put to them that he had himself acknowledged and signed a statement to the effect that he knew perfectly well that by propagating Freemasonry he was acting against religion. 'I'm not interested in your silly word-games! Are you telling me that I no longer understand my own words?' was Cagliostro's indignant and irritated response to these tactics.

(123) Acts of faith, hope and charity, cf. *Vie de Joseph Balsamo*, p. 173.

(124) 'Would you believe that when he was questioned on the cardinal virtues he replied that they were the same as the theological virtues; that the sacrament of confirmation was simply the confirmation of baptism; and that he didn't even know how many cardinal sins there were!' the Jesuit father who authored the *Vie de Joseph Balsamo* wrote indignantly. Evidently these shortcomings in Cagliostro's theological knowledge merited torture and 'exemplary death'.

(125) *Vie de Joseph Balsamo*, p. 173. Éliphas Lévi, an imaginative man, who often spoke on behalf of people he was supposed to be quoting, tells the following story on this subject which certainly conveys the right spirit even if it didn't actually happen: 'Some of the judges were irritated with him and asked him brusquely for the names of the seven deadly sins. He named lust, envy, greed, gluttony and sloth. 'You forgot pride and wrath', said one of the judges. 'Pardon me', the defendant replied, 'I didn't actually forget them but I didn't want to name them out of respect and fear of offending you'.'

(126) Cf. *Vie de Joseph Balsamo*, p. 175.

(127) *Vie de Joseph Balsamo*, p. 216. Gagnière, loc. cit., pp. 49-50.

(128) *Vie de Joseph Balsamo*, p. 178.

(129) *Vie de Joseph Balsamo*, p. 176-177.

(130) 'Prove to us that your husband is an uneducated man', one of the judges said to her, 'that he owed his oratorical successes solely to the artificial excitation of alcohol, and the success of his various magical demonstrations solely to conjuring tricks, and you will save him from being condemned for sorcery. We're not interested in pursuing legal proceedings against a charlatan – that's not something that worries us, and it's none of our business'. And on another occasion: 'If we really had some hard evidence of his knowledge, some actual unarguable facts about God's protection of him and his works, if his predictions and his various actions are genuine and miraculous then this

Chapter IX

would certainly be a matter for further enquiry and would have to be approached as a matter of divinely-inspired mysticism and no longer as *goetia*. Your husband would be a saint'. And the poor captive Countess, with no one to help her, interrogated separately, did everything she could to save her husband and to save herself, but everything was arranged so that her answers got both of them into even more trouble.

(131) *Vie de Joseph Balsamo*, p. 214.

(132) It is not the gentle author of the *Vie de Joseph Balsamo* who has revealed this to us, although certain phrases of his book and certain actions by Cagliostro suddenly become easier to understand when one admits the possibility of torture having been used. But the letters of Semproni (see earlier in this chapter) are sufficient to prove it. The procedures of the Inquisition are well known and they did not change: 'The legal procedures of the Inquisition certainly didn't allow for any form of debate: these were not conventional lawsuits where there was a to-and-fro of argument between the plaintiff and the defendant. The proceedings were always held *in camera* and were based on documents that the defendant never saw. No defence counsel was permitted. Denunciations were accepted as sworn witness-statements, and the defendant was not allowed to challenge them. Informers were paid. Finally the defendant had to admit to guilt if he wanted any sort of leniency from the judges. The concept of a 'concluding appearance' in court was also denied to defendants like Cagliostro where there was a possibility of extracting further confessions, with the option of a short visit to the torture-chamber to jog their memories', Gagnière, loc. cit., p. 50.

(133) *Vie de Joseph Balsamo*, pp. 204, 206, 217. Gagnière, loc. cit., pp. 54, 55. Letters of Semproni, see earlier in this chapter.

(134) He still engaged in occasional outbursts which he quickly mastered, but these were increasingly rare, *Vie de Joseph Balsamo*, p. 215.

(135) *Vie de Joseph Balsamo*, foreword, xxiii.

(136) It is sad to see even liberal and enlightened authors such as Gagnière espousing these opinions and not understanding the dramas that must have been present within Cagliostro's heart.

(137) We have seen how affected by these reports Sarrasin and Lavater were. The *Testament de mort*, the *Confessions* and the *Vie de Joseph Balsamo*, all translated into many languages, date from this time.

(138) Note that this was a religious advocate and a *Monsignor* of the Curia, not a conventional lawyer.

(139) No defence counsel was allowed, as we have mentioned above.

(140) Cagliostro, having been formally recognised as a heretic, 'fell within the scope of all the penalties and censures leading to an exemplary death' (phrase taken from the official text of the sentence). The General Decrees (the *Bandi Generali*) distinguished two kinds of death penalty: the *pena della vita*, which involved hanging or decapitation, and the *morte exemplare*, the exemplary death sentence, i.e. burning at the stake, breaking on the wheel, quartering, disembowelment etc. (Gagnière, op. cit., p. 51). 'Heresy', says the *Manuel des Inquisiteurs*, is the greatest of crimes, and death does not expiate it. It must be pursued even as far as the grave. Death is closely interlinked with the acts and thoughts of the living person. If he has already been buried then he must be pulled out of the earth that covers him and dragged wretchedly through the streets, then thrown onto the rubbish-heap to serve as a terrible warning to the people'. The Curia's lawyers were certainly not exaggerating when they described the horrors that awaited Cagliostro.

(141) *Vie de Joseph Balsamo*, p. 216.

(142) 'The presence of Pope Pius VII proves how much political importance he attached to the whole affair. It was unprecedented for the Sovereign Pontiff to deign to witness the appearance in court of a heretic', Gagnière, loc. cit. p. 50.

(143) The Bull *In eminenti* of Clement XII dated 26th April 1738, confirmed by the Edict of 14th January 1739, forbids under penalty of exemplary death any affiliation with Freemasonry and imposes upon everyone an obligation of denunciation. The Bull of Benedict XIV *Providas Romanorum* of 18th May 1751 confirms the previous edicts. As proof of the wisdom of these edicts is cited the fact that 'no one knows for sure whether the Masonic sect is innocent or criminal' (*Vie de Joseph Balsamo*, p. V). As

proof that the edicts were inspired by the Holy Spirit the Jesuit father Marcello, author of the *Vie de Joseph Balsamo*, cites the fact that several princes, including the Ottoman Sultan Mahmut I in 1748, have acted in the same way and proscribed the Freemasons (*Vie de Joseph Balsamo*, p. 88).

(144) *Vie de Joseph Balsamo*, pp. 220-221. Gagnière provides a shorter version of this sentence which he says is *verbatim*, and which is identical as to sense but differs in terminology.

(145) Year 1791, no. 34, p. 129, 'The Roman eagle is armed with the claws of superstition: pity him who falls into its merciless grasp', id., ibid.

(146) *Vie de Joseph Balsamo*, Notice, pp. 5 & 6.

(147) Gagnière, loc. cit., p. 54.

(148) 'This manuscript entitled *La Maçonnerie Égyptienne...* will be burned publicly by the hand of the executioner along with the instruments belonging to this sect', Sentence imposed on Cagliostro, in *Vie de Joseph Balsamo*, p. 221. On 4th May 1791 someone wrote as follows from Rome to Paris: 'Yesterday they posted the sentence ordering that the papers and personal effects of Signor Cagliostro be burnt by the hand of the executioner. This was done this morning on the Piazza della Minerva. It took about forty-five minutes. The people used it as an excuse for a party. Every time something was thrown onto the fire – books, signs, Masonic licences, Masonic cordons or what-not – the crowd clapped and cheered', *Gazette Nationale (Moniteur universel)*, no. 159 of Wednesday 8th June 1791.

(149) Gagnière, loc. cit., p. 54.

(150) Gagnière thinks Cagliostro was well treated! 'They didn't even put him in leg-irons', he says, loc. cit., p. 43. After everything we have said about the procedures of the Inquisition this would not be an adequate argument even if what he says is true – but it isn't, as we know that Cagliostro was shackled in his dungeon, cf. Borowski, op. cit., p. 134.

(151) As we have shown, Cagliostro was arrested for his beliefs and for the role he had played in Europe, not for an illegal act, e.g. founding a Masonic lodge on Roman territory. Even the Inquisition's investigators were forced to admit this. 'The causes of his arrest are questionable', writes a contemporary. 'He was accused of being a bad Catholic, of not going to Mass and of not fasting on Fridays', Borowski, op. cit., p. 134.

(152) See the Appendix to this book. The news was spread by *Kracas*, the Vatican's semi-official newspaper.

(153) Lavater, after being informed of this by Hirt, passed the news on to Sarrasin by a card which will be found in the *Archives Sarrasin*, vol. VII, shelf-mark 39, and then confirmed it to him following a conversation with Hirt after the latter's return from Rome (*Archives Sarrasin*, vol. VII, shelf-mark 40). Hirt repeated that the execution was not in public, but that it definitely happened, that everyone knew about it, and he himself had heard the news from a very reputable source. This has served as a pretext for lovers of the miraculous, who cannot accept that a man like Cagliostro could possibly be mortal, to spin a yarn that he had escaped in his confessor's clothes and that in his cell there had been found just one disfigured corpse (that of the priest) clad in Cagliostro's own clothes. And so we find here and there, depending on the needs of various interested parties, the idea that Cagliostro escaped and became immortal. Éliphas Lévi has foolishly propagated this disrespectful legend.

(154) The only proof we have of the accuracy of this information is the entry in the pontifical registers. The letters of Lavater give a more recent date for Cagliostro's death. In any case, the precise date and time are of secondary importance: what really matters is the admission that Cagliostro was murdered, an event that crowned his martyrdom.

(155) Cf. Appendix.

(156) Cf. Appendix.

(157) p. 52. This is a study from which we have very often quoted.

(158) Gagnière, loc. cit., p. 56.

(159) This historic event, unknown up to now, is confirmed by the Milan Archives and was revealed for the first time by Gagnière, loc. cit., p. 56. It should be compared with the destruction of the Bastille after Cagliostro's arrest.

(160) Rodocanachi, *Le Château Saint-Ange*, Paris, 1909, p. 238.

Chapter IX

(161) Gagnière, loc. cit., p. 52.

(162) Figuier, *Histoire du merveilleux*, Paris, 1861, vol. IV, p. 128.

(163) The Treaty of Boulogne was actually imposed on 23rd June 1796, but when the Pope failed to comply with all his undertakings Napoleon sent his troops to Rome (January 1797). The Treaty of Tolentino was imposed in February 1797: Generals Victor and Duphot stayed in Rome to oversee its implementation. The Pope had Duphot assassinated, and on 10th February 1798 Berthier entered Rome. The Pope was exiled to Siena, then Florence, and then the Dauphiné. He died in Valence.

CHAPTER X

—

SOME OBSERVATIONS UPON THE LIFE AND THE DEATH OF CAGLIOSTRO

THE SPIRIT OF THE SHADOWS

Thus died the divinely-inspired Cagliostro, that Being of Light and Goodness, thrown as prey to the Roman she-wolf which avenged herself upon him for all her terrors and defeats. Delivered up, if not actually betrayed, by those whom he loved the most, abandoned by those upon whom he had heaped the greatest blessings [1], hunted down not for his deeds but for his originality of mind, arrested by an abuse of power, condemned to sufferings out of all proportion to the offences of which he was wrongly accused, tortured without pity, he ended a life of apostleship and selfless charity with a brutal martyrdom.

If he had been guilty in Palermo, Rome, Paris [2], or London, of even the most minor of the offences of which he was accused then he would have found judges and punishments enough, but no criminal court – not a single one, anywhere – found him to be in the wrong [3]. It fell to the so-called representative of his God, to the alleged defenders of the eternal verities that Cagliostro embodied, to kill him in defiance of any semblance of justice.

But what did justice matter to these people? Everything and everybody was the same to the Inquisitors: whatever the actions or beliefs of their victim; whether Cagliostro was a heretic or not; whether he practised white magic or black; whether he was a saint or a non-believer; whether his morals were pure or depraved – the Cardinals couldn't care less. Cagliostro was a threat to the power of Rome, so he had to be removed. From the moment of his arrest his death was a foregone conclusion.

His judges knew perfectly well that he taught the existence of God, the immortality of the soul, respect for the law, even respect for their religion [4]. They knew also that his life had been a model of philanthropy and wisdom, that he restored health to crippled bodies and sight to the spiritually blind. They knew that his disciples, far from being plunged by him into utter darkness, drew from his words and his personal example the most powerful virtues and the most vibrant energies. They knew that only too well, and that was exactly what they were afraid of.

That an extraordinary man who was not a practising Catholic [5], who did not declare himself to be a submissive son of the Roman Church, should propagate a doctrine that was all the more worrying for being closer to true Christianity and all the more threatening because it appealed to everyone without distinction of race, nation or religion [6] – *that* was where the real and terrible danger lay, *that* was their real objection, and *that* was the sole and shameful reason for their hatred and eagerness to destroy him. Rome was fighting a losing battle for retention of its temporal power, its worldly goods, its monopoly. It was Christ himself whom the priests pursued in the person of Cagliostro, and it was the spirit of the true liberator that they sought to eliminate in His true earthly representative.

'Crucify him!' they cried, repeating the ancient formula, 'crucify him! For we have found this man a pestilent fellow, and a mover of sedition amongst all the Jews throughout the world, and a ringleader of the sect of the Nazarenes, who also hath gone about to profane the temple, whom we took, and would have judged according to our law'. [7]

NOTES

(1) The Order of Malta, the Freemasons and his disciples, remained passive spectators of these events or even disowned him, the Russians repudiated him, Strasbourg forgot him, France expelled him, and London delivered him up to Rome.

(2) In Paris, at the time of the Diamond Necklace Affair, a complaint for 'impiety and profanation' was lodged against him (*Gazette de Leyde*, no. XVI of 21st February 1786). He was found not guilty of this, just like all the other things he was accused of doing or being, so Rome couldn't even claim the novelty of having charged him with something he hadn't been charged with before.

(3) 'Did the judges of Rome really have any right to pursue him for crimes committed outside their territory and for which they had no evidence? Yet it was in Rome that he was condemned', *Vie de Joseph Balsamo*, Notice, p. iv. Even the French translator felt obliged to acknowledge this abuse of power.

(4) *Liber memorialis*, French translation, Paris, 1910, p. 45, Abbé Georgel, *Mémoires*, Paris, 1817, vol. II, p. 45, *Mémoire contre le Procureur général*, Paris, 1780, pp. 6 & 75, *Rituel de la Maçonnerie Égyptienne*, Ms. Papus, pp. 5, 84, etc.

(5) Donato, the Sardinian Minister in Rome, reports that Cagliostro was arrested either for being a Freemason 'or for stopping his wife from going to Confession', cf. Borowski, op. cit., p. 134.

(6) *Rituel de la Maçonnerie Égyptienne*, Ms. Papus, p. 83. 'He didn't criticise any religion. Indeed, he even wanted people to respect the dominant religion. Divinity, he said, prefers the pure and simple worship of natural religion, but she does not take offence at what mankind has added to it at various times, in the light of changing circumstances and conditions, in their efforts to worship the Creator and give thanks to Him', Georgel, *Mémoires*, Paris, 1817, vol. II, p. 46.

(7) Acts of the Apostles, XXIV.5-6.

CHAPTER XI

–

WAS CAGLIOSTRO REALLY JOSEPH BALSAMO?

After the Diamond Necklace Affair, Cagliostro's acquittal, and the lawsuits that he brought against Chesnon and De Launay these two characters, finding themselves under threat for a change, defended themselves vigorously. They began by 'buying' Morande and then, in a joint enterprise, set out to show that Cagliostro, though honourably acquitted by the law-courts of Paris, was an impostor. Here's how they conducted their campaign.

In 1786 the Paris Police Commissary Fontaine, one of Chesnon's colleagues, found in his archives a file dating from February 1773. His eye was caught by the words 'Feliciani, wife of Balsamo'. He told Chesnon about it. Morande pounced on it and immediately announced [1] that Cagliostro was actually a 'wretched dauber' called Balsamo, who was already known to the police in both London and Paris. He collected evidence, published article after article [2], got his network of correspondents busy, and spread the news around the Lodges which proceeded to have some fun with it [3].

But the fact – of scant interest to the general public – that Cagliostro was an ordinary mortal, born of Italian parents and not the son of the Sharif of Mecca, the sort of story that would do nothing more than bring a smile to peoples' lips, was not enough. They had to prove that the man they had identified as Balsamo was still a practising criminal. They set to work digging up everything they could about Balsamo, including police reports, letters showing him in the worst possible light, rumours, accusations and tall stories [4]. These piled up all the more readily as there was no Joseph Balsamo present to lodge a protest and, of course, Cagliostro himself had no reason to get involved. He was content to declare, whenever an opportunity presented itself [5], that he was not called Balsamo any more than he was called Thiscio or Baltimore.

In 1787 Goethe intervened in this debate, pretentiously publishing a family-tree of J. Balsamo [6], a genuine character no doubt but someone whose genealogy, however meticulously compiled, proves nothing about Cagliostro. Goethe himself however believed that by doing this he had made a substantial contribution to the enlightenment of humanity. His role was, however, an insignificant one. Goethe had simply been passing through Palermo when someone showed him the Balsamo file and the related family-tree. He went to see the family, giving the mother and her children some false hopes [7], and making a generous donation using someone else's money. That was all he did. He didn't even add any documents to the file that had already been compiled by the lawyer who was chaperoning him, whose name he doesn't even tell us.

On the basis of this evidence and certain investigations in Italy it has been established that someone called Giuseppe Balsamo certainly was born in Palermo on 2nd June 1743, that he left there as a very young man, and that he got married in Rome in 1768 to someone called Lorenza Feliciani, the daughter of a goldsmith. He then disappears from history until 1771 when he turns up in London [8]. We find him again in Paris in 1773, when he had a brush with a rich idler who had made passes at his wife. In fact, he had to take the man to court to stop the would-be seducer and recover his conquest. After that he disappears from history.

Those are the facts that we have about Balsamo, clear and complete, as they appear in the official documents [9]. They seem precise enough, and indisputably establish the existence, genealogy and adventures of someone called Giuseppe (Joseph) Balsamo [10]. But what parallels are there between the life of this character and that of Cagliostro, and what evidence have his enemies relied upon to prove that these two people were one and the same? We shall list these points of similarity below, analysing each of their arguments as we go.

When Morande had announced that Police Commissary Fontaine's Balsamo and Cagliostro were actually one and the same person an anonymous correspondent (whom we now know to be a French subject called Bernard, a calligrapher and teacher of languages) wrote to Fontaine from Palermo [11] stating that a Signor Bracconieri had assured him that Cagliostro was none other than his nephew J. Balsamo:

1. because his nephew, an adventurer whose age corresponded to Cagliostro's, had wandered around Europe, just like the other Balsamo had, under various assumed names [12];
2. because his physical description – 'small, very dark, with a flattened nose and an ugly face' – corresponded to that of Cagliostro [13];
3. because if his wife, who was baptismally Lorenza (just Lorenza?), was now known as Serafina Feliciani it was because she'd borrowed these names from Balsamo's aunt Serafina Bracconieri and her mother-in-law Felicia Balsamo [14], just as he himself had taken his name Cagliostro from that of his godmother [15];
4. because he'd been told in 1784 (if he was not mistaken) that Balsamo had returned to Naples, had been in Morocco, and was calling himself Count Cagliostro;
5. finally, because he'd read in a Florentine newspaper, the *Gazette de Florence* of 31st October 1786, that certain letters of Cagliostro's had borne the signature 'Balsamo'. The newspaper found the case proven: Cagliostro was J. Balsamo [16].

Bernard, the author of the letter, claimed to have been acting as a true patriot who was seeking to defend Frenchmen of good reputation and respectable position against whom Cagliostro had made shameful accusations (i.e. Chesnon and De Launay). He hoped that the evidence he was providing would confirm Fontaine's suspicions regarding the identity of Balsamo and Cagliostro [17]. His explanation of why he was not signing the letter and was sending it regardless shows some naivety: the letter was obviously of considerable interest to De Launay, Chesnon and Fontaine as police-officers and it would have been obvious to them that the sender was a hard-working employee well worthy of promotion.

Bernard summoned Bracconieri before Maître Gugino, Advocate-Fiscal of the Court of Palermo on 9th March 1787 to obtain a notarised statement. Bracconieri repeated the claims, even though they were unsupported by any evidence and rested solely upon vague suppositions about the possible identity of the two men. Bernard refrained from also summoning the *Gazette de Florence*, since in the interim he would have undoubtedly received some explanations about the origins of the newspaper-article, nor did he mention the letters allegedly by Cagliostro and signed 'Balsamo', which he would have been obliged to produce but was obviously unable to [18].

All in all, what came out of all these revelations? Certainly no formal evidence of identity. Let's summarise the various points:

Chapter XI

J. BALSAMO	CAGLIOSTRO
Born in Palermo.	Place of birth unknown. Claims to have been born in Medina.
Born 2nd June 1748 [19].	1749 (according to his own statement).
Married in Rome on 20th April 1768.	Married in Rome in 1770.
Married Donna Lorenza (Feliciani?), illiterate.	Married Serafina Feliciani, illiterate.
Balsamo only spoke Italian.	Cagliostro spoke French, Italian, Portuguese, Latin, etc.
Balsamo was very dark, ugly, with a flattened nose.	Cagliostro was fresh-faced with a fair complexion, very pleasant to look at, good-looking even.
Balsamo's godmother was called Cagliostro.	Cagliostro said that he had chosen the name himself: he didn't know his real name.

Glancing at the above table we can see that any putative identification only rests on an approximation in dates; the resemblance of the surnames of the two women; and the existence of the name Cagliostro in a branch of the Balsamo family. That is not very much: apart from that there are no parallels, just descriptions that do not match, differences in detail, the denials by Cagliostro, the formal assertion by Sachi which contradicts that of Bracconieri, and the absence of any official documents (deeds, letters, witness-statements) that would support the assumption. In the papers of Cagliostro which were twice seized from him without warning, i.e. in Paris in 1784 and in Rome in 1789, we find no trace of anyone called Balsamo [20]. These observations would seem to prevail in number and importance over the preceding objections and suggest that the three points of resemblance mentioned are purely fortuitous.

One way of clearing the matter up once and for all would have been to confront Cagliostro with his so-called uncle and with his alleged mother, who were still living in 1787, and about which so much has been said. If Palermo was too far to travel then he could have been confronted with Duplessis, Buhot [21], and especially with Fontaine, whose job it was to identify people, but neither Fontaine in 1787 nor the Inquisition in 1791 did so. Why not? The answer is obvious: the story was so dubious that they were frightened of seeing it collapse in front of the stark facts. A little obscurity suited them better.

And that obscurity has remained: today the protagonists are no longer with us and it is therefore impossible for us to resolve the question. It is true that we have only raised objections, not provided a decisive refutation of the possible identity, but it will readily be conceded that the opposing theory rests on quite specious and vague arguments. We will acknowledge that, at a pinch, it is possible, even probable, but in no way can we or should we say in all historical sincerity that anyone has ever proved the identity of Balsamo and Cagliostro. If we have proved that then our goal has been attained.

But, subject to these caveats, let's for a moment accept this possibility. Let's accept that Count Cagliostro was born Joseph Balsamo. What harm does that do to his standing, and in what way would that force us to modify the judgement that posterity has made on his subsequent actions? What if he *was* the son of a solicitor, a gendarme or a farm-labourer, what does it matter to us? Even if people in the 18th century worried about such matters this isn't a scruple that should stop us in our tracks today. Epictetus was a slave, born the son of a slave, but are his name and moral teachings in any way tarnished by those facts? Whether Cagliostro had a wayward childhood and was of an independent character; whether his constant running-away scandalised those close to him, his uncle in particular, who was unable to turn him into the exemplary clerk that he himself was [22]; whether he travelled little or a lot; whether he married the daughter of a goldsmith, technically middle-class [23] but poor, rather than a wealthy heiress – all these facts are of no importance for humanity. What interests the historian is what he did when he entered the arena of social combat and became involved with the passions, struggles and sufferings of his fellow-men.

Even so, we are not prepared to blindly accept all the allegations with which certain people have tried to sully this obscure period of his youth. We need not pay any heed to the whimsical calumnies; the odious and gratuitous allegations; the inventions of lampoonists manufactured from day to day and often recounted without even a pretence of evidence, and often contradictory; the tales of brigands; and the obscene stories designed to titillate the readers of the *Courrier de l'Europe* or scandalise the pious readers of the *Vie de Joseph Balsamo* [24]. All these outrageous stories, repeated without evidence, are not even worthy of discussion. Sachi can tell us anything he likes about Don Thiscio of Barcelona, and the *Vie de Joseph Balsamo* can then impute all these things to Cagliostro, while a lampoonist can depict Balsamo as a cut-throat, a forger of counterfeit bills or a procurer, and if he gives us as his guarantee only his own word – and that is often the case – or, perhaps, the 'authority' of yet another anonymous lampoonist [25], then all we can do is pass over these things in silence.

We know that Joseph Balsamo's mother retained the most tender memories of him and expressed a wish to hold him in her arms again before she died [26]. She sent him her blessing and asked for his. Bracconieri does not depict his nephew as a good-for-nothing: he tells us only about him running away from the various monasteries where he'd been locked up and his involvement with Marano in a search for a hidden treasure, and he tells the story simply and without romantic embellishment. In Naples, in Palermo even, in Rome, Balsamo enjoyed the regard and friendship of persons of high rank, and does not seem to have been a dishonest person. These are the positive testimonies in his favour.

In everything that was said against Balsamo only one thing seems important, only one document exists, only one charge dominates all the rest and and deserves to be examined [27], and that is the Duplessis-Balsamo affair, the legal action that Joseph Balsamo brought in Paris against the seducer of his wife. Here also let us automatically assume that this document is not a forgery [28].

What does it tell us about him? Here we have a banal love-affair involving a rich and brilliant seducer who offers his services as the protector of a stranger struggling to make a living as an inventor and who finds himself attracted to his charming wife. A husband wrapped up in his work, often absent, with a vain and naive wife; a moment of weakness after a long period of resistance that proved difficult to sustain; remorse; then the impoverished foreigner of a husband suddenly coming to his senses, vigorously employing all the means at his disposal to fight a rich man in his own country; finally tearing his wife away from her seducer and the dangerous road upon which she had embarked, forgiving her, and taking her away with him to a place far from danger and temptation. Is there

Chapter XI

anything defamatory in all this? Though the woman's honour might be in question, what does it tell us about the husband's dignity and morals?

Some might say that it does reveal the duplicity and dissimulation of Cagliostro because he always denied both his use of the name Balsamo and his involvement in this little adventure. Yes, Cagliostro certainly did say that his name wasn't Balsamo [29], either because it wasn't or because, forsaken and rejected by the Balsamos, he had severed all social connections with a family to which he had never really belonged in a spiritual sense: after all, his life and true personality really began for him when, free at last, he first appeared in Courland. It was then that he had assumed the name of Cagliostro [30]. By rejecting the name of Balsamo under which his wife had compromised herself, Cagliostro (if we still accept here the Balsamo hypothesis and the truth of the Duplessis story) engaged in work of mercy. He acted as a noble-hearted man eager to avoid the remorse and shame of the woman who had betrayed him. Is this not the ultimate in charity and forgiveness, to assume the defence against the world of a woman who had caused him so much pain? And isn't that so very typical of the generous character and wisdom that we so often see displayed in the actions of Cagliostro?

Let's try to summarise these long and tedious discussions. All things considered, no one has ever proved that Balsamo and Cagliostro were the same person: neither Morande, nor Goethe, nor Fontaine nor the Inquisitors uncovered any documents sufficiently detailed to remove any lingering doubts. But even if we accept that they were the same person, and even if we accept the file compiled by Fontaine on the Duplessis-Balsamo affair as authentic, we cannot find in what little we know about Balsamo's life anything definite that was criminal or even blameworthy, or any act irreconcilable with the exceptional character and virtues of the man who, in public life, we have admired under the name of Cagliostro [31]. If he adopted a fictitious name and threw a veil of mystery over his origins which has never been removed then it was less for his own sake than for that of others. An untameable child who rebelled against all discipline, already gifted with qualities that attracted attention and brought him into conflict, he shook off the yoke that others wished to impose on him. Could a man who spoke to the greatest of men, to geniuses, with so much pride and independence of spirit really be expected to submit to the discipline of brutal and ignorant monks? Abandoned by his own family, he rejected their name so as to be able to *forgive* them. Deceived by the woman he had chosen, he saved her and succeeded in concealing her fault: the more she recognised and acknowledged her weakness, the more consideration he showed her. Is that not the natural conduct of someone who, as we have seen, always returned good for evil when persecuted, who spread goodness and illumination on those very people who did nothing but mock him?

At the beginning of this chapter we said that the question of the unknown life of Cagliostro was of no importance, and we say it again now at the end, hoping to have proved it. Even if we join his enemies in accepting, without proof, that Balsamo really was Cagliostro, we do not find in this hypothesis anything which in any way sullies the beauty and nobility of his remarkable life.

NOTES

(1) Their tactics were extremely skilful: Morande wrote initially in the *Courrier de l'Europe* (27th February 1787), without evidence but on the basis, so he said, of confidences entrusted to him, that Cagliostro had often called himself Balsamo, especially in London where he had already lived in 1771. It was only then that Fontaine stated, as a striking confirmation of Morande's revelations, that the man

called Balsamo, whose wife was called Feliciani, had also been involved with the police in Paris in 1773.

(2) In the *Courrier de Londres* (February to June 1787), in the *Gazette de Leyde*, and in the *Notizie del Mondo* of Florence (no. 83 of 1786).

(3) 21st November 1786 Cagliostro was received into the Lodge *Antiquity* of the Scottish Rite. A caricature of this meeting subsequently appeared (Cagliostro unmasked, etc.) which was reproduced in the *Monist*, July 1903.

(4) *Ma correspondance*, Years 1785, 1786 and 1787.

(5) *Lettre au peuple anglais*, 1787, pp. 56-57.

(6) Goethe, who found the enigmatic Cagliostro frankly annoying, had no objection to publishing this story to prove to his friends (and especially his lady-friends) that he'd been the only person to have seen through Cagliostro and had not allowed himself to be taken in by a joker who had bedazzled everyone else, cf. Goethe, *Voyage en Italie*, pp. 34 et seq.

(7) False information about their son whom he claimed to know, and an illusory promise to obtain a study-grant for one of their children.

(8) This presence in London in 1771 has not been proved, cf. *Lettre au peuple anglais*.

(9) *Dossier du Commissaire Fontaines (Enquête Gugino)* in Campardon, *Marie-Antoinette et le Procès du Collier*, Paris, Plon, 1863, pp. 410 et seq. *Déposition Bracconieri* in *Courrier de l'Europe* of 15th June 1787. *Actes officiels d'origine ecclésiastique:* extracts from death, marriage & birth certificates, reproduced in the Appendix to this book.

(10) We should note that we could certainly, in the same way, simply on the word of Sachi, identify Cagliostro with a certain Thiscio of Naples, the son of a wig-maker, tell the story of his origins and journey through life, which would have been a perfectly accurate account, and impute to Cagliostro all the responsibility for the life of this individual until 1778. The method would have been the same, and meaningful discussion just as difficult.

(11) Letter of 2nd November 1780 to Fontaine, Rue de la Verrerie (received 3rd December 1786). *Arch. Nat.*, Y. 13125.

(12) 'The last time he saw him, in Naples in 1773, he was calling himself the Marquis de Pellegrini', id. ibid.

(13) It is useless to point out the inadequacy and even the self-contradictory nature of the descriptions, cf. Chapter II of this book, 'Portrait'. A German jeweller in Palermo, Mathieu Novarrchy, who often met Balsamo around 1768, had seen on the snuffbox of one of his customers, Baron Irobio, in 1784, a pen-and-ink portrait of Cagliostro, half-length and not coloured, and found that the two heads resembled each other, 'without however being able to confirm the precise conformity of the two physiognomies', *Courrier de l'Europe*, 12th June 1786, *Enquête Gugino*, p. 393.

(14) *Courrier de l'Europe*, 15th June 1787, *Déposition Bracconieri*, p. 402. An imprecise statement, even from the Balsamo point of view, as we know full well from the marriage certificate of Balsamo (see Appendix) that Balsamo's wife was called Lorenza Feliciani.

(15) Balsamo was held over the baptismal font by J. Basile who was standing in for his godmother Vincentia Cagliostro.

(16) *Lettre Bernard*, Arch. Nat., Y. 13125. The newspaper in question was *Le Notizie del Mondo*, no. 83 of 17th October 1786, and the article, which we have managed to find, is a 'communiqué' from Paris, simply repeating something from the *Courrier de l'Europe*.

(17) *Courrier de l'Europe*, 1787, p. 393, col. I. The phrase in the Bernard letter, 'You yourselves have said, etc.' clearly indicates that he was responding to a request for information.

(18) Compare the *Déposition Bracconieri* in *Courrier de l'Europe*, no. 48, p. 401.

(19) We must point out that the Balsamo documents themselves are not very precise. There are grounds for discussion, e.g. the version of the Holy Office gives his date of birth as 8th June instead of the 2nd; says that the church where he was married was Saint-Sauveur-aux-Champs instead of Santa-Maria-in-Monticelli as stated in the certificate (cf. Appendix); gives the name of Balsamo's wife sometimes as just Lorenza (Bracconieri), sometimes as Feliciana (Sartines), sometimes as Feliciani

Chapter XI

(as in the certificate); and says that Bracconieri met Balsamo in Naples in 1773, i.e. the same year that the Fontaine dossier says he was in Paris.

(20) We know he had very important (indeed, 'irreplaceable') papers, that they were thoroughly examined, that they were not returned to him in Paris, and that in Rome, although warned in advance, he did not destroy any documents or conceal any of his files.

(21) Buhot and Fontaine must have seen Cagliostro very often in Paris in 1784, and yet it never occurred to them to try and identify him as Balsamo.

(22) Antonio Bracconieri was a clerk with the business-house of Aubert & Cie. in Palermo. Pierre Balsamo died a few months after the birth of his son, Joseph. The child was given to J. Bracconieri, his great-uncle, and then, when he died, to Antonio Bracconieri. The two uncles got rid of the child by initially placing him in the Saint-Roch seminary in Palermo, which he ran away from in 1755 to return home. After this escapade he was put under judicial supervision and sent to the Benedictine Bonfratelli Fathers near Caltagirone (1756). He didn't stay there very long either and, turning his back on monasticism and rejected by his own family, began a wandering life at the age of 14. Another version of his childhood says that in 1754 he was already a boarder at Caltagirone. In 1755 he was then sent as a penitent, once again as a boarder, to the Capuchins in Georgenti, and that it was from there that he escaped and finally gained his freedom, cf. *Lettre écrite d'Aix-les-Bains à M. de Beaumarchais*, 1788, p. 9.

(23) Testimony of A. Bracconieri, cf. *Courrier de l'Europe* of 15th June 1787.

(24) The *Vie de Joseph Balsamo*, the last of the series, accumulates these turpitudes and expands gleefully upon them. The author refrains from quoting any references. To do so he would of course have had to call upon the 'authority' of Morande, Sachi, Madame de la Motte, or the paid informers of the Inquisition, and the lies would no longer have had any verisimilitude. In spite of this precaution one's mind still boggles when one reads this hodgepodge. Sometimes the young Balsamo seems to be prematurely gifted with extraordinary devilish powers (p. 5), at other times he appears as a charlatan exploiting the superstitious credulity of the naive *Palermitani* and taking people for a ride in phantasmagorical adventures like the Marano treasure-hunt. An actor and a swindler in one case, a genuine wizard in another, the mass of contradictions are obviously of no importance to the author as long as he can pile up the complaints, charges and allegations. A measure of agreement between the different stories would however have been welcome.

(25) The *Vie de Joseph Balsamo* abounds in borrowings of this kind from the *Mémoires authentiques*, the *Confession de Cagliostro*, *Ma Correspondance et la Suite*, etc. without indicating their origins.

(26) Goethe, *Voyage en Italie*, pp. 24, 31-32.

(27) We won't mention J. Balsamo's so-called creditor in London in 1771-1772. Whether he was actually in London at that time is doubtful. No allegation was substantiated and no witnesses could be found to testify against him. Cagliostro rebutted all these stories in his *Lettre au peuple anglais*, pp. 58-59. He asked for a Dr. Bénamore [sic] to be questioned because this doctor, cited by Morande as a witness for the prosecution, was ready to certify that he never had any business with anyone called Balsamo, that he did not know Balsamo, and that he was seeing Count Cagliostro for the first time (1786).

(28) We would be fully justified in doubting it. It was exhumed late in the day as a means of defence by Chesnon and did not emerge from any general investigation: the story is therefore suspect. The descriptions of Balsamo and his wife should have been well established in 1773 during their expulsion from Paris. When Cagliostro received a visit in Strasbourg from Desbrugnières (the police-agent who had come *incognito* to examine him); when he arrived in Paris in 1781; when he was arrested and questioned by the Paris police about the Diamond Necklace Affair in 1785, along with his wife – on all these occasions the appropriate police-registers of Italians and quack-doctors were examined, yet on none of these occasions did any of the descriptions catch anyone's eye, nor was any reference to anyone called Balsamo found. If Balsamo had returned with his name changed to Cagliostro then would his wife also have retained her surname of Feliciani? Cagliostro himself pointed all this out in his *Lettre au peuple anglais*, pp. 63-64. The Fontaine dossier deals entirely with events that occurred

Cagliostro – The Unknown Master

in 1773, but it was in 1773 that Bracconieri says he met Balsamo in Naples (*Courrier de l'Europe*, 1787, no. 48). As for the evidence based on the signature of J. Balsamo, which in any case is not found in the Archives in document Y. 13125, and which, according to Fontaine – appointing himself a handwriting-expert for the occasion – was in the same hand as the Cagliostro signatures in the interrogations of 1784, it has no value even if the document is genuine, and even less so if it is apocryphal, which it probably is.

(29) He could have added that he wasn't Belmonte, Pellegrini, etc. either. 'I styled myself Count Cagliostro on orders from above', he told Countess von der Recke, 'although it is not my real title. Whether my true quality is higher or lower than that which I bestowed upon myself is something that the public will perhaps learn one day'. Cagliostro also said that he 'had already in former times served the same superior spirit, the Grand Copht, under the name of Federico Gualdi', a statement which, if correct, can certainly be explained. But Cagliostro's words were probably misreported. We find this anecdote in Borowski, *Cagliostro, einer der merkwürdigsten...*, 1790, p. 67 (following the account in the book by Madam von der Recke). [Gualdi was an Italian alchemist and engineer, born around 1600].

(30) This would be a quite natural choice if we accept the Balsamo hypothesis, cf. Appendix p. 296. The pamphlet *Lettre écrite d'Aix*, 1788, p. 15, gravely explains how Balsamo formed this pseudonym from two Italian roots, *Cagliare* and *ostro*, meaning 'I desire the purple!' [i.e. of royalty]. It will readily be seen what mountains of stupidity and deceit one has to clear away to find even a few fragments of the truth about Cagliostro.

(31) Accepting the idea that Cagliostro and Balsamo were one and the same person would also, however, help to explain Cagliostro's use of certain names and titles, even from a purely social point of view, and also shed exceptional light upon his relationship with the Order of Malta, cf. 'Titles of nobility and armorial bearings of the Balsamo and Cagliostro families', in the Appendix to this book.

AFTERWORD
THE UNKNOWN MASTER

It didn't matter to Cagliostro's disciples when or for how long he slept and it shouldn't matter to history what he got up during those years of his childhood for which the historical record remains silent. Drying people's tears, lifting up those who'd stumbled, giving the wayward traveller the strength and courage to continue until dawn, sowing joy and beauty in the darkness, bringing shafts of light to the heroic skies, acting as the glorious cup-bearer of the beverage of immortality – that is surely what matters to humanity about the life of Cagliostro, and that is what our planet will remember him for.

Those were the precious diamonds that Nature concealed within his breast and which characterised every act of his life. We can learn to read these letters of light and to hear these voices of the Earth, and fathom what they have to say about him. Even if our eyes are still quite blurred and our ears not yet attuned to understanding everything they have to say, then at least we're not relying on the tired phrases of hack-journalists or police-reports to tell us his name, his titles, his nationality, his racial origin and other trivia, for it will be Cagliostro himself who will be speaking to us.

Let us reflect therefore upon the successive scenes of this wonderful life, a life that we have tried in the pages of this book to restore in its true light; let us reflect upon those ten years of teaching, philanthropy and martyrdom; let us see once more the crowds on their knees, and those great men and women who seemed so small beside him; let us look again at this Great Being, who was as sublime in love as he was in wisdom; and in the clarity of this luminous vision let us glance once more at those pages, so odiously ridiculed, in which Cagliostro tells us about himself [1]. What shall we find there?

I am not of any specific hour or place: my spiritual being lives its eternal existence beyond time, beyond space, and if I sink deeply into my thoughts and then rise again through the course of the ages, if I stretch forth my spirit towards a form of existence that is far removed from what you can perceive, then I can become whatever I wish to be. I am a conscious part of the Absolute Being and I regulate my actions according to the medium that happens to surround me. My name is that of my present purpose, and I can choose my own name just as I can choose my own purpose, because I am free. My country is wherever I temporarily set my feet. Set your age from yesterday if you wish, by simply removing those years lived by your ancestors who were complete strangers to you, or from tomorrow by removing the illusory pride of a grandeur that might never be yours. As for me, I am what I am.

I have only one father. Various experiences in my life have made me sceptical about this whole subject of great and powerful verities, but the mysteries of my origin in this father and the links that bind me to Him are – and shall ever be – my secrets. Let those who are called to fathom them and to foresee them, as I have done, understand me and approve me.

As for the place and the hour where my material body was formed on this Earth some forty years ago or the family that I chose for that purpose, I do not wish to know those things. I do not wish to remember myself as I was in the past because I do not want to increase the already heavy responsibilities of those who knew me, for so it is written: 'Thou shalt not curse the deaf, nor put a stumblingblock before the blind' [2].

I was not born of the flesh, nor of the will of man: I was born of the spirit. My name, that which is mine and of me, that which I chose in order to appear amongst you, is that to which I laid claim. The name by which I was called at birth, the name that was given to me in my youth, those names under which, at sundry times and places, I have been known... I have abandoned all of them, as I would have abandoned clothing that was worn out and therefore no longer of any use.

Here I am. I am noble, and a traveller. I speak and your soul trembles when it recognises ancient words. A voice that is within you, which had kept silent for so long, answers the call of my own. I act, and peace floods back into your souls, health into your bodies, and hope and courage into your hearts.

All men are my brothers. All countries are dear to me. I pass through them only so that, everywhere, the Spirit can descend and find its way towards you. I ask the kings, whose power I respect, only for their hospitality on their soil, and when it is granted to me I pass through, doing as much good as I can to those around me. But that is all I do – I pass through. Am I not a noble traveller?

Like the wind from the South [3], *like the lovely light of the Midi which characterises complete knowledge of things and active communion with God, I come towards the North, towards the fog and the cold, shedding everywhere as I pass something of myself, expending myself, decreasing myself at every step, but leaving you with a little more clarity, a little more warmth, a little more strength, until I am finally stopped and fixed definitively at the end of my career, at that hour when the Rose shall finally bloom upon the Cross.*

For I am Cagliostro.

What more could you ask for? If you were truly children of God, if your hearts were not so vain and questioning, then you would have understood me already!

But I know that you need details, signs and parables, so listen! Since you wish to do so, let us travel together far, very far into the past.

All light comes from the East, and every initiation comes from Egypt. Once upon a time I was three years old, just as you were once, then seven, then of manly age, and when I reached that age I stopped counting. Three septenaries make twenty-one years, and it is then that human development is fully achieved. In my early childhood, under the laws of rigour and justice, I suffered in exile [4], *just as Israel did amongst the nations. But just as Israel had with her the presence of God, as a Metatron to keep her feet upon His path, so in the same way a powerful angel took care of me* [5], *directed my every act, illuminated my soul, and developed the latent powers within me. He was my Master and my guide.*

My powers of reasoning were formed and made specific. I questioned myself, I studied myself, I became aware of everything around me. I went on journeys – not just one but many – journeys around the little room of my quiet reflections, journeys around the temples, journeys to the four corners of the Earth, but when I wanted to penetrate to the origins of my being and to rise towards God in the fervour of my soul then my impotent reason fell silent and abandoned me to my conjectures.

A love that drew me impulsively towards every creature with an irresistible ambition and a profound feeling of entitlement to everything from Earth to Heaven propelled me, nay hurled me towards life, and the progressive experience of my forces, their sphere of action, their interplay and their limits was the struggle that I had to bear in the face of the powers of the world. I was abandoned and tempted in the desert [6], *I fought with the angel like Jacob, I fought with men and demons, and once vanquished they taught me the secrets of the world of darkness so that I would never go astray on any of those dark roads from which one does not return.*

One day – after so many journeys and oh so many years! – the heavens finally crowned my efforts. They remembered their faithful servant and, adorned in bridal clothes, I was granted the favour, like Moses, of being allowed into the presence of the Eternal [7]. *I then received a new name and a unique mission. Now free and a master of life, I dreamed only of doing the work of God. I knew that He would confirm me in my acts and words, as I would confirm Him in His name and His kingdom upon Earth, for there are beings that no longer have a guardian angel* [8], *and now I too was one of those.*

That was my childhood, my youth, just as your restless minds, so eager for knowledge, so eager for explanations, have claimed it to be. But how many years it lasted, whether it was spent in the country of your fathers or in some other part of the world, what does that matter to you? Am I not a free man? Judge my morals, my actions, and tell me if they are good, tell me if you have ever seen more powerful ones, and do not concern yourself with my nationality, my status in society or my religion.

If, continuing on the happy course of his travels, one of you should one day come ashore in those same lands of the East where I was born then you have only to remember me, you have only to say my name, and the servants of my Father shall open before you the doors of the Holy City. Then return, and ask your brothers and sisters whether I ever abused amongst you an honour that I did not earn or ever took from you anything that did not rightfully belong to me.

Cagliostro

NOTES
(1) *Mémoire pour le comte de Cagliostro accusé contre le Procureur général*, Paris(?), 1786, p. 12 et seq.
(2) Leviticus XIX.14.
(3) Cagliostro, according to two Italian roots, can be interpreted as 'the wind of the south', 'that which is fixed', or 'that which softens and moderates'.
(4) Medina, *Mémoire pour le comte de Cagliostro accusé contre le Procureur général*, p. 12.
(5) Althotas, loc. cit., p. 13.
(6) Trebizond, loc. cit., p. 16.
(7) Mecca, loc. cit., p. 15.
(8) Death of Althotas, loc. cit., p. 19.

APPENDIX

PART I
SPECIFIC DOCUMENTS ON THE ORIGINS AND PERSON OF CAGLIOSTRO

PART II
GENERAL DOCUMENTS – LETTERS AND REFERENCE MATERIAL

APPENDIX PART I
SPECIFIC DOCUMENTS ON THE ORIGINS AND PERSON OF CAGLIOSTRO

I. CAGLIOSTRO'S SIGNATURES.

Very few of Cagliostro's signatures have survived: he wrote little and signed his letters either with his first name alone [1] or with his seal, consisting of a snake pierced by an arrow, imprinted on green wax. This seal, the motif of which we illustrate here, was used on the manuscript of the Ritual of Egyptian Freemasonry [2]. The cursive monogram with which Cagliostro identified himself and which constituted his mystical signature is found at the end of an Italian letter that Cagliostro wrote to Countess von der Recke in 1779 and which will be found below. The eccentricities of Cagliostro's spelling have been retained.

Cara Figlia e Sorella,

In questa potrete imaginarvi, se ho della stima per Voi, mai ho scritto a donne, e per questo è il primo vincolo che rompo in voi perche vi stimo, e il futuro sarà che vi dara prove del mio operare. Et intanto cara, non vi dimenticate i miei consigli e l'amore fraternale. Il silenzio è quello che vi indurrà alla vera strata dei Sabbini, e vi farà unire alla gloria celeste, e sarete sodisfatta dai trovagli chez fatto avete.

Sicche sappiata, cara Sorella, che io sono il medesimo sempre per voi, e avrò tutta la cura possibile per farvi contenta; ma il silenzzio ritorno arreplicarvi.

Ed intanto v'incarico imbasciatrice per tutta la logia dei F∴ e S∴, acciò l'abbracciate per me, e specialmente il vostro Caro Padre e Madre e Sorella, alli quale farete tutto quello che il vostro cuore vi dirà, e direre che spero in breve tempo di abbracciarli di presenza. Ma nel tempo istesso v'incarico di pregare al Grande Iddio per me, perche mi ritrovo circondato di nemici, e pieno di amarezzi, in unione di mia moglie vostra cara sorella; ma bisognia sofrire con pasienzza, e battere l'ingnioranzza prufanesca.

Per adesso non posso dirvi di piu ma fra poco vi dirò di piu. E con questo finisco con darvi i saluti di mia moglie, come il consimile osserva con tutti i F∴ e S∴. E per non piu dilungarmi, mi resto con abbracciarvi di quore, comé osservo con tutti i F∴ e S∴, e non vi dimentichiate di me ut Deus.

Vostro per sempre che vi ama di quore. [3].

Translation:
My dear Daughter and Sister,

From this letter you will be able to see for yourself the high esteem in which I hold you, for this is the first time I have ever written to a woman. This is the first bond that I am breaking on your behalf, and I do it because I respect you. The second bond I am breaking is that I shall be giving you some proof of the effectiveness of my work. Meanwhile, my dear, do not forget my advice and my fraternal love. Remember, it is silence that will bring you onto the true path of the Sabine Women, and which one day will unite you with the Celestial Glory so that, ultimately, you will be very well pleased with all your efforts.

Appendices

You will find, my dear Sister, that I am always the same for you and that I will take all possible care to ensure your fulfilment, but I must once again commend to you the need to remain silent.

Meanwhile I am appointing you my ambassadress for the whole lodge of Brothers and Sisters to embrace it in my name, and especially your dear father, mother and sister, for whom you must do everything that your heart tells you to do. Tell them that I hope to soon embrace them personally. But for now I request you to pray to Almighty God on my behalf, because I am surrounded by enemies and find myself full of sorrows, along with my wife your dear Sister. But one must suffer in patience and overcome the ignorance of the profane.

For the time being I cannot tell you any more, but in a short while I shall do so. I conclude this letter by sending you my wife's greetings, as she sends greetings also to all the Brothers and Sisters. And not to continue this letter any further I shall stop here and embrace you warmly as I do also all the Brothers and Sisters. And do not forget me ut Deus [like God].

Vostro per sempre che vi ama di quore.

1255 (1).

We find this same sign, preceded by interlaced lines which seem to me to be the monogram of his initials L.c.d.C (i.e. 'Le comte de Cagliostro'), at the end of a letter of ntroduction written by someone else and merely signed by Cagliostro [4]. Here is this variant:

Those are two very rare documents, but the following signature, in which his name and title are written out in full, is rarer still. We found it in the *Archives Nationales*, at the end of the report on the interrogation of Cagliostro (shelf-mark: X^2 b, 1417) [5].

II. CERTIFICATE OF BAPTISM

Document stating that Joseph Balsamo, son of Pietro Balsamo and Felicia Bracconeri (sic) was baptised on 8th June 1743 in the metropolitan church of Palermo in the presence of Giovanni Baptista Barone, godfather, and Vincentia Cagliostro, godmother, the latter being replaced by Josepha Basile, who was provided with a procuration for that purpose.

From the archives of the metropolitan church of Palermo, Legalised Copy (Author's personal collection).

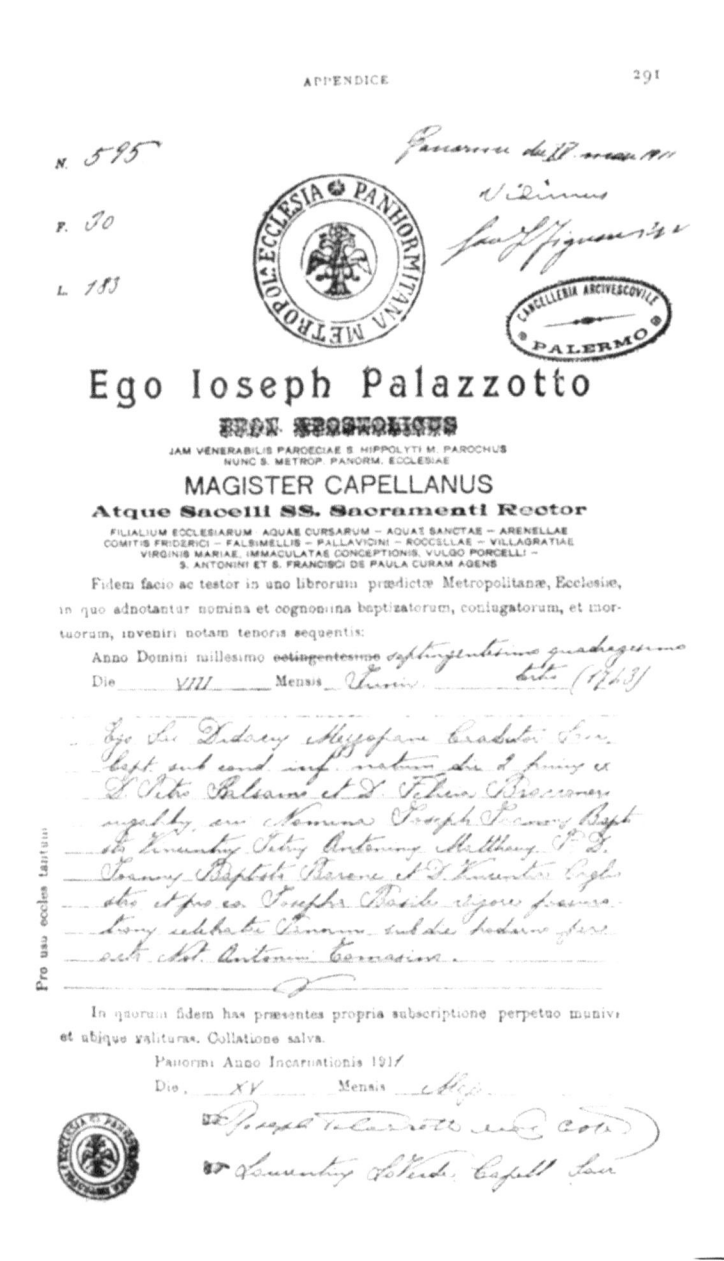

III. CERTIFICATE OF MARRIAGE

Document stating that Joseph Balsamo, son of Pietro (of Palermo), and Laurentia Feliciani, daughter of Joseph (of Rome), received the sacrament of marriage in the church of Santa Maria de Monticelli in Rome on 20th April 1768.

From the Parish Archives of Santa Maria de Monticelli in Rome, volume running from 1751 to 1785, Folio 53, Legalised Copy (Author's personal collection).

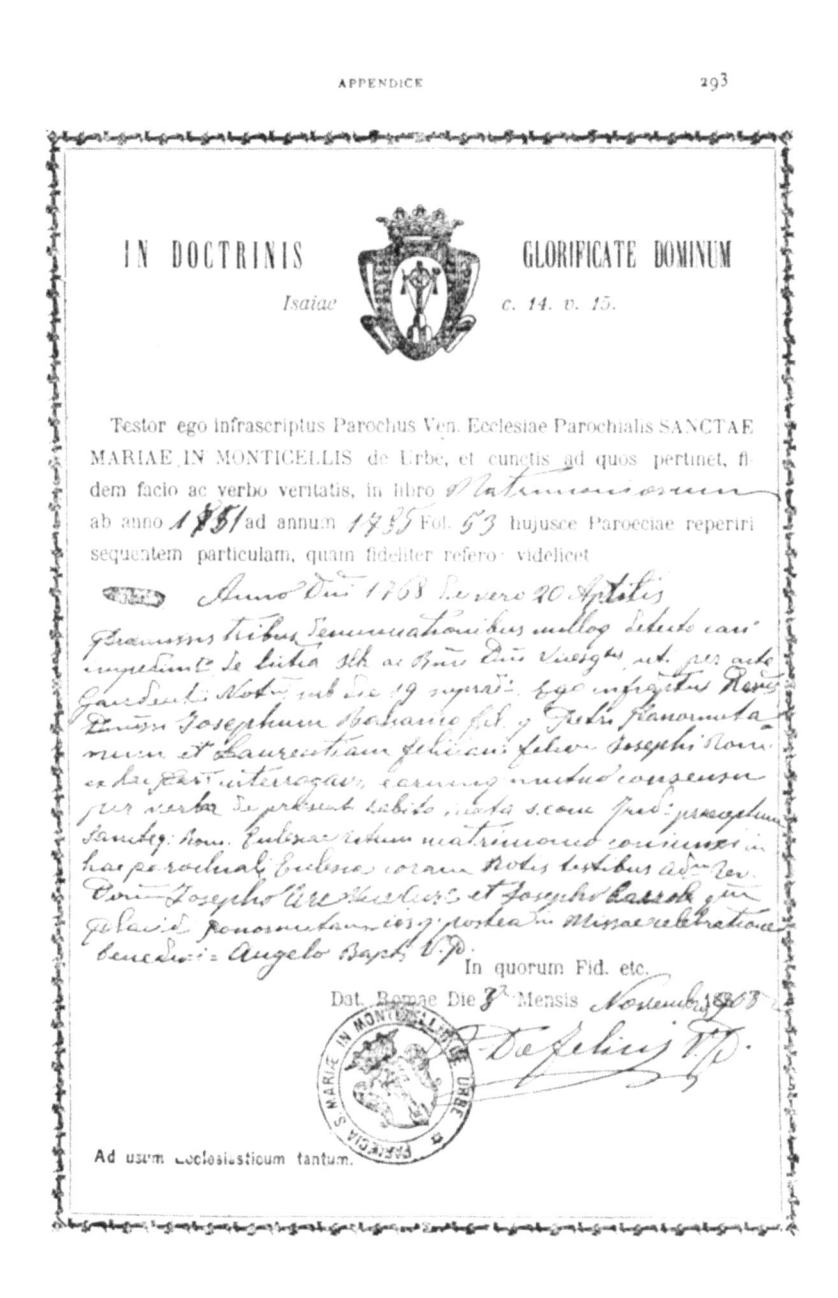

IV. DEATH CERTIFICATE.

The death certificate of Cagliostro will be found in the Register of Deaths of the Church of Santa Maria Assunta in San Leo (Book III, pp. 25-26). We have been able to obtain a legalised copy bearing the two seals of Santa Maria and San Leo. Here is this interesting text, followed by a full translation.

Anno Domini 1795, die 28 mensis Augusti.

Joseph Balsamus, vulgo Conte di Cagliostro, patria Panormitanus, baptismo christianus, doctrina incredulus, hoereticus, mala fama famosus post disseminata per varias Europae provincias impia dogmata sectae Ægypticae, cui prope innumeram asseclarum turbam prestigiis, se praedicante, conciliavit, passus varia discrimina vitae e quibus arte sua veteratoria evasit incollumis : tandem sacros^{tae} Inquisitionis sententia relegatus, dum viveret, ad perpetuam carcerem in arce hujus civitatis (si forte resipisceret) pari obstinatione carceris incommodis toleratis annos 4, menses 4, dies 5, correptus ad ultimum vehementi apoplexiae morbo, secundum duritiem mentis et impenitens cor, nullo dato poenitentiae signo illamentatus moritur extra comm. S. Matris Eccles^{ae}, annos natus 52, mens : 2, dies 28. Nascitur infelix, vixit infelicior, obiit infelicissime die 26 augusti anni suprad: sub horam 3 cum dimidio noctis. Qua die indicta fuit publica supplicatio si forte Misericors Deus respiceret ad figmentum man : suar :

Ei tanquam haeretico, excommunicato, impaenitente denegatur ecclesiastica sepultura. Cadaver tumulatur ad ipsum supercilium montis qua vergit ad occidentem aequa fere distantia inter duo munimenta habendis excubiis destinata vulgo nuncupata Il Palazzetto et Il Casino in solo R. C. A. die 28 praedict. hora 23.

In quorum fidem, etc.

Aloysius Marini Archip. M^n pp^e.

TRANSLATION

On the 28th August in the year of grace 1795, Joseph Balsamo, known as the Conte di Cagliostro, born in Palermo, baptised a Christian but a notorious non-believer and heretic, after having propagated all over Europe the impious dogmas of the Egyptian sect, and having acquired, through his fame and eloquence, an almost innumerable crowd of followers; having undergone various mishaps from which he emerged safe and sound thanks to his magical arts; having been finally condemned by sentence of the Holy Inquisition to perpetual imprisonment in a fortress of this city in the doubtful hope that he would eventually repent; and having with the same obstinacy borne the sufferings of prison for a period of 4 years, 4 months and 5 days, but being finally struck down by a violent attack of apoplexy, which is not unexpected in a man with such stubbornness of heart and unrepentance of soul, died without having given any sign of repentance [6] and without showing any regrets, outside the Communion of our Holy Mother Church, at the age of 52 years, 2 months and 28 days. He was born in misery, lived in greater misery, and died in the greatest misery on 26th August of the aforesaid year at 3 o'clock in the morning. This day, a public supplication was ordered to petition God to, if it were possible, show mercy upon this piece of clay kneaded by His hands.

As a heretic, excommunicated and unrepentant, burial in consecrated ground was denied to him: instead he was buried at the very top of the hill on the side where it inclines towards the west, more or less equidistant from the two structures which were built for the sentinels and which are known as *Il Palazzetto* and *Il Casino*, on the soil of the Roman Apostolic Curia, on the 28th day of this month at 11 o'clock in the evening.

In witness whereof… etc.
Aloysius Marini, arch-priest

V. NOTES ON THE BALSAMO, BRACCONIERI AND CAGLIOSTRO FAMILIES

The Balsamo family was of noble origin, and some of its members had served in official capacities in Sicily for several centuries. During the reign of Ferdinand the Catholic, Giacomo Balsamo was a captain, commander of Milazzo and Patti (1517) and lord of Mirto and Taormina. In 1613 Pietro Balsamo, Marchese della Limina, the so-called *Straticote* of Messina, accepted the principality of Roccafiorita and the Spanish Order of San Giacomo. In 1759 Francesco Balsamo bought the principality of Castellaci and was senator and syndic of Messina: he had two sons, Giuseppe Balsamo, Barone de Cattafi, and Giambattista Balsamo, Marchese de Montefiorito, Pronotary of the Kingdom in 1773. To this same family of Balsamo belonged Brother Giordano Salvo Balsamo, Grand Prior of Messina in the Order of Malta in 1618, as well as several Knights of Malta [7].

But these were not their only titles of nobility: the mother of Joseph Balsamo belonged, through her father, to the Bracconieris, an extremely well-known family of the high nobility of Sicily. In 1439 Simone Bracconieri acquired the barony of Piscopo and was lord of the manor of Castroreale: the armorial bearings of the Bracconieri are known to us [8]. Through her mother Felicia she belonged to the Cagliostro family (9): her mother's brother, Giuseppe Cagliostro of Messina, was property-manager to the Prince of Villafranca, and it was as his heir that Joseph Balsamo added his name to his own.

As for his coat of arms, which is that of the Balsamo family and which we reproduce here, they are composed of *an Italian shield party per fess, the chief per pale, 1st a bird sable on a field or, 2nd gules, 3rd azure, surmounted by a Count's coronet.* These armorial bearings are somewhat coarsely reproduced around a portrait of Cagliostro which was found by Signor Alessandro Scala and which now forms part of our collection [10].

NOTES

(1) Letter to his wife signed 'Il tuo Alessandro' (Collection of the Vicomte Morel de Vindé, dated 4th February 1788?) Monsieur Charavay says, in the *Amateur d'autographes* of 15th February 1900, p. 35, that he has seen several similar signatures but that Cagliostro signatures are almost impossible to track down.

(2) Cf. p. 148 of this book.

(3) Von der Recke, *Nachricht von des berüchtigten*, pp. 147-148. Countess von der Recke provides a translation of this letter into German.

(4) *Archives Sarrasin*, Basel, Letter dated from Strasbourg, 2nd April 1783.
(5) The learned and very amiable director of the *Archives Sarrasin*, Monsieur Déjean, kindly allowed us to reproduce it and facilitated the task for us. We would like to express our thanks to him here.
(6) Either this statement is untrue or Cagliostro's alleged retractions, confessions and abjurations listed in the trial proceedings in Rome are incorrect. Cagliostro was either a hardened and unrepentant non-believer or a repentant heretic humbly begging forgiveness – but he cannot have been both at the same time!
(7) This sheds singular light on the relations between Cagliostro and the Order of Malta.
(8) *Argent two dogs passant gules alternating with two stars of the same, one in chief and the other in the centre*, cf. Alexandro Scala, *Rivista del Collegio araldico*, Rome, Oct. 1903, no. 48, p. 605.
(9) There were two Cagliostro families in Messina in 1788. Cf. *Courrier de l'Europe*, 1788, issue of 15th June, p. 393, col. 2, Letter from Bracconieri.
(10) Alexandro Scala, op. cit., p. 603.

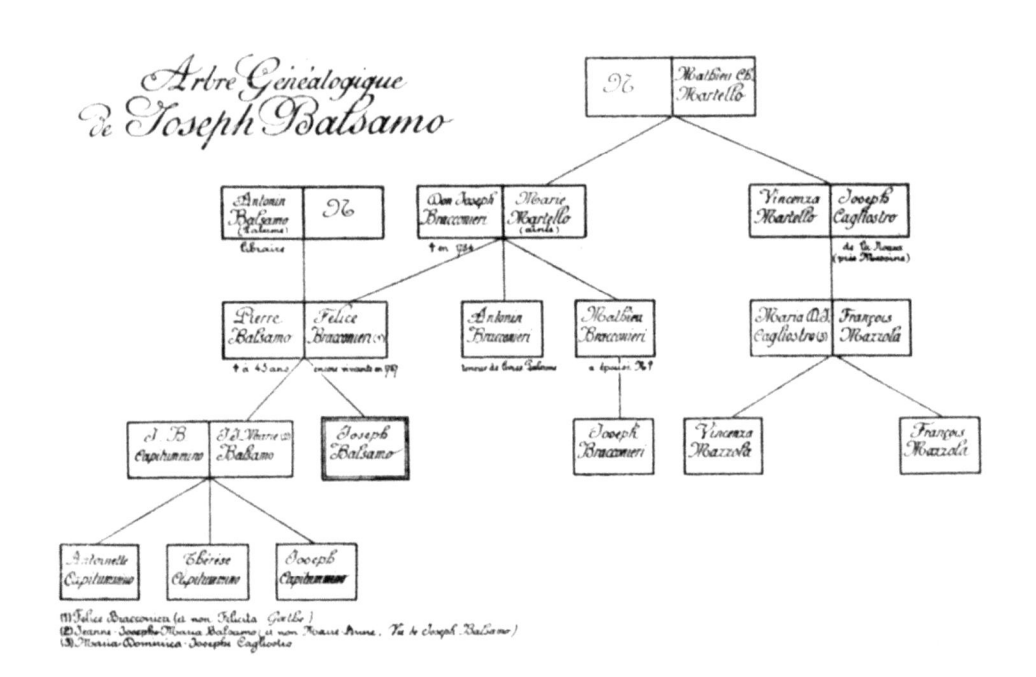

APPENDIX PART II
GENERAL DOCUMENTS – LETTERS AND REFERENCE MATERIAL

I. SOME OF CAGLIOSTRO'S MEDICINAL FORMULAS AND PREPARATIONS FROM HIS TIME IN STRASBOURG (1781).

Some prescriptions made up at the Hecht pharmacy in Strasbourg by Dr. Martius, at that time the dispenser at that firm, cf. Dr. Martius, *Erinnerungen aus meinem neunzigjährigen Leben*, Leipzig, 1847, pp. 74-77.

PURGATIVE HERBAL TEA. Rp: Herbæ Cichorii, Acetosæ, Violarum Agrimoniae, Calcitropiæ, Ononidis ana Mpj. Radic. Cichorii, Acetosæ Fragaræ, Ononidis, Calcitropæ, ana ℨ jj.
Semin. Anisi, Coriandri ana ℨ jjj.
Flor. Rosarum rubr. ℨ □ cc. m. bull. per 1/4 horam in Libris XVI. aquæ fontanae. In colat. refrigeratae infrinde per 24 horas. Fol. Sennæ electae ℨ jj. Col. d. in 4 lagenas.

POMADE FOR THE FACE. Rp: Olei amygdale dulcium ℨ vjjj. Spermat. ceti ℨ jv. Ceræ albæ ℨ jj. Alumin. Camphoræ ana ℨ jj. M. f. ceratum et in capsul. effunde.

PECTORAL ELECTUARY WITH MANNA. Rp: Mannæ Calabrin. ℨ jj. Dissolv. in aq. font. ℨ j □. adde olei sacchari [1] cand. pulv. succ. liquirit ana ℨ □ M. f. Electuarium.

STOMACHIC PILLS. Rp: Aloe hepaticae ℨ j. Diagrydii, Rad. Turpethi, Agarici, Trochisc. Alkand. ana, 3. □. Gum. Mastichi 3 jjj. Rhabarb. optim, Myrobalan. citr, Chebul ex Ind; Herb. Marrubii albi, Semina Fœniculi ana 3 j. Cinnamoni, Macis, Lignis Santelli albi, Flor. Lavendulæ, Hbæ Osari, Croci orientalis, Caryophillor. Nucis Moschat; Sem. Rut. Siler. mont; herb. Euphrasiæ Cuberar; Myrrhæ electæ ana 3 □. M. f. Pulvis and cum mucilagine Tragaeanth. f. pill. pond. gr. V. Fol. aur. obduc.

TURPENTINE PILLS. Rp: Terebinth. venet ℨ j. Sacchar. albi ℨ jj. Cinnamon 3 j. M. f. cum pulv. Rad. Althaæ et Mucilagine Tragacanthæ pill, pond. V. obduc. Fol. aur.

CANADA BALSAM PILLS. Rp: Balsami de Canada ℨ j. Sacchari Albi ℨ jj. Cinnamon. 3 j. Myrrh. electæ gr. XII. Pulv. rad. Althaæ q. s. m. f. c. Mucilagine Tragacanthæ pill. pond. gr. V. obduc. Fol. aur [1].

PURGATIVE POWDER (from the first prescription). Rp: Pulv. folior. semi. radic. Fallopæ, cremor. tartar. ana ℨ jj. Semin. Anisi, Fœniculi ana ℨ □. Diagrydii sulph. 3 jjj M. f. pulv. d. 3 j. pro die.

PURGATIVE POWDER (from the final presciption). Rp: pulver. prœcedent. ℨ v.jj. 3 jjj admisc. pulv. Cinnamoni ℨ □.

OLEUM SACCHARI (or: Oleo-Sacchari). This oil, derived from sugar alone, was intended to be used by ladies as a sweet to aid digestion and was packaged in elegant bottles. To prepare it, a hard-boiled egg was first sliced in two. The yoke was then carefully scooped out and the space thus created was filled with the most beautiful white candy-sugar. The two halves of the egg were then immediately closed and the reconstituted egg bound up with wire. The egg was then placed in a covered vase made of glass or porcelain which was put in a cool dark place. The sugar would gradually dissolve [2].

NOTES
(1) It should be noted that all Cagliostro's pills weighed five grains and were carefully gilded.
(2) In the *Pharmacopoea Wurtemberg* of 1771 (p. 105) we find a similar process for preparing *Oleum myrrhæ per deliquium.*

II. LETTER FROM CARDINAL DE ROHAN ABOUT CAGLIOSTRO

On several occasions Cardinal de Rohan wrote letters of defence or introduction for Cagliostro [1]. The letter we reproduce here is interesting from three points of view:
1. it proves that, eight years after his stay in Strasbourg, and despite the Diamond Necklace Affair, the exiling of Cagliostro and the smear campaign carried out against him, the Cardinal still had the same respectful affection for his Master and friend as he'd had at the beginning of their relationship; 2. the tenor of this little-known letter is almost the same as that to be found in the memoirs of Madam de Créquy, and indeed could well be the authentic and original document [2], the de Créquy letter being only a pastiche of it adapted to suit the events of 1781;
3. according to the date and text it is probable that this letter was written to the Archbishop of Lyons at the time when Cagliostro was preparing to return to France in the belief that his petition to the Estates-General would be successful and that the arbitrary decree that prohibited his entry to France would be revoked. Cagliostro wanted to return to Lyons, and the Cardinal de Rohan wanted to make it easier for him. Here is his letter of recommendation:

Monseigneur,
You have often heard me speak of Count Cagliostro. As I have always spoken about his excellent qualities you will know of his love for doing good and about his virtues, which have earned and won the esteem of the most distinguished people in Alsace, and my own devotion in particular. I understand that he is currently living in Lyons under the name of Count Phœnix, and I would like to recommend him to you with the greatest enthusiasm. Whatever you could do for him would help him win the attention of a wider public. I would also ask you to tell Monsieur Caze about him. I am sure that you will develop the same feelings towards this good man that I am expressing to you. It is with a feeling of veneration that I have observed his consistent inclination towards what he thinks is good and just. I have told you everything you need to know to be able to show a particular esteem and friendship towards him, but I have not told you everything about my high regard for him.
I think Abbé Maury would have preferred us to have been in Paris [3]. I hope and desire that Cagliostro is successful in his petition, but in any case we have not done his cause any harm. I have also written in his favour to Monsieur Séguier and to Cardinal de Luynes.
You seem to think that Alsace is already resounding with rumours of war. I would like to bet that there will be war, and yet I am intimately persuaded that there will not be.
Farewell, Monseigneur, as you know I have been devoted to you for a long time now and so I shall always be, and with all my heart,
Saverne, 7th December 1789.

NOTES
(1) Letter to the Royal Praetor, Saverne, 17th July 1781, manuscripts in the Library of Strasbourg, bundle AA, 2110, document 2, Letter to the Marquise de Créquy in 1781, reported in her memoirs, and several times reproduced, cf. D'Alméras, *Cagliostro*, Paris, 1904, p. 200, amongst others.
(2) This letter is from the collection of Monsieur Alfred Sensier who authorised its reproduction in the *Revue des documents historiques*: it is from there that we have extracted it.
(3) The Cardinal had been elected a Deputy in the Estates-General. It was probably his presence in this assembly that encouraged Cagliostro to address his petition to the Estates-General.

III. LETTER FROM BARBIER DE TINAN, MUSTER-MASTER, TO THE EDITOR OF THE *CORRESPONDANCE SECRÈTE DE NEUWIED*.

Strasbourg, 21st December 1786

I am utterly astonished, Sir, that a man of letters who every day gives evidence of his ability to fill with interesting material the periodical that he is in charge of should stoop to the level of wanting to feed the malignity of the public at the expense of a man that he does not even know. I would never have believed that you would end up echoing the author of the Courrier de l'Europe and would add to the venom that his pen has distilled, in a fashion as wrongful as it is malicious, upon Count Cagliostro.

Be assured that whatever someone in London may have written to you about the alleged scorn that Cagliostro has suffered due to all these vain attacks is utterly without foundation. I am convinced that the opposite is actually the case, and the fact that we see Monsieur d'Éprémesnil, whose reputation is above reproach, and other distinguished people giving him tokens of the highest esteem and the most constant attachment is surely sufficient to counterbalance the words of Monsieur Morande and at least cause you to suspend judgement, instead of condemning him in advance to the fate of Schröpfer and Zannowich? [1]

Have no fears for him, Sir, regarding the loss of everyday resources that you assume he is suffering. You are quite wrong in that respect. I, who know Count Cagliostro well, and who like him very much and am proud of that fact, defy you to show me just one person who has agreed to contribute either directly or indirectly to his expenses since his arrival in France. It is not just from today that spiteful people have attacked him and that various people have been quoted as having supported him financially from their own personal fortunes, but there is not one of them who is not in a position to affirm, in the most solemn way possible, that nothing is less true than this allegation.

I shall not undertake, Sir, to tell you everything that is on my mind on the subject of Count Cagliostro. You seem to be too biased against him for my testimony alone to cause you to pass from the very greatest estrangement to the esteem that he deserves. I would like only to urge you to display greater moderation in his regard, both through fear of making a precipitate judgement about him and out of consideration for the many people worthy of esteem and respect who, for a long time now, have professed for him a public attachment and whom it would be very wrong to accuse of blindness in their choice of friends,

I have the honour to be, Sir, etc.
BARBIER DE TINAN, Muster-Master [2].

NOTES

(1) Amongst other nonsense it was said that Cagliostro was the brother of the impostor and adventurer Stefan Zannowich, the self-styled Prince of Albania, who long deceived the aristocracy of Poland before finally killing himself, cf. Borowski, *Cagliostro*, p. 29. [Johann Georg Schröpfer (1730-1774) was a German illusionist, Freemason and occultist. He was a pioneer of séances as a form of entertainment which he staged at his Leipzig coffee-shop using a magic-lantern to simulate ghosts. Schröpfer was allegedly driven mad by his own illusions and shot himself after promising an audience that he would come back from the dead].
(2) *Archives Sarrasin*, Basel, vol. XXXIII, document 16, 2 pp.

IV. LICENCE OF THE MOTHER-LODGE OF THE EGYPTIAN RITE FOUNDED IN LYONS BY THE GRAND COPHT

Glory.   Wisdom.

Union.

Benevolence.   Prosperity.

We, the Grand Copht, founder and Grandmaster of High Egyptian Freemasonry in all parts of the globe both oriental and occidental, hereby make known to all to whom these presents may come:

That since, during our sojourn in Lyons, several members of a lodge of this Orient following the ordinary rite and bearing the distinctive title of *La Sagesse* informed us of their burning desire to submit to our regime and to receive from us the necessary illumination and powers to know, profess and disseminate Freemasonry in its primitive true form and purity, we have readily granted their wish, having been persuaded that, by giving them this mark of benevolence and confidence, we shall have the double satisfaction of having worked for the glory of Almighty God and for the good of humanity.

For these reasons, having sufficiently established and noted with respect to the Worshipful Master and several members of the aforesaid lodge, the power and the authority which we hold for this purpose, we, with the assistance of these same brothers, do hereby found and create in perpetuity at the Orient of Lyons the present Egyptian Lodge and do constitute it the Mother-Lodge for the whole of the Orient and Occident. We attribute to it from this point onwards the distinctive title of *La Sagesse triomphante* and appoint as its perpetual and irremovable officers the following:

J. M. S. C. [1] Worshipful Master.   substitute: G. M. [2]
B. M. [3] Orator;   substitute: J. [4]
D. Secretary.   substitute A. [5]
A. [6] Keeper of the Seals.   substitute B. R.
Other members: B.G.I., M.C. and F.T.

We grant to these officers, once and for all, the right and power to hold meetings of the Egyptian Lodge with the brothers who are subject to their direction; to arrange the reception of Egyptian Apprentices, Fellow Crafts and Master Freemasons; to dispatch certificates; to maintain relations and correspondence with all the Freemasons of our Rite and the lodges upon which they depend wherever upon the Earth they might be situated; to affiliate, after due examination and the formalities prescribed by us, those lodges of the ordinary rite that might wish to embrace our regime; in a word to generally exert all the rights which can and do belong to a just and perfect Egyptian lodge enjoying the title, prerogatives and authority of Mother-Lodge.

We nevertheless enjoin the Worshipful Masters, officers and members of the lodge to take unceasing care and to devote their scrupulous attention to the work of the lodge, so that the work of reception and all other tasks generally of whatsoever nature are performed in conformity with the regulations and statutes separately dispatched by us under our signature, our Great Seal and the Seal of our Arms. We further enjoin each brother to walk constantly in the narrow path of virtue, and to show by the regularity of his conduct that he cherishes and understands the precepts of our Order.

To validate these precepts we have signed them with our hand and have affixed to them the Great Seal granted by us to this Mother-Lodge, as well as our Masonic and Profane Seals.

Done at the Orient of Lyons [7].

NOTES
(1) J.- M. Saint-Costar.
(2) Gabriel Magneval.
(3) B. Magneval.
(4) Journet *fils*.
(5) Aubergenois.
(6) Alquier.
(7) *Rituel de la Maçonnerie Égyptienne*, Manuscript from the Library of Papus, p. 91 et seq.

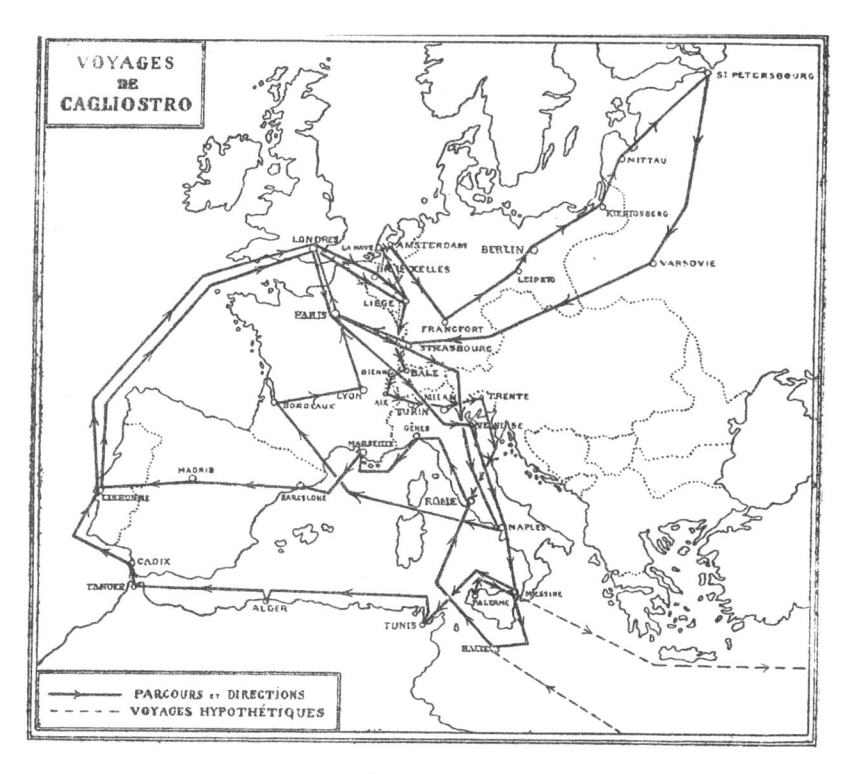

Map of Cagliostro's travels.

BIBLIOGRAPHY AND ICONOGRAPHY OF DOCUMENTS RELATING TO CAGLIOSTRO

n.d. = no date
n.p. = no place of publication
n.n. = no name of publisher

WORKS IN FRENCH

Works by or about Cagliostro:

1. Anonymous. L'arrivée du fameux Cagliostro annoncée par lui-même d'après une lettre écrite du Tirol.
n.p., n.d., (but at end of book: Paris, 1789, Garnery), octavo, 15 pp.

2. Cagliostro. Lettre du comte de Cagliostro au peuple anglais pour servir de suite à ses mémoires.
n.p., 1786 (Paris), octavo, 92 pp.
n.p., n.d., (1787), quarto, 78 pp. + 1.
Bibl. Nat.. K. 10191.

3. Cagliostro. Lettre écrite à M... par M. le comte de Cagliostro, de Londres, le 20 juin 1780.
Quarto, 4 pp.

Bibl. de l'Arsenal, Mss. 12457, folios 21 et seq.
This letter is better known as the *Lettre au peuple français* and was also published under the title of *Traduction d'une lettre du comte de Cagliostro à M. M... trouvée dans les décombres de la Bastille*. Cf. Traduction...

4. Cagliostro. Pétition du comte de Cagliostro aux États Généraux de France.
Rome, 1789. Cited in a manuscript preceding the *Rituel de la Maçonnerie égyptienne*. Bibliothèque Papus. Mss.

5. Cagliostro. Lettre écrite à Morande in : Public Advertiser, no. 16306.
London, 1786.

6. Cagliostro. Rituel de la Maçonnerie égyptienne. Cf. Manuscrits.
Some fragments of the Ritual appeared in *Initiation* in 1906-1907-1908.

7. Cagliostro. Cartel à Morande, printed in London, 3rd September 1786.

8. Cagliostro. Deuxième cartel à Morande.

These two dubious documents are presumably open letters written to Morande which appear in extract in the *Public Advertiser* and the *Courrier de l'Europe* and in full in the *Lettre au peuple anglais*. We have severe doubts that they were ever printed separately as the author of this citation alleges. Preface to the Mss. Of Egyptian Freemasonry, Bibl. Papus.

9. Cagliostro. Mémoire pour le comte de Cagliostro accusé contre M. le Procureur général accusateur.
Paris, Lottin, 1786, octavo, 51 pp.
Paris, n.n., 1786, quarto.
n.p. 1786, sixteenmo, 80 pp.

10. Cagliostro. Mémoire pour le comte de Cagliostro demandeur contre Me Chesnon, et le Sieur de Launay, gouverneur de la Bastille.
Paris, 1786, Lottin, octavo, 64 pp.
Paris, 1788, Lottin, quarto, 37 pp.

11. Cagliostro. Requête au Parlement les chambres assemblées, signifiée le 24 février 1786 par le comte de Cagliostro.
Paris, 1786, quarto, 4 pp.
Liège, 1786, octavo, 4 pp.

12. Cagliostro. Requête à joindre au mémoire du comte de Cagliostro. À Nos seigneurs...
Paris, 30th May 1786, quarto, 11 pp.
Paris, 30th May 1786, octavo.

13. Cagliostro. Réponse à la pièce importante dans l'affaire De Launay... par le comte de Cagliostro.
Paris, Lottin, 1787, quarto, 25 pp.

14. Cagliostro. Requête au roi pour le comte de Cagliostro, contre Me Chesnon et de Launay.
Paris, Lottin, 1st February 1787, quarto, 72 pp.

15. Cagliostro. Deuxième requête au roi pour le comte de Cagliostro contre M. Chesnon (1).
Paris, Lottin, (15th February), 1787, quarto, 8 pp.

16. Cagliostro. Confessions (apocryphal). Cf. Confessions.

17. Cagliostro. Lettre écrite d'Aix (apocryphal). Cf. Lettre.

18. Cagliostro. Mémoires authentiques (apocryphal). Cf. Mémoires.

19. Cagliostro. Testament de mort (apocryphal). Cf. Testament.

20. Anonymous. Cagliostro (Alexandre, comte de). Notice extraite d'un dictionnaire

biographique contemporain.
n.p., n.d., (1787 or 1788) quarto, 2 pp.

21. Anonymous (Comte Moszyński). Cagliostro démasqué à Varsovie ou Relation authentique de ses opérations dans cette capitale en 1780 par un témoin oculaire.
n.p., 1786, duodecimo, III + 62 pp. + 1.
Translated into German by J. F. Bertrich, n.p., 1789.

22. Anonymous (R...). Le Charlatan démasqué ou les aventures et exploits du comte de Cagliostro précédé d'une lettre de Mirabeau.
Frankfurt am Main, 1786, octavo.
Frankfurt am Main, 1786, sixteenmo, 62 pp.
By a 'mischievous abbé', Cf. Borowski, p. 29.
This was also translated into German.

23. Anonymous. Confessions du comte de C... avec l'histoire de ses voyages en Russie, Turquie.... etc., et dans les pyramides d'Égypte.
Cairo and Paris, 1787, duodecimo.
Cairo and Paris, 1787, quarto, 57 pp.
Cairo and Paris, 1787, new edition.
Bibl. Nat., Y^2 23627.

24. D'Alméras. Cagliostro.
Paris, Soc. franç. d'imprimerie, 1904, sixteenmo, 384 pp.

25. De Mirabeau. Lettre du comte de Mirabeau à M.M... sur MM. de Cagliostro et Lavater.
Berlin, chez Fr. de Lagarde, 1786, octavo, 48-xiii pp.
Frankfurt am Main, 1786, sixteenmo, 30 pp.
There is also a German edition. Berlin, 1786, octavo, 103 pp.

26. Anonymous. La dernière pièce du fameux Collier.
n.p., n.d. (Paris 1786), octavo, 45 pp.
Paris, 1787, quarto, 34 pp.

27. De Saint-Félix. Aventures de Cagliostro.
Paris, Hachette, 1854, duodecimo, 160 pp.
Paris, Hachette, 1855, duodecimo, 160 pp.

28. Haven (Dr Marc). L'Évangile de Cagliostro retrouvé, traduit et publié avec une introduction et un portrait.
Paris, Librairie Hermétique, 1910, sixteenmo, 86 pp.

29. Anonymous (Manuel L.-P.). Lettre d'un garde du roi pour servir de suite aux mémoires sur Cagliostro.
n.p., 1786, octavo.
London, 1786, sixteenmo, 1 + 34 pp. (2nd edition).

Bibliography and Iconography

Cf. *La magie de Cagliostro.*

30. Anonymous. Lettre écrite de Aix-les-Bains en Savoie à M. de Beaumarchais, par M. Cagliostro contenant des faits intéressants... (Apocryphal).
Kell, 1788, octavo, 16 pp.
Bibl. Nat., Ln[27] 1318.

31. Anonymous (Morande). Ma correspondance avec le comte de Cagliostro.
Milan (Paris), n.d., quarto, 38 pp., 1st edition.
Milan (Paris) 1786, quarto, 38 pp., 2nd edition.

32. Anonymous (Morande.) Suite de ma correspondance avec le comte de Cagliostro par lequel il est prouvé que le comte et le sieur Balsamo, etc.
Milan (Paris), 1786, quarto, 16 pp., Aux dépens de la société Cagliostrienne, Hamburg, 1786, octavo, 96 pp. Contains *Ma Correspondance* and the *Suite réunies.*

33. Anonymous. La magie de Cagliostro dévoilée par lui-même, ou révélation des intrigues mises en usage dans l'affaire du Collier.
London (Paris), 1789, octavo, 49 pp.
Bibl. Nat., Lb[39] 11101.
Republication under a different title of *Lettre d'un garde du roi.*

34. Anonymous. Mémoire pour servir à l'histoire du comte de Caglyostro [sic] au sujet de l'affaire du Cardinal de Rohan, évêque et prince de Strasbourg.
Strasbourg, 1786, octavo, 40 pp.
Republication under a different title of the *Mémoires authentiques.*

35. Anonymous (De Luchet). Mémoires authentiques pour servir à l'histoire du comte de Cagliostro faisant suite au Mémoire de la Comtesse de la Motte-Valois.
n.p., 1785, duodecimo (Paris), 1st edition.
London, 1785, octavo (Paris), 1st edition.
2nd edition: n.p., 1786, octavo (Paris), 36 pp.
New edition, n.p., 1786, sixteenmo, 66 pp.
Strasbourg, 1786, octavo.
Hamburg, Fauche, 1786, octavo, 95 pp.
For information about the author De Luchet see Grimm, *Corresp. littéraire*, Paris 1813, octavo, vol. III, pp. 248 & 424.

36. Motus (P. J. N.). Réflexions sur le mémoire ou roman qui a paru en février 1780 pour le comte de Cagliostro.
Medina (Paris), 1786, octavo, 48 pp.

37. Anonymous. Procès comique et instructif pendant entre le fameux Cagliostro et le sieur de Morande.
1st part (the only part to appear).
London, 1787.

38. Anonymous. Procès de Joseph Balsamo surnommé le comte de Cagliostro, commencé devant le Tribunal de la Sainte-Inquisition en décembre 1790 et jugé définitivement le 7 avril 1791.
Liège, Tutot, 1791, duodecimo, 295 pp.
This is the *Vie de Joseph Balsamo* under another title.

39. Anonymous. Les Prodiges de Cagliostro (J. Balsamo) à Strasbourg, Bordeaux, Paris.
n.p., n.d., duodecimo.

40. Anonymous. Les Prophéties de saint Cagliostro et son arrivée à Paris.
n.d. (around 1786), duodecimo.
Cited in: Catalogue Astier, Paris, 1856, octavo, p. 18, no. 135.

41. Sachi (Carlo). Mémoire sur le comte de Cagliostro.
Partially quoted by Madame de la Motte in her *Sommaire* and her *Réponse*. — Drafted by the advocate Rochebourne.
Strasbourg, sixteenmo, 1782.

42. Spach. Cagliostro à Strasbourg (Talk given on the 9th November 1889).
Œuvres, Paris and Strasbourg, Berger-Levrault, 1871, octavo. Vol. V. Biographies Alsaciennes, pp. 61-80.

43. Anonymous. Testament de mort et déclarations faites par Cagliostro, de la secte des illuminés et se disant chef de la Loge égyptienne...
Paris, 1791, octavo, 44 pp.
Bibl. Nat., K. 10192 bis.

44. Anonymous. Traduction d'une lettre du comte de Cagliostro à M. M... trouvée dans les décombres de la Bastille.
Paris, impr. de Lourmel, n.d., octavo, 7 pp.
Bibl. Nat., Lb[39], 7384.
This is the *Lettre au Peuple français*.

45. Anonymous (Father Marcello S.J.). Vie de Joseph Balsamo, connu sous le nom de comte de Cagliostro, extraite de la procédure instruite contre lui à Rome en 1790, imprimé à la Chambre apostolique.
Paris, Onfroy and Strasbourg, Treuttel & Wurtz.
1st edition, 1791, octavo, 1 f., portrait, xxvi-239 pp.
2nd edition, ibid., 1791.
There are translations into Italian and German.

WORKS IN LANGUAGES OTHER THAN FRENCH

46. Anonymous. Gli arcani svelati o sia il Cagliostrismo smascherato dove si dimostrano i fonti dell'impieta della pretesa scienza occulta...
Venice, at the author's expense, 1791, octavo, 180 pp.

47. Anonymous (Ludw. E. Borowski). Cagliostro, einer der merkwürdigsten Abentheurer

unsres Iahrhunderts. Seine Geschichte, nebst Raisonnement...
Königsberg, 1790, G.-L. Hartung, small sixteenmo, portrait, title-page, vi-190 pp.
2nd edition, same year, other details as above.

48. Anonymous (J-F. Bertuch.) Cagliostro in Warschau oder Tagebuch... aus dem französichen übersetzt (Cagliostro démasqué à Varsovie).
Königsberg, 1785, octavo.
n.p., 1786, octavo.
Strasbourg, 1786, octavo (No. 27 of Hayn), 11 ff. 44 pp.

49. Cagliostro (Madame). Auch noch etwas für ordens und nichtordens Leute durch das Rosensystem numehro beyderley Geschlechte.
Philadelphia, 178... (sic), octavo in 2 parts. 1, vii-272 & ii-302 pp.

50. Anonymous (Father Marcello S.J.). Compendio della vita et delle geste di Giuseppe Balsamo, denominato il conte Cagliostro che siè estratta dal processo contro di lui formato in Roma Tanno 1790.
Roma, Stamperia della rev. Camera apostolica, 1791, octavo, 216 pp.
The same book is also found, with the same publication details, under the title *Vita di Giuseppe Balsamo*.
Id. Venice, 1791, octavo, 216 pp.
This book was translated into French, German and Spanish.

51. Anonymous. Compendio de la vida y hechos de Jos. Balsamo llamado el conde Calliostro.
Seville, 1791, octavo.
Spanish translation of the previous entry.

52. Anonymous. Corrispondenza segreta sulla vita publica e privata del conte di Cagliostro con le sue aventure e viaggi in diverse parti del mondo.
Venice, 1791, duodecimo.
n.p. (Venice), 1791, octavo, at the author's expense (with portrait and plates).

53. Anonymous (Bode). Ein paar Tröpflein aus dem Brunnen der Wahrheit ausgegossen vor dem neuen Thaumaturgen Cagliostro.
An Vorgebirge, 1781, octavo, 46 pp. (Frankfurt am Main, Brönnert).

54. Anonymous. Der entlarvte Charlatan.
Frankfurt am Main, 1787, octavo, 87 pp.
German translation of *Le Charlatan démasqué*.

55. Funck-Brentano. Cagliostro and Company. (Extracts from *L'Affaire du Collier*).
Translated by O. Maidment.
London, 1902, small sixteenmo, 10 plates.

56. Hildebrandt (L.). Merkwürdige Abenteuer des Grafen Alex. von Cagliostro.
Quedlinburg, n.d. (1839), octavo, 224 pp.

57. Hugo Hayn. Vier neue Curiositäten Bibliographien.
Jena, 1905, Schmidts, octavo, 88 pp.
Containts in part III, pp. 25-55, a bibliography on the Diamond Necklace Affair and on Cagliostro.
Bibl. Nat., 8° Q. 3395.

58. Anonymous. Kurzer Begriff von dem Lebe und den Thaten des J. Balsamo.
Rome (Zürich, Orell), 1791, octavo, 231 pp.
Graz, n.d. (1792), octavo.
German translation of the *Vie de Joseph Balsamo*.

59. Anonymous. Kurzgefasste Beschreibung des Lebens Jos. Balsamo... aus dem lateinischen (sic) übersetzt.
Augsburg, 1791, octavo, 112 + 120 pp.
Ibid., same date, octavo, J. Nepom. Stage, translated from the Italian.
Ibid., same date, octavo, 2nd edition.
Translation of the *Vie de Joseph Balsamo*.

60. Anonymous. Ist Kagliostro chef der Illuminaten? oder das Buch....
Gotha, Ettinger, 1790, sixteenmo, xvi-228 pp.
Translation by J.-J. Bode with notes of *Essai sur la secte des Illuminés* by De Luchet.

61. Anonymous. Istoria critica della vita del Conte di Cagliostro e della contessa sua Moglie prigionieri... alla Bastiglia.
n.p., 1786, duodecimo.

62. Anonymous. Lebensgeschichte Gefangennehmung und gerichtliches Verhör des Grafen Cagliostro von ihm selbst geschrieben.
Vienna, 1786, octavo.
Translation from French of *Mémoires authentiques*.

63. Anonymous. Leben und Thaten des Joseph Balsamo sogenannten Grafen Cagliostro; nebst einigen Nachrichten über die Beschaffenheit und den Zustand des Freymaurersekten...
Translated from the Italian by C. J. J. (Chr. J. Jagermann), Frankenthal, 1791, octavo, xii-171 pp.
Id. — Zurich, 1791, octavo, xii-171 pp.
Id. — Weimar, chez Hoffmann, 1791, octavo, in 2 parts.
Id. — Augsburg & Vienna, 1791 (Cf. Tschink).
Id. — Mannheim, Löjfer, 1814, octavo.

64. Anonymous. (Clementi Vannetti.) Liber memorialis de Caleostro cum esset Roboreti (L'Évangile de Cagliostro).
(At the end of the book: Mori, printed by Steph. Tedolini, 1789), small octavo, 31 pages.
Id. — Venice, n.d. (1791), J. Sfort, octavo, 36 pp., portrait.
Bibl. Nat.: refused (1T).

A French translation of this by Dr. Marc Haven was published in Paris, 1910, sixteenmo.

65. Anonymous (Lucia ?). The life of the count Cagliostro (1776-1787) dedicated to Mme la comtesse de Cagliostro.
London, T. Hookham, 1787, octavo, viii-xii-127 pp.
A rare defence of Cagliostro probably attributable to O'Reilly or one of his friends.

66. Anonymous (Cagliostro). Manifesto for the Freemasons (in English and code) in :
Morning Herald, London, 1786, issue of 2nd November.

67. Anonymous. Manifesto di Giuseppe Balsamo denominato il conte Cagliostro o sue difese contro il di lui processo formato dalla S. Inquisizione di Roma.
Translation from the French.
n.p., 1790, octavo, 33 pp.
Bibl. Nat., K. 15148.

68. Anonymous. Memoiren von Cagliostro.
Edited by Paul Bernstein.
Leipzig & Berlin, n.d.., octavo.

69. Anonymous. Memorie del conte di Cagliostro prigioniero alla Bastiglia e supposto implicato nel processo dei cardinale di Rohano.
n.p., 1786, duodecimo.
n.p., 1786, octavo, 100 pp.

70. Anonymous. Nachrichten æchte von dem Grafen Cagliostro aus der Handschrift seines entflohenen Kammerdieners.
Berlin, 1786, octavo, 2 copperplate engravings.

71. Anonymous. Nachrichten glaubwürdige zur Geschichte des Grafen Cagliostro.
Translation of the *Mémoires authentiques*.
n.p., 1786, octavo.

72. Anonymous. Saggio storico del conte di Cagliostro e della contessa sua moglie.
Cosmopoli, 1791, octavo, 56 pp., two badly-executed portraits.

73. E. Tschink (Cajetan). Unparteyische Prüfung des zu Rom erschienen kurzen Inbegriffs von dem Leben und Thaten Jos. Balsamo's.
Vienna, Kaiserer, 1791, octavo.
Translation of the *Vie de Joseph Balsamo*.

74. Anonymous. Vertheidigungschrift für den Grafen Alexander von Cagliostro.
n.p. (Basel), 1786, octavo.
German translation of the *Mémoire du comte de Cagliostro contre le procureur général...*
The other memoirs and petitions relating to the trial have also been translated into German.
Id. — Frankfurt am Main, 1786, octavo.

75. Von de Recke. Nachricht von des berüchtigten Cagliostro's Aufenthalte in Mitau im Jahre 1779 und von dessen magischen Operationen.
Berlin & Stettin, Friedrich Nicolai, 1787.
Small octavo, xxxii-168 pp.

76. Von der Recke. Geschiedverhaal van het verblijf van dem besuchter Graaf von Cagliostro...
Amsterdam, P. Boddaert... 1791, LXII-221 pp., octavo, portrait engraved by Tokke.
A Dutch translation of the previous entry.

WORKS IN FRENCH
II. Part-studies — References — Newspaper articles

77. Anonymous (Thory). Acta Latomorum.
Paris. 1812, 2 vols., octavo.
Vol. II, pp. 109 et seq. Discussion with the *Philalèthes*.

78. Anonymous. Cagliostro et l'affaire du Collier in: Revue du psychisme expérimental.
Nos. 4 & 5 of Year 1, Paris, 1911, with engravings.

79. Beugnot (comte). Mémoires (1783-1815).
Paris, Dentu. 1866, 2 vols. octavo. Several reprintings.
Vol. I. Diamond Necklace Affair: pp. 1-80.
Bibl. Nat., 8° La^{31} 7.

80. Bulau (Fréd.). — Personnages énigmatiques.
Paris, Poulet Malassis, 1861, 3 vols., duodecimo.
Vol I, pp. 306-329.

81. Gampardon (Émile). Marie-Antoinette et le procès du Collier.
Paris, Plon, 1863, octavo.
P. 36. Count Cagliostro.
Pp. 337 et seq. Interrogation of Cagliostro in the Bastille.
Pp. 410 et seq. Documents relating to Commissary Fontaine.

82. Courrier de l'Europe, Morande's newspaper, twice-weekly.
London, quarto.
Issues from 22nd August 1786 to 25th June 1787.
Bibl. Nat., Nd. 34.

83. Damman (W.) Cagliostro au Ban de la Roche.
Article in: Revue Alsacienne illustrée, 1910, no. 11.

84. De Bachaumont. Mémoires secrets pour servir à l'histoire de la République des lettres en France depuis 1762 jusqu'à nos jours.
London, 1783, 33 vols., duodecimo.

See vols. XVII & XXXIII.
Bibl. Nat., Z. 16858-16891.

85. De Gleichen (C.-H.).—Souvenirs.
P. Techener, 1868, duodecimo, 227 pp.
Cf. pp. 135 et seq.
This was also published in German, Leipzig, 1847, large octavo.

86. De La Motte-Valois (comte). Mémoires inédits sur sa vie et son époque.
Paris, Poulet Malassis, 1858, duodecimo.

87. D'Oberkirch (baronne). — Mémoires sur la cour de Louis XVI.
Brussels, Comptoir des éditeurs, 1854, 2 vols., octavo.
Vol. I, chap. vii.
Bibl. Nat., 8° Lb^{39} 66.

88. Dugast de Bois Saint-Just. Paris, Versailles et les provinces au XVIII siècle.
Paris, Gosselin, 1823, 3 vols., octavo.
A chapter on Cagliostro in vol. I, p. 329.
Bibl. Nat.. 8° La^{30}8A.

89. La Feuille Villageoise. A weekly newspaper published by Cérutti.
1791, no. 34, p. 129.
Bibl. Nat., LC^2 463.

90. Figuier. Histoire du merveilleux.
Paris, Hachette, 1861, 4 vols., sixteenmo.
Vol. IV, pp. 1 et seq.

91. Anonymous. Une fille de Cagliostro.
Article in: *Le Figaro* of 13th May 1858.

92. F. Funck-Brentano. L'affaire du Collier.
Paris, Hachette 1902, 4th edition, octavo, 352 pp.
Pp. 86 et seq.

93. Gagnière (A.). Cagliostro et les Francs-Maçons devant l'Inquisition.
Article: in *Nouvelle Revue*, 1903, pp. 25-56, octavo.

94. Gazette nationale ou Moniteur Universel. Issues of 8th June 1791 (no. 159) and 6th October 1795 (no. 14).
Bibl. Mat., Lc^2 113.

95. Gazette d'Amsterdam, for the years 1785-1786.
Bibl. Nat., Inv^{re} G. 4385.

96. Georgel (Abbé). Mémoires pour servir à l'histoire des événements de la fin du XVIII

siècle.
Paris, 1817, 6 vols., octavo.

97. Grimm & Diderot. Correspondance littéraire, philosophique et critique adressée à un souverain depuis 1753 jusqu'en 1790.
Paris, Longchamps, 1813, 4 vols. octavo.
Bibl. Nat., Z, 15488-15492.

98. Haven (Dr. Marc). Les Critiques de Cagliostro.
Article in: *Initiation*, February 1910.

99. Haven (Dr. Marc). Quelques documents nouveaux sur le comte de Cagliostro.
Article in: *Initiation*, December 1905.

100. Heyking. Le comte de Cagliostro parmi les Russes.
Article in: *Initiation*, August 1898.

101. Journal de Paris. Supplements of Monday 31st December 1781 and Monday 27th January 1783 containing the letters by Wieland and Sarrazin.
Quarto.
Bibl. Nat. Lc² 80.

102. Labande. Un diplomate français à la cour de Catherine II (1775-1780).
Paris, Plon, 1901, 2 vols., octavo.

103. Anonymous (De Laborde). Lettres d'un voyageur français en Suisse adressées à Mme M... en 1781.
Geneva, 1783, 2 vols., octavo, and Geneva, 1784, 3 vols., octavo. Vol. I.

104. Lenotre. Paris révolutionnaire. Vieilles maisons, vieux papiers, 1re série.
Paris, Perrin, 1900, octavo.
Pp. 161-172: La maison de Cagliostro (Cagliostro's house).

105. Le Roy de Ste-Croix. Les quatre cardinaux de Rohan.
Strasbourg, 1881, octavo, 202 pp.
Bibl. Nat., 4°. Lm³ 2594.

106. Ma Correspondance (twice-weekly newspaper), 1785-1786.
2 vols., duodecimo, I, nos. 1-52. II, 53-106.
Bibl. Nat., Lc² 93.

107. Mercure de France (Le). (Magazine).
1785-86-87, & May 1791.
Bibl. Nat., Lc² 39.

108. Métra. Correspondance secrète, politique et littéraire (1775-1793).
Neuwied, 1793, 19 vols., small octavo. Cf : vol. XVIII.

Bibl. Nat., Lc² 77.

109. Nouvelles politiques publiées à Leyde. Magazine, 1786.
Bibl. Nat., Inv^re M. 9961-9968.

110. Anonymous. Personnages bizarres et singuliers.
Paris, 1868, duodecimo.
Contains a study of Cagliostro.

111. The Public Advertiser (Journal).
London, 1786, no. 16306, challenge to Morande.

112. Robertson. Mémoires récréatifs scientifiques, etc... du physicien aéronaute E.-G. Robertson (Robert).
Paris, 1831, 2 vols., octavo.

113. Robiquet. Théveneau de Morande.
Paris, Quantin, octavo.
Cf. pp. 189 et seq.
Bibl. Nat., Ln²⁷ LnST, 33240.

114. Rodocanachi. Le Château Saint-Ange.
Paris, Hachette, folio, 1909.
Cf. p. 238.
Bibl. Nat., Fol. K. 317.

115. Anonymous. Travaux de Cagliostro à Lyons.
Article in *Initiation*, March 1906.

WORKS IN LANGUAGES OTHER THAN FRENCH

116. Ademollo (A). Cagliostro e i Liberi Muratori.
Article in *Nuova Antologia*, Rome, 1881. vol. XXVI, fascicule VIII, p. 622.
Bibl. Nat., 8° Z. 41.

117. Allgemeine Encyclopädie des Wissenschaften und Kunst von Ersch und Gruber.
Halle.
Contains, in cahier C, pp. 75 et seq., a bibliography on Cagliostro.

118. Allgemeine Zeitung (Revue.)
Year 1894. Supplements nos. 64, 65 & 67. Letters from Burkli about Cagliostro.

119. Berlinische Monatsschrift (Gedike & J. E. Biester).
Berlin, 1784, December, pp. 538 et seq. A visit to Cagliostro.
1786, May, pp. 385, 398. Article by Countess von der Recke.
1787, November, pp. 449, 458. Article on his visit to Switzerland.

120. Bucholz (C. F.) Historiche Denkwürdigkeiten aus Kriminal Prozessen... II Theile.

Perth, K. A. Hartleben. 1816, octavo.
Part I no. 2, pp. 34, 73.

121. Bulau (Fred). Geschichten geheime und räthselhafte Menschen.
Leipzig, F.-A. Brockhaus, 1850, octavo. Cf. vol. I.

122. Carlyle. Count Cagliostro. Flight First and Flight Last.
Articles in: Fraser's Magazine, July 1883, pp. 19-28, & August 1823, pp. 132, 155.
All these articles were collectively reprinted in vol. III of Critical and miscellaneous essays of Carlyle, London, 1847.
Bibl. Nat., Z. 44799.

123. Cesari (Ant.). Vita di Clementi Vannetti.
Verona, 1818, octavo, 187 pp. Cf. pp. 120 et seq. Cagliostro's stay in Rovereto.

124. Il Chracas (or Krakas). (Newspaper.)
Years 1790 & 1795. Articles on the trial and death of Cagliostro.

125. Cummerow. Graf Cagliostro alias Joseph Balsamo aus Palermo.
Article in: Westermann's Monatschrift, Braunschweig, Year 1893.

126. Deutscher Merkur, edited by Wieland.
Year 1791. Biography of Cagliostro.

127. Deutsches Museum (Magazine.)
1787, no. 13, pp. 387 et seq.
Letter from Schlosser about Cagliostro.

128. D. P. (Picenardi). Del Cagliostro secondo i documenti diplomatici sardi.
Article in: Curiosità e ricerche di Storia Subalpina.

129. Ephemeriden der Freymaurerei (Magazine.)
Contains, on p. 109, the letter from Chevalier Langlois about his cure.

130. Ephemeriden der Menschheit (Magazine.)
Year 1782, vol. II, pp. 471-484.
Contains an article on Cagliostro.

131. Evans (Henry Ridgely). Cagliostro, a study in charlatanism.
Article in: *The Monist*, Vol. XIII, July 1903.
Chicago, octavo, pp. 523-552, with engravings.

132. Frankfürter gelehrte Anzeiger (Magazine.)
Frankfurt am Main, 1787, issue of 5th June. Article on Cagliostro.

133. Funk (Heinrich). Die Wanderjahre der Frau von Branconi.
Article in: Westermann's Monatschriften, November 1895.

134. Funk (Heinrich). Lavater und Cagliostro.
Article in: Nord und Süd Berliner.
Berlin, October 1897.

135. Funk (Heinrich). Cagliostro à Strasbourg.
Article in: Archiv. für Kultur-Geschichte, 1906, vol. III, pp. 223-234.

136. Goethe (J. W.) Neue Schriften.
Berlin, J. F. Unger, 1794-1800, seven vols., octavo.
Vol. I, no. 2. Balsamo's family-tree.

137. Das Graue Ungeheuer (Newspaper.)
Editor: Wekherlin, small octavo.
1785, vol. V, no. 15, pp. 331 & 1786, vol. VII, no. 20. p. 157.
Articles against Cagliostro.

138. Hartmann (Dr Franz). Cagliostro. Article which fiirst appeared in *The Occult Review* translated in *La Verdad*, Year V, no. 60, April 1910, pp. 543-546. 2 columns with an unusual portrait.

139. Hesekiel (G.). Abenteuerliche Gesellen.
Berlin, 1862, octavo, 2 vols.
Vol. I, no. 2 : Cagliostro.

140. Hegner (Ulrich). Beiträge zur wahren Kenntnis und wahren Darstellung Joh. Kaspar Lavaters aus Briefen seiner Freunde.
Contains, pp. 137 et seq., a letter from Matthaei to Lavater about Cagliostro.

141. Journal von und für Deutschland.
December 1788, pp. 516-520. Article on Cagliostro.

142. Kekule von Stradonitz (Stephan). Goethe als Genealog.
Berlin, 1900, square sixteenmo, 18 pp.
Genealogy of J. Balsamo.

143. Langmesser. Jacob Sarrasin der Freund Lavaters (Thesis).
Zurich, 1899, large octavo, pp. 24-153.

144. Martins (Dr. Em. Wilhelm). Erinnerungen aus meinem neunzigjährigen Leben.
Leipzig, Leop. Voss, 1847, small octavo.
Cf. pp. 74-77.

145. Medizinisches Wochenblatt (Revue).
Frankfurt am Main, octavo. Cf. issue of 11 February 1786.

146. Meiners (C.) Briefe über die Schweiz (6 parts, 4 volumes).

Vienna, 1791, octavo, illustrated. 2nd part.

147. Anonymous. Menschen berühmte und ihre Geschichte.
Berlin, 1894, octavo in 10 parts.
Contains a study of Cagliostro by Bernstein.

148. Oberrheinische Mannigfaltigkeiten (Newspaper.)
1781, 2nd quarter, part I, p. 113, part XI, p. 161.

149. Pitaval (Der neue). Translation into German from French of Le nouveau Pitaval by Hitzig & Wilibald.
Leipzig, 1845, octavo, vol. I, p. 1.
Cagliostro and the Diamong Necklace affair.
Another translation by Lud. Hain under the title *Lebensbeschreibungen und Criminalprozesse* was published in Leipzig by Kollman in 1846,
3 vols., octavo, cf. vol II. Cagliostro.

150. Richard (H.-A.-O.) Cahiers de lecture, IV fascicules (all that appeared).
Gotha, Ettinger, 1786, octavo.
Contains a study of Cagliostro.

151. Scala (Alessandro). Lo Stemma del conte Cagliostro.
Article in: Rivista del Collegio Araldico.
Rome, 1905, Year III, no. 10, October.

152. Schlosser. Schreiben an Herrn N... über eine in dem Grauen Ungeheuer no. 20 enthaltene Stelle um Grafen Cagliostro. Article in: Deutsches Museum, January 1787, no.13, p. 387 et seq.

153. Schultz (Em.) Cagliostro und Consorten.
Berlin, 1894, octavo, 10 pp.
Article in a magazine.

154. Seyboth (Ad.) Das alte Strassburg.
Strasbourg, S. A (1890) Heitz, quarto, cf. p. 236.

155. Sierke (E). Schwärmer und Schwindler am Ende des 18e Iahrhunderts.
Leipzig, 1874, large octavo.

156. Silvagni (D). La Corte et la Società Romana.
Florence, 1882, octavo.
Vol. I, p. 298.

157. Sommi Picenardi (Marchese). Ricordo di Cagliostro a San Leo.
Article in: *Rivista di Scienze Storiche*, Pavia, June 1905.

158. Sylvestre (Julien). Interessante Enthüllungen.

London & Berlin, H. F. Smith. n.d. (1860), octavo, pp. 95- 101. Note on Cagliostro.

159. Türler (Dr Heinrich) Neues Berner Taschenbuch (1901).
Bern, K. J. Wyss, 1900, sixteenmo.
Cf. pp. 110-118, Cagliostro in Bienne.

160. Von der Recke. Etwas ueber des Herrn Oberhofprediger J. Aug. Stark Vertheidigungschrift nebst einigen andern nöthigen Erläuterungen.
Berlin, Ebend, 1787, octavo.

161. Weisstein (G.) Cagliostro à Strasbourg.
Article in: Elsass Lothringische Zeitung, 1882, no. 37.

MANUSCRIPTS

162. Private library of Dr. Papus. *Rituel de la maçonnerie égyptienne* by Cagliostro. The original quarto is lost. The Papus Library copy is a folio but the pagination follows the original. This is the copy we have been able to inspect thanks to the kindness of our friend Papus. René Philipon has another copy.
Some fragments were published in *Initiation*, August 1906 to April 1908.

163. Archives Nationales. Interrogations of Cagliostro in the Bastille. X^2B 1417 (formerly F^7 4445 B & 4450). Fontaine's document on the J. Balsamo affair. Y. 13125. Other documents on the Diamond Necklace Affair as it relates to Cagliostro. O^1 598.

164. Bibliothèque de l'Arsenal. Manuscripts of the Bastille.
Classification: 1785. B.
I. Mss. 12457. Five documents om the detention of Cagliostro and the Countess in the Bastille.
II. Mss. 12458. 12459. Catalogue of pamphlets, brochures, memoirs and lampoons relating to Cagliostro and the Diamond Necklace Affair in the Bibliothèque de l'Arsenal.
III. Mss. 12517. Note relating to the illness of the Countess in the Bastille, folio 126.
(Classification: 1786. B.)

165. Bibliothèque Nationale. Mss. in French, 6685. Diary of the bookseller Hardy.

166. Bibliothèque de la ville de Paris. Manuscrits. Dossier Target. In the Reserve.

167. Bibliothèque de la ville de Bâle. Archives Sarrasin. Comprising the diary of Sarrasin and his correspondence. These archives, formerly conserved by the Sarrasin famiy, have been donated to the City of Basel. We find there letters by Sarrasin, and above all letters addressed to him by Lavater, Matthaei, De Gingin, etc., which shed remarkable light on the life and activities of Cagliostro. There is also a letter from Cagliostro, a letter from his wife, some portraits and some documents.

168. Bibliothèque de la ville de Strasbourg. Manuscrits. Bundle AA 2110. Documents, leters and reports on the Ostertag affair and the Sachi affair, a letter about Cagliostro from the Cardinal de Rohan, from Barbier de Tinan and other officials.

169. Bibliotheca. Naz. Vittorio Emanuele à Rome. Cod. Mss. 245. Scritture circa il processo di Giuseppe Balsamo.
Information taken from the work of Rodocanachi on the Castel Sant'Angelo.

170. Private library of M. Bréghot du Lut (at Confolens, Drôme). Letters from Salzmann to Willermoz about his visit to Cagliostro in 1780.

PORTRAITS OF CAGLIOSTRO
171. Bust by Houdon. This is currently (1912) in the Museum of Aix-en-Provence: no. 776. A plaster-cast was given to Me Thilorier and in 1902 formed part of the collections of Monsieur Storelli in Blois.

172. Portrait. I. Drawn from nature by Guérin, engraved Devère, Paris, available from the artist, 17 Rue des Grands-Degrés, and from Mademoiselle Le Beau, merchant at the Palais Royal.
Announced as a novelty in the *Mercure de France* of 18 March 1786, with these lines:

L'homme dans chaque siècle a connu les prestiges ;
Ce docteur que tu vois a profité des siens :
Il étudia l'homme et, grand magicien,
Sur l'ignorance humaine il fonda ses prodiges.

(In each century man has achieved various kinds of fame. This doctor you're looking at certainly made the best of his. He studied man and, being a great magician, based his 'miracles' on human credulity).
Quarto.

173. Idem, drawn by Guérin and engraved by Thœnert.
Octavo.

174. Idem, drawn by Guérin and engraved by Duhamel.
Paris, Esnault & Rapilly.
Quarto.

175. Portrait. — II. Engraved portrait: Le comte de Cagliostro.
On sale in Augsburg, duodecimo.

175b, Idem — IIb. Engraved portrait, octavo. Legend reads, 'Pour savoir ce qu'il est, il faudrait être lui-même', ('You would need to be him to understand what he is') .

176. Portrait. — III. Engraved portrait, hand-coloured with the coat of arms of Cagliostro.

177. Portrait. — IV. Engraved portrait in blue by Pariset after a painting by Boudeville, sixteenmo.
'Dedicated to Madame Seraphina Felichiani [sic]' with these verses:
Du comte Cagliostro dévoilons le mystère.

Il veut, c'est pour le bien; il peut, c'est pour le faire.
('Let's unveil the mystery of Count Cagliostro. If he wants to do something, he does it for the common good. If he can do something, then he'll do it').
Bibl. Nat. Estampes. Collect. Hennin. 138.

178. Portrait. — V. Portrait engraved by Vinsac after a portrait from nature by Pujos (1786).
Mezzotint. Cagliostro is shown wearing a fur-coat.

178b. Idem. — Vb. The same. 'S^a W^a Evans, sculp^t· A. Loosjes. P. Z., exc$^{t.}$'
Engraved portrait.

179. Portrait. — VI. Portrait engraved by Bonneville, Paris, rue du Théâtre Français.
Octavo.

180. Portrait. — VII. Mezzotint portrait with, below, the words 'le comte de Cagliostro' and these verses :
De l'ami des humains reconnaissez les traits.
Tous ses jours sont marqués par de nouveaux bienfaits,
Il prolonge la vie, il secourt l'indigence,
Le plaisir d'être utile est seul sa récompense.
('Recognise the features of a true friend of humanity. All his days are marked by new acts of kindness. He prolongs people's lives, helps the poor. The pleasure of being useful is his sole reward'.)
Engraved by J.-B. Chapuy. 'Brion de la Tour del$^{t.}$'
Basset, rue Saint-Jacques.
Quarto.

181. Portrait. — VIII. Physiognotrace (4T). Black silhouette.

182. Portrait. — IX. Lithograph portrait by Wittmann.
The same produced as a lithograph by the printer Aubert (cabinet de lecture).

183. Portrait. — X. Portrait engraved by Bollinger, octagonal frame.
Zwickau, Gabr. Schumann.

184. Portrait. — XI. Portrait engraved by Leclère after a contemporary painting, Collection de la galerie historique de Versailles, folio.
Portrait in town-dress, head lowered.

185. Portrait. — XII. Portrait engraved by R.-S. Marcuard after a painting by F. Bartolozzi, 1786.
Folio, also exists in monochrome.
Bibl. Nat. Collect. Caffarelli Calamy.

186. Idem, in bistre.

187. Idem, in colour.
At the bottom, 4 lines of verse in English:
Behold this wondrous man. whose talents sublime
His skill each day doth eager death disarm,
His noble soul, sordid int'rest doth decline,
Humanity alone his breast doth warm.

These are translated into French thus:
Voilà l'homme étonnant, dont le talent sublime
De la mort, chaque jour, trompe l'avidité,
Et qu'aucun intérêt n'anime
Que celui de l'humanité.

188. Portrait.— XIII. Full-length portrait, engraved by Sasso, drawn by Bosio.
Quarto.

PORTRAITS OF THE COUNTESS CAGLIOSTRO
189. Portrait. — I. Portrait, quarto, oval, half-length portrait in bistre.
Paris, Alibert.

190. Portrait. — II. Mezzotint portrait.
Octavo.

191. Portrait. — III. Engraved portrait hand-coloured.

MISCELLANEOUS SUBJECTS
192. Drawing. Cagliostro reveals to Marie-Antoinette (?) and her entourage an apparition in a carafe: no legend.
Contemporary pen-and-ink drawing, 56 x 79 mm.
Catal. Rosenthal.

CARICATURES
193. I. 'The new idol', depicting Count Callimasse.
Folio, 30 x 40 cm, surrounded by a black line. Engraving formed from some twenty small distinct subjects, each with its own legend.
At the bottom the legend: Symbolic portrait of the Count Callimasse.
(Around 1786).

194. II. Making a Free mason. The Celebrated Dr comte de Cagliostro and his assistant making the necessary preparations for admission into the anc. order of Egyptian Free Freemasonry.
Quarto, 2 pages, coloured.
(Collection Astier. Catal. p. 41, no. 343).

195. III. A Masonic anecdote which happened in London on 1st November 1786 to Bro. Balsamo, self-styled Prince of Trebizond.
London, 1786.

Folio, coloured, description in English and French.
(34 lines of English verse).
(Collection Astier. Catal. p. 42, no. 344.)

196. IV. Frontispice of: Nachrichten ächte... (Mémoires authentiques.) Berlin, 1786. Cagliostro is depicted naked and surrounded by adoring females. He is seated on a sphere with a snake in his hand and his head surrounded by a nimbus.

WORKS OF THE IMAGINATION

197. Anicet Dumanoir. La Fiole de Cagliostro. Vaudeville, 1835, quarto.

198. Antony Béraud & Léopold Cagliostro, melodrama, octavo.

199. Bell (Georges). Le miroir de Cagliostro. Paris. 1860, duodecimo.

200. Bréval (Jean). Cagliostro. Conte du lundi. Journal d'Alsace-Lorraine, 14 March 1910.

201. Anonymous. Cagliostro ou l'Intrigant. Paris, 1834, 2 vols., octavo.

202. Anonymous. Cagliostro und die Hexe. Comedy, Kehl, 1874, octavo.

203. Catherine II of Russia. Der Betrüger. Der Verblendte. Der Sibirische Schamon, comedies.
Riga, 1787, & Berlin, 1788, octavo.

204. De Créquy (marquise) (Apocryphal: Comte de Courchamps). Le paradis sur Terre ('an extract from some unpublished memoirs of Cagliostro').
In: *Souvenirs*, Paris, 1834, 3 vols., octavo.
Vol. III, 323-359.
Conte fantastique.

205. Dumas (Alexandre). Mémoires d'un médecin. Joseph Balsamo (3 vols.). Le Collier de la Reine (5 vols.).

206. Dumas (Alex.) fils. Joseph Balsamo, a drama in 5 acts, 1878.

207. Dupaty & De Reveroni. Cagliostro ou les Illuminés, comic opera, Paris, 1810, octavo.

208. Gérard de Nerval. Les Illuminés. Paris, Lévy, 1868, eighteenmo.

209. Goethe. Le Grand Cophte, comedie, in: Vol. I of the Œuvres dramatiques, Paris, 1825, Santelet.
The original German edition dates from 1792.

210. Giseke (R.). Diebeiden Cagliostro, drama, Leipzig, 1858, octavo.

211. Griesinger (Th.) Cagliostriana, novel, Stuttgart, 1844.

212. Anonymous (Natale Roviglio). Il Cagliostro, comedy in 5 acts. n.p., 1791, octavo, 71 pp. With 2 portraits.

213. Mendès &Lesclide. La divine aventure. Paris, 1881, duodecimo.

214. Mundt (Th.) Cagliostro in Petersburg, novel, Prague, 1858, octavo.

215. Scribe. Cagliostro, comic opera, 1844.

NOTES

(1T) The BN can refuse the legal deposit of works if their form would make long-term conservation problematical.
(2) For the discussions surrounding the Diamond Necklace Affair the following works can be profitably consulted along with the numerous memoirs of the various accused:
- *Pièce importante dans l'Affaire du Collier pour de Launay*, 1789. quarto.
- *Sommaire pour la comtesse de Valois-La Motte*. 1786, quarto.
- *Réponse de Madame de La Motte au mémoire de Cagliostro*. 1786, octavo, quarto, sixteenmo.
- *Mémoires justificatifs de Madame de La Motte*. 1789, London, octavo.
- *Vie de Jeanne de Saint-Rémy de Valois*. 1793, 2 vols. octavo.
(3T) The physiognotrace (or physionotrace) is an instrument designed to trace a person's physiognomy, especially the profile, in the form of a silhouette. Based on the pantograph, it was invented by Gilles-Louis Chrétien in 1783-84.

INDEX

Numbers in Roman type are page-numbers, while italics indicate footnotes, e.g. 42/*31* refers to footnote 31 on page 42.

Acta Latomorum **42**/*31*, **139**/*15*, **143**/*81*, **143**/*89-94*, **256**
Acton (Minister to the Queen of Naples) **203**
Acts of the Apostles quoted **9, 84**/*56*, **143**/*87*, **222**/*7*
Agrippa, Henry Cornelius **19**
Ailly, Madame d' (disciple) 148
Aix-les-Bains **198, 229**/*22*, **251**
Albani, Cardinal **199**
Albertus Magnus **19**
Alchemy **5, 6, 16, 19, 25, 29, 34, 61, 66, 71, 72, 75, 76, 79, 80, 87**/*105*, **89**/*128*, **89**/*129*, **90**/*150*, **113**/*54*, **145, 188, 192**/*58*, **211**/*48*, **230**/*29*
Alembert, Jean le Rond d' **70**
Alméras, d' **27**/*12*, **55**/*1*, **87**/*112*, **114**/*61*, **117**/*116*, **245**/*1*, **250**
Alquier **119, 130, 247**/*6*
Amiens **41**/*13*
Angels **21, 60, 62, 64, 65, 67, 83**/*42*, **85**/*64*, **127, 139**/*19T*, **141, 142, 169**/*29*, **171**/*69*, **232, 233**
Antinori (Bailiff of Malta) **200**
Antonelli, Cardinal **203**
Apollonius of Tyana **16, 19**
Aquino, Chevalier d' **30, 30**/*3*, **31**/*4*, **110**
Arabic language **38, 43**/*58*, **109, 168**/*17*
Aracoeli (prison) **202**
Arras **122**
Artois, Comte d' **42**/*27*, **146**
Astrology **55**/*9*, **90**/*138*
Aubergenois **130, 247**/*5*
Aufklärer **122**
Augeard, Madame (patient) **95, 146**
Augustus II of Poland **122**
Auret, Madame d' (disciple) **148**
Aylett (lawyer) **48, 51, 55**/*7*
Aymar, Abbé d' (Grand-Vicar to Cardinal de Rohan) **105**

Badioli **50**
Balsamo, Giordono Salvo **241**
Balsamo, Francesco **241**
Balsamo, Giacomo **241**

Balsamo, Joseph (Giuseppe) **5, 215/*109*, 223, 224, 241, 253, 255, 264**
Balsamo, Pietro **239, 241**
Bar-sur-Aube **156**
Barbier de Tinan (Muster-Master) **97, 115/*90*, 116/*97*, 116/*101-104*, 165, 190/*29*, 245, 263**
Barcelona **226**
Barry, Madame du **181-2**
Barthélemy, François, French Minister in London **177-8, 182**
Basel **94, 95, 110, 111/*5, 17, 22-23*, 118/*126 & 128*, 175/*135-6*, 188, Chapter IX** *passim*
Basle (see Basel)
Bastille **28/*21*, 33, 142/*71*, 156ff, 177ff, 201, 212/*56*, 214/*77*, 215/*104*, 218/*159*, 248, 249, 252, 256, 263**
Baussan, Marquise de (disciple) **148**
Beaumarchais, Pierre-Auguste Caron de **158, 170/*39*, 181-2, 189/*17*, 190/*18 & 22*, 229/*22*, 251**
Beaumarchais, boulevard (Paris) **145**
Béguin, Mathieu **97**
Benedetti, Luca Antonio (Papal lawyer) **200, 202, 213/*75***
Benedict XIV, Pope **207, 217/*143***
Bercy, Marquise de (disciple) **148**
Bergeret de Frouville **177-8**
Bergmann (Attorney-General of Riga and Masonic commentator) **88/*116***
Bern **122, 194, 195, 209/*10***
Bernard, police-agent **40/*1*, 224, 228/*16 & 17***
Berne, see Bern
Bernis, François-Joachim de (French Ambassador to Rome) **200 et seq.**
Bette d'Étienville, quoted **150**
Beugnot, Count (memorialist) **43/*59*, 111/*26*, 149-50, 152, 168/*17*, 210/*22*, 256**
Bibliotheca Tabernensis **180/*57***
Biel, see Bienne
Bielefeld, Major **122**
Bienne Chapter IX *passim*, **263**
Blache, Madame de la (disciple) **148**
Blessig, Professor Laurent (philosopher) **69, 110/*1*, 113/*46***
Blévary, Madame de **46, 51, 55/*8***
Bode (pamphleteer) **37, 43/*58*, 87/*105*, 253, 254**
Bœhmer (Royal Jeweller) **151 et seq.**
Boissière (bookseller and crook) **182**
Bonfratelli, Order of **120, 229/*22***
Bordeaux **84/*57*, 112/*31*, 120-1, 124, 146, 152, 171/*62*, 185, 191/*35*, 252**
Borri, Joseph-François (alchemist and heretic) **25**
Boulainvilliers, Marquise de **149-50**
Boulogne **164 et seq., 178, 180**
Boulogne, Treaty of **219/*163***
Bourrée, Marc-Daniel, see Corbéron, Chevalier de
Boursenne, Madame de (disciple) **148**
Bouturlin, Madame (patient) **73**
Bracconieri, Antonio **185, 224 et seq.**

Bracconieri, Simone **241**
Branconi, Marquise de **37, 195 et seq., 260**
Breitinger, Professor (philologist) **97, 194**
Breteuil, Baron de **27/*2*, 156, 163, 173/*105*, 175/*127*, 177 et seq., 200 et seq.**
Brice de Beauregard, Comte **65-6**
Brienne, Comtesse de (disciple) **148**
Brissac, Comtesse de (disciple) **148**
Broad, Mr. (perjuror) **48, 51**
Brussels **50, 56/*28***
Bruyère, Dr. de la (medical doctor) **124**
Buhot, Inspector (police-officer) **225**
Buoncompagni, Cardinal **199**
Burckhardt (member of the Sarrasin circle) **194**
Bürkli **93, 95, 107**

Cabala **16, 17, 18, 52, 56/*33*, 89/*128***
Cabale de Cagliostro, La **55/14**
Cadet Corps, St. Petersburg **86/*91***
Cagliostro, Count:
    appearance, character and accomplishments **Chapter II**
  early life **Chapter I**
  identity and family background **Chapter XI**
  in London **Chapters III and VIII**
  in Lyons **Chapter VI**
  in Paris **Chapter VII**
  in Rome **Chapter IX** *partim*
  in Russia **Chapter IV**
  in Strasbourg **Chapter V**
  in Switzerland **Chapter IX** *partim*
  trial and death **200-208**
Cagliostro, Countess **36, Chapter III** *passim*, **79, 97, 105 et seq., 208**
Cahagnet, Louis (cabinet-maker and writer on spiritualism) **65, 85/*58T***
Cambis, de (patient) **107, 117/*112 & 122***
Campanella, Cardinal **203**
Campardon, Émile (historian) **25, 41/*13***
Carlyle, Thomas (traducer of Cagliostro) **27/*3*, 139/*17*, 142/*67*, 260**
Casanova, Giacomo **41/*9*, 212/*58***
Catherine the Great, Empress of Russia **70-74, 87/*104*, 88/*116*, 89/*124***
Cesi, Prince Frederico **200**
Chaise-Dieu, La **188/*2***
Chanet, residence of the Marquise de Branconi **196, 210/*26***
Chardon (jeweller) **199**
Chartres, duc de **42/*27*, 121, 146**
Châtelet, Le (prison) **156, 164, 191/*33***
Chefdebien, Marquis (Secretary-General of the Convention) **134**
Chesnon (Police Commissary) **29, 34, 156-7, 163 et seq., 177, 184, 186, 223, 224, 229/*28*, 249**

Chevaliers de l'Aigle Noir **139**/*35*
Chevaliers d'Orient **121**
Choiseul, Comtesse de (disciple) **148**
Choiseul, Duc de **43**/*47*
Christianity **97, 123, 200, 205, 221, 240**
Christie's auction house **188**
Clement XII, Pope **207, 217**/*143*
Clermont, Chapter of **121**
Coffee, Cagliostro's love of **37, 101**
Colonge (member of *La Sagesse*) **130**
Columbus, Christopher **52**
Chambre des Quinze Strasbourg) **104, 115**/*90*
Contades, Maréchal de (Governor of Alsace) **97, 105, 109**
Convention of the *Philalèthes* **133 et seq.**
Copht, the Grand (title of Cagliostro) **64, 71, 83**/*42*, **130, 131, 146, 154, 230**/*29*, **246**
Corbéron, Chevalier de **72, 75, 87**/*103*
Courrier de l'Europe (newspaper) **13, 29, 40**/*1*, **52, 90**/*144*, **172**/*89*, **182 et seq., 199, 226, 227**/*1*, **245, 249, 256**
Créquy, Marquise de (memorialist) **42**/*25*, **89**/*130*, **244, 267**
Crisp, Marshal of the Prison of the King's Bench **51**
Croix, Madame de la (follower of de Saint-Martin) **119**
Crookes, William (chemist and physicist) **91**/*57*
D'Oliva affair, the **151 et seq., 171**/*62*
Dampierre, Baron de **97**
Delorme (Deputy Governor of the Bastille) **157**
Delorme, J.-B. ('The American') **124**
Desbrugnières (police-agent) **108, 156, 162-3, 229**/*28*
Desport, see Ort, de l'
Dessalles, Comtesse (disciple) **148**
Deux-Ponts, duc de **75**
Diamond Necklace affair **7, 13, 19, 24, 26, 27**/*6*, **28**/*23*, **34, 37-8, 59, 75, 91**/*158*, **130, 149ff, 222**/*2*, **223, 229**/*28*, **244, 254, 256, 263, 268**/*2*
Diderot **70, 121, 258**
Dietrich, Baronesse von (patient) **95**
Doillot (lawyer) **157**
Doves (term for psychic intermediaries) **61ff, 125, 133, 154, 171**/*69*, **201**
Dubourg (French Embassy notaire) **56**/*32*, **191**/*32*
Dumas, Alexandre **24-5, 267**
Dunkirk **122**
Dunning (lawyer) **51**
Duplessis **225-7**
Dupotet, Baron (crystal-gazer) **66**

Egg, Alchemical **90**/*150*
Egypt **30, 84**/*50*, **113**/*52*, **232**
Egyptian Rite **5, 7, 24, 44**/*69*, **59, 61, 64, 68-9, 77, 82**/*23*, *24 & 26*, **84**/*49 & 50*, **85**/*64*, *65*, *66 & 68*, **99, 100, 114**/*71*, **119, 120, 126 et seq., 147, 152, 168**/*23*, *27 & 28*, **169**/*32 &*

34, 174/*118*, 194, 201 et seq., 236, 240, 246, 247, 248, 249, 252, 263, 266
Ehrmann, Professor **97**
Elect Cohens **121, 139**/*35*
Elixir, the **61, 76, 93, 95, 96, 201**
Erlach de la Fare, Madame d' (disciple) **148**
Espinchal, Comtesse d' (disciple) **148**
Évangile de Cagliostro, L' **17, 27**/*1*, **35, 198-9**
Évreux, Madame d' (disciple) **148**
Exemplary death **207, 216**/*124*, **217**/*140 & 143*

Fage, Madame de la **101**
Falk, Rabbi Samuel **119, 138**/*10T*
Fasting **141**/*53*, **204, 218**/*151*
Feliciani, Lorenza, see Cagliostro, Countess
Feminine Masonry **148 et seq.**
Fénix, Count (pseudonym of Cagliostro) **81**/*5*
Figuier, Louis (populariser of science) **19, 66, 257**
Finguerlin (betrayer of Freemasonry) **125, 130**
Flournoy **34, 41**/*11T*
Fontaine, Police Commissary **25, 223 et seq., 256, 263**
Forain, Jean-Louis (illustrator) **187**
Fournié, Abbé **124**
Frankfurt-am-Main **119**
French Revolution **6, 19, 23, 24, 26, 41**/*13*, **62, 139**/*24*, **162**
Friedrichs, Dr. (Masonic historian) **70, 86**/*91*, **88**/*116*, **89**/*128*
Fry, Mary, see Scott & Fry affair
Funck-Brentano, Frantz (author) **13, 25, 28**/*23*, **149, 156, 160**
Galaizière, Chaumont de la (Intendant of Strasbourg) **97, 112**/*36*
Ganges, Monsieur de (Madame de la Motte victim) **151**
Gaudicheau, Madame (sister of Miss Fry) **51**
Gazette de Florence **224**
Gazette de Leyde **149**
Geber (alchemist) **72**
Gelagin (patient) **73**
Genlis, Marquise de (disciple) **148**
Georgel, Abbé (memorialist) **167, 170**/*57*, **171**/*65 & 67*, **173**/*101*, **175**/*131*, **222**/*6*, **257**
Gérard, de (Royal Praetor) **97, 117**/*123*
Gichtel **84**/*56*, **85**/*64*
Gingin, de (member of the Sarrasin circle) **194, 198, 211**/*40 & 46*, **212**/*50 & 56*, **214**/*87*, **263**
Gleichen, Baron de **25, 35, 42**/*31*, **93-4, 116**/*105*, **119, 134-5, 143**/*88*, **257**
Goethe **111**/*16*, **112**/*32*, **173**/*104*, **195, 209**/*9*, **210**/*24 & 25, 30, 34*, **223, 227, 228**/*6*, **261, 267**
Golitsyn, General **72, 87**/*105*
Gordon, Lord George **13, 177 et seq., 187, 192**/*46*, **193**
Gouttes Jaunes, see Yellow Drops
Grand Lodge (Holland) **122**

Grand Lodge (London) **119, 121**
  Grand Orient of France **121, 122, 169/*34*, 194**
Grand Orient of Warsaw **89/*127*, 122**
Grasset Dr. Joseph (neurologist) **67, 85/*63T***
Grilloni (Adjutant, Corsican Guard) **204**
Grimm, Friedrich Melchior Baron von **70, 191/*41*, 251, 258**
Grœbel, Catherine (patient and famous cure) **101 et seq.**
Gros Cagliostro, Le (fortune-telling book) **55/*14***
Grotthaus, Frau von (cousin of Countess Von der Recke) **68**
Gualdi, Federico (occultist) **25, 230/*29***
Gugino (advocate-fiscal to the Court of Palermo) **224, 228/*9 & 13***
Gustav III of Sweden **88/*123***

Haas, Professor (member of the Sarrasin circle) **194**
Hallopeau, Professor F.-H. (dermatologist) **88/*115***
Hamburg **122, 190/*29***
Harat, Count (pseudonym of Cagliostro) **81/*5***
Haven, Marc (Dr. Emmanuel Lalande) **15-18**
Hazenbach family **194**
Helium **91/*157***
Henry of Prussia, Prince **140/*36*, 193-4**
Herder, Johann Gottfried (philosopher) **112/*32***
Hermeticism **19, 20, 30, 34, 44/*66*, 61, 72, 75 et seq., 114/*65*, 132, 140/*47*, 169/*32***
Hervier, Père (hypnotist) **84-5/*57***
Heyking, Baron von **71 et seq.**
Hinz (notary) **68, 81/*13***
Houdon (sculptor) **40/*3*, 169/*33*, 209/*19*, 264 and illustrations on pages 35, 150**
Howarth (arbitrator) **49-51**
Howen, Chamberlain von **61, 68, 71, 81/*14*, 82/*21***
Hund, Baron von **122, 139/*33***
Hypnosis and hypnotism **19, 22, 66-7, 79, 85/*57*, 100, 171/*69***

Iamblichus (neo-Platonist) **83/*28 & 41***
Illuminés of Avignon **28/*18*, 121, 122, 143/*85*, 169/*34*, 254**
In eminenti (Papal Bull) **217/*143***
Inquisition **6, 7, 24, 64, 76, 126, 133, 175/*137*, 188, 191/*35*, 199, 202 et seq., 225, 229/*24*, 240, 252, 257**
Isleniev, Ivan (patient) **73 et seq.**

Jacquet, Dr. (dermatologist) **88/*115***
Jaquaut (assistant to Cagliostro) **113/*58***
Jena **81/*14***
Jesuits **25, 59, 69, 80/*4*, 107, 122, 206, 216/*124*, 218/*143***
Jesus, Society of, see Jesuits
Jews **29, 40, 44/*67*, 140/*49*, 222**
Joseph II, Emperor **122, 199, 210/*25*, 213/*64***
Journets, the (members of *La Sagesse*) **130, 247/*4***

Kabbala, see Cabala
Kayserling, Frau von **68**
Képinska, Mademoiselle **90/***134*
King of France, see Louis XVI
Kirchberger **84/***49*, **133, 141/***57*, **142/***63*, **143/***76*
Königsberg **59, 80/***4*
Korff, Major von **68, 80/***4*

Labande, L. H. (biographer of De Corbéron) **87/***103*, **258**
Labarthe (correspondent with Séguier) **37, 95, 114/***74*
Laborde Jean-Benjamin de (tax-farmer, composer, author and Freemason) **38, 41/***8*, **65, 66, 136, 143/***83*, **168/***23*, **258**
Laffrey, Abbé de (member of the *Convention*) **136**
Lamballe, Prince de **83/***36*
Lamothe-Langon, Baron de (memorialist) **108**
Langlois, Chevalier de (Captain of Dragoons) **95, 165, 260**
Laporte (lawyer) **150-1**
Laroche, Sophie (traveller and friend of Cagliostro) **42/***34* & *40*, **43/***41*, **193**
Launay, De (Governor of the Bastille) 157 et seq., **177, 181, 184, 186, 223-4, 249, 268/***2*
Lauraguais, Comte de (enemy of Morande) **186, 191/***42*, **192/***42*
Lavater (theologian and physiognomist) **26, 28/***17T*, **60, 85/***64*, **97, 165, 167, 190** et seq., **209/***16*, **210/***25*, **212/***56*, **213/***76*, **214/***83*, **217/***137*, **218/***153* & *154*, **250, 261, 263**
Lecoulteux de la Novaye (Freemason) **150**
Leidnerin, Magdalene (midwife) **101**
Leipzig **119, 246**
Lenotre **41/***15*, **42/***25*, **145, 167/***5*, **258**
Lettres de cachet **156, 158, 164, 173/***103*, **174/***122*, **178 et seq.**
Lévi, Éliphas (occultist) **82/***23*, **83/***37*, **216/***125*, **218/***153*
Lieb, Dr. (member of Cagliostro's lodge in Courland) **68**
Loménie, Marquise de (disciple) **148**
Loras, de (Freemason & member of the Order of Malta) **203**
Loth, Father (Freemason) **150**
Lotteries **19, 45, 46 et seq., 56/***34*
Louis XV **28/***16*, **181, 182**
Louis XVI **36, 62, 167/***5*, **201, 257**
Loutherbourg family **192/***58*, **193 et seq., 210/***35*, **211/***40, 44, 46* & *48*, **212/***54*
Lubel (artist and Freemason) **202-3, 214/***96*
Luminous Stone **76, 91/***157*
Lutzelbourg, Comte de **97**
Lyons **17, 45, 60, 62, 64, 84/***49*, **100, 112/***31*, **Chapter VI** *passim*, **146 et seq., 151-3, 168/***21*, **175/***32* & *38*, **185, 187, 190/***29*, **191/***35*, **195, 244, 246-7, 259**

Madariaga, Salvador de **138/***9T*
Magnetism, Animal **65 et seq., 100, 114/***68*, **124, 171/***69*, **175/***131*
Magneval family **130, 247/***2* & *3*
Maître Philippe de Lyon (Nizier Anthelme Philippe, healer) **7, 13, 16, 17**
Majorca **31/***5*

Malta **30, 116/***96*
Malta, Order of **30/***3,* **200, 203, 213/***72,* **222/***1,* **230/***31,* **241, 242/***7*
Mansfield, Lord **49**
Marat, Jean-Paul (physician, scientist, journalist and politician) **41/***13*
Marcello, Father (Jesuit and biographer of Cagliostro) **25, 211/***44,* **216/***119,* **218/***143,* **252, 253**
Maria Theresa, Empress **65, 170/***54T,* **212/***57*
Marie-Antoinette (Queen of France) **27/***11,* **Chapter VII** *passim,* **177, 256, 266**
Marschall (ritualist) **122**
Martinez de Pasqually **121, 139/***33,* **143/***85*
Martius, Dr. E.W. (pharmacist) **113/***46,* **114/***65 & 68,* **243**
Masonic Lodges by name:
    Au bon pasteur, Warsaw **89/***128*
    Charles of the Three Helmets (Templar lodge) Warsaw **75, 90/***138*
    Die Große Landesloge, Berlin **71**
        L'Amitié, Bordeaux **121, 139/***35*
    L'Espérance, London **119-20**
    La Constance, Maastricht **122**
    Lacorne **121**
    La Loge Française, Bordeaux **121**
    La Parfaite Égalité, Liège **119**
    La Sagesse, Lyons **124-5, 130, 138/***3,* **139/***35,* **140/***39 & 47,* **142/***72,* **246**
    La Sagesse Triomphante, Lyons **124-5, 130 et seq., 142/***62 & 71,* **143/***80,* **159, 246**
    Le Parfait Silence, Lyons **124, 139/***34 & 35,* **142/***62,* **143/***80*
        Perfect Union, Naples **120**
Massini, Marchese **200**
Matousky (crook) **182**
Mecca **223, 233/***7*
Medem family of Von, **61, 68, 81/***10 & 11, 13, 14,* **82/***24,* **84/***51,* **112/***32*
Meiners **27/***2,* **87/***107,* **190/***29,* **261**
Melissino, General (ritualist) **72, 87/***103*
Melissino, Rite of **72**
Mesmer, Franz (physician) **124, 134**
Mesmerism **67, 143/***85*
Messina **30, 241, 242/***9*
Meta-elements **91/***157*
Mirabeau **88/***120,* **90/***144,* **113/***43,* **173/***104,* **190/***18,* **250**
Miromesnil, de (Keeper of the Seals) **146**
Mittau **59 et seq., 68-71, 74, 76, 81/***14,* **85/***76,* **86/***90,* **86/***93*
Montbruel, Chevalier de (patient) **95**
Montchenin, Madame de (disciple) **148**
Montesquieu **70**
Morande **24, 27/***6,* **29, 45 et seq., 85/***74,* **88/***117,* **90/***144,* **169/***38,* **181 et seq., 211/***48,* **223 et seq., 245, 248, 249, 251, 256, 259**
Morin, Abdré Saturnin (animal magnetiser) **65, 66**
Morning Herald **187, 255**
Moszyński Count **34, 78 et seq., 84/***56,* **90/***135,* **90/***141 & 149,* **91/***151,* **250**

Motte, Count de la ('Momotte') **150**
Motte, Madame de la **13, 24, 27/6, 29, 34, 36, 37, 88/*117*, 91/*158*, 114/*63*, 116/*100*, 130, Chapter VII** *passim*, **182, 191/*35*, 229/*24*, 251, 252, 257, 268**
Mundt, Theodore (novelist) **88/*118*, 268**

Naples **29, 30, 31/*4*, 110, 120, 203, 214/*90*, 224, 226, 228/*10* & *12*, 229/*19*, 230/*28***
Napoleon Bonaparte **209, 219/*163***
Narbonne, Vicomte de **104 et seq.**
Nerval, Gérard de **24, 25, 169/*34*, 267**
Neuchâtel **193 et seq., 210/*26***
Neuve-Saint-Gilles, rue (Paris) **150**
Neva, River **73**
Newgate prison **185**
Nicolai, Friedrich (founder of the Aufklärer) **69, 86/*86*, 88/*116*, 122, 256**
Noirot, Catherine, see Grœbel, Catherine
Normandez, de (Spanish chargé d'affaires) **75, 88/*122***
Nostradamus **19**
Nuremberg **119**

O'Reilly (friend and tavern-owner) **50, 55/*2*, 56/*29* & *32*, 191/*32*, 255**
O'Reilly's Tavern, Great Queen Street **187**
Oberkirch, d', Madame (memorialist) **89/*132*, 96, 167, 169/*33*, 257**
Occultism **5-8, 13, 16, 17, 19ff, 25, 34, 39, 44/*70*, 60, 76, 82/*23*, 89/*128*, 90/*138*, 98, 113/*52*, 120, 139/*33*, 146, 154, 246/*1*, 252**
Oleum Sacchari (remedy) **114/*65*, 244**
Olomier, Comte d' **150**
Orléans, Duc d' **83/*36*, 119, 121**
Ort, Monsieur de l' (King's Lieutenant) **97, 109**
Orvillers, Marquise d' (Cagliostro's landlady in Paris) **145**
Ostertag, Dr. (obstetrician) **101 et seq.**

Palermo **6, 7, 120, 221, 223, 224, 225, 226, 228/*13*, 229/*22*, 238, 239, 240, 260**
Palingenesis **91/*158***
Palle, Cortile delle **203**
Papus (Dr. Gérard Encausse) **7, 13, 16, 17, 89/*132*, 249, 263**
Paracelsus **17, 19**
Parlement de Paris **13, 172/*85*, 190/*22*, 249**
Passy **163, 165, 174/*113***
Paul, Bro. de (Marseilles Freemason) **136**
Pergolezzi **55/*7*, 186**
Péricaud (biographer of Cagliostro) **124-5, 130**
Pernety, Abbé **122, 139/*22***
Perrin, Messrs. (merchants of Lyons) **151**
Philalèthes, Les **42/*31*, 121, 133 et seq., 168/*23*, 194, 202, 256**
Philippon (member of *La Sagesse*) **130**
Phoenix, Count (see Fénix, Count)
Pink Powder, The **55/*13*, 100**

Pinto, Grandmaster **30**
Piquais (lawyer) **191/***33*
Pius VII, Pope **217/***142*
Planta Monsieur de (business-manager of Cardinal de Rohan) **145, 151**
Poisson, Albert (alchemist) 17, 89/*132*
Poland, King of, see Poniatowski, Stanislaw August
Polignac, Comtesse de (disciple) **148, 214/***87*
Polygon of Grasset **67, 85/***63T*
Poniatowski, Stanislaw August (King of Poland) **77 et seq., 90/***138*
Poni☐ski, Prince **68 et seq., 75 et seq.**
Pope, Alexander **145**
Potemkin, Prince **72, 74, 87/***104 & 05*
Powder of Projection (see also Pink Powder) **61, 79**
Prague **122**
Prediction and forecasting distinguished **52 et seq.**
Priddle (lawyer) **49, 56/***32*, **185-6, 191/***36*
Prost de Royer, Worshipful Master **64, 125, 140/***45*
Prussia **80/***2*, **86/***93 & 102*, **88/***122 & 123*, **122, 193, 194**
Psychometry **41/***13*, **84/***56*, **140/***44*
Puységur, Marquis de (magnetic healer) **66, 114/***68*

Queen of France, see Marie-Antoinette

Radioactivity **91/***157*
Ramond de Carbonnières **98, 145, 164, 170/***61*, **175/***131*
Ramond (Freemason of Besançon) **136**
Recke, Countess von der **59 et seq., 68-9, 112/***32*, **119, 236, 256, 259, 263**
Reformed Templars **122**
Regeneration of humanity **67, 72, 103, 110, 126 et seq., 141/***52, 53 & 58*, **147-8**
Reich, Baronne de **97**
Rétaux de Villette, Antoine **130, 150 et seq.**
Reynolds (lawyer) **48 et seq., 56/***17*
Rezzonico della Torre, Principessa **200**
Rhodes **30**
Rigollet (member of *La Sagesse*) **142/***72*
Ritter, Abraham (servant of the Loutherbourgs) **198**
Rockhalt (Cagliostro's country-house) **194 et seq., 209/***11*
Rogerson, Dr. John (physician to the Russian Empress) **74, 88/***115 & 119*, **169/***38*
Rohan, Cardinal de **13, 26, 43/***44*, **64, 78, 89/***132*, **96 et seq., Chapter VII** *passim*, **177, 201, 244, 251**
Rome **5, 25, 30, 33, 37, 64, 85/***61*, **107, 119, 125, 130, 139/***20*, **140/***46*, **175/***137*, **181, 188, 191/***35*, **199 et seq., 221, 222, 223, 225, 226, 229/***20*, **239, 242, 252**
Rosicrucian Brotherhood **8, 40, 113/***52*
Rousseau, Jean-Jacques **70**
Roveredo **41/***5*, **42/***22*, **43/***44 & 58*, **198 et seq.**
Russia **34, 42/***25*, **45, Chapter IV** *passim*, **97, 116, 122, 139/***34*, **146, 169/***38*, **222/***1*

Index

Sachi, Carlo **24, 27/*6*, 29, 36, 42/*37*, 105ff, 113/*58*, 114/*69*, 116/*100 & 101*, 139/*17*, 157, 185-6, 191/*35 & 36*, 225-6, 228/*10*, 229/*24*, 252, 263**
Saint-Claude, rue (Paris) **145, 157, 167/*5***
Saint-Costar (banker and Freemason) **130, 135, 140/*47*, 247/*1***
Saint-Denis **164, 174/*113*, 180**
Saint-Félix, Jules de **25, 27/*13*, 111/*28*, 250**
Saint-Germain, Comte de **28/*16*, 34, 40, 119-20, 169/*35***
Saint-Hilaire, de (captain of dragoons) **181**
Saint-Martin, Louis-Claude de (philosopher) **119, 121, 124, 139/*29*, 141/*56 & 57*, 142/*63*, 143/*76***
Saint-Pierre-le-Vieux, Church of (Strasbourg) **97, 102, 112/*32***
Saint-Rémy, Jeanne de, see Motte, Madame de la
Saisseval, Marquis de **150**
Salzmann (Freemason) **84/*50*, 86/*80*, 87/*104*, 89/*126 &131*, 97, 98, 112/*31 &32*, 113/*55 &56*, 117/*112*, 138/*14*, 139/*34*, 264**
San Leo, Fortress of **7, 207-9, 240, 262**
San Maurizio, Francesco da (Capuchin) **201-3**
Sant'Angelo, Fortress of **203, 207, 215/*104*, 264**
Santa Croce, Principessa **200**
Sarrasin family **Chapter V *passim*, 165, 167, 175/*129*, 187, 190/*29*, 193-7, 261, 263**
Saunders (bailiff) **48 et seq.**
Savalette de Langes **134**
Saverne **42/*27*, 96, 105, 116, 152, 162, 170/*45 & 57*, 173/*100*, 188/*1*, 244**
Scala, Alessandro **241, 262**
Schlosser (Goethe's brother-in-law) **44/*65*, 82/*17*, 111/*16*, 190/*29*, 260, 262**
Schmidt, Pastor Christian Gottlieb **195**
Scott & Fry affair **46 et seq.**
Scott, 'Lady', see Scott & Fry affair
Scott, 'Milord', see Scott & Fry affair
Schröder (ritualist) **122**
Schröpfer, Johann Georg (ritualist) **122, 139/*33*, 143/*85*, 245, 246/*1***
Schuabé (obstetrician) **101**
Schwander (Aulic Counsellor) **68, 81/*13***
Scieffort **60, 119, 122**
Séguier (archaeologist) **37, 95, 244**
Sheridan (lawyer) **50**
Simon Magus **19, 40**
Smith, Helene (psychic artist) **34, 41/*11T***
Société de magnétisme de Paris **66**
Soderini, Contessa **200**
Solve et coagula **113/*54***
Sommi Picenardi, Marchese **215/*109*, 262**
Sotomajor, Don Jaime de Majonès de Lima de **31**
Soubise, Prince de (patient) **94-6, 146, 173/*109***
Spain **30, 75, 105**
St. Petersburg **37, 68, 70 et seq., 86/*90*, 87/*105*, 88/*123*, 95, 112/*31*, 121, 131, 214**
Stark, Dr. (philosopher and occultist) **60, 81/*9*, 112/*31*, 263**

Strasbourg **34, 45, 50, 60 et seq. 79 et seq., Chapter V** *passim*, **120 et seq., 146 et seq., 159, 165, 185, 191/***35***, 195, 197, 199, 201, 229/***28***, 243-5, 251-2, 261-3**
Straub (company director and friend) **97, 109, 110, 111/***24*
Strict Observance, Order of **119**
Stroganov, Baron (patient) **73**
Swedenborg, Emanuel (mystic) **60, 124, 169/***29*
Switzerland **35, 122, 193 et seq., 259**
Sylvestre, Monsieur (complainant) **185, 262**

Talismans **77, 84/***56***, 119, 126**
Tanganelli (secretary to the Marchese Vivaldi) **200, 202, 203**
Target (Cardinal de Rohan's lawyer) **159, 170/***52* **&** *61***, 173/***93* **&** *94***, 263**
Tarot **7, 16, 28/***20*
Templars **20, 75, 122, 216/***120*
Terrasson de Sénevas (member of *La Sagesse*) **130**
Theological Society, The **187**
Theurgy **66, 72, 80, 84/***43***, 91/***155***, 124, 148, 205**
Théveneau, Charles, see Morande
Thilorier, Maître (Cagliostro's lawyer) **28/***22***, 38, 43/***61***, 111/***22***, 157, 163-5, 177, 180, 197, 264**
Thiscio (alleged surname of Cagliostro) **29, 223, 226, 228/***10*
Touchon (pastor) **97, 194**
Tour, Mademoiselle de la **91/***158***, 154ff, 171/***69***, 172/***86*
Transmission of powers **84/***49***, 128**
Trento **198ff, 213/***65***,** *67* **&** *69***, 215/***103*
Trévières, Madame de (disciple) **148**
Trevisan, Bernard of (alchemist) **72**
Trianon, Le **156**
Turin **198, 213/***59*

Ullmann, Jean-Daniel **97**

Valencia (Spain) **105-6**
Vasconcellos, Don Luis de Lima **31/***5*
Venice **27/***1***, 199, 203, 252, 253, 254**
Vergennes, de **114/***61***, 146, 190/***22*
Visconti, Abbé Quirino **200**
Vismes, de (Grand-Secretary of the Egyptian Rite) **136, 142/***73***, 168/***23***, 197**
Vitellini **46-9, 51, 55/***2* **&** *10*
Vivaldi, Marchese **200ff**
Vola (Cagliostro's country-house) **76, 78, 80**
Voltaire **70, 189/***16***, 190/***18*
Vrai Cagliostro, Le (fortune-telling book) **55/***14*

Wallace (lawyer) **51**
Warsaw **62, 65, 68, 75ff, 122, 139/***34*
Weishaupt, Adam **60, 122**

Index

Wieland (editor of the *Deutscher Merkur*) **95, 111/*24*, 258, 260**
Wieland, Colonel **111/*24***
Wildermett, Sigismund **194, 211/*43***
Willermoz **84/*50*, 86/*80*, 89/*126*, 89/*131*, 112/*31*, 113/*55 & 56*, 117/*112*, 122, 124, 138/*14*, 139/*35*, 140/*39*, 142/*71*, 264**
Wilzen, Treasure of **61, 84/*51***
Wine of Egypt (remedy) **89/*130*, 100, 108, 114/*67***
Wittel (obstetrician) **101**

Ximenes, Thomas **119, 138/*9T***

Yellow Drops (remedy) **89/*130*, 100, 108, 114/*69***

Zaegelins (curé) **102, 104**
Zannowich (impostor) **245, 246/*1***
Zelada, Cardinal Francesco Saderio **203-4, 207**
Zinnendorf (ritualist) **122**
Zuckmantel, Baron de **97**